Urban Transformations in Sierra Leone

Urban Transformations in Sierra Leone

Knowledge co-production and partnerships for a just city

Edited by Joseph M. Macarthy, Braima Koroma, Andrea Rigon, Alexandre Apsan Frediani and Andrea Klingel

Executive Editor: Andrea Rigon

First published in 2024 by
UCL Press
University College London
Gower Street
London WC1E 6BT

Available to download free: www.uclpress.co.uk

ISBN: 978-1-80008-687-6 (Hbk.)
ISBN: 978-1-80008-686-9 (Pbk.)
ISBN: 978-1-80008-685-2 (PDF)
ISBN: 978-1-80008-688-3 (epub)
DOI: 10.14324/111.9781800086852

This book is dedicated to the resilient residents of Freetown, including those in informal settlements and throughout the city, whose daily experiences and aspirations are at the core of urban transformations in Sierra Leone.

Contents

Part II: Knowledge contributions

Part III: Learning and action

List of figures

List of tables

List of abbreviations

AAP	action area plan
AAPS	Association of African Planning Schools
AP	assistive products
APHRC	African Population and Health Research Centre
ARISE	Accountability and Responsiveness in Informal Settlements for Equity
ARUA	African Research Universities Alliance
ASF-UK	Architecture San Frontières – United Kingdom
AT	assistive technology
AURI	African Urban Research Institute
CAAP	community action area plan
CbD	Change by Design
CBD	central business district
CBDRMC	community-based disaster risk management committees
CBO	community based organisation
CDMC	community disaster management committee
CHAI-SL	Clinton Health Action Initiative – Sierra Leone
CHWs	community health workers
CiLP	City Learning Platform
CKG	Crab Town, Kolleh Town and Gray Bush
CLGF	Chiefdom and Local Government Framework
CODOHSAPA	Centre of Dialogue on Human Settlement and Poverty Alleviation
CoLP	Community Learning Platform
COMAHS	College of Medicine and Allied Health Sciences
COVID-19	coronavirus disease
CRS	Catholic Relief Services
CSOs	civil society organisations
DAG	development action group
DePAC	Development and Planning in African Cities

DMD	disaster management department
DPOs	disabled people's organisations
DPU	Development Planning Unit
DRM	disaster risk management
DRR	disaster risk reduction
EPA	environment protection agency
ESAs	external support agencies
ESD	environment and sustainable development
ESRC	Economic and Social Research Council
FCC	Freetown City Council
FCDO	Foreign, Commonwealth and Development Office
FCI	The Four Cities Initiative
FEDURP	Federation of Urban and Rural Poor
FHS	Future Health Systems
FIA	Freetown Improvement Act
FIAR	Freetown Improvement Act and Rules
FSP	Freetown Structure Plan
FTF	Fordibambi Trust Fund
GATE	Global Cooperation on Assistive Technology
GCRF	Global Challenge Research Fund
GDI	Global Disability Innovation Hub
GDP	gross domestic product
GHG	greenhouse gas emissions
GOSL	Government of Sierra Leone
GPS	global positioning system
HDCA	Human Development and Capability Association
HEPPO	Help Empower Polio People's Organisation
HIV/AIDS	human immunodeficiency virus/acquired immunodeficiency syndrome
IDRC	International Development Research Council
IDS	Institute of Development Studies
IFRC	International Federation of Red Crescent
IGDS	Institute of Geography and Development Studies
IIED	International Institute of Environment and Development
INGO	international non-governmental organisation
IOM	International Organisation for Migration
JHU	Johns Hopkins University

KNOW	Knowledge in Action for Urban Equality
LGAF	Land Governance Assessment Framework
LIS	land information systems
LMICs	low- and middle-income countries
LSHTM	London School of Hygiene and Tropical Medicine
MDAs	ministries, departments and agencies
MLCPE	Ministry of Lands, Country Planning and the Environment
MLHCP	Ministry of Lands, Housing and Country Planning
MoHS	Ministry of Health and Sanitation
MOOC	massive open online course
MPs	members of parliament
MTCC	mass transit cable car
MTNDP	medium term national development plan
NDAR	national disability assistive technology and rehabilitation
NDCs	nationally determined contributions
NDMP	national disaster management policy
NEPA	National Environment Protection Agency
NGOs	non-governmental organisation
NIHR	National Institute of Health Research
NLPSL	National Land Policy of Sierra Leone
NPF	national platform
NSC	National Steering Committee
NU	Njala University
ODA	Official Development Assistance
OECD	Organisation for Economic Cooperation and Development
ONS	Office of National Security
PERAV	Portee Response Alliance Volunteers
PESIA	Platforms for Energy Security, Innovation and Access
PSPP	Pull Slum Pan Pipul
rATA	rapid assistive technology assessment
RBA	right based approach
RUSLP	Resilient Urban Sierra Leone Project
SDGs	sustainable development goals
SDI	Slum Dwellers International
SGP	Small Grants Programme

SLRTC	Sierra Leone Road Transport Corporation
SLURC	Sierra Leone Urban Research Centre
SSL	Statistics Sierra Leone
tCO2e	tonnes of carbon dioxide equivalent
TCPA	Town and Country Planning Act
T-SUM	Transition to Sustainable Urban Mobility
UCL	University College London
UCLG	united cities and local government
UHC	universal health coverage
UKRI	United Kingdom Research Institute
UN	United Nations
UNDESA	United Nations Department of Economic and Social Affairs
UNGA	United Nations General Assembly
WASH	water, sanitation and hygiene
WHO	World Health Organization
YMCA-SL	Young Men's Christian Association – Sierra Leone

List of contributors

Adriana Allen is Professor of Development Planning and Urban Sustainability at the Bartlett Development Planning Unit, UCL and former president of Habitat International Coalition. Originally from Argentina, she is an academic activist with over 35 years of international experience in research, pedagogy, advocacy, advisory and capacity-building undertakings in almost 30 countries across the Global South. Through the lens of land, housing, risk, water, sanitation, food and health, her work adopts a feminist political ecology perspective to look at the interface between everyday city-making practices, planned interventions and their capacity to generate transformative spaces, places and social relations. She has worked for various international and bilateral organisations and in collaboration with UN Special Rapporteurs to advance urban justice through advocacy and policy-evidence. Her most recent books include *Untamed Urbanisms* (2016), *Environmental Justice and Resilience in the Global South* (2017), *Urban Water Trajectories* (2017), *Handbook of Urban Global Health* (2019) and *The Routledge Handbook of Urban Resilience* (2020).

Hawanatu Bangura is a graduate student pursuing a master's degree in sustainable communities at Michigan Technological University (MTU), in the USA. Added to her studies, she is currently working as a teaching and research assistant in the Department of Social Sciences at MTU, where she works on energy transition projects and teaches human geography, global issues and related topics. Over the years, she has collaborated closely with local and national governments in Sierra Leone and international partners such as UCL and the Global Disability Innovation Hub (GDI Hub) in the UK. She has worked in areas of sustainable urban mobility and transport, environmental management, disaster risk reduction, disability, urban health and wellbeing.

Stephanie Butcher is a lecturer in Global Sustainable Development at the University of Sheffield. Her work focuses on informality and urban inequalities, especially housing and infrastructure in cities of the Global South, with a particular interest in social mobilisations, community-led planning and identity and diversity. She has worked on collaborative research and action projects in several urban areas across sub-Saharan Africa and South Asia. She holds a PhD in development planning from the Bartlett Development Planning Unit, UCL.

Clemence Cavoli is Assistant Professor at the Centre for Transport Studies, part of the Civil, Environmental, Geomatic Engineering Department of UCL. She researches and teaches environmental and transport policymaking and planning, in particular at the urban level. Her work is highly interdisciplinary and aims to transform governance processes across levels (supranational, national and subnational) and sectors. She is a political scientist and historian by background, expert in multi-level governance linked to sustainable development and innovative policymaking and planning. She specialises in environmental and transport policies and in developing transformative governance for cities, in particular linked with urban mobility. Her research and teaching work has a strong interdisciplinary component and a focus on policy impact. She coordinates the Transitions to Sustainable Urban Mobility in sub-Saharan Africa (T-SUM) project.

Alphajoh Cham is an urban planner, environmental researcher, policy specialist and public health specialist. He holds a BSc (Hons) in zoology (USL), an MSc (Ing.) in regional planning and environmental management (Germany) and a PhD in public/environmental health (USA). He is currently the Director of Planning, Policy and Project Development, as well as the Project Coordinator of the Sierra Leone Land Administration Project at the Ministry of Lands, Housing and Country Planning (MLHCP). He has over 20 years working and research experience in land use planning, environmental management and planning, natural resource (land) management, land governance policy development, project management, monitoring and evaluation. He has been very instrumental in the development and formulation of the comprehensive National Land Policy 2015 for Sierra Leone and served as the national coordinator for its implementation. He was an expert investigator in the development of the Land Governance Assessment Framework (LGAF) for Sierra Leone. He coordinated the European Union Urban Planning Project and has been the focal point for the

UN-Habitat in Sierra Leone, supervising the implementation of the New Urban Agenda in Sierra Leone and coordinating the development of the National Urban Policy.

Alexandria Z. W. Chong is a doctoral researcher at the Bartlett Development Planning Unit, UCL. She is also a research assistant for the T-SUM project. Her doctoral research interrogates transport as a social equity issue in Singapore through a critical feminist lens. Alexandria holds an MSc in spatial planning from UCL and an MArch from the Singapore University of Technology and Design.

Camila Cociña is a researcher at the International Institute for Environment and Development (IIED). She co-convenes the housing justice programme of work at IIED. She holds a PhD in development planning from the Bartlett Development Planning Unit, UCL. Her work focuses on housing justice, urban equality, gender, informality and local governance. She has worked on several collaborative initiatives with communities, researchers, civil society groups, international agencies and governments across Latin America, West Africa and Southeast Asia. Camila is a member of the Radical Housing Journal editorial collective. She is currently based in Santiago, Chile.

Abu Conteh is a senior researcher and head of the Urban Health Cluster at the Sierra Leone Urban Research Centre (SLURC). His research interests include gender and intersectionality, and social determinants of health. He has worked extensively with local and external partners on research focusing on health accountability, health and wellbeing, vaccine equity and epidemic preparedness. Part of his research collaborations include the Accountability for Equity Hub (ARISE), led by the Liverpool School of Tropical Medicine; the Shock Tactics project, led by the Institute of Development Studies; and the Future Health Systems, jointly with Johns Hopkins University. His recent work with the London School of Hygiene and Tropical Medicine explored perceptions of COVID-19 response and the gendered relations shaping COVID-19 vaccine uptake in informal settlements in Freetown. Abu is currently a PhD candidate at the Liverpool School of Tropical Medicine and his research explores non-communicable disease experiences and health seeking priorities.

Yirah Oryanks Conteh is a BSc degree holder in community development study and the national chairman of the Federation of Urban and Rural Poor Sierra Leone (FEDURP-SL) working with a supporting NGO, Centre of

Dialogue on Human Settlement and Poverty Alleviation (CODOHSAPA), an affiliate of Slum Dwellers International (SDI). He is a member of the SDI board and council and the Head of Mapping and Profiling of the coordinating team of SDI. Yirah has been in FEDURP-SL for over fifteen years, working with different partners in the development of his country such as SLURC, Catholic Relief Service (CRS), Freetown City Council (FCC) and United Nation Capital Development Fund (UNCDF). Most of the work his organisation is doing is advocacy and dialogue with city stakeholders to improve the urban poor in all informal settlements in Sierra Leone.

Beatrice De Carli is Reader in Urbanism at the School of Art, Architecture and Design, London Metropolitan University. She previously held positions at Politecnico di Milano and the University of Sheffield. In addition to her academic roles, Beatrice serves as a Managing Associate for Architecture Sans Frontières UK, a non-profit organisation specialising in community-led design and planning. Her work employs a collaborative, design-based approach to tackle issues of social and environmental justice in city-making, with a focus on contested and fragile urban contexts.

Alexandre Apsan Frediani is a principal researcher at the Human Settlements Group of the IIED, in London. Alexandre co-leads the housing justice thematic work of IIED, where he runs research and projects to strengthen the capabilities of grassroots groups to contest housing injustices, influence governance systems and build global alliances for housing justice. Alexandre specialises on issues around human development in cities of the Global South and his work has explored participatory approaches to planning and design of interventions in informal settlements in cities in Latin America and sub-Saharan Africa. Alexandre is an advisor of Architecture Sans Frontières UK, part of the boards of Habitat International Coalition and SLURC and a fellow of the Human Development and Capability Association (HDCA).

Pascale Hofmann is Associate Professor at the Development Planning Unit, UCL and joint programme leader of the MSc in environment and sustainable development. Her expertise lies within the field of urban environmental planning and management and urban sustainability. She has over 20 years of experience conducting research and consultancy work in the urban global south and Europe. Most of her research centres on infrastructure and service provision arrangements in urban and peri-urban contexts with a keen interest to explore the scope for equitable and sustainable access to services in a changing climate. Her research is particularly concerned with the dialectics of policy-driven and everyday practices and the implications on people and the environment to generate knowledge towards integrated multi-actor approaches and pathways.

Andrea Klingel is Director of Operations at SLURC. Originally from Germany, she has over 25 years' experience in international project and programme management in the private, public and third sector in the UK and almost six years in Sierra Leone. Andrea specialises in complex projects, managing a wide variety of stakeholders, building and strengthening vital relationships for SLURC's work ranging from ministerial to community level. While her main scope of work entails all organisational operations at SLURC, she oversaw national coordination directly on projects including the African Cities Research Consortium project and the World Bank funded consultancies to develop a flood risk assessment and management plans for secondary cities in Sierra Leone and spatial development plans for secondary cities in Sierra Leone. She is also the safeguarding lead at SLURC with several years' experience in safeguarding and policy.

Braima Koroma is Director of Research and Training at SLURC. His work focuses on urban livelihoods and the city economy, environmental management, vulnerability and adaptation to climate change, urban planning and development impact evaluation. He has provided consulting services with various national government ministries, departments and agencies, as well as international organisations and institutions including the African Development Bank, the World Bank, the Japan International Cooperation Agency, the Department for International Development, the German Agency for Technical Cooperation, United Nations, amongst others. With his extensive interdisciplinary research experience, he has published widely to engage both academic and non-academic audiences.

Amadu Kamara Labor is a dedicated Research Officer at SLURC. He holds a BA in development studies from the University of Makeni, Sierra Leone and a BSc in agricultural education from the Ernest Bai Koroma University of Science and Technology, Sierra Leone. His diverse academic achievements provide crucial skills for his current role. Early in his career, he was an essential member of the Federation of Urban and Rural Poor (FEDURP). This experience allowed him to gain valuable insights into the challenges faced by underprivileged urban populations, setting the stage for future endeavours. He is currently leading the Beyond the Networked City Project, which focuses on water, sanitation and energy delivery to marginalised urban communities. He also leads the consortium Platforms for Energy Security, Innovation and Access (PESIA), piloting a community kitchen at Portee-Rokupa, a community-driven solution for urban poor. Throughout his career, his growing passion for research aligns with his belief that it empowers understanding and shapes the world.

Rita Lambert is Associate Professor at the Bartlett Development Planning Unit at UCL. She is an urban development planner and architect by training with over 20 years of academic and practical experience in diverse geographies from Latin America, Africa and Southeast Asia. Her research, teaching and external engagements are intertwined and based on feminist political ecology, environmental justice and systemic thinking. She is committed to advancing conceptualisation of planning and developing methodologies for observing complex urban processes, locating action and advancing equitable and sustainable urban futures. She seeks to make visible mechanisms that (re)produce territories where people and ecosystems are kept in permanent conditions of vulnerability. Her contributions are on peripheral urbanisation, governance and urban and environmental planning through the analysis of life sustaining themes (like water, energy, housing, food, ecological systems) as well as a better understanding of how policies and everyday practice interact to create risk and violence.

Joseph M. Macarthy is Executive Director of SLURC. He holds a PhD in urban planning and management from Newcastle University, specialising in the intersections between housing and informal settlements, mobility and transport, urban vulnerability and resilience, public health and the management of climate change adaptation. He is the co-investigator for the T-SUM project, as well as the research lead for the Knowledge in Action for Urban Equality (KNOW) project in Freetown. Joseph was the lead local consultant in the preparation of the European Commission-funded Freetown Structure Plan (2013) and currently provides volunteer service to the UNDP as a member of the National Steering Committee (NSC) of the Small Grants Programme (SGP) in Sierra Leone.

Alexander Macfarlane is the media and digital learning producer at the Bartlett Development Planning Unit, UCL. He holds an MSc degree in social development practice and has an interest in grassroots and citizens' media and communication practices and how they can challenge dominant discourses. As an experienced photographer and videographer, Alexander has helped plan and deliver training and workshops that have built on the existing body of literature on participatory visual and storytelling methodologies in order to explore the interface between grassroots digital media practice and urban planning.

Blessing Mberu is Senior Research Scientist and Head of Population Dynamics and Urbanisation Research at the African Population and Health Research Center, Nairobi. He is honorary professor of demography and population studies, University of Witwatersrand, Johannesburg. Professor Mberu was a graduate assistant in 1988 and a senior lecturer between 1999 and 2002 in the Department of Sociology, Abia State University. He earned MA and PhD degrees in sociology, with specialisation in demography from Brown University. Prior to his time at Brown University, he obtained a BSc degree in sociology from Imo State University, Nigeria (then located in Okigwe) and a master's degree in sociology from the University of Ibadan, Nigeria. He was in the International Advisory Board of SLURC, Freetown and Executive Board and Expert Advisory Council of the International Society for Urban Health. His research work covers migration, urbanisation, urban health, urban slums and urban poverty across sub-Saharan Africa.

Milimer Morgado is a climate change and sustainable infrastructure professional with a proven track record in driving green city action plans and sustainable infrastructure investment globally, through policy dialogues, capacity-building and technical assistance to governments. She has worked in private consultancies, non-profit organisations and academia, enabling a holistic approach to sustainability by combining technical knowledge with socio-economic factors. Milimer has worked with over 20 cities and regional governments, building institutional capacity across Europe, Latin America, Asia and Africa to achieve net zero and climate resilience. This has been achieved through expertly leading and supporting a diverse portfolio of capacity-building projects on decarbonisation pathways and climate adaptation for clients, including Germany's International Climate Initiative (IKI), the Green Climate Fund (GCF), the UNDP and the UK PACT (Partnering for Accelerated Climate Transitions).

Nancy Odendaal is Professor of Urban Studies at the University of Cape Town (UCT) and the University of Basel. She is based at the African Centre for Cities at UCT and teaches on the critical urbanisms programme at the University of Basel. Up until July 2024, she was professor of city and regional planning and director of the School of Architecture, Planning and Geomatics, also at UCT. Her research and teaching interests are at the intersection of urban studies and postcolonial science and technology studies. Her recent book, *Disrupted Urbanism: Situated smart initiatives in African cities*, was published by Bristol University Press, in January 2023. In it she examines how endogenous platform applications in African cities, not only enable more sustainable livelihoods but could potentially have spatial impacts.

Emmanuel Osuteye is Associate Professor of Urbanisation and Sustainable Development, based at The Bartlett Developing Planning Unit, UCL. His research interests focus on studying the governance, policy and institutional aspects of disaster risk and risk management, climate change adaptation and resilience, and community-led development in low-income urban centres, particularly in Africa (and has extensive in-country field experience in several countries). He regularly provides technical inputs to sustainable development policy formulation & implementation processes and has worked with the AUDA-NEPAD, UNDP, UNEP and UN-Habitat. He is a contributing author to the IPCC's 6th Assessment Report on Climate Change (Working Group 2 – on impact, adaptation and vulnerability) and also serves as a technical advisor on urban resilience to the African Union (Department of Agriculture, Rural Development, Blue Economy and Sustainable Environment).

Daniel Oviedo is Associate Professor of Development Planning at the Bartlett Development Planning Unit at UCL. He specialises in the social, economic and spatial analysis of inequalities related to urban and interurban transport in rapidly growing cities across Latin America, sub-Saharan Africa and South Asia. He is the principal investigator of the On the Way to School (OWS) project and the UCL Inclusive Mobility (E)Innovations platform (IME). He is also the co-director of the UCL-Osaka Walking Cities Lab and a founding member of the International Network for Transport and Accessibility in Low-Income Communities in Latin America and the Caribbean (INTALInC). Daniel has been an advisor for various national governments, including Colombia, Peru, Panama, Nigeria and Sierra Leone, in addition to international organisations such as the Inter-American Development Bank and the World Bank, on issues related to transport, poverty, accessibility and social exclusion.

Francis Anthony Reffell is the founder and Executive Director of Centre of Dialogue on Human Settlement and Poverty Alleviation (CODOHSAPA). He is a social justice and development professional with over 20 years of working experience in the NGO sector, serving in various capacities in both local and international agencies. Has an MSc in rural development and BA general in geography and sociology. He pioneered the establishment of Federation of Urban and Rural Poor (FEDURP), a network of savings groups operating in rural and urban settings across the country with a mission to provide a platform for voice and space for poor populations and communities to drive their own development agenda. Through this space, Francis has dedicated his career to working on creating the space and voice of the poor and marginalised population and localities, which commands the value of restoration of hope and transformative change and development.

Andrea Rigon is a founder of SLURC. He is currently based at Politecnico di Milano and has been Professor of Participatory Development Planning at the Bartlett Development Planning Unit, UCL. His professional and research work spans 15 countries and focuses on how power relations affect the participation of different people and social groups in decision-making processes at different scales. He is interested in how residents' participation is managed within urban development projects, particularly in informal settlements and what the effects are on in/equality and social exclusion. He chairs CatalyticAction, a charity and design studio using participatory design to deliver dignified built environment in humanitarian or vulnerable contexts. In his work, he developed intersectional participatory methods and is now applying them to intersectional climate justice. He is currently working on young people participation in urban governance through digital platforms in Indonesia and Lebanon.

Alexander Stone is a communications professional focusing on participatory visual methodologies and creating inclusive, human-centred content. He holds an MSc in environment and sustainable development from the Development Planning Unit at UCL. He spent two years as a programme assistant at SLURC in Freetown and currently works as a story producer for an NGO which fights for the rights of people with disabilities. A keen photographer and videographer, Alexander continues to combine his passion for images with his storytelling work to raise the voices of marginalised groups at home in London and further afield.

Joanna Stroud is Head of Online Learning at UCL and has worked at a number of research intensive and teaching institutions in the UK. At UCL she has established and leads a unit responsible for the design and development of online courses, providing guidance relating to online pedagogies and learning design, technology and course production management processes. She co-ordinated the strategic, pedagogic and developmental components of UCL's move to online teaching as part of its COVID-19 response and has supported a series of projects in humanitarian contexts, including educational interventions around preventable blindness and major Ebola and Zika epidemics.

Irene Vance has several decades of experience working with international development agencies and UK grant-making organisations. As International Grant Manager at Comic Relief, a major UK charity, she managed a six-figure grant portfolio across African cities. She has served on grant-making advisory panels, including the Jersey Overseas Fund for financial inclusion. Irene's international experience extends to collaborations with donors such as UN-Habitat, the InterAmerican Development Bank, The Nordic Fund, Sida and private investors, developing sustainable financial models for micro and small business development, housing microfinance and incremental slum upgrading. She has overseen projects in Central American transitions from donor initiatives to financially sustainable foundations. Currently, Irene is Head of Project Delivery at the African Cities Research Consortium, based at Manchester University.

Ignacia Ossul Vermehren is a gender and humanitarian analyst for UN Women Somalia. She is a programme specialist and researcher promoting gender equality and disability inclusion in development and humanitarian action. Prior to joining UN Women Somalia, she was part of Oxfam's Global Gender in Emergency team deployed to Ukraine and the Earthquake response in Syria. She participated in Global Disability Hub's AT2030 initiative as a research fellow working in Indonesia and Sierra Leone. She holds a PhD in development planning from UCL.

Julian Walker is Professor of Inclusive Social Policy at the Bartlett Development Planning Unit at UCL. He has a background in social anthropology and research and practice experience in several fields. These include, gender policy and planning, disability and child rights, urban displacement – including involuntary resettlement and forced eviction – and pro-poor livelihoods and employment rights. He is interested in how gender and social diversity relate to citizenship practices.

Michael Walls is Professor of Development Politics and Economy and Director of UCL's Bartlett Development Planning Unit. He has thirteen years' experience in senior management in the private sector and teaches market-led approaches to development. Over the past 20 years, his research has focused on the political economy of the Somali Horn of Africa and the impact of climate change on urbanisation. He was chief observer for the international observation missions to Somaliland's 2021 local council and parliamentary elections and the 2017 presidential election and has coordinated missions since 2005. In addition, he is a member of the board of SLURC, which aims to build research capacity and to conduct research in the informal settlements of Sierra Leone, and was a co-investigator in a research project examining complex land markets in Uganda and Somaliland.

Julia Wesely is a postdoctoral researcher at the Institute of Landscape Planning at the University of Natural Resources and Life Sciences in Vienna, who holds a PhD in development planning from The Bartlett Development Planning Unit at UCL. Her research, teaching and public engagement focuses on the intersections of urban (in)equality, environmental (in)justice and critical pedagogy. Julia has worked in collaboration with universities, civil society organisations, NGOs and social movements from several Latin American, African and European cities. She is part of the Early Career Researcher Collective Overlooked Cities, which seeks to draw attention to people, places and practices that are marginalised, off-the-map and under-theorised in 'global' urban studies.

Annie Wilkinson is a research fellow at the Institute of Development Studies, University of Sussex. She is an anthropologist and health systems researcher. She conducts interdisciplinary and participatory research on global health challenges and has expertise in urban health, zoonotic disease, drug resistance and epidemic preparedness. She has worked mostly in West Africa – especially Sierra Leone – and within emergency humanitarian and epidemic response. Her current research explores institutional arrangements around health and disease in informal urban settlements and the governance of infection control. She has advised governments and international organisations on responses to the West African Ebola epidemic and COVID-19.

Yasmina Yusuf is an independent consultant with a focus on environmental planning in the Global South. She has experience measuring cities' greenhouse gas emissions and has worked with big data sets such as Environmental Insights Explorer to support cities in identifying policy interventions that encourage active travel. Prior to this, she was a researcher and project manager on the Transitions to Sustainable Urban Mobility project and a fellow based at SLURC. She also spent three years at Oxford Policy Management, where she managed and implemented research programmes related to economic development. She has a master's degree in urban and regional planning from the University of California, Los Angeles and a master's degree in social development practice from UCL.

Preface

Urban Transformations in Sierra Leone: Knowledge co-production and partnerships for a just city is a testament to the collaborative efforts, research insights and transformative practices that have evolved through collective work of SLURC and its partners since its inception in 2015. Edited by Joseph M. Macarthy, Braima Koroma, Andrea Rigon, Alexandre Apsan Frediani and Andrea Klingel, this book brings together a diverse array of experts and practitioners to delve into the critical issues surrounding urban transformations in Sierra Leone.

The chapters presented in this book reflect a deep commitment to fostering knowledge co-production and equitable partnerships as essential elements in shaping a more just and equitable urban landscape for all residents. The narratives, research findings and transformative practices shared in this book are an accumulation of the research endeavours conducted by SLURC and its partners over the years, reflecting a wealth of knowledge and experience gained through rigorous inquiry and community engagement.

As the editors of this book, we acknowledge the pivotal role that SLURC and its partners have played in advancing the discourse on urban development in Sierra Leone. The insights presented in this book are a result of the dedication, expertise and collaborative spirit of all those involved in the research work conducted by SLURC and its partners, highlighting the importance of inclusive and sustainable urban development strategies that prioritise social justice and equity in the rapidly evolving context of cities like Freetown.

The book is divided into four distinct parts, each offering a unique perspective on urban transformations in Sierra Leone. In Part I, we provide a comprehensive overview of the context in which urban transformations take place, exploring the concept of knowledge co-production in urban Africa to an in-depth introduction to the city and detailing the story of SLURC and its impactful research work. In Part II, we delve into innovative approaches and practices. This part explores research-based training, principles of co-learning for environmental justice, participatory photography for inclusive neighbourhood planning and the role of community action area planning in empowering the urban poor and fostering inclusive urban development. Part III focuses on knowledge contributions, highlighting critical issues such as urban health priorities, resilience-building, urban livelihoods, empowerment in urban humanitarian responses, community-led planning and sustainable mobility, offering valuable insights for addressing key challenges in urban development. In Part IV, we shift the focus towards learning through the lens of SLURC, featuring reflections from key figures such as Michael Walls, Blessing Uchenna Mberu and Nancy Odendaal, among others. Their insights underscore the transformative impact of SLURC's work in the global context, emphasising the importance of knowledge exchange, activism and impactful partnerships in driving positive urban transformations.

Through the diverse perspectives and experiences shared in this book, we aim to inspire policymakers, researchers and community stakeholders to engage in collaborative efforts towards creating a more inclusive, resilient and sustainable urban environment in Sierra Leone. We invite readers to immerse themselves in the narratives, research findings and transformative practices presented in this volume and join us in our shared dedication to fostering knowledge co-production and partnerships for a more just and equitable city in Sierra Leone. Together, let us embark on a journey of learning, understanding and action towards shaping urban transformations that prioritise the wellbeing and prosperity of all residents in Sierra Leone, building upon the foundation of research work conducted by SLURC and its partners.

Foreword

It is with great pleasure and enthusiasm that I write the foreword for this groundbreaking book. As the mayor of the municipality of Freetown, I am deeply committed to the development and progress of our city and this book aligns perfectly with our vision for a just and sustainable urban future.

Sierra Leone, like many other developing countries, is experiencing rapid urbanisation. Our cities are growing at an unprecedented rate, presenting both opportunities and challenges. It is essential that we navigate this transformation in a way that promotes social equity, economic prosperity and environmental sustainability. This book not only recognises the urgency of this task but also provides a comprehensive and innovative framework to achieve it.

The concept of knowledge co-production is central to the approach outlined in this book. It emphasises the importance of collaboration and partnership between different stakeholders, including government institutions, academia, civil society organisations and local communities. This inclusive and participatory approach ensures that the knowledge and expertise of all relevant actors are harnessed, leading to more informed and effective decision-making processes.

Furthermore, this book highlights the significance of partnerships in driving urban transformations. It emphasises the need for multi-stakeholder collaborations that transcend traditional boundaries and foster innovative solutions. By working together, we can leverage the strengths and resources of different actors to address the complex challenges we face. This book provides valuable insights and case studies that demonstrate the power of partnerships in creating a just city.

One of the key strengths of this book is its focus on the context of Sierra Leone. It recognises that urban transformations cannot be approached in a one-size-fits-all manner but must be tailored to the specific needs and realities of our country. By highlighting the experiences and lessons learned from Sierra Leone, this book offers a unique perspective that can inform urban development strategies not only in our country but also in other similar contexts.

As the mayor of Freetown, I am particularly excited about the potential impact of this book on our city. As both the capital and largest city in Sierra Leone, Freetown is at the forefront of urban transformations in our country. We are already implementing various initiatives to promote sustainable urban development and this book contributes to the body of knowledge and ideas required to enhance our efforts.

I would like to express my sincere gratitude to the editors, Joseph M. Macarthy, Braima Koroma, Andrea Rigon, Alexandre Apsan Frediani and Andrea Klingel, for their outstanding work in compiling this book. Their dedication and expertise have resulted in a comprehensive and insightful resource that will undoubtedly contribute to the advancement of urban transformations in Sierra Leone. This book is a must-read for anyone interested in urban development, social justice and sustainability. It offers a roadmap for creating inclusive, equitable and sustainable cities and will be a valuable input in our journey to transform Freetown.

Yvonne Aki-Sawyerr, mayor of the municipality of Freetown

Acknowledgements

We extend our thanks to all the individuals who have shared their reflections, experiences and perspectives in the various chapters of this book, contributing to a diverse and comprehensive understanding of urban development in Sierra Leone.

We would like to thank the reviewers and editors who have provided valuable feedback, guidance and support throughout the process of compiling and editing this book. Their expertise and insights have been invaluable in ensuring the quality and relevance of the content presented in this book.

We express our gratitude to the readers, policymakers, researchers, practitioners and community stakeholders who engage with the ideas in this book. Your commitment to fostering inclusive and sustainable urban development in Sierra Leone is essential in driving positive change and creating a more just and equitable city for all residents.

We extend our heartfelt gratitude to all those who have contributed to this collaborative effort. Your collective contributions have ignited a spark of change and progress in urban development in Sierra Leone and we are excited for the journey ahead as we work towards a more just and equitable urban future.

Introduction

Joseph M. Macarthy, Braima Koroma,
Andrea Rigon, Alexandre Apsan Frediani and
Andrea Klingel

With a population now exceeding one million people, Freetown is confronted with significant challenges related to the provision of services, housing and infrastructure for its residents, which are further exacerbated by the impacts of climate change. A substantial portion of Freetown's population already resides in informal settlements, with the informal economy estimated to provide employment for up to 70% of the city's inhabitants.

In 2015, the Sierra Leone Urban Research Centre (SLURC) was established with the primary objective of engaging with the growing urban challenges in Sierra Leone through research, capacity building and advocacy activities. SLURC was founded as a partnership between the Institute of Geography and Development Studies of Njala University and the Bartlett Development Planning Unit of UCL. Since its establishment, SLURC has conducted research in various areas, including urban health, urban livelihoods and city economy, land and housing, urban vulnerability and resilience, urban services and infrastructure, and urban mobility and transport. SLURC has become a platform for dialogue among urban stakeholders to negotiate the future of the city.

This book shares the journey of SLURC so far, presenting the key findings generated by its diverse research projects while reflecting on the partnerships it has fostered throughout this process. By bringing together research from different sectors, the book advances knowledge about Freetown and makes a significant contribution to the understanding of contemporary African cities. It also demonstrates the potential of transdisciplinary work and a commitment to collaboration across sectors to co-produce a more sustainable urban future.

The book makes three main contributions. Firstly, it provides a systematic account of the key processes shaping and driving urban development in Freetown, shedding light on their impact on the wellbeing of those living in informal settlements. Secondly, it draws on the experiences of SLURC to illustrate the challenges and opportunities associated with knowledge co-production methodologies in informing urban transformations. Finally, it reflects on the role of partnerships facilitated by and with higher education institutions in influencing policy and planning processes to contribute to national development priorities and global urban agendas, such as the New Urban Agenda and Sustainable Development Goal 11.

The book offers a comprehensive overview of the various urban research projects conducted at SLURC and reflects on the processes and impact of this institution. Despite their diversity, all the research findings outlined in this book are linked to SLURC's mission of improving the wellbeing of residents in informal settlements, which, in turn, contributes to the overall wellbeing of the city.

The book is divided into four parts. The first part, 'Setting the scene', begins with an introduction to knowledge co-production and equitable partnerships in urban Africa (Chapter 1). This is followed by Chapter 2 on urban development in Freetown; Chapter 3 delves into the history of the Sierra Leone Urban Research Centre. This part concludes with a discussion on the terminology used to describe slums and informal settlements.

Part II, 'Knowledge contributions', presents the key policy-relevant findings from various research projects undertaken by SLURC. It includes chapters on analysing urban livelihoods (Chapter 4), understanding Freetown's urban health priorities and challenges (Chapter 5), assessing Freetown's development trajectory from a sustainable mobility perspective (Chapter 6), highlighting the strategic importance of knowledge production on assistive technology, disability and informality (Chapter 7), exploring political spaces to address risk traps (Chapter 8), exploring the impact of community-led planning in Freetown (Chapter 9) and examining the role of empowerment in urban humanitarian responses in Freetown (Chapter 10).

In Part III, 'Learning and action', six chapters analyse the different strategies and approaches employed by SLURC and its partners to generate knowledge about the city and foster action. This includes a reflection on SLURC's programme of research-based training (Chapter 11), an exploration of the MSc ESD/SLURC Learning Alliance and principles of co-learning for environmental justice (Chapter 12), the use of participatory photography for inclusive neighbourhood planning (Chapter 13), the development and implementation of a massive open online course (Chapter 14), the role of community action area planning in expanding the participatory capabilities of the urban poor (Chapter 15) and the establishment of city and community learning platforms (Chapter 16).

Finally, Part IV, 'Learning through SLURC', offers brief reflections on SLURC's impact and role, drawing on the personal experiences of a range of internal and external stakeholders. The book concludes with an appendix that provides protocols for research partnerships developed by SLURC and its research partners.

This book represents a complex collective effort to synthesise the multifaceted work undertaken by SLURC since its inception in 2015. The editors are the four founders, the two Sierra Leone directors, Joseph M. Macarthy and Braima Koroma, along with the two Principal Investigators of the initial start-up grant based at UCL, Alexandre Apsan Frediani and Andrea Rigon. Andrea Klingel, the recently recruited Director of Operations, was added to the editorial team because of her important role in producing the book, particularly in tracking the progress and submissions of the contributions. Andrea Rigon takes on the role of executive editor, leading the editing of chapters and proposal development.

In summary, this book sheds light on the urban transformations taking place in Freetown, Sierra Leone and the role of knowledge co-production and partnerships in fostering a more just city. It provides insights into the key processes shaping urban development, explores the challenges and opportunities of knowledge co-production methodologies and reflects on the impact of partnerships facilitated by higher education institutions. By sharing the research findings and experiences of SLURC, this book contributes to the understanding of African cities and offers valuable lessons for urban practitioners, policymakers and researchers.

Part I
Setting the scene

1
Knowledge co-production and equitable partnership in urban Africa
Andrea Rigon and Alexandre Apsan Frediani

Introduction

The Sierra Leone Urban Research Centre's (SLURC) mission of working for the wellbeing of the residents of informal settlements is grounded in the view that urban residents should have meaningful and equitable opportunities to be involved in city-making. From the perspective of a research institution, this means putting knowledge co-production at the centre and seeing co-production as a 'strategy to challenge existing epistemic injustice' (Castán Broto et al., 2022, p. 10). We view knowledge co-production as being at the service of a just co-production of the city. With that in mind, SLURC's research and learning initiatives have been informed and driven by the motivation to co-produce knowledge in ways that enhance the recognition of the needs and aspirations of those living in informal settlements. At the same time, SLURC has also been motivated to build partnerships with equivalence with institutions and collectives locally, regionally as well as internationally.

This chapter frames the work of SLURC within debates on knowledge co-production and equitable partnerships in urban Africa. It defines the values and principles embedded in this normative approach that underpinned SLURC's foundation and operation. We also reflect on some of the complexities and challenges that emerge from linking this approach to knowledge production and partnership building with the efforts to improve the wellbeing of the urban inhabitants of Sierra Leone, especially those living in informal settlements. These reflections are then deepened throughout the various other contributions in this book. Part II, 'Knowledge contributions' discusses the knowledge outcomes of this co-production process, while Part III, 'Learning and action' discusses the mechanisms and methodologies of the co-production.

Co-producing knowledge and the city

SLURC has been operating in the interlinkages between two aspects of co-production: knowledge co-production and co-production of the city. Knowledge co-production is a way of working with partners to define research objectives and questions and to generate new knowledge by combining the approaches and epistemologies of the different actors involved (Padan, 2020). However, different actors can also jointly co-produce the city, democratising city-making. In some cases, co-production can focus on specific projects aimed, for example, at specific services. As discussed below, one criticism concerns the extent to which co-production is instrumentally used by government to deliver services at lower cost.

This concern opens a debate on whether co-production is always a normative and intentional approach to transforming a place and its unequal power relations, in order to achieve positive co-creation of the city (Mitlin, 2018). Even if this is the case, as has been recently argued (Castán Broto et al., 2022), African cities have been co-produced 'from below' long before these intentional, normative co-production attempts. Whether those in charge want it or not, African cities are always co-produced to some extent because there are large areas where state policy and interventions are limited, whereas the contribution from below is strong. The everyday lived dynamics and experiences of the urban inhabitants produce African cities (Pieterse & Simone, 2013).

However, this co-production is taking place in the context of very unequal conditions. The question is whether this co-production from below is recognised and therefore, whether urban administration and policies reflect the needs of this large number of city makers, or whether these voices are completely ignored.[1] This is where knowledge co-production can help address epistemic injustice. It can recognise these voices and make them central to the discussion between different interests and visions of what a good city is. This is fundamental because how we *know* the city (whose perspective and vision we adopt) defines the kind of city that is produced and for whom. Therefore, epistemic injustice is directly linked to structural injustice.

This point is also important because urban planning and development in African cities is still overcoming a legacy of colonial spatial structure and planning regulations (Watson, 2014b). Post-independence urbanisation took place on the basis of – and is often exacerbated by – pre-existing patterns of exclusion and segregation. The spatial inequality and segregation of African cities is an urban form that hides the poor, who often live on small marginal lands (Rigon, Koroma, Macarthy & Frediani, 2018). Many civil servants and local authorities understand planning in terms of restoring a social order lost during the rapid growth of cities. This technocratic perspective views planning as an exclusively technical and neutral process that professionals must perform *for* people, rather than *with* people (Rigon et al., 2015).

Even when colonial and similar post-colonial planning models are rejected, planning is still seen as the technical implementation of a master plan. Several cities are preparing new plans through a process of privatising planning. Here, master plans are developed by a few multi-national consultancy companies that produce standardised plans, reproducing dominant planning principles, often exported from Europe (Rigon et al., 2018). These are plans prepared with little participation or democratic control, through processes that do not recognise the role of people's agency in making the city and the needs for a political, negotiated process. These plans are, consequently, disjointed from the reality of most urban residents. Co-production is therefore a necessary process for going beyond enforced universal models based on unrealistic, unsustainable and exclusionary 'urban fantasies', based on the model of Dubai, Shanghai or Singapore (Watson, 2014a).

In many African cities, there are urban residents who build their houses and provide their own services through various forms of individual and collective action. This self-help approach is a major force that shapes and makes African cities. Therefore, there is a lot of urban development and planning taking place outside the control of city authorities. For example, under the umbrella of Slum Dwellers International (SDI), national federations of the urban poor organise themselves into saving groups and generate their own censuses and data to negotiate with policymakers. Residents in informal settlements also initiate their own slum-upgrading processes (Mitlin & Satterthwaite, 2004).

The centrality of such 'agency from below' in planning and managing cities can contribute to the emergence of a hybrid urbanism that can find new models and concepts appropriate for the specific needs of diverse African cities, leaving behind European models. The value of citizen participation in local governance and planning is increasingly recognised in different African countries, presenting opportunities. However, a range of inequalities in African cities generates social, economic and political barriers that can turn them into archipelagos where people live in certain islands without necessarily meeting people from other islands: areas/ settlements, social classes, etc.

It is in this space, between opening opportunities for collaborative governance and urban fragmentation, that there is scope for the knowledge co-production processes facilitated by institutions such as SLURC. These processes include the creation of meetings between these different urban islands. It is important to note that, even if people do not talk to each other, such islands are part of an integrated urban system. For example, Chapter 4 demonstrates how the livelihoods of those living in informal settlements contribute to the wellbeing and economy of the entire city and thus how policies that undermine these livelihoods negatively affect the entire city. In this sense, co-production can bring 'different stakeholder groups together in an attempt to overcome often longstanding antagonisms and wide asymmetries of power by working or researching together to improve outcomes' (Simon, Palmer, Riise, Smit & Valencia, 2018, p. 481). At the same time, for co-production to take place, 'it is not always necessary for the state and its citizens to work under one organisational framework or to be focused on the same specific project, or even the same geography' (Lines & Makau, 2018, p. 421). Co-production does not only happen in formal facilitated spaces; it is an ecosystem of actors in which research institutions play an important role in documenting new knowledge and practices, particularly recognising those of subaltern groups and in encouraging information flows in multiple directions. Finally, the scale of co-production processes and the relationship between these are fundamental to the outcomes. The challenge is connecting the work at neighbourhood scale with processes at city level. Other chapters will engage with SLURC's strategy of working in-depth and long-term in specific settlements and then using the outputs of this process to influence city-level conversation and policy.

Another key pillar shaping co-production in African cities is the condition of the knowledge landscape within which co-production takes place. Through the lens of southern urban theory and practice, various academics have been arguing that dominant modes of knowledge production have failed to generate thick analysis of experiences and processes taking in place in African cities (Parnell & Pieterse, 2014; Bhan, 2019). Instead of focusing on contextual and historicised analysis of the everyday practices of city-making, the main sources of knowledge used to inform decision-making processes often re-affirm the theoretical lens and explanatory frameworks developed by privileged and dominant knowledge producers. It is within this context that knowledge co-production emerges as a response to challenge existing epistemic injustices about urban Africa.

From SLURC's perspective, challenging the asymmetries of power in the process of knowledge production about Freetown has been a critical condition, as well as a way to promote more democratic, equitable and sustainable urban development. By producing knowledge not only *about* but *with* marginalised voices and perspectives, knowledge co-production aims to generate alternative visions of the city, creating a richer and more expanded vocabulary and more responsive devices to give a direction to collective city-making. Knowledge co-production processes are also a terrain with more equitable conditions for dialogue, enabling different actors to get to know and listen to each other and negotiate/disagree, while building a framework for the discussion.

SLURC aims to address the unequal opportunities for participating meaningfully in the co-production of the city by reconfiguring the process of knowledge production and centring it around the knowledge processes of those living in informal settlements in Freetown. In this sense, democratisation of knowledge production aims to make the playing-field of engagement between informal dwellers and more powerful actors in the city (such as the government) more equitable. Although it may initially be difficult to enable these fairer conditions of engagement, over time these participatory spaces have been shown to change the relationship between citizens and government towards a different form of participatory citizenship (Hickey & Mohan, 2004, Gaventa & Barrett, 2012). These spaces can become more empowering and transform the way in which residents exercise their citizenship. Citizens start to expect continuous involvement in decisions affecting their lives (Cornwall & Coelho, 2006).

There are two important criticisms of co-production that need to be addressed. First, there is the view that by taking responsibility away from government and making service delivery more efficient, co-production is an approach aligned with the most extreme neoliberal perspectives (Ostrom, 1996). However, co-production becomes essential in cities like Freetown where the government alone is unable to provide services. We believe that it is important to continuously reflect on who bears the costs of co-production and ensure it is not a way to further shift the burden on the poorest, but rather a tool to involve them in urban governance and use limited government resources better.

Second, co-production is criticised as contributing to depoliticisation as it avoids conflict with authorities, whereas conflict is an important form of city production. In her analysis of the movements of slum-dwellers and their organisations, Mitlin argues that there is not a dichotomy whereby working collaboratively to co-produce urban services excludes more conflict-oriented action. Instead, these are all part of an array of approaches available in the complex strategies that urban dwellers and their organisations employ, which involves shifting from contention, collaboration, subversion and resistance (Mitlin, 2018).

An important side of knowledge co-production, central to this book, is its connection with learning. Linked to the point made by Parnell and Pieterse, McFarlane noted that learning can challenge and transform how we know and see the city. Therefore, learning in cities 'cannot simply be restricted to the domain of specialist and expertise knowledge... We need to repeatedly ask who "we" – critical urban researchers, planners and so on – learn from, with, for what ends and under what conditions of power and inclusion' (McFarlane, 2018, pp. 323–324). Crucially, we also need to reflect on *how* we learn to co-produce and cultivate a partnership, by constantly reflecting on power relations and the unequal burdens of co-production (Oliver, Kothari & Mays, 2019). A partnership like SLURC also implies first unlearning, then relearning how to work together. This is a process in which the entire institution is involved. From small things like booking flights with routes that minimise visa requirements, to identifying common priorities and language.

Partnership with equivalence

As we defined it, co-production is a process of collaborating with partners to define research agendas and generate new knowledge based on merging the approaches and epistemologies of the different participating actors. This makes the relations between the partners involved the centre of the co-production process. Therefore, partnerships are central to making co-production processes transformational, that is, transforming power relations and the actors themselves (Padan, 2020). For this reason, this second part of the chapter focuses on partnerships. Complex sets of partnerships characterise knowledge co-production efforts and their interface with power relations between actors at city, national and international scales. There are partnerships between research institutions based in the Global North and in African cities; partnerships amongst research institutions in African cities; partnerships between research institutions, non-governmental organisations, urban communities and government.

This book adopts the concept of 'partnership with equivalence' developed by Caren Levy (2020). This is defined as those partnerships that recognise the diverse skills, knowledge and values brought by different urban actors and are formed through mutual respect, transparency and accountability, and a commitment to learn together. The Knowledge in Action for Urban Equality (KNOW) project spells out eight principles to make such partnerships flourish and these have been a compass to guide the establishment of the complex networks of partnerships that enabled the co-production of the knowledge presented in this book. Partnerships with equivalence are: based on a shared vision and common purpose; based upon co-produced knowledge; founded on mutual respect; grounded in inclusivity and open to new actors; co-constructed as durable, strategic and long-term; rooted in the local governance context; transparent and accountable; embrace different forms of engagement (Knowledge in Action for Urban Equality, 2020).

As SLURC was formed through a partnership between higher education institutions and researchers based in the UK and Sierra Leone – involving a series of Freetown grassroots and civil society actors – it has been crucial for us (the SLURC team) to reflect about the nature and quality of these international, as well as local, relationships. A significant part of the research conducted by SLURC in African cities involves researchers based in institutions outside the continent. We started from a joint understanding that international research collaborations can reinforce rather than remedy the epistemic injustice discussed above and often prevents research from becoming part of co-produced solutions.

In many sub-Saharan countries in Africa, we often witnessed foreign researchers hiring local academics as individual consultants to do their data collection and fulfil other research needs. Local academics are usually happy to join such projects if paid international rates and those targeted by international researchers are often amongst the best academics in the country. Their time and input are desperately needed by their universities to train new generations and by other local organisations including the government. However, there may be greater incentives to conduct work which responds to external research agendas in projects that often have little benefit for local universities and leave little legacy.

It takes Global North academics two emails to agree a daily fee with an African colleague; while it takes months or years to develop a strategic partnership with a local research institution in which research agendas and the terms of engagement are openly discussed and arrangements are identified for the benefit of all parties. If northern researchers do not want to take resources away from Global South higher education and government institutions by buying people out from their critical work, then a long-term partnership approach is the only viable option.

These partnerships and institutional arrangements need to be set in such a way that they allow knowledge to contribute positively to urban transformations (Rigon, Macarthy, Koroma, Walker & Frediani, 2017). An important dimension of these partnerships involves developing institutional capabilities that can make future collaboration more equal. For African institutions, this could mean having the structure to receive and administrate significant funding and or being able to lead on a joint proposal. In the Global North, institutions may need to develop internal processes that recognise a diversity of contexts and requirement and, for example, fully support the application for visas for southern partners to rebalance the administrative burden that otherwise furthers inequalities by, for instance, using up the limited time of African scholars.

Importantly, partnerships of equivalence cannot solve the structural and power differentials or epistemological differences. Rather, they offer a framework for these to be continuously discussed, by acknowledging and dealing with conflict, and for the partnership practice to adapt in relation to such discussions.

At a city level, we argue that research institutions can play the important role of brokering relationships and facilitating platforms so that other actors can feel comfortable when negotiating important issues of the city, creating space for co-production. For example, urban marginal communities often mistrust local authorities which may enforce evictions or interventions that can affect the livelihoods of their residents. By listening and working with such communities and their organisations, research institutions can become perceived as a safe place for these discussions. Similarly, government and other institutions often see research institutions as a neutral space. However, in this brokering role, research institutions should be aware that 'research in itself is a powerful intervention, even if carried out at a distance, which has traditionally benefitted the researcher, and the knowledge base of the dominant group in society' (Smith, 1999, p. 176). This implies constant self-reflection on the normative positioning of research institutions in knowledge co-production processes.

In the history of SLURC itself, there have already been three moments where local partnerships were established. Firstly, in its formation stage, the scope and approach of SLURC's work were defined through dialogue and in partnership with other Freetown based civil society groups working to improve the wellbeing of informal settlements' dwellers. The second moment produced a deeper level of partnership with residents and groups in four informal settlements, where SLURC conducted most of its research and capacity building activities: Cockle Bay, Dworzark, Portee-Rokupa and Moyiba. Most recently, SLURC started to support the formation of community learning platforms in informal settlements in Freetown as well as the City Learning Platform, involving representatives of informal settlements, government authorities, development agencies, NGOs and professional urban development practitioners.

A key ingredient that cuts across SLURC partnerships at local and international levels has been a commitment to solidarity. Iris Marion Young (2011, p. 120) defines solidarity as 'a relationship among separate and dissimilar actors who decide to stand together, for one another'. Young asserts how 'solidarity need not connote homogeneity or symmetry among those in relation' (2011, p. 120) and it is precisely that heterogeneity that makes solidarity a powerful political project. This is an ongoing process. Solidarity, she continues, 'must always be *forged* and *reforged*. Solidarity is firm but fragile. It looks to the future because it must constantly be renewed' (Young, 2011, p. 120). Such a project is only made possible by building trust and mutual responsiveness: necessary mechanisms for building collaborations that recognise difference. For SLURC, it has been crucial to build solidarity at neighbourhood and city-level among actors advocating for more equitable urban development. At the same time, SLURC has been part of international solidarity partnerships focused on urgently prioritising the needs and aspirations of those living in informal settlements among international actors and processes.

Conclusion

Bringing together the co-production of cities and knowledge through partnerships with equivalence has meant SLURC recognising marginality as a site for emancipatory planning and practice. SLURC's approach resonates with what bell hooks (1990, p. 145) has termed 'the margin as a space of radical openness'. For SLURC, this meant a constant effort to understand, and bring to the centre of its work, subaltern rationalities and practices (Chattopadhyay & Sakar, 2005). This includes everyday knowledge, ways of doing things and practise of self-organisation and resistance. The aim has been to understand what those rationalities and practices might mean for urban planning (Miraftab, 2009). To engage meaningfully with the subaltern on the margins, partnerships must face existing structures of power and oppression, which means – to return to hooks (1990, p. 145) – seeking to create material spaces 'where there is unlimited access to the pleasure and power of knowing, where transformation is possible'.

This trajectory of SLURC has meant that its activities have been able to create not only positive and reciprocal relationships, but also infrastructures of collaborations of urban research and practice. These infrastructures have the potential to affect and transform the landscape of how decisions and policies are made in Freetown. SLURC's key challenge ahead is to continue nurturing these practices and spaces of co-production, retaining their radical and emancipatory potential, while enhancing their ability to affect structural change that leads to more equitable and just urban development in Sierra Leone.

Note

1 Some may not define these processes as co-production, making a rigid distinction between a) *city-making* that happens in a more heterogenous and conflictual form, where the state may not acknowledge how some residents make the city; and b) *co-production* where there is that positive and normative connotation.

References

Bhan, G. (2019). Notes on Southern urban practices. *Environment and Urbanization, 31*(2), 639–654.

Castán Broto, V., Ortiz, C., Lipietz, B., Osuteye, E., Johnson, C., Kombe, W., . . . Levy, C. (2022). Co-production outcomes for urban equality: learning from different trajectories of citizens' involvement in urban change. *Current Research in Environmental Sustainability, 4*, 100179. https://doi.org/10.1016/j.crsust.2022.100179

Chattopadhyay, S., & Sarkar, B. (2005). Introduction: the subaltern and the popular. *Postcolonial Studies*, 8:4, 357-363, https://doi.org/10.1080/13688790500375066

Cornwall, A., & Coelho, V. S. P. (2006). *Spaces for Change? The politics of citizen participation in new democratic arenas*. London: Zed.

Gaventa, J., & Barrett, G. (2012). Mapping the outcomes of citizen engagement. *World Development, 40*(12), 2399–2410. https://doi.org/10.1016/j.worlddev.2012.05.014

Hickey, S., & Mohan, G. (Eds). (2004). *Participation: From tyranny to transformation? Exploring new approaches to participation in development*. London: Zed.

hooks, b. (1990). *Yearning: Race, gender, and cultural politics*. Boston: South End Press.

Knowledge in Action for Urban Equality. (2020). *Partnerships for Urban Equality*. International Engagement Brief #1. London: Bartlett Development Planning Unit.

Levy, C. (2020). Framing the agenda: What do we mean by 'partnerships with equivalence' for the pursuit of urban equality? In *Partnerships for Urban Equality*. International Engagement Brief #1. London: Bartlett Development Planning Unit.

Lines, K., & Makau, J. (2018). Taking the long view: 20 years of Muungano wa Wanavijiji, the Kenyan federation of slum dwellers. *Environment and Urbanization, 30*(2), 407–424. https://doi.org/10.1177/0956247818785327

McFarlane, C. (2018). Learning from the city: a politics of urban learning in planning. In M. Gunder, A. Madanipour, & V. Watson (Eds), *The Routledge Handbook of Planning Theory* (pp. 323–333). London: Routledge.

Miraftab, F. (2009). Insurgent planning: situating radical planning in the global South. *Planning Theory*, 8(1), 32–50. http://www.jstor.org/stable/26165884

Mitlin, D. (2018). Beyond contention: urban social movements and their multiple approaches to secure transformation. *Environment and Urbanization*, 30(2), 557–574. https://doi.org/10.1177/0956247818791012

Oliver, K., Kothari, A., & Mays, N. (2019). Coming to terms with the hidden costs of co-production. London School of Economics blog, 19 June. Accessed 25 June 2024. https://blogs.lse.ac.uk/impactofsocialsciences/2019/06/19/coming-to-terms-with-the-hidden-costs-of-co-production/

Ostrom, E. (1996). Crossing the great divide: coproduction, synergy, and development. *World Development*, 24(6), 1073–1087. https://doi.org/10.1016/0305-750X(96)00023-X

Padan, Y. (2020). Guide # 3: Co-producing knowledge. *Practicing Ethics: Guides*. https://www.urban-know.com/_files/ugd/623440_67fbdaf836574ccc869a1f7f7ec80c0d.pdf

Parnell, S., & Pieterse, E. A. (2014). *Africa's Urban Revolution*. London: Zed.

Pieterse, E. A., & Simone, A. M. (2013). *Rogue Urbanism: Emergent African cities*. Johannesburg: Jacana Media.

Rigon, A., Abah, O. S., Dangoji, S., Walker, J., Frediani, A. A., Ogunleye, O., & Hirst, L. (2015). Well-being and citizenship in urban Nigeria. ICF International, UCL Development Planning Unit: London, UK. https://discovery.ucl.ac.uk/id/eprint/1474968/

Rigon, A., Koroma, B., Macarthy, J., & Frediani, A. A. (2018). The politics of urban management and planning in African cities. In T. Binns, K. Lynch, & E. Nel (Eds), *The Routledge Handbook of African Development* (pp. 415–425). New York: Routledge.

Rigon, A., Macarthy, J., Koroma, B., Walker, J., & Frediani, A. A. (2017). Partnering with higher education institutions for social and environmental justice in the Global South: lessons from the Sierra Leone Urban Research Centre. *DPU News* (62). Accessed 25 June 2024. https://www.ucl.ac.uk/bartlett/development/sites/bartlett/files/dpunews_62_web.pdf

Satterthwaite, D., & Mitlin, D. (Eds). (2004). *Empowering Squatter Citizen: local government, civil society and urban poverty reduction*. London: Routledge. https://doi.org/10.4324/9781849771108

Simon, D., Palmer, H., Riise, J., Smit, W., & Valencia, S. (2018). The challenges of transdisciplinary knowledge production: from unilocal to comparative research. *Environment and Urbanization*, 30(2), 481–500. https://doi.org/10.1177/0956247818787177

Smith, L. T. (1999). *Decolonizing Methodologies: Research and indigenous peoples*. London: Zed Books.

Watson, V. (2014a). African urban fantasies: dreams or nightmares? *Environment and Urbanization*, 26(1), 215–231. https://doi.org/10.1177/0956247813513705

Watson, V. (2014b). Learning planning from the south: ideas from new urban frontiers. In S. Parnell & S. Oldfield (Eds), *The Routledge Handbook on Cities of the Global South* (pp. 98–108). London: Routledge.

Young, I. M. (2011). *Responsibility for Justice*. New York: Oxford University Press.

2
An introduction to the city of Freetown
Alexandre Apsan Frediani

Introduction

The trajectory of Freetown's urban development is at the centre of contemporary political contestations in Sierra Leone. The city is home to over one million inhabitants and the population is expected to double in size over the next 20 years (by 2040), is responsible for 30% of the nation's GDP. The city's development has been marked by colonial legacies, as well as eleven years of civil war, the Ebola epidemic, the 2017 mudslide, annual flooding and most recently the COVID-19 pandemic. Freetown is conditioned by deep social and environmental disparities, but it is also a vibrant, dynamic and contested site of narratives and politics. For the national government, Freetown is key for the advancement of the national economy. The city mayor's vision is promoted through the 'transform Freetown' agenda, which has become the means through which the Freetown City Council can gain leverage to influence the future trajectory of the city. However, in the middle of the power struggles between national and local governments, local and international civil society actors are forging horizontal networks and experimenting with participatory planning instruments to bring about change on the ground, while gaining legitimacy and recognition to influence urban development. As mega projects are being considered for Freetown by local and national governments, it is crucial for research to continue to examine how policy and planning can promote more inclusive and sustainable urban development.

Urban context

Freetown is the capital and largest city of Sierra Leone, located in the western area of the country, by the Atlantic Ocean. The city has a distinct geographical terrain, with much development having taken place on steep mountainous slopes or on reclaimed land at sea level. Its geographical precarity, with the Atlantic Ocean to the west and mountains to the east, constrain and impact urban expansion, especially in the southern part of the city.

The city was established in 1787 by the Sierra Leone Company to settle 1,600 freed slaves from the West Indies and Nova Scotia (Canada). The area was previously inhabited by local Temne tribes, who were displaced by the British in 1807 and prohibited from settling within an eleven-mile radius. In 1808, the British took responsibility for Sierra Leone, establishing a Crown colony in and around Freetown. This social-spatial segregation deepened at the beginning of the twentieth century when the colonial government created a 'mosquito-free zone for privileged inhabitants' (Goerg, 1998, p. 7). In 1902, construction started on a new residential site for Europeans only, located by the hills, six miles out of Freetown.

The boundaries of the city extended after independence in 1961 (see Figure 2.1), followed by rapid population growth. From 1901 until 1985, the Freetown population grew from 67,782 to nearly 500,000 inhabitants. In the following 30 years, the population doubled and there are now more than one million people living in the city (Lynch, Nel & Binns, 2020).

After independence, urban development in Freetown was driven by positivist ideals of planning and the aspiration to build a modern city. The 1963 Borys Plan for a Contemporary City was an example of this attempt to enhance city competitiveness (Macarthy et al., 2022). At the same time, in the 1980s, there were initial attempts of the Sierra Leonean government to implement structural adjustment programmes (SAPs) in conjunction with the International Monetary Fund (IMF) and the World Bank. In common with other contexts, the focus on liberalisation of trade and reduction of welfare system via SAPs led to weakened local industries, resulting in growth of unemployment and lack of social protection in cities. As a result, SAPs have been often characterised as an impediment to the redistributive power of cities (Riddell, 1997).

In this post-independence period, the eleven-year civil war and the West African Ebola virus epidemic were key milestones in Freetown's development. The civil war started in 1991 and generated an estimated

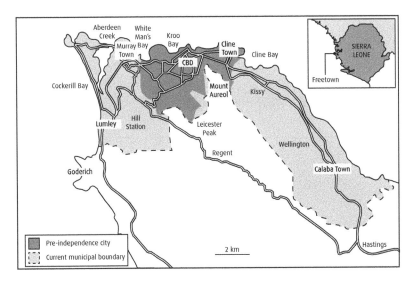

Figure 2.1 Urban growth of Freetown. Source: © Chris Gardner in Lynch, Nel & Binns (2020, p. 4)

500,000 internally displaced persons (IDPs). Most of them sought refuge in Freetown. When the war ended in 2002, many IDPs remained in the city, as did ex-combatants who experienced challenges returning to hometowns, often outside of Freetown. This resulted not only in rapid population growth, but also in a dramatic increase in population density. Data from Statistics Sierra Leone (2017), shows that 'in 1985, the population density in Freetown and surrounding rural areas was 769 people per square kilometre, rising to 1,360 in 2004 and 2,154 in 2015' (Lynch, Nel & Binns, 2020, p. 8). Growth in population numbers and density took place mostly in the low-income informal settlements of the city, located by the coast and on the hillsides.

In 2014, Sierra Leone was affected by the Ebola epidemic. For the first time an Ebola epidemic reached urban centres and Freetown's geography. The epidemic had several negative impacts on the living conditions in Freetown. It constrained urban mobility, compromised local livelihoods, disrupted education and put extra burden on an already fragile health system. The majority of Ebola treatment centres were situated in rural areas external to the city and movement between districts was strictly controlled. Following the epidemic, inward migration to Freetown was triggered predominantly by job losses after the closure of two of Sierra Leone's main iron ore mines.

Since the end of the Ebola epidemic in 2016, Freetown has continued to play a key role in Sierra Leonean economic development. At the time of writing, the city houses 15% of the country's population and accounts for 30% of its GDP. According to the World Bank, 'rapid urbanization is now Sierra Leone's biggest growth narrative for the 21st century' (World Bank, 2018a, p. 49).

Political context

There are two main parties in Sierra Leone shaping its political context: the current ruling Sierra Leone People's Party (SLPP) and the All People's Congress (APC). Historically, SLPP has had a stronghold in the south of the country with the Mende ethnic group and APC has relied on the Limba and Temne groups in the north of the country. The 2018 general election resulted in a peaceful transition of power from APC to SLPP, as the SLPP Presidential candidate Julius Maada Bio was elected with a slight margin. However, the parliament was dominated by an APC majority. This APC majority was short lived as the legitimacy of the votes (being 'free and fair') was contested for most candidates in courts of law, leading to victories being overturned for some and re-run elections for a few constituencies. Since mid-2019, the SLPP have had a slim majority in parliament. Freetown has been a swing region and in 2018 Yvonne Aki-Sawyerr from APC party was elected mayor of Freetown municipality.

Within this contested political context, two key and interconnected processes have been affecting the operations of Freetown City Council: decentralisation and tax reform. In 2004 the country embarked on an ambitious programme of decentralisation, which included the enactment of the 2004 Local Government Act, re-establishing local councils and requiring these to formulate development plans. On paper, the act – which had implications for several ministries – required devolution to take place with the expectation that this would generate a more responsive and efficient service delivery in local areas and support local economic development. Freetown was one of the six elected town/city councils established by the act. Councils were divided into wards, with each ward having a ward development committee, with the objective to link grassroots level planning with local government actions. Apart from the political and administrative reforms, the act also aimed to establish fiscal decentralisation, by granting local council powers to raise their own revenues (Edwards, Yilmaz & Boex, 2015).

This process triggered efforts to strengthen Freetown's planning system and led to the development of Freetown structure plan for 2013–2028 and a spatial development strategy. However, in practice various functions have not been devolved[1] to Freetown City Council (FCC). In 2020, 15 years after the enactment of the Local Governments Act, only 43 of the 79 functions were fully devolved. Some of the outstanding functions include strategic local plans, issuance of building permits and preparation of land use plans (Koroma, Macarthy & Yusuf, 2020). Furthermore, citizen participation is rarely seen as a priority in the government's activities. Action on the ground continues to be driven by diverse actors without coordination, 'resulting often in chaotic development, diseconomies and negative externalities' (Macarthy, Frediani & Kamara, 2019, p. 13). FCC lacks capacity to take on new functions, due to the lack of fiscal decentralisation and of incentives to retain qualified human resources in local government posts. The Freetown structure plan has still not attained parliamentary assent, limiting the possibility for the City Council to drive the processes of change (Macarthy, Frediani & Kamara, 2019).

Within this context, reforms to Sierra Leone's tax system have become a central stage for political disputes. After inheriting a declining economy from the stagnation of the mining sector (caused by low prices for iron ore and rutile), the 2018 SLPP elected national government committed to implement a fiscal adjustment framework supported by the World Bank and the IMF. The framework provides a commitment to improve the nation's tax revenue performance and it is part of a series of World Bank and IMF budgetary support to the Sierra Leone national government. This included a US$325 million funding package from the World Bank agreed in March 2019 and a US$143 million IMF loan approved in June 2020. One of the key features of these initiatives has been the emphasis on property taxation to increase local government revenue (World Bank, n.d.). The new property rate reform system as part of the Mayor's Transform Freetown initiative aims to increasing the potential for tax revenue fivefold.

Even within this wider political context encouraging local authorities to boost revenue collection, national government pushed back efforts of Freetown's mayor to establish a more equitable property tax system in the country's capital. However, the mayor managed to get the reform through and there are estimates that suggest that it could increase the city council's revenue five-fold when fully operational (Oxford Analytica, 2020; for more on the Freetown new property tax system see Grieco et al., 2019). Nevertheless, the deepened political polarisation of the 2023 national elections, as well as recent urban unrests demonstrate that there are growing social and political tensions in the country and in Freetown's politics.

Urban challenges

The increased emphasis on Freetown's role in the country's economic growth has resulted in amplified commitment to the city's infrastructure development. This has stimulated the city's high-end real estate market and increased demand for large scale property development. In turn, the pressure to access land to enable property development in inner city areas of Freetown has similarly increased, resulting in a greater threat of eviction for residents from coastal informal settlements. The World Bank estimates that 'the monetary loss due to very low and stagnant land prices in slum areas could equal almost US$58 million' (World Bank, 2019, p. 37). While this figure fails to recognise the economic value and levels of productivity within informal settlements, it illustrates the narrative that fuels the threat of eviction and displacement. At the same time, the formal real estate market continues to be deeply exclusionary, as existing challenges around access to mortgages and high land transaction costs[2] have resulted in insufficient investment in affordable housing developments. These factors contributed to a sharp (much faster than price inflation) increase in rent prices: rental prices increased at around 650% between 2003 and 2011, while price inflation was approximately 36%. The average monthly rent in the formal market for a three-bedroom apartment in central and western Freetown ranges from US$3,000 to US$5,000: affordable to only 3% of Sierra Leone's households (World Bank, 2019).

This emphasis on Freetown as pivotal to economic growth has not translated into a fairer urban development trajectory, as the urban poor have experienced continued threats to their security of tenure, as well as deepened exposure to social, environmental and economic risks. Informal settlements (slums) constitute 36% of all settlements in the city (World Bank, 2019, see Figure 2.2). To date, the most detailed published profile of Freetown's informal settlements was conducted by the Centre of Dialogue on Human Settlement and Poverty Alleviation (CODOHSAPA), involving eight communities. The profile demonstrated that residents of informal settlements comprise diverse ethnic identities, but the majority were Temne and 69% of those profiled were Muslim. Most of the residents were tenants living in an average household size of seven people per household. Only 51% of households enumerated had access to electricity (CODOHSAPA, 2019).

As informal settlements are located by the coastal area and hillsides, their residents are exposed to the constant threat of environmental risks, such as flooding and landslides. These threats have intensified due to continuous hillside deforestation by unregulated low-income as well as

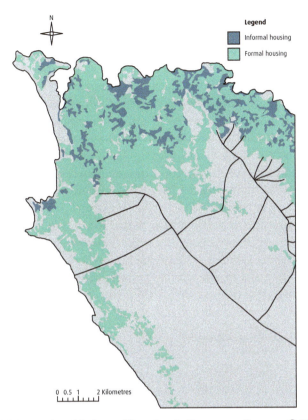

Figure 2.2 Formal and informal housing in Freetown. Source: © World Bank (2019, p. 32)

middle- and high-income settlements. The Regent landslide in August 2017 destroyed 400 buildings, affected 5,000 people and claimed the lives of an estimated 1,100. It highlighted the urgent need for planning to promote urban resilience and risk reduction. Meanwhile, the rising sea-level owing to climate change is expected to affect mostly the urban poor. A scenario for 2050 estimates that 85% of the 2,380 buildings affected will be in informal settlements (World Bank, 2018b). Apart from the large-scale disasters, the existing pattern of urbanisation has reproduced 'urban risk traps', exposing the urban poor to the cumulative deterioration of their lives and assets generated by everyday risks and small disasters (Allen et al., 2020).

   In 2015, 35% of the population of Freetown was living below the multidimensional poverty line. While 2018 national statistics show a slight reduction in income poverty, it is extremely likely that the COVID-19 pandemic has had an adverse impact. Sierra Leone's GDP shrank by 3.1% in 2020 (IMF, 2020), leading to a loss of more than 15% of projected domestic revenues (Oxford Analytica, 2020). Meanwhile, most of Freetown is affected by the lack of access to adequate water and sanitation services. With 39% of households instead relying on public taps, only 22% of residents have access to improved, private sanitation facilities and only 3% of urban households have access to piped indoor drinking water. Just 40% of the city's waste is collected (World Bank, 2018a). As a result, lack of access to adequate services is one of the main drivers of health risks for residents of Freetown's informal settlements (Macarthy et al., 2018). These risks are particularly experienced by women and girls residing in informal settlements. For example, when water scarcity is great, women and girls can be subjected to more violence or coerced into sexual activity in exchange for water (Freetown Wash Consortium & Liberia Wash Consortium, 2015; Conteh, Kamara & Saidu, 2020).[3]

Livelihoods in the city are predominantly informal, often precarious, insecure and stigmatised. In the western area, where Freetown is located, more than 60% of the labour force work in the

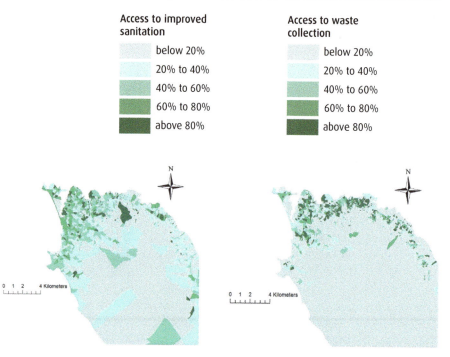

Figure 2.3 Access to improved sanitation and waste collection (% of households) in Freetown. Source: © World Bank (2019, p. 83)

informal sector (Koroma et al., 2018). In some sectors, the percentage of informal activities is even higher. In the transport sector (the second-highest generator of jobs in Freetown), 85% of jobs generated are informal and in the construction sector, 72% of jobs are informal and 8% are unpaid (T-SUM city brief). Meanwhile, under the narrative of beautification, government authorities have often criminalised informal activities in the city. They have been prohibited and sanctioned in various ways, such as banning motorcycle taxis or street traders from operating in some parts of the city (Enria, 2018). However, informal livelihood activities are an integral part of the functioning of the city's economy and they play important roles in securing a basic income and social protection for Freetown inhabitants. This is especially the case for 'open access' livelihood activities, such as cockle picking, trading, sand mining, stone quarrying and fishing, which can be accessed by those with limited assets (Rigon, Walker & Koroma, 2020; City Learning Platform, 2020).

Another key driver of inequality in Freetown is uneven access to transport. Public transport is very limited in the city; in 2019 the city had only 66 public buses (World Bank, 2019). The main form of collective transport is *okadas* (motorcycle taxis) and *kekehs* (three-wheelers). These forms of transportation are often preferred by Freetown residents, as they can navigate congested roads and access unpaved hilly areas (Koroma et al., 2020). However, those living in hilly and peripheral areas of the city are particularly isolated from transport connections. Residents of large parts of the city must spend more than 60 minutes to access inner city areas. Location and gender have a direct impact on costs of services, as providers charge more for those living in hard-to-reach places and tend to be less willing to negotiate prices with women (Oviedo Hernandez et al., 2022). These mobility injustices provide some insights into the motivations of those choosing to live in coastal settlements that are closer to inner city areas, even if these areas are prone to both disasters and everyday risks.

Political factors shaping whether urban challenges are addressed

Local urban stakeholders, Freetown City Council and national development priorities have recently brought new impetus towards more inclusive urban development. This has generated opportunities to reinvigorate urban planning efforts in the city. In response to humanitarian crises – landslides, flooding; the Ebola and COVID-19 pandemics – community groups from informal settlements have demonstrated great ability to mobilise and coordinate actions, build resilience and have a significant role in responding to and mitigating risks at the community level. The establishment and operations of community disaster management committees across many Freetown informal settlements is evidence of communities' capabilities to mobilise, plan and act collectively (Macarthy et al., 2017; Osuteye et al., 2020). While these committees have emerged out of the lack of government's capacity to address the needs of those living in conditions of informality, if supported, they create potential opportunities for more community-led forms of urban governance (see Chapter 9 for more on this). At city level, there is a dynamic and well networked urban community of practice in Freetown, aiming to improve quality of life for those in informal settlements. This network is a legacy of the Pull Slum Pan Pipul (PSPP) partnership in Freetown, involving various civil society organisations[4] funded by Comic Relief between 2015–2019. Relationships established through the PSPP initiatives continue to collaborate through the City Learning Platform initiative, co-chaired by the FCC and Sierra Leone Urban Research Centre (SLURC). This promotes more collaborative and participatory solutions for improving living conditions in Freetown's informal settlements involving community residents (City Learning Platform, 2019).

The City Learning Platform is connected to the mayor's 'Transform Freetown' initiative launched in 2019, bringing together urban stakeholders to define, coordinate and implement a shared agenda for the city. This initiative has been able to generate a lot of political traction and has helped to highlight the need for coordinated and planned efforts to address urban development challenges in Freetown.

At the national level, the Ministry of Lands and Country Planning has been leading efforts to develop policies relevant to urban development, such as the National Housing Policy (2006) and National Land Policy (2015). The Ministry of Planning and Development has also co-ordinated the production of the national development plan (2019–2023). Furthermore, a national urban policy is being considered by the national government (with support from UN-Habitat), which could have a substantial impact in increasing the role of national government in directing Freetown's future development.

Nevertheless, political energy seems to currently gravitate around large scale and highly visible urban projects, such as the mayor's mass transit cable car project (Atkins, 2020) or the president's US$2 billion Freetown-Lungi bridge (Reuters, 2019), rather than more comprehensive and coordinated action. Given that by 2040 Freetown's size is expected to double, it is crucial that local, municipal and national efforts are galvanised and synergised to respond to this challenge and to bring about more equitable and sustainable urban development.

Notes

1   In 2019, the government devolved all remaining functions in Schedule 2 of the Local Government Act (2004) to the local councils. However, in practise, some these functions are still performed by ministries, departments and agencies.
2   According to the World Bank (2019), property transfers in Freetown typically cost almost 11% of property value, compared to an average of approximately 8% across sub-Saharan Africa. In 2006, there were only 200 registered property transactions in Freetown.
3   For another account of some of these processes, see the video produced by MSc in Environment and Sustainable Development students of The Bartlett Development Planning Unit, University College London in partnership with the Sierra Leone Urban Research Centre: https://www .youtube.com/watch?v=DAU0Xz2xCsg&feature=youtu.be;
4   Organisations funded by Comic Relief include: YMCA Sierra Leone; Centre of Dialogue on Human Settlement and Poverty Alleviation (CODOHSAPA); Restless Development (RD); Youth Development Movement (YDM); Bangladesh Rural Advancement Committee (BRAC); and the Sierra Leone Urban Studies Centre (SLURC).

References

Allen, A., Osuteye, E., Koroma, B., & Lambert, R. (2020). Unlocking urban risk trajectories in Freetown's informal settlements. In UN-Habitat (Ed.), *Breaking Cycles of Risk Accumulation in African Cities* (pp. 54–61). United Nations Human Settlements Programme (UN-Habitat).

Atkins, W. (2020). Freetown eyes a green post-Covid future. FDI Intelligence, 9 September. Accessed 25 June 2024. https://www.fdiintelligence.com/content/interview/freetown-eyes-a-green -postcovid-future-78379

City Learning Platform. (2019). Practitioner brief 1#: principles of engagement for the city learning platform. 1. Practitioner brief. Freetown: Sierra Leone Urban Research Centre (SLURC). Accessed 25 June 2024. https://www.slurc.org/uploads/1/0/9/7/109761391/cilp_pb_web .pdf

City Learning Platform. (2020). Practitioner brief 2#: community livelihoods opportunities. 2. Practitioner brief. Freetown: Sierra Leone Urban Research Centre (SLURC). Accessed 25 June 2024. https://www.slurc.org/uploads/1/0/9/7/109761391/cilp_pb_n2_final.pdf

CODOHSAPA. (2019). Community profiling enumeration report. Freetown: Centre of Dialogue on Human Settlement and Poverty Alleviation (CODOHSAPA) and Federation of Urban and Rural Poor (FEDURP). Accessed 27 September 2023. https:// codohsapa.org/wp-content/uploads/2020/09/CODOHSAPA_FEDURP-Enumeration-Report__2019.pdf

Conteh, A., Kamara, M. S., & Saidu, S. (2020). COVID-19 response and protracted exclusion of informal residents: why should it matter to city authorities in Freetown, Sierra Leone? *Arise News & Events* (blog), 22 July 2020. Accessed 25 June 2024. http://www.ariseconsortium.org /covid-19-response-and-protracted-exclusion-of-informal-residents-why-should-it-matter-to -city-authorities-in-freetown-sierra-leone/.

Edwards, B., Yilmaz, S., & Boex, J. (2015). Decentralization as a post-conflict strategy: local government discretion and accountability in Sierra Leone. *Public Administration and Development*, 35(1): 46–60. https://doi.org/10.1002/pad.1707

Enria, L. (2018). *The Politics of Work in a Post-Conflict State: Youth, labour and violence in Sierra Leone*. Melton: James Currey.

Freetown Wash Consortium & Liberia Wash Consortium. (2015). Prioritising water, sanitation and hygiene in Ebola recovery: for health, life and dignity. Oxfam International, 9 July. Accessed 25 June 2024. https://www.oxfam.org/en/research/prioritizing-water-sanitation-and-hygiene-ebola-recovery

Goerg, O. (1998). From Hill Station (Freetown) to Downtown Conakry (First Ward): comparing French and British approaches to segregation in colonial cities at the beginning of the twentieth century. *Canadian Journal of African Studies/La Revue Canadienne Des Études Africaines*, *32*(1): 1–31. https://doi.org/10.1080/00083968.1998.10751128

Grieco, K., Kamara, A. B., Meriggi, N. F., Michel, J., Prichard, W., & Stewart-Wilson, G. (2019). Simplifying property tax administration in Africa: piloting a points-based valuation in Freetown, Sierra Leone. Summary brief 19. Brighton: International Centre for Tax and Development. Accessed 25 June 2024. https://www.ictd.ac/publication/simplifying-property-tax-administration-africa-piloting-points-based-valuation-freetown-sierra-leone/

IMF (International Monetary Fund). (2020). Real GDP growth: annual percentage change. Accessed 25 June 2024. https://www.imf.org/external/datamapper/NGDP_RPCH@WEO/SLE?year=2020

Koroma, B., Macarthy, J. M., & Yusuf, Y. (2020). When tax hits home: institutional barriers to decentralisation in Freetown. Urbanet, Spotlight on decentralisation. Accessed 24 January 2024. https://www.urbanet.info/when-tax-hits-home-decentralisation-in-freetown/

Koroma, B., Macarthy, J. M., Yusuf, Y., Sellu, S. A., Hernandez, D. O., Cavoli, C., Jones, P., & Levy, C. (2020). City profile Freetown: base conditions of mobility, accessibility and land use. T-SUM. London: UCL.

Koroma, B., Rigon, A., Walker, J., & Sellu, S. A. (2018). Urban livelihoods in Freetown's informal settlements. Freetown: Sierra Leone Urban Research Centre (SLURC).

Lynch, K., Nel, E., & Binns, T. (2020). Transforming Freetown: dilemmas of planning and development in a west African city. *Cities*, *101* (June): 102694. https://doi.org/10.1016/j.cities.2020.102694

Macarthy, J. M., Frediani, A. A, & Kamara, S. F. (2019). Report on the role of community action area planning in expanding the participatory capabilities of the urban poor. Freetown: SLURC. Accessed 25 June 2024. https://www.slurc.org/uploads/1/0/9/7/109761391/caap_research_report_final__web_quality_.pdf

Macarthy, J. M., Frediani, A .A., Kamara, S. F., & Morgado, M. (2017). Exploring the role of empowerment in urban humanitarian responses in Freetown. International Institute for Environment and Development (IIED) working paper. London: IIED. Accessed 25 June 2024. https://pubs.iied.org/10845IIED/

Macarthy, J. M., Conteh, A., Sellu, S. A., & Heinrich, L. (2018). Health impacts of the living conditions of people residing in informal settlements in Freetown. Report on the future health systems (FHS) Research in Freetown. Freetown: SLURC.

Macarthy, M., Koroma, B., Cociña, C., Butcher, S., & Frediani, A. A. (2022). The 'slow anatomy of change': urban knowledge trajectories towards an inclusive settlement upgrading agenda in Freetown, Sierra Leone. *Environment and Urbanization*, *34*(2): 294–312. https://doi.org/10.1177/09562478221106611

Osuteye, E., Koroma, B., Macarthy, J. M., Kamara, S. F., & Conteh, A. (2020). Fighting COVID-19 in Freetown, Sierra Leone: the critical role of community organisations in a growing pandemic. *Open Health*, *1*(1), 51–63. https://doi.org/10.1515/openhe-2020–0005

Oviedo Hernandez, D., Cavoli, C., Jones, P., Levy, C., Sabogal, O., Koroma, B., Macarthy, J. M., & Arroyo, F. (2022). Accessibility and sustainable mobility transitions in sub-Saharan Africa: insights from Freetown. *Journal of Transport Geography*, *105*: 103464.

Oxford Analytica. (2020). Sierra Leone's revenue problems are likely to mount. Oxford Analytica Daily Brief, 1 July 2020. Accessed 25 June 2024. https://dailybrief.oxan.com/Analysis/DB253563/Sierra-Leones-revenue-problems-are-likely-to-mount

Reuters. (2019). Sierra Leone president opens bids for 7 km airport bridge. 19 June. Accessed 25 June 2024. https://www.reuters.com/article/us-leone-bridge-idUSKCN1TK2OD/

Riddell, B. (1997). Structural adjustment programmes and the city in tropical Africa. *Urban Studies*, *34*(8), 1297–1307.

Rigon, A., Walker, J., & Koroma, B. (2020). Beyond formal and informal: understanding urban informalities from Freetown. *Cities*, *105*: 102848. https://doi.org/10.1016/j.cities.2020.102848

Statistics Sierra Leone. (2017). 2015 population and housing census: thematic report on migration and urbanization. Freetown: Statistics Sierra Leone.

World Bank. (2018a). Reviving Urban Development: The importance of Freetown for the national economy. Sierra Leone Economic Update. Washington, DC: World Bank Group. Accessed 25 June 2024. https://openknowledge.worldbank.org/bitstream/handle/10986/30032/127049 -WP-PUBLIC-SierraLeoneEconomicUpdatev.pdf?sequence=1&isAllowed=y

World Bank. (2018b). Sierra Leone multi-city hazard review and risk assessment (vol. 2): Freetown City hazard and risk assessment: final report. Washington, DC: World Bank Group. Accessed 25 June 2024. https://documents.worldbank.org/en/publication/documents-reports/docum entdetail/151281549319565369/Freetown-City-Hazard-and-Risk-Assessment-Final-Report

World Bank. (2019). Freetown: Options for growth and resilience. Urban sector review. Washington, DC: World Bank Group. Accessed 25 June 2024. http://documents1.worldbank.org/curated /en/994221549486063300/pdf/127039-REVISED-PUBLIC2-14-19-Freetown-Report-Final -web2.pdf

World Bank. (n.d.). Sierra Leone Tax Reform. Engagement Note. Washington DC: World Bank Group. Accessed 6 August 2024. http://documents1.worldbank.org/curated/ en/307101560154425941/pdf/Sierra-Leone-Tax-Reform-Engagement-Note.pdf

2.1

Editorial position on the use of the terms 'slums' and 'informal settlements'

Andrea Rigon, Joseph M. Macarthy, Braima Koroma, Alexandre Apsan Frediani and Andrea Klingel

We are aware that definitions of 'slums' and 'informal settlements' are contested. According to UN-Habitat (2007), slums refer to settlements characterised by the lack of at least one of the following features:

- durable housing which protects against extreme climate conditions
- sufficient living space (not more than three people sharing a room)
- easy access to safe, sufficient and affordable water
- access to adequate sanitation
- security of tenure that prevents forced evictions.

In contrast, informal settlements have been defined (UN, 1997) more narrowly as:

- areas where groups of housing units have been constructed on land that the occupants have no legal claim to, or occupy illegally
- unplanned settlements and areas where housing is not in compliance with current planning and building regulations (unauthorised housing).

This book wants to demonstrate that there are contentious politics built around these terminologies. The term 'slum' typically carries derogatory connotations and thus its use can imply that a settlement needs replacement, or can legitimise the eviction of its residents. However, it is a difficult term to avoid in practice.

First, some networks of informal neighbourhood organisations, including in Freetown, choose to identify themselves with a positive use of the term 'slum'. This has the political aims of neutralising such negative connotations by re-appropriating the term, fostering slum dwellers into a collective identity and appealing to international human rights legislation which refers to slum dwellers. One of the most successful of such networks is the National Slum Dwellers Federation in India, part of a wider federation which is also active in Freetown in the form of FEDURP. Second, the only global estimates for housing deficiencies available, collected by the United Nations, are for what it term 'slums'. Third, given that many housing developments of the middle classes and urban elites meet many of the criteria generally linked to settlement informality – for example, unclear tenure, lack of conformity with local government planning norms, and location on unsuitable land – it may be important to distinguish between these informal middle- and high-income settlements, and 'slums' as informal settlements of the poor.

The 2014 Millennium Development Goals Report of the United Nations Statistics Division (2015) estimated that three quarters of the total urban population in Sierra Leone live in areas classified as 'slums'. However, other stakeholders working with the urban poor felt that the international UN-Habitat definition did not reflect the city's local realities because the socio-economic, environmental and cultural context of Sierra Leone is in many ways different from other countries used to formulate such a definition. A working group led by SLURC worked on a local definition for Freetown, which found consensus amongst several key stakeholders. Based on this, the working group defined a slum in Freetown as an area in which:

- a significant proportion (over 60%) of houses have insecure tenure
- the majority of houses are semi-permanent structures (where semi-permanent refers to homes built with materials including, but not limited to, cardboard and iron sheets aka 'pan body');
- roads within the settlement are inaccessible for motor vehicles
- populations are highly vulnerable to risks including disaster and disease
- the majority of residents are unemployed or are working in the informal sector – where the informal sector is defined as businesses that either are not registered to pay taxes (not including market dues), or employ fewer than six people
- the settlement is a distinct group of over 40 structures, with a population exceeding 300. However, if a given settlement meets all the criteria except for this one, it can be defined as a 'slum pocket'.

As 'slum' was the term used by many NGOs and grassroots organisations, SLURC has been working with the term and has helped develop a tailored definition for its analytical use in identifying these settlements. In some cases the literature identifies precarious settlements as slums, but we feel that this reinforces a discourse of temporary settlement, potentially exploited by those wanting to evict and displace residents, whereas the reality is that some of these settlements have been present for decades. Low-income, informal settlement seems to us the most appropriate and complete term, as it clarifies that SLURC does not directly focus on high-income settlements that may have been built without planning permissions but focuses on those with poor and vulnerable communities. However, this wording is quite long for repeated use in a text. 'Slum' is also used by the institutions with whom we work, or whose work we use, including the World Bank, UN-Habitat, central government, local and international NGOs and, of course, the residents and their own organisations.

Informal settlements/slums are and have been approached in quite different ways in terms of their treatment in city development strategies and through the planning and governance of cities. At one extreme, historic approaches that equated development with a particular Western model of modernity (Escobar, 1995) often saw informal settlements as a sign of underdevelopment and responded to them through strategies of demolition and eviction. In many contexts, such approaches to urban development remain and are arguably resurgent. These approaches view city development as processes of 'beautification' or urban regeneration, with aspirations towards the 'world class city' (Ghertner, 2011). This prioritises conformity with technical masterplans over the lived realities of many poor citizens. Such approaches typically still deal with slums/informal settlements through processes of eviction (Fahra, 2011). Such evictions are often justified either on the basis of the need to clear land to make space for infrastructure development (with land occupied by informal settlements normally the easiest to clear and the cheapest to acquire), or more directly with the rationale of eliminating informal settlements as intrinsically unruly or unsafe spaces which are seen as a blight on city development (Bahn, 2009; Watson, 2009). It is also worth noting that although such rationales for the eviction of informal settlements are generally made on the basis of 'public interest' arguments, actual underlying motivations for displacing informal settlements (which are often on central city land with high potential value) may also relate to private interests and profit through real estate speculation, made possible by clearing land of informal residents, at times in collusion with the state (Smith, 1996; Lees et al., 2016; Oliver-Smith, 2010).

As reflected in this editorial position, for SLURC and our partners it is crucial to be aware of the politics involved in the concepts used in our work. The choice of terminologies such as 'slum' or 'informal settlement' is not a purely academic or technical decision. It has substantial implications to how alliances are forged and how decisions are made in the city. Therefore, it is crucial for us to continue debating and making decisions around their use with our key partners, striving for more equitable and sustainable urban development in Freetown.

References

Bahn, G. (2009). 'This is no longer the city I once knew'. Evictions, the urban poor and the right to the city in millennial Delhi, *Environment and Urbanization*, 21(1): 127–142.

Escobar, A. (1995). *Encountering development: The making and unmaking of the third world*. Princeton, NJ: Princeton University Press.

Farha, L. (2011). Forced evictions: global crisis, global solutions. Nairobi: UN-HABITAT.

Ghertner, D. A. (2011). Rule by aesthetics: world-class city making in Dehli. In A. Roy & A. Ong (Eds), *Worlding Cities: Asian experiments and the art of being global* (pp. 279–306). Oxford: Wiley-Blackwell.

Lees, L., Shin, H. B., & López-Morales, E. (2016). *Planetary Gentrifications: Uneven development and displacement*. Bristol: Polity Press.

Oliver-Smith, A. (2010). *Defying Displacement: Grassroots resistance and the critique of development*. Austin, TX: University of Texas Press.

Smith, N. (1996). *The New Urban Frontier: Gentrification and the revanchist city*. London: Routledge.

UN-Habitat. (2007). State of the World's Cities Report 2006–2007. Nairobi: UN-Habitat.

United Nations. (1997). Glossary of Environment Statistics, Studies in Methods, Series F, No. 67. United Nations, New York.

United Nations Statistics Division. (2015). The Millennium Development Goals Report 2014. https://www.un.org/millenniumgoals/2014%20MDG%20report/MDG%202014%20English%20web.pdf

Watson, V. (2009). 'The planned city sweeps the poor away...' : Urban planning and 21st century urbanisation, *Progress in Planning, 72*: 151–193

2.2
Informal settlement profiles: Cockle Bay, Dworzark, Portee-Rokupa and Moyiba

Braima Koroma, Joseph M. Macarthy,
Andrea Rigon, Alexandre Apsan Frediani and
Andrea Klingel

This chapter comprises in-depth profiles of the four settlements where SLURC concentrates its research. They represent a diverse mix of important characteristics which offer a good representation of the informal settlements in Freetown.

Cockle Bay informal settlement

Cockle Bay informal settlement is located along the Aberdeen Creek on the western coast of Freetown. It is predominantly built on land that lies between 0–1 metres above sea level reclaimed from the low-lying mangrove forest. This geographical location makes the settlement highly susceptible to coastal flooding and rising sea levels (ASF UK & SLURC, 2018, p. 20). Cockle Bay is approximately 5 km from the city centre and is estimated to have a population of 20,000 inhabitants, residing in 1,350 households within 540 structures (SDI, 2017; Allen et al., 2017).

The name Cockle Bay originated from cockle production that once was the primary source of income for the community during the 1990s and 2000s. However, production has significantly declined in recent years owing to the destruction of the mangrove forest ecosystem. The settlement has been occupied since the 1940s, with initial residents residing mainly along the shore of the Aberdeen Creek. In 1955, makeshift houses started to be constructed and during the civil war from 1992 to 2002, Cockle

Informal Settlements
Cockle Bay
Dworzark
Moyiba
Portee-Rokupa
OpenStreetMap

0   1   2 km

Map data from OpenStreetMap.
http://www.openstreetmap.org/copyright

Figure 2.4 Map of Freetown showing Cockle Bay, Dworzark, Moyiba and Portee-Rokupa. Source: © Ansumana Tarawally.
Map data: © OpenStreetMap contributors.
https://www.openstreetmap.org/copyright

Bay became a preferred location for resettlement for the rural population migrating to Freetown.

Cockle Bay informal settlement is unofficially divided into four distinct zones: Kola Tree, Jai Mata, Mafengbeh and Elet View. Each zone has its own characteristics and features that shape the dynamics of the settlement. Mafengbeh, the heart of Cockle Bay, is the most populous area and exhibits a diverse range of community residences. It serves as a hub for community activities, including a school, mosque, bakery, cinema, football field and sports bar. The main access point to Mafengbeh is from Byrne Lane, located at the top of a steep hill. A taxi and motorcycle stand provide transportation for residents to Wilkinson Road and beyond. While a few relatively affluent houses can be found in this zone, the majority of dwellings consist of poor, corrugated iron homes.

Elet View stands out as the most organised and least densely populated zone within Cockle Bay. It features walkable alleyways often used by motorbikes and a significant number of concrete block homes. The zone offers spaces for residents to engage in crop cultivation. Elet View is locally considered the most affluent neighbourhood within the settlement, although it has undergone extensive land reclamation over

Map of Cockle Bay

Informal Settlement
Cockle Bay
OpenStreetMap
0 75 150 m

Map data from OpenStreetMap. https://
www.openstreetmap.org/copyright

Figure 2.5 Map of Cockle Bay. Source: © Ansumana Tarawally.
Map data: © OpenStreetMap contributors
https://www.openstreetmap.org/copyright

the years. Notably, access to the zone is challenging as unlike Kola Tree and Mafengbeh it has no existing road around it. Instead, people access Elet View through a few, small pedestrian footpaths or roads that lead to Mafengbeh or Thompson Bay.

Kola Tree, situated under the slope, represents the densest part of Cockle Bay. The zone has evolved around the presence of a church, mosque and access roads. At the foot of the hillslopes that separate the formal and informal areas of the settlement, residents in Kola Tree engage in market gardening practices, utilising the available space for cultivation.

Jai Mata, the smallest zone in Cockle Bay, is located in close proximity to the Aberdeen bridge. Despite its size, it is densely populated and often inaccessible. The houses in Jai Mata are typically constructed with cement and covered by corrugated iron sheets. This zone is particularly vulnerable to flooding during high tides, prompting significant efforts to establish tidal defences, known within the community as the Wharf.

The land in Cockle Bay is predominantly owned by Freetown City Council, with the Sierra Leone River Estuary (SLRE) wetlands classified as being under state ownership. In common to other informal settlements in Freetown, housing in Cockle Bay consists of mixed forms, with approximately four out of ten households classified as pan-bodies (structures made with wood and corrugated iron sheets) and some houses are constructed from concrete blocks (Leong et al., 2018). However, tenure insecurity has hindered housing upgrades, with residents refraining from investing due to concerns about eviction (Leong et al., 2018).

The settlement faces inherent complexities and contestations due to persistent threats of eviction, as it is considered both risk-prone (particularly to floods and disease outbreaks) and in need of ecological protection under the SLRE. Consequently, Freetown City Council has prioritised upgrading or resettlement in the Freetown Structural Plan (2014–2028). Although large-scale evictions have not yet occurred, the limited communication with residents regarding these threats has led to Cockle Bay being labelled a 'grey space' (Yiftachel, 2009). The use of risk-based politics by the Environmental Protection Agency (EPA) and Freetown City Council has left residents in a state of uncertainty, discouraging them from constructing permanent dwellings. This undermines their adaptive capacity and increases their vulnerability to risks, reinforcing the perception of being highly at risk (Leong et al., 2018; Allen et al., 2020).

Like other informal settlements in Freetown, the majority of Cockle Bay residents lack formal land claims. In an attempt to secure tenure, residents have paid city rates to Freetown City Council or applied for legal tenure status from the Ministry of Lands, Housing, and Country Planning (MLHCP). However, these applications are often rejected or left pending, exacerbating the struggle for legitimacy and tenure security (Leong et al., 2018). It is important to note that the distinction between formal and informal is not a clear dichotomy, but rather a continuum. The historical and systematic lack of recognition by all levels of government has resulted in Cockle Bay being framed as 'illegal' and deemed ineligible for adequate service provision.

Cockle Bay suffers from inadequate infrastructure and a lack of basic services, with only 9% of households having access to electricity. Waste management practices are poor due to a lack of formal waste collection services; residents often resort to dumping waste in open spaces or water bodies, leading to environmental degradation and health hazards. Healthcare facilities are non-existent and there is limited access to clean water and sanitation. Residents rely on communal water sources, such as public taps and wells, which may not always provide safe drinking water. Hygiene practices, such as handwashing, are often compromised due to the lack of access to clean water and sanitation facilities. Most households lack access to proper toilets or sanitation systems. Open defecation is prevalent, which poses significant health risks and contributes to environmental pollution. The settlement's low-lying location, proximity to the coast, and inadequate drainage contribute to localised flood risks during heavy rains, as well as the prevalence of waterborne diseases such as cholera, and potential fires. The lack of proper drainage systems and the haphazard construction of houses further increase the vulnerability of residents.

In terms of mobility and transport, the primary modes of public transportation to and from Cockle Bay are motorbikes (okada) and tricycles (kekeh). Access to the community is restricted to the Aberdeen Ferry Road and the lanes connecting to Byrne Lane, where residents can find other public and private transport options such as poda-poda (public minibuses) and taxis. Walking is the predominant mode of transport within the community, with most paths consisting of a combination of rubble and dirt, occasionally adorned with cockle shells.

The economy of Cockle Bay relies heavily on sand mining, petty trading structured in self-owned micro-and-small enterprises within and outside the settlement, fishing and the declining cockle production industry (Koroma et al., 2018). Sand mining, which takes place during low tides in the lagoon of Aberdeen Creek, has become the main subsistence livelihood. However, the National Protected Area Authority (NPAA) prohibits residents from extracting sand for sale and closely monitors any violations (Koroma et al., 2018). Overexploitation of resources and increasing restrictions on sand mining have led to decreases in available sand close to Cockle Bay.

In terms of governance, Cockle Bay has a multi-layered community governance structure, including an elected development committee, traditional leaders, religious representatives, and elected officials. Trust within the community governance system often depends on specific circumstances and positions. Additionally, various NGOs and organisations such as the Ward Development Committee and Community Development Committee, Community Disaster Management Committee (CDMC), FEDURP, Fordibambi Trust Fund (FTF), WASH-Consortium, YMCA and Restless Development are present in the settlement, which demonstrates the commitment of external organisations to support the community.

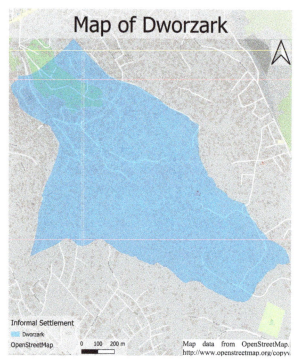

Figure 2.6 Map of Dworzark. Source: © Ansumana Tarawally.
Map data: © OpenStreetMap contributors.
https://www.openstreetmap.org/copyright

Dworzark

Dworzark is the largest informal settlement in Freetown and spans an area of approximately 126 hectares. It is situated in constituency 127, between wards 434 and 435. The settlement is bordered by Somalia Town to the east, Leicester to the south, New England Ville to the west and Brookfields to the north. Located about 5 km from the central business district (CBD), Dworzark can be accessed via the George Brook Road, the only formal road leading to the community.

The settlement is positioned on the northernmost fringe of the peninsular mountain, characterised by a varied topography ranging from 57 m at its lowest point to 316 m at the highest. In some areas, the slope reaches a steep gradient of up to 71% due to deforestation, soil erosion, stone mining, and the construction of houses in unstable locations. These factors have resulted in frequent flooding, mudslides, and rock falls (Cumming and Harrison, 2012, p. 15). Dworzark is also marked by large boulders and a natural drain that collects water from upstream communities into George Brook River. Housing in the settlement is predominantly poorly constructed, utilising materials such as mud bricks and corrugated iron sheets. Contested land ownership hampers investment in improved housing and public infrastructure development.

For convenience, the community has informally divided itself into twelve zones named after countries. Higher terrain zones include Nigeria, USA, Spain, Cameroon, and Germany, while the urban core zones with the highest housing density are France, Italy, England, Brazil, Morocco, Argentina, and Holland.

Dworzark's history goes back to the 1930s and 1940s, when people sought livelihood opportunities in or near Freetown's CBD. In 1941, part of the land owned by the Dworzark family was sold to Freetown Cold Storage Limited, which established the Coca Cola bottling plant to supply carbonated drinks to the city. This led to an influx of people working in these companies and providing services to them. In 1945, the Dworzark Company was established, primarily involved in agriculture and stone extraction for Freetown's construction. As the years went by, the settlement began to form as employees of these companies chose to reside in the community. A school and a church were built in the 1960s, but since the 1980s, rapid urbanisation has outpaced investments in social infrastructure.

The population of Dworzark is estimated to be around 50,000 residents, with 2,003 structures and 5,236 households. This translates to an average household size of approximately nine persons per household (CRS, 2019). The high population density in Dworzark poses significant challenges in terms of access to basic services and infrastructure. With limited resources and inadequate investment in social amenities, the community struggles to meet the needs of its residents. The overcrowded housing conditions and lack of proper sanitation facilities further exacerbate health and hygiene issues.

Land tenure and shelter security in Dworzark vary, with some residents legally owning land through title and permission. Approximately 50% of the settlement is privately owned, 25% is owned by the municipality, and 25% is customary land (SDI, 2017). However, land ownership disputes are common, hindering investments in improved housing and public infrastructure development (Koroma et al., 2018, p. 10).

In terms of mobility and transport, Dworzark has a variety of public transportation options, including minibuses (poda-poda), motorbikes (okada), tricycles (kekeh), and taxis. However, vehicular movement within the community is restricted due to the lack of formal roads, steep gradients, houses obstructing roads, and roads demarcated on large boulders.

Unemployment is high in the community, particularly among the youth, and many residents engage in informal trade. The settlement's proximity to the CBD provides opportunities for residents to engage in informal trade and seek employment. The most common livelihood activities in Dworzark include petty trading, manual labour jobs such as stone mining and construction work, and home-based enterprises. While there is a formal market in the community, it is inadequate considering the number of people and businesses in need of commercial space. Some residents have taken advantage of this by running shops on the ground floors of their properties. Additionally, women in the community are involved in agricultural activities along the banks of the George Brook Stream, which flows through Dworzark and empties into Kroo Bay, another informal settlement in Freetown.

Access to basic services in Dworzark is limited. There is a community health centre along the main access road, but residents in areas with poor access face challenges in reaching it. The environment in the settlement is poorly managed, with no designated waste-dumping site. As a result, household waste is often deposited openly along the George Brook Stream, leading to clogged drains and an increased risk of flooding. Community groups are responsible for maintaining the drains to prevent flooding.

Dworzark is prone to various environmental hazards and risks. Fire outbreaks, floods (especially for residents living along the George Brook Stream), rock falls (due to erosion and construction on steep hillsides) and waterborne disease outbreaks are common. Although the number of fatalities from these risks may be relatively low, the overall vulnerability of the settlement is significant when considering the cumulative effect of losses from these disasters.

Dworzark is also home to the Federation of Urban and Rural Poor (FEDURP) and has an active set of YMCA Youth groups, which undertake activities that focus on alleviating specific physical risks within their communities. These include disaster prevention, such as breaking and removing large boulders and clearing the existing drainage channels of waste; as well as raising awareness and lobbying the local authorities to support these efforts through waste collection services (Cumming, 2012).

NGOs play an active role in the community, addressing various sectors such as health, education, disaster and risk management, sanitation and water, child protection, and gender issues. Organisations such as Save the Children, BRAC, CRS, Concern Worldwide, and YMCA are actively involved in supporting the community. Dworzark also has

Figure 2.7 Map of Portee-Rokupa. Source: © Ansumana Tarawally. Map data: © OpenStreetMap contributors. https://www.openstreetmap .org/copyright

a community disaster management committee (CDMC) and a system of community health workers (CHWs) to address recurring natural disasters and health problems.

Portee-Rokupa

Portee-Rokupa is a coastal settlement nestled in a small bay near a beach and located in the eastern part of Freetown, about 10 km from Freetown's city centre. Politically, Portee-Rokupa is divided into two separate wards, Portee and Rokupa, with the wharf area serving as a shared space that unifies the community. It shares borders with Kuntolor to the south, Congo water to the east, Grassfield to the west and the mouth of the Rokel river to the north where it meets the Atlantic Ocean. The geography of the area is characterised by sandy soil and rocky slopes. While officially divided into Portee and Rokupa in 2004, the community is often referred to as one entity. It falls within two separate wards, each with its own parliamentarian, councillor and tribal chiefs. The ward development committee established by the FCC also plays a role in the community's governance.

The settlement has a history dating back to the 1940s, with immigration mainly from the Port Loko district throughout the twentieth century. However, in the 1990s, the population experienced significant growth due to an influx of people displaced by the civil war in Sierra Leone. This has led to overcrowding and a concentration of poverty in the informal part of Portee-Rokupa. Unemployment, illiteracy, poor hygiene, inadequate skills, and low political participation are major challenges faced by the community.

According to population projections from Statistics Sierra Leone in 2012, Ward 354 (Rokupa) had a population of 18,763, while Ward 355 (Portee) had a population of 24,855. A study conducted by the YMCA and CODOHSAPA in 2015 found that 6,069 people reside in the poorest part of the settlement, often referred to as the 'informal' areas. Unofficially, the settlement is divided into four zones: Benk, Portee Wharf, Rokupa Wharf, and Mefleh.

The most densely populated area of Portee-Rokupa is Rokupa Wharf, originating from 1942–45 when a pepper seller named Phybian Cole established the first settlement. This zone is characterised by poor housing conditions and steep topographic features. The roads are unpaved and suffer from a severely inadequate drainage system. The community is highly vulnerable to natural disasters, particularly flooding along the coastal areas. Fishing and petty trading are the main livelihood activities in Rokupa Wharf.

The oldest part of the informal settlement is Portee Wharf, which was originally a resting place for fishermen and hosted businesses in the early 1940s, before being developed into a residential area. It is located at the centre of the settlement, sharing boundaries with Rokupa Wharf and Benk. Portee Wharf has a high population density compared to other zones. Access to this area is challenging, as it can only be reached through a steep stairway constructed with large rocks. Portee Wharf serves as the main fishing community and acts as a landing site at Kissy, in the east end of Freetown.

Benk zone, established in the late 1970s, is the smallest of the four zones in Portee-Rokupa. It is located on the fringe of the Portee Wharf zone. The settlement lacks essential amenities such as safe drinking water, schools, healthcare facilities, and improved sanitation. Additionally, the community is inaccessible by road.

The largest and most recent zone is Mefleh, which was established c.2002 by a man named Pa Mefleh who dug a water well, attracting people from the formal part of the community to fetch water or wash their clothes. Mefleh zone expanded rapidly during the aftermath of the civil war in the early 2000s. However, this zone also faces accessibility challenges. Its topography and proximity to the sea make it prone to flooding, particularly during high tides or heavy rainfall.

Despite its vibrancy, the informal areas of Portee-Rokupa face significant challenges in terms of limited space for social infrastructure expansion. Schools, health centres, community centres, markets, and sewerage systems are lacking. Access to essential services such as water and electricity is also limited, with no pipe-borne water supply available. Residents rely on hand-dug wells, which are often close to the sea, resulting in salty water. In some cases, residents must travel long distances outside the community to purchase water.

The housing conditions in Portee-Rokupa are severely overcrowded, exacerbating the challenges of inadequate sanitation. Many residents rely on hanging toilets, which are often shared and constructed with sticks and sacks over the sea. These toilets are poorly built, managed and neglected by users. In some cases, resident's resort to using the sea as a makeshift toilet, particularly in houses with limited space for proper sanitation facilities. The lack of access to water and proper sanitation contributes to the frequent occurrence of waterborne diseases.

Portee-Rokupa is characterised by small houses made of concrete or mud blocks with plastering, often located close together. The housing conditions are generally poor, with a significant number of makeshift structures made from corrugated iron sheets, wooden planks, mud bricks, broken stone, zinc, tarpaulin, concrete/cement, cardboard/plastic/cartoon, and even car tyres. Brick houses are mostly found outside the slum, particularly in the areas leading to the upper parts of the community. Access to services and amenities is generally inadequate.

The settlement is situated in a low-lying area distinguished by high levels of poverty and inequality, unemployment, illiteracy, limited skills, low political participation, and poor hygiene. Due to poverty, housing shortages, high rental costs, and limited available land, many residents engage in land reclamation, particularly along the seafront, to construct their makeshift dwellings. The poor living conditions, high population density and lack of improvement in services and infrastructure contribute to worsening socioeconomic conditions in the informal part of the settlement. There is a lack of space for social infrastructure facilities such as schools, health centres and markets and there is no sewerage system. Sewage from the upper, better-planned areas of the east end of Freetown empties nearby the cliff situated in the informal settlement. Limited access to essential services such as water and electricity is a common challenge for local residents. As a result, residents often must walk long distances or climb steep slopes to access these services in the formal part of the settlement.

Portee-Rokupa is not accessible by road and access to the community is only possible via a very steep stairway constructed from large rocks. Walking is the primary mode of transportation, followed by minibuses (poda-poda), motorcycles (kekehs) and shared taxis. Most residents in the informal part of Portee-Rokupa have workplaces that are not too far from the community and they prefer to trek or walk rather than use other modes of transportation.

Safeguarding public and environmental health poses significant challenges in the informal settlement of Portee-Rokupa. The community lacks formal land titles, leading to housing shortages and high rental costs. As a result, many residents resort to traditional land reclamation at the seafront to build their makeshift dwellings. The informal part of Portee-Rokupa lacks a dedicated healthcare facility. Residents must walk to the formal part of the settlement to seek medical services, with an average walking time of 15 to 30 minutes. This limited access to healthcare exacerbates the prevalence of diseases such as malaria and typhoid in the community.

Water access and quality are also major concerns. There are approximately 60 water points serving the population of 7,000, including hand pumps, public taps, protected and unprotected wells, springs, and a water tank. While most households report satisfactory water quality, 12.1% consider it to be bad, with only 7.9% rating it as good (SLURC, 2022). Sanitation facilities in Portee-Rokupa primarily consist of hanging toilets, which are makeshift structures made from sticks and empty sacks. These toilets hang over the edge of the sea or stream and are connected directly to the sea through pipes. They are poorly built, unmanaged and uncared for by users. Some residents without toilets resort to using the sea as a means of waste disposal. Waste generated in the community is often dumped into the sea and waterways, or in communal refuse dumps and open spaces. Limited financial resources among households make it difficult to afford proper waste disposal, leading to the common practice of depositing waste along the coast. This waste is sometimes used by seaside dwellers for land reclamation from the sea.

Petty trading and fishing are the primary sources of livelihood for the community in Portee-Rokupa. Fishing plays a crucial role in the lives of the residents and has contributed to the settlement's identity as

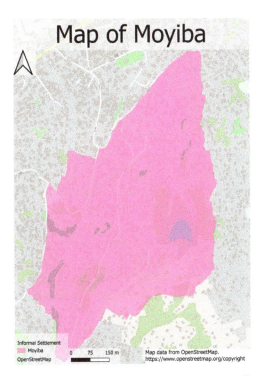

Figure 2.8 Map of Moyiba. Source: © Ansumana Tarawally. Map data: © OpenStreetMap contributors. https://www.openstreetmap.org /copyright

a fishing community. Portee-Rokupa has emerged as one of the largest fishing communities along the coastline in the east end of Freetown, benefiting from its strategic location near major transport routes and the seafront connecting the Port Loko district. The fishery sector in Portee-Rokupa encompasses various activities, including fishing, fish processing through smoking, and the sale of both raw and smoked fish. Fishing is carried out using different types of boats, mainly large 'Ghana' boats with a crew of 25–30, and 'Capital' boats with a crew of about six. The combination of a strategic location, close proximity to transport routes and access to both sheltered bay areas and the open sea has contributed to the growth of the fishing industry in Portee-Rokupa. It serves as a vital source of income and employment for the community, with entire households often involved in different aspects of the fishing value chain. The community's reputation as a fishing hub attracts customers from various locations, further supporting the local economy.

Portee-Rokupa faces significant environmental risks, primarily due to its location beneath a cliff that hangs over the settlement. The population residing on the plateau above contribute to the contamination and waste that ends up in the low-lying informal settlements. To meet their housing needs, residents resort to reclaiming land at the seafront, resulting in tenure insecurity and a reluctance to invest in gradual housing upgrades. These makeshift structures are highly vulnerable to flooding and lack access to essential services. The community has experienced various disaster events, including mudslides, seasonal flooding and the impact of the Ebola outbreak. These incidents have led to loss of life, displacement and further exacerbation of the community's vulnerabilities. Poor sanitation practices, contaminated water sources, limited access to safe drinking water, coastal pollution and inadequate waste management contribute to the environmental risks faced by Portee-Rokupa. The high population density of the settlement amplifies these challenges. Due to its vulnerable location along the coastline, Portee-Rokupa is particularly susceptible to seasonal flooding caused by inadequate drainage networks. The settlement also faces erosion, illegal waste dumping, the danger of loose boulders from cliffs, fire outbreaks (often resulting from improper fuel storage) and occupational risks for fisherfolk, such as marine accidents.

Moyiba

Moyiba is an informal settlement located in the east of Freetown, about 5 km away from the CBD. According to the most recent census recorded in 2015, the settlement has 37,000 residents, half of whom are young people. Originally established as a farming community in 1929, it later transformed with the establishment of a quarry in 1966 to support the construction of major infrastructure projects in Freetown, such the main trunk roads, Queen Elizabeth Quay, Congo Cross Bridge, National Stadium and the Youyi Building.

The houses in Moyiba primarily are built with mud-brick walls and corrugated iron sheets, with a few makeshift structures, commonly called 'pan-bodi' (corrugated iron houses). There is a lack of formal land title deeds with most plots informally owned by individuals/families and/ or occupied by tenants and the community has no clear boundaries. Neighbouring communities include Kissy Mamba Ridge, Kissy Brook, Kortright, Mount Aureol and Blackhall Road. However, the settlement's hillside location poses risks such as landslides, rockfalls, road accidents, and mudslides, particularly during the rainy season.

Due to its unplanned nature, Moyiba faces challenges in terms of infrastructure and service provision. The settlement has precarious road networks, with one main unpaved road serving as the primary artery. The rugged terrain makes vehicular access difficult, leading to limited public transport and emergency services options. As a result, many residents rely on footpaths to access the community. The overall road network in Freetown is inadequate, covering only 5% of the city's land compared to the recommended 30% (Oviedo et al., 2021). This further exacerbates the accessibility issues faced by informal hillside settlements like Moyiba.

Access to basic services in Moyiba is limited. Water is primarily obtained through community water points, a piped water supply and a dam. The community has poor access to drinking water. The existing water supply from a dam further upstream is only available for a limited period in the rainy season due to extensive deforestation, leading to the rapid drying up of the inflow stream to the dam. Access to electricity is also limited. Sanitation facilities are inadequate, with residents relying on pit latrines, 'flying toilets' (defecation into polythene bags that are subsequently dumped along drainage channels) and open defecation. These poor sanitation practices contribute to water contamination and the prevalence of water-related diseases such as cholera, typhoid and malaria.

The main source of livelihood is stone mining, but this often results in further damage to the ecosystem and landscape. Stone quarrying is increasingly in competition for land with housing, as the settlement of Moyiba continues to grow up the hill toward the quarry (Koroma et al., 2018). Education and healthcare services in Moyiba are provided through 23 schools (four secondary and 19 primary) and one health centre. However, the overall infrastructure and service provision remain a challenge for the residents of Moyiba.

References

Allen, A., Koroma, B., Manda, M., Osuteye, E., & Lambert, R. (2020). Urban risk readdressed: bridging resilience-seeking practices in African cities. In M. A. Burayidi, J. Twigg, C. Wamsler & A. Allen (Eds), *The Routledge Handbook of Urban Resilience* (pp. 331–348). London: Routledge.

Allen, A., Koroma. B., Osuteye, E., & Rigon, A. (2017). Urban risk in Freetown's informal settlements: making the invisible visible. Policy brief No. 6, April 2017. Accessed 25 June 2024. https://assets.publishing.service.gov.uk/media/5a02fc65ed915d0ade60dab3/UrbanArk_briefing_6_web_1_.pdf

ASF UK & SLURC. (2018). Change by design: Dworzark Community Action Area Plan 2018. Freetown: SLURC.

CRS (Catholic Relief Services). (2019). Disaster risk reduction and resilience in Dworzark informal settlement. Catholic Relief Services.

Cumming, A. (2012). Youth volunteerism and disaster risk reduction. Y-Care International. Accessed 25 June 2024. https://www.preventionweb.net/files/29460_29460youthvolunteerismanddisasterri.pdf

Koroma, B., Rigon, A., Walker, J., & Sellu, S. A. (2018). Urban livelihoods in Freetown's informal settlements. Publication 005. Freetown: SLURC. Accessed 25 June 2024. https://www.slurc.org/uploads/1/0/9/7/109761391/urban_livelihoods_in_informal_settlements_-_report_web_quality.pdf

Leong, M., Kim, H., Lui, Y. R., Korsi, S., Tang, T. C., Chen, et al. (2018). Fieldwork data collected in Cockle Bay, Freetown as part of the ESD MSC DPU-SLURC Learning Alliance: co-learning for action: from risk mitigation to transformative action to disrupt urban risk traps in Freetown.

Oviedo, D., Okyere, S. A., Nieto, M., Kusi, L. F., Kita, M. Yusuf, Y., & Koroma, B. (2021). Walking off the beaten path: everyday walking environment and practices in informal settlements in Freetown. *Journal of Research in Transportation Business and Management, 40*: 100630. https://doi.org/10.1016/j.rtbm.2021.100630

SDI (Slum Dwellers International). (2017). Know your city: Dworzark. SDI. Accessed 5 June 2023. https://sdinet.org/settlement/1860/13581265

SLURC (Sierra Leone Urban Research Centre). (2022). Portee-Rokupa settlement profile. Freetown: SLURC.

Yiftachel, O. (2009). Critical theory and 'gray space': mobilisation of the colonized. *City*, *13*(2–3), 246–263.

3

The story of SLURC

Joseph M. Macarthy, Braima Koroma,
Andrea Rigon and Alexandre Apsan Frediani

Introduction

Some debates on the role of higher education institutions call for them to serve as knowledge hubs and to engage more directly with urban actors to address intractable societal problems. The expertise that already exists outside of universities should be harnessed and deployed into problem discovery and the creation of cutting-edge scientific knowledge for addressing real-life societal problems (Evans & Marvin, 2006; May & Perry, 2011). Of particular importance is the role that university partnerships with other urban stakeholders can play in improving the knowledge base for urban development. The Sierra Leone Urban Research Centre (SLURC) operates at the intersection between academia and society to drive urban transformation in Sierra Leone.

The urban population in Sierra Leone has been growing rapidly from 18.9% of the country's total population in 1963 (when the first population census was held) to 41.0% in 2015. Freetown is located on the western edge of the country and has become almost entirely urban, accounting for a significant proportion of Sierra Leone's urban population. However, urban population growth in Freetown and other Sierra Leonean cities and towns is happening without significant economic growth with persistent levels of poverty and inequality. The country's estimated urban population of nearly three million in 2015 (or 40.9% of the national population) is expected to rise to 3.7 million by 2025, bringing serious challenges relating to housing, service delivery, health, disaster risks and safety and security. The introduction of the Local Government Act in 2004 triggered significant political and administrative reforms based on a decentralised system of governance, albeit implementation remains limited. At the local level in Freetown is the Freetown City Council (FCC), the city's highest development authority responsible for, amongst other functions, waste collection/disposal, street cleaning and cleaning of faecal sludge. Several functions such as education, health, policing and security are held by the central government, even though some NGOs and other bodies also play a critical role in the city's development process. Increasing the knowledge base on the urban in Sierra Leone and the capacity to manage the related challenges is therefore imperative.

Freetown is characterised by high levels of inequality, with a significant proportion of its residents classified as poor, making access to basic services such as housing, water and energy problematic. The city's hilly topography creates a spatial divide for service delivery, thereby challenging access to and connectivity with some areas of the city, preserving existing inequalities and fragmentation.

Since its inception, SLURC has been developing a research network integrated with Freetown's informal settlements and their organisations. Over the years, SLURC has successfully built relationships with local, mainly informal, communities, including setting up a research and training agenda relevant to the needs of residents.

This chapter narrates SLURC's journey in the first nine years, which involves its setting up and infancy (or coming into being) as a globally connected research organisation that delivers high-quality research, builds the capacity of urban professionals and communities, and works with other urban actors to advocate for urban social justice. This chapter discusses the opportunities and challenges of running a strategic research partnership integrated with public institutions, civil society and community organisations. The chapter also reflects on the key impacts of the centre and the institutional challenges faced.

Connection and partnership development

SLURC was set up in relation to the scarcity and limited reliability of data on Freetown. In 2013, invited by Comic Relief UK, academics from Njala University and the Bartlett Development Planning Unit at UCL conducted a study on the state of urban knowledge in Freetown, including an inventory of available data on the city's informal settlements. The study included an assessment of the available knowledge, the methods that produced it, its validity, and identified the key knowledge gaps. Key findings included that data on urban development issues in Freetown was scarce and isolated and that the only state-led information collected on informal settlements was in the form of national population censuses, which are too infrequent to provide a clear and correct picture of the many challenges faced by the residents. The report further noted that much of the data collected and analysed in relation to available studies was not disaggregated to provide a clear understanding of the diverse characteristics needed for policy formulation and practice. Other crucial findings related to broad inconsistencies and gaps in the available knowledge and evident methodological issues that weakened the reliability of existing research, making it difficult to use it to inform development programmes. The report also found a major constraint to be the limited technical capacities of institutions with responsibility for spatial development, in particular surveying, urban design, town planning, architectural and structural engineering as well as the lack of skilled professionals in Sierra Leone who could provide training. A few NGOs paid for their staff to attend professional courses overseas but did not necessarily focus on the skills needed for urban development and planning.

Based on the identified gaps in knowledge and capacity for urban transformation in Sierra Leone, Comic Relief became interested in funding more research led by UCL to support the development of NGO-led interventions in Freetown's informal settlements. However, this risked reproducing the existing dependence on international actors. Therefore, the conversation evolved into proposing the setting up of a centre that would generate a locally relevant research agenda, deliver high-quality research jointly with urban stakeholders, freely disseminate the research outputs, build the capacity of urban professionals and community actors, and work in partnership with urban actors to advocate for urban justice. The proposal also involved a focus on building local research capacity, including the skills for using the research evidence in policy and planning to help improve the wellbeing of people living in urban informal settlements. The idea was to also establish a resource centre for the collection, organisation and dissemination of research outputs, such as reports, handbooks, training manuals, books, journal articles, policy/issue briefs, leaflets, posters and videos, as well as other related forms of knowledge on urban Sierra Leone.

In 2014, a full proposal was submitted to Comic Relief by Njala University and the Bartlett Development Planning Unit for the setting up of a research centre in Freetown. SLURC was established with a three-year core grant from Comic Relief in August 2015. The project aim was to establish SLURC as a globally connected urban research centre to generate evidence, share urban knowledge, build a strong research and analysis capacity and influence the country's urban policy and practice toward improving the wellbeing of residents living in precarious informal settlements. SLURC was set up as an autonomous and locally based institution, officially registered as a non-profit organisation (company limited by guarantee) with the Office of the Administrator and Registrar General (Freetown) in August 2015. In 2019, at the end of the Comic Relief (UK) core funding, SLURC re-registered with the Corporate Affairs Commission. In parallel, the nature of the partnership has been consistently reviewed over the years to ensure SLURC's sustainability, for example expanding the membership of the board.

SLURC in action

SLURC was founded to respond to the growing urban development challenges in Sierra Leone. The initial funding was linked to a large consortium called the 'Pull Slum Pan Pipul' (Krio for 'pull the slum out of the people') cluster which consisted of three local and three international NGOs funded by Comic Relief to improve the life and wellbeing of people living in Freetown's informal settlements. This consortium created a space for SLURC to build important relationships with both the partners and communities in informal settlements, allowing the setting up of a local research and capacity-building agenda relevant to the needs and aspirations of residents. The central assumption for establishing SLURC is that knowledge and research capacity are 'essential enablers' to transformative positive urban change.

SLURC was set up as a financially independent legal entity linked to the Institute of Geography and Development Studies at Njala University, while being operationally based in Freetown. In the first three years, SLURC was controlled by a management board comprising Njala University and the Bartlett Development Planning Unit with equal votes and a co-management structure. In parallel to the management board, an international advisory board of five eminent academics provided guidance to the management board and helped SLURC grow during its first three years. The advisory board had one representative each from Njala University and the Bartlett Development Planning Unit, nominated from among its most senior management team. The other three members were chosen from among distinguished urban experts across Africa. Their role was to lend their knowledge, experience and skills to the management board.

The management board also comprised two urban academics, each nominated by Njala University and UCL. Their key role was to provide strategic leadership for the running of SLURC. The UCL representatives initially had specific responsibilities to build the institutional and operational capacity of the centre, while progressively withdrawing from daily management. They were to serve only in their standard role as board members by the end of the Comic Relief project. A local civil society representative was added to the management board to ensure accountability and the operational flexibility needed to implement complex practice-oriented research projects. A project manager, hired by the Bartlett Development Planning Unit, was seconded to the centre full-time to provide operational support to the management board in implementing the core grant. During the first five years, SLURC enjoyed sustained support from the leadership of Njala University, whose Deputy Vice Chancellor, Dean of the School of Environmental Sciences and the Director of the Institute of Geography and Development Studies were actively involved in the management of the centre. However, getting SLURC established was not an easy task as this involved serious negotiations between the leaderships of Njala University and the Bartlett Development Planning Unit to secure agreements that described the broad objectives of setting up the centre and the lines of management: a top requirement of the funder.

SLURC was formally launched in January 2016, following a delay partially linked to the uncertainties in the immediate aftermath of the 2014–2016 Ebola crisis in Sierra Leone. In full attendance were a mix of urban stakeholders drawn mainly from among local and international academics, public officials (local and national), civil society (particularly NGOs and the media), the private sector and local community representatives and their groups (CBOs). The gathering created a forum for participants to hold meaningful exchanges and share experiences of dealing with some of the major challenges of urban growth and discuss the role of research evidence and training in building more inclusive and sustainable cities and towns in Sierra Leone. This engagement was essential since a critical part of SLURC's work concerns fostering relationships among urban stakeholders while exploring opportunities for collaborative engagements for transformative change in Sierra Leone. The launch was accompanied by the first meeting of SLURC's advisory board, comprising professor Michael Walls (UCL), professor Ibidun Adelekan (Ibadan University, Nigeria), professor Alpha Lakoh (NU), professor Blessing Mberu (African Population and Health Research Centre (APHRC), Kenya) and professor Nancy Odendaal (University of Cape Town, South Africa and Association of African Planning

Schools (AAPS)). Following this, SLURC was once again launched globally through a press conference in October 2016 at the Habitat III conference in Quito, Ecuador. The session enabled an engagement with the global public on SLURC's research, describing it as a new mode of knowledge co-production through partnering with relevant public institutions (local and national), civil society, the private sector and local communities and their groups.

SLURC's first organised global engagement was an international networking event planned as part of Habitat III in Quito. Through its global partnerships, this event allowed the participation of five other urban alliances from the Observatory of Evictions (São Paulo), CLIMA Sin Riesgo (Lima), CityLab (Cape Town), Engaged Learning Sheffield (Sheffield) and Habitat International Coalition Action Research Partnerships (Global) who shared their insights and made recommendations on how urban learning alliances can play active roles in the implementation of the UN's New Urban Agenda. Other SLURC activities in Quito included a meeting with Cities Alliance to explore their future work plans regarding slum upgrading. It also included the prospect of extending funding to support urban development initiatives in Sierra Leone and meetings with the Secretary for Territory and Housing of the Quito Municipality and the officials from the Government of Kenya in charge of slum-dwellers. The latter meetings provided insights into how good quality data can lead to evidence-based decisions, allowing city authorities and other urban stakeholders to improve a city.

SLURC's way of working

Based on the analysis of existing urban knowledge, the feasibility study initially proposed three thematic research areas for SLURC: land and housing, vulnerability and resilience, and livelihoods and the city economy. Cockle Bay, Moyiba, Dworzark and Portee-Rokupa were the four informal settlements in which all initial research activities were grounded. These communities represent the diversity of Freetown's informal settlements and the different research projects have allowed the creation of multiple layers of knowledge, which provided a comprehensive and transdisciplinary understanding of the settlements to inform policies at the city scale. SLURC has now extended its work to 20 informal settlements, often tailoring research and practices to suit the immediate need and scale of those particular contexts. Moreover, because Freetown and the other urban areas in Sierra Leone were severely affected by the

Ebola epidemic, urban health was added as a fourth research theme during the proposal development. In 2019, two other themes: mobility and transport, and urban services and infrastructure, were added, reflecting the adaptability and flexibility of the centre to take up new and emerging concerns. Since 2016, SLURC has carried out a series of research projects relating to the six thematic areas. Each research theme had training activities at its core to upskill researchers and other actors concerning theories, methods and policy related to these issues. SLURC training bring together community members, NGO staff, government officials and academics. It is often the first time that they have had a chance to meet, work together and learn from each other.

Important elements of SLURC's work include building relationships between urban stakeholders, looking out for synergies and exploring collaboration opportunities to enhance the impact of SLURC and its partners in decisions relating to urban problems and urban development issues. The aim is to help improve the life and wellbeing of people in deprived urban informal settlements. SLURC's research approach, which is based on knowledge co-production and capacity building, has allowed it to gain the trust and confidence of local communities, NGOs, public officials, and international organisations and is therefore capable of brokering relationships that can foster transformation in urban Sierra Leone. SLURC uses participatory action research to understand the key challenges faced by residents in marginalised urban settings, who struggle daily with health and social inequalities and problems of access to housing and other social services. This involves working with community residents, and community and city governance actors to co-produce knowledge and action for change. SLURC capitalised on the relationships its consortium partners had built with the informal settlements over many years of working with their residents.

Through its participatory action research, which involves working directly with the residents, SLURC was able to gain acceptance by the local community structure, including the chiefs, elders, youth groups, community disaster management committees (CDMCs), women's groups, religious groups and members of the Federation of the Urban and Rural Poor (FEDURP). Some community actors, along with public officials and civil society actors, were part of international knowledge exchange visits organised by SLURC to Kampala (Uganda), Lusaka (Zambia), Karonga and Mzuzu (Malawi) and Cape Town (South Africa). These visits generated learnings and fruitful exchanges on cutting-edge initiatives for improving the lives of people living in informal settlements. SLURC's work showcases how knowledge can be co-produced involving actors from different levels and backgrounds and how to use such opportunities to address the different capacities of these actors. Furthermore, it illustrates how building strategic relations between universities, public officials, civil society, community residents and their groups can create openings to promote the voices of marginalised groups and communities, influence policy decisions, and foster the development of an inclusive city.

In 2016, SLURC's knowledge exchange involved organising a delegation to Habitat III in Quito which included the Mayor of Freetown, who not only met with the UN Secretary-General but was invited to be a speaker at the special session on urban rules and legislations, thus raising the profile of Freetown and its concerns at international level. Over the years, SLURC has benefited significantly from the Bartlett Development Planning Unit's international networks, including the International Institute for Environment and Development (IIED), Cities Alliance, and international donors. The Bartlett Development Planning Unit was particularly instrumental in the recruitment of the International Advisory Committee, linking SLURC up with a variety of experts, such as Arif Hassan, who shared lessons from setting up an Urban Resource Centre in Karachi, and Melanie Lombard from the Global Urban Research Centre, University of Manchester.

Since its foundation in 2015, SLURC has worked on several multi-country research and capacity-building grants with institutions including UCL, the Institute of Development Studies (IDS) at the University of Sussex, Global Disability Innovation Hub (GDI), IIED, Architecture Sans Frontières UK (ASF-UK), Development Action Group (DAG) South Africa, Liverpool School of Tropical Medicine (LSTM), London School of Hygiene and Tropical Medicine (LSHTM), the University of Manchester, University of Bristol, King's College London, John Hopkins University (JHU), York University in Canada, Osaka University in Japan, University of Lagos, University of Ghana, Loughborough University, The World Bank, United Cities and Local Governments (UCLG), national NGOs such as Catholic Relief Services Sierra Leone, and networks of marginalised communities. In total, SLURC has successfully run 33 research and capacity building projects receiving total funding of USD 2.5million (in addition to the initial Comic Relief grant of over USD 1,000,000), with many more in the pipeline.

In 2017, SLURC and the Bartlett Development Planning Unit's master's degree programme in environment and sustainable development (MSc ESD) established a Learning Alliance to support transformative actions towards building a socially and environmentally just Freetown. The four-year Learning Alliance brought together over

120 MSc students and staff of the ESD practice module to work directly with SLURC, FEDURP, the Centre of Dialogue on Human Settlement and Poverty Alleviation (CODOHSAPA), and residents of selected informal settlements to co-produce contextual knowledge on a variety of issues relating to the settlements and to facilitate knowledge exchange, including exploring joint solutions to the challenges. Over the years, the teams have conducted research on nine themes (including land and housing, waste management, sanitation, mobility and transport, and energy transition, amongst others) in eight informal settlements (Cockle Bay, Moyiba, Dworzark, Kroo Bay, Colbot, CKG, Portee-Rokupa and Susan's Bay). The key outputs included 15 policy briefs, 17 videos and three reports on how to build a more socially and environmentally just Freetown.

SLURC situates its work within national and global discourses through bi-annual conferences, first held in August 2017 on Freetown's informal economy. The one-day conference was attended by diverse participants from central government, ministries, departments and agencies, local councils, local and international academics, civil society, private sector, and local community residents. The conference enabled a detailed examination of the evidence from SLURC's research and identified outstanding cases of noteworthy lessons to inform policy reforms and practice while networking. Two conferences convened in 2019 and 2022 built on these earlier achievements. In 2019, the second conference on 'Urban Transformations in Sierra Leone: Lessons from SLURC's research in Freetown' included a high-level delegation visit from UCL. It came at an interesting moment for urban planning and development in Sierra Leone, with both the Transform Freetown Framework and Mid-Term National Development Plan in their implementation phases. However, the conference also came at a time of huge global challenges with a disproportionately negative impact on poorer countries, exacerbating deeply entrenched inequalities. The third bi-annual conference, delayed due to the COVID-19 pandemic, was held in September 2022 with the theme 'Tackling Urban Inequalities: Pathways for Housing Justice and Inclusive Urban Development in Sierra Leone'. This third conference facilitated dialogues on policy solutions and approaches to reducing inequalities and fostering inclusive growth in urban Sierra Leone.

In 2019, SLURC shifted from core funding to project funding which allowed it to engage in a variety of research projects, often in partnership with foreign-based universities. SLURC's transition to project funding was swift due to its reputation for high-quality outputs. There were, however, concerns about its ability to continue raising funds considering its overreliance on funding from the UK (96% of SLURC's budget), which implemented drastic cuts to its Official Development Assistance (ODA) in 2021. While SLURC managed to overcome the UK financial cuts unharmed with its sustainability plan and risk reserves intact, a key lesson learned was the urgent need to diversify its funding sources, which involved exploring collaborations with institutions based in the US and other European and African countries.

Outcome and impact

SLURC's team of trusted local researchers has produced several research outputs linked to the different projects and research themes, either implemented alone or jointly with international colleagues. A key feature of all SLURC's research is that rigorous ethical procedures have guided it. SLURC has developed specific modes of engagement negotiated with all its main international partners (see Appendix 1 on Protocols for research partnerships). SLURC's outputs and ideas have been applied in teaching a range of development courses at Njala University and other tertiary institutions. SLURC's participation in the Knowledge in Action for Urban Equality (KNOW) project led by the Bartlett Development Planning Unit enabled support for the development of a curriculum for an innovative master's degree in 'Development and Planning in African Cities' (MSc DePAC). This academic programme was to be domiciled within the IGDS and run jointly by NU and the DPU. It assists students and those who already have careers in other disciplines, both in Sierra Leone and elsewhere in Africa, who were interested in acquiring the technical and practical skills needed to engage with the various influencers shaping the urban environment. A preliminary step for developing the masters programme was the creation of a massive open online course (MOOC) on 'Development and Planning in African Cities' by SLURC and the Bartlett Development Planning Unit in 2018. The MOOC raised SLURC's profile with urban experts internationally, attracting 6,900 participants from 120 countries. The course draws upon the insights of SLURC staff, urban experts at the Bartlett Development Planning Unit, as well as key stakeholders and partners in Sierra Leone. Amongst other achievements, the course became the most-downloaded resource on the UCL Open Education repository and has been awarded a UCL Faculty Education Award. SLURC aligned the MOOC with a wider learning and educational strategy that builds the capacities of urban practitioners to foster pathways to urban equality.

SLURC has positioned itself as a centre of research excellence that is contributing considerably to existing knowledge on urban Sierra Leone, prioritising the underserved urban informal settlements. This has allowed SLURC to influence policy and practice enabling improvements in the wellbeing of people living in informal settlements. Through its training programmes and advocacy activities, SLURC has established itself as an institution trusted by communities, civil society, government (national and local) and international organisations and is therefore capable of brokering relationships that can transform urban development paths in Sierra Leone. SLURC's most important policy inputs were in the design of the Transform Freetown Agenda, specifically in the Environmental Management and Urban Planning and Housing working groups; the land policy review by the Ministry of Lands, Housing and Country Planning; and the current national disaster management policy of Sierra Leone. SLURC also made significant contributions as part of a sub-cluster working group (land and housing) in the preparation of the Medium-Term National Development Plan (2018–2023). For the first time, informal settlements are recognised at the national level not only in the national land and disaster management policies, but also in the Medium-Term National Development Plan. The Transform Freetown Plan also acknowledges informal settlements as spaces for improvement, leading to synergies being developed between the FCC and the Federation of the Urban and Rural Poor (FEDURP).

In 2019, an external evaluation identified SLURC's role in acting as a facilitator of dialogue as one of its biggest impacts. SLURC's work in bringing public officials, policy makers, civil society organisations, academia, the private sector and local community residents together to discuss pertinent issues relating to deprived spaces, has led to a shift in thinking and practice by the central and local governments and other urban stakeholders towards informal settlements. As shown in Mayor Aki-Sawyerr's Transform Freetown Agenda, slum upgrading is specifically cited ahead of forced eviction. SLURC's and FCC's ongoing City Learning Platform activities in Freetown have brought together informal settlement dwellers, government officials, city authorities, private sector, academia and international and national NGOs. They foster dialogue on the problems in the city, allow ideas to be shared, generate new knowledge through the encounters and exchanges, and promote just urban development that prioritises the needs and aspirations of informal settlement dwellers.

The impact of SLURC's work as a leading knowledge centre in urban Sierra Leone was publicly recognised by the Freetown City Mayor Yvonne Aki-Sawyerr during SLURC's second national conference in July 2019, when the mayor openly acknowledged using the research evidence in the design of the Transform Freetown Plan. A similar statement by the Director of Policy and Planning within the Ministry of Lands, Housing and Country Planning highlighted SLURC's significant contribution to advancing the knowledge on several urban development issues and policies. Various NGOs and community groups also alluded to SLURC's role in the increased visibility of the intractable challenges in informal settlements, including their different needs, aspirations and the capacity to influence policy and planning.

This international academic engagement has allowed SLURC directors and researchers to co-author academic book chapters and papers, and speak at conferences hosted by IIED in London, the African Centre for Cities in Cape Town, the International Institutes on Human Settlements (IIHS), the Development Studies Association, the Association of African Planning Schools (AAPS) conference in Tanzania, Africa Research Universities Alliance (ARUA) conference, and the Africa Urban Research Institute (AURI) conference in Cape Town SA, amongst others. SLURC has also organised joint webinar sessions with Habitat International Coalition, ARUA, Centre of Excellent Urbanisation and Habitable Cities, University of Lagos and many more. Sustaining this international profile is essential for SLURC's continued growth.

Key challenges

SLURC's establishment was faced with some challenges. The initial discussions regarding the involvement of staff from Njala University did not fully anticipate the exact workload that this would entail. So, while seven days a month were assigned to each director for their involvement with SLURC, it soon became obvious that more of their time was needed considering the increasing number of funding opportunities that emerged. Besides, as urban research was a completely new experience in Sierra Leone, given the country's extensive focus on rural development – and with the urban not being a vital part of the curriculum at most local universities – finding candidates with the requisite skills and knowledge to take up the different positions created at SLURC proved difficult. It involved massive investment in staff training to develop autonomous researchers. This also had a gender challenge, as it was difficult to identify qualified female candidates. Promising graduates were hired and trained, but retention proved difficult as the centre could not afford the same salaries as international organisations, leading to staff moving into higher paying sectors and institutions. This prompted a constant focus on building staff capacity, which was not easily funded by donors.

As the centre migrated from core funding to project funding, the issue of sustainability became very important. However, with the COVID-19 crisis, which weakened the economic base of many countries, the prospects of raising additional research funds became extremely difficult. Countries such as the UK, where the centre draws more than 90% of its funds, cut its international funding support. SLURC has had to act more strategically by reshaping both its organisational structure and its strategies to enable it to adapt to the wavering funding climate. Another challenge was the enormous time commitment to building the centre's institutional structure, consisting of formal and informal rules and procedures. This involved holding a series of management meetings and consultations to define the organisational structure and employee roles, recruitment processes, contracts, financial management procedures, policies, staff mentoring and retention, networking and several other activities, at the expense of taking time away from research and training. Moreover, it has been difficult to fund knowledge management and dissemination with funders interested in funding new research, compared to the important work of making existing knowledge available across different research teams and urban stakeholders. Finally, Sierra Leone is considered one of the most difficult countries in which to run a business. Establishing a centre presented major challenges. For example, despite significant investment, energy supply and internet connections were often poor, making it difficult to collaborate internationally. .

Conclusion

The rapid urbanisation of Freetown is associated with some specific fragility challenges. Locating and accessing relevant knowledge on urban issues is a key challenge faced by city authorities, policy makers, civil society and academics in Sierra Leone. SLURC has been responding to this challenge through research, training and knowledge management. The centre also operates a physical and online resource unit, to expand access to the centre's outputs and other relevant urban knowledge. SLURC is committed to advancing an urban development agenda that works towards building an equitable, inclusive and sustainable urban Sierra Leone. Its six thematic research areas focus on harnessing evidence and learning from the contributions of informal settlement dwellers on city development and the challenges they face, including ways to ensure their rights across the country.

SLURC's work demonstrates that cities and towns can be made more inclusive and productive if deliberate efforts are taken to build on the ingenuity, knowledge and capacity of local community actors as well as enhancing the scale and efficacy of their community-led solutions. Its work, which involves building a community of practice, focuses on promoting collaborative solutions to address socio-economic inequalities in urban Sierra Leone, bringing academic expertise to support ongoing interventions on the ground. SLURC's partnership with public officials, civil society and community residents adds value to research activities in the informal settlements. Its engagement with communities in research and capacity building aids the development of policy solutions for some of the intractable challenges faced in the city. SLURC strives to shape and inform policy and planning by providing periodic outputs in the form of reports. It empowers communities through advocacy materials and policy briefs, while convening platforms for collective discussions on important urban problems. Its collaborative engagement creates opportunities for government MDAs, the public sector, academics, civil society, the private sector, and community residents to discuss and identify clear and compelling visions and objectives for transforming their communities. Finally and most importantly, SLURC has radically changed the political economy of international research. Research agendas were dictated by principal investigators based in the Global North that were buying the best local academics out of their important work to support their government and from training a new generation to respond to the concerns of foreign academics. Now, SLURC is in a position to use its research base to establish locally relevant research agendas and negotiate international research projects in such a way to respond to the grounded concerns of local partner communities.

References

Evans, R., & Marvin, S. (2006). Researching the sustainable city: three modes of interdisciplinarity. *Environment and Planning A: Economy and space*, 38(6), 1009–1028.
May, T., & Perry, B. (2011). *Social Research and Reflexivity: Content, context and consequences*. London: Sage.

Part II
Knowledge contributions

4
Urban livelihoods
Andrea Rigon, Braima Koroma and Julian Walker

Introduction

This chapter[1] presents a succinct summary of research findings on the livelihoods of the residents of informal settlement and their role in the wellbeing of Freetown's residents. It seeks to disaggregate the ways that different groups of women and men participate in, and benefit from, these livelihood activities, as well as their impact on the wider settlements and city. The chapter considers how these findings relate with theory on informality and the governance of informal economic activities.

The focus of this study on *informality* encompasses both the distinction drawn between informal and formal settlements (a spatial dimension) and between informal and formal economic activities (economic dimension).

Informal settlements/slums have been approached in quite different ways in terms of their treatment in city development strategies. These often prioritise conformity with technical masterplans over the lived realities of many poor citizens. Such approaches typically still deal with slums/informal settlements through processes of eviction (Fahra, 2011). Such evictions are often justified either on the basis of the need to clear land to make space for infrastructure development (with land occupied by informal settlements normally the easiest to clear and the cheapest to acquire); or more directly, with the rationale of eliminating informal settlements as intrinsically unruly or unsafe spaces, which are seen as a blight on city development (Bahn, 2009; Watson, 2009; Bahn, 2016).

On the other hand, there are consolidated approaches that focus on upgrading slums by improving the conditions and lives of people living in them, rather than by improving these spaces by removing slum dwellers (Payne & Majale, 2004; Burra, 2005; Boonyabancha, 2009). Such in-situ approaches to informal settlement upgrading have encompassed a range of approaches linked to housing and settlement upgrading, including special planning zones and dual building standards; state and civil society support to housing upgrading; community-led upgrading that leverage residents' own resources and capacity, enabling private housing markets to meet the needs of the poor, or, the incremental extension of basic infrastructure.

The informal economy has been broadly defined as 'the diversified set of economic activities, enterprises, jobs, and workers that are not regulated or protected by the state' (ILO, 2002). However, if we apply this to the broad definition of informality, it would encompass most of the Sierra Leone economy, where self-employment and working for a family member make up 87.7% of the labour force. Note that although not all family work is necessarily informal, it is a good proxy for informal employment. This definition also throws up several issues. One is the extent to which boundaries between the formal and the informal can in practice be drawn. For example, economic activities may be regulated in some ways (e.g. taxation) but not in others (e.g. social protection of workers or quality control of output). Moreover, even where economic activities are *officially* regulated by the state, this may not be applied in practice, drawing a distinction between formal regulation and de facto informality. In many contexts this de facto informality is accompanied by the increasing informality of the de jure governance regimes, where public officials govern in ways that contradict formal laws and procedures (Meagher, 2007, p. 406). Another blurring of the boundaries can be found in the institutional and spatial 'sites' of informal economic activities. Much informal employment now takes place in 'formal' enterprises (Williams & Lansky, 2013). On the other hand, informal economic activities can be widespread in formal areas of the city, while, equally, formal economic activities and employment may be based in informal settlements (e.g. official public employment of teachers or officials in slums). Our findings interrogate the utility of the in/formal urban divide and explore in/formal relations.

Research approach and methodology

The research combined the sustainable livelihoods framework, a people-centred analysis of value chains, and gender analysis. The research aimed at exploring how economic relations work as systems, and how women and men negotiate these systems. The research standpoint was to approach formality and informality as characteristics of different elements in an interconnected system.

An influential approach to understanding economic systems and their impact on people's lives and wellbeing is the analysis of livelihoods. Livelihoods are defined as comprising '…people, their capabilities and their means of living, including food, income and assets', including both tangible and intangible assets (Chambers & Conway, 1992, p. ii). A key element of livelihoods analysis is examining how 'capital assets' (natural, social, physical, financial and human) are used in livelihoods strategies, as well as how they may be built or depleted by livelihoods strategies or context-specific processes.

The concept of livelihoods helps paint a picture of the ways in which people construct a living, putting women and men, and their agency, at the centre of analysis. At the same time, it examines the context that poor women and men need to navigate. It aims to pinpoint and understand resources or capital (such as economic, social and symbolic resources), activities and strategies that lead to the construction of household livelihoods, as well as the challenges which affect the sustainability of livelihoods in the face of economic troubles and severe household shocks (Scoones, 1998; Carney, 1999, 2002; Farrington, Rasamut, & Walker, 2002; Rakodi & Lloyd-Jones, 2002).

Livelihoods analysis also provides a holistic understanding of intra- and inter-household relationships and their impact on livelihood activities. Livelihoods in urban spaces utilise, amongst other things, an array of social networks, land, financial capital and technology to earn income and access goods.

Another approach to understanding local economic systems and how women and men negotiate them, is the analysis of value chains which focuses on products or sectors of production. Tracking these sheds light on the activities and outcomes of groups of women and men involved in sectors of production. Value chains are also a way to understand how the city is produced through interactions of formal and informal practices (Palat Narayanan & Véron, 2018). In this vein, a value chain describes 'the full range of activities which are required to bring a product or service from conception, through the different phases of production (involving a combination of physical transformation and the input of various producer services), delivery to final consumers, and final disposal after use' (Kaplinsky & Morris, 2002, p. 4).

Mapping value chains helps to identify the chain's links and actors, their functions, degrees of power, and relationships. Visualising the stages of production and the flows between these stages enables an exploration of the livelihood system beyond its core value chain to include a wider set of relations, including regulations and connections to other sectors and dimensions of people's lives. As such, a value chain analysis adds a comparative dimension of the different groups of women and men engaged in a sector and explores the way that relations between them are structured. In contrast, a key focus of value chain analysis is to identify inequalities between nodes in value chains – in terms of decision-making power or profit generated – and to highlight that high- and low-value nodes are often associated with different categories of people.

The analysis of livelihoods systems presented in this chapter engages with the ways that livelihoods are structured around social and political power relations, which may offer structural advantages to some while keeping others in poverty. The analysis includes an understanding of the capital assets available to people working within the systems and the relationships and flows between actors at different nodes in the value chains. Building on this context, we explain the livelihood strategies of people in terms of their agency (the decisions and choices that they make about how to engage in livelihoods) and their circumstances (the specific connections and opportunities that influence these decisions). We then explore the various outcomes of these livelihood systems and the choices of women and men working within then. Cutting across all these areas of analysis is gender relations and a consideration of how each area of analysis plays out across different (individual, settlement and city) scales. In particular, we use value chain mapping to track power relations between different actors, daily activity charts to track time spend in different activities, and life histories to reveal the gendered nature of these livelihood sectors.

The research focused on four informal/slum settlements in Freetown (embedded cases) which were selected from among the 68 settlements identified as slums which formed the initial sampling frame. These included two coastal settlements: Cockle Bay and Portee-Rokupa from the West and East of Freetown respectively; and two hillside/hilly settlements: Dworzark and Moyiba, also from the West and East of Freetown, respectively. In terms of the value chains/livelihood systems selected in the settlements, we focused on sectors that characterised the settlements in that they were typical forms of livelihood and/or linked to the collective identity of the settlement, and because they employed large numbers of people, specifically poorer residents. This chapter will present in some detail only two sectors (stone quarrying in Moyiba and fishing in Portee-Rokupa) but will draw on evidence from all the sectors (sand mining in Cockle Bay and stone quarrying in Dworzark) in the overall findings.

The livelihoods systems

Stone quarrying in Moyiba

Moyiba is situated in a hilly area on the eastern side of Freetown, 5 km from the city centre. The settlement has approximately 37,000 residents of which half are young people. It was a farming community until 1966 when a large-scale, mechanised stone quarry was established. This closed in 2002 due to the civil war. Since then, self-employed informal workers have taken over quarrying activities, where a significant section of residents (women, men and children) derive their livelihood. Work in the quarry is sometimes suspended by public authorities, for example in 2014 after an accident, or the following year due to a land dispute. At times, quarrying activities are suspended due to heavy rains. Nonetheless, the booming Freetown construction activities make quarrying an attractive livelihood.

As outlined in Figure 4.1 and Table 4.1, this value chain links several actors and activities, starting with the initial extraction of rock and ending with the use of the stones and gravel produced in local and citywide construction projects.

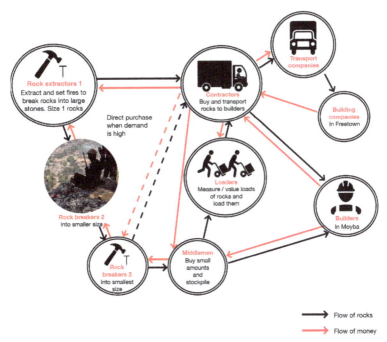

Figure 4.1 Stone quarrying value chain in Moyiba (Freetown).
Source: © Authors

Table 4.1 Actors and processes in the quarrying sector in Moyiba. Source: © Authors

Stages	Actors	Processes and relations
'Boss-Boss' Breaking a large boulder into rocks that can be transported from the site. It requires an investment of at least USD 260 for the purchase of the required tools.	Men, particularly young able-bodied men.	An agreement is made that Boss-Boss stone extractors will receive a share of the processed stones from the women stone breakers. Boss-Boss men then sell on the processed stones to contractors or to petty buyers.
'Cut-Cut' Breaking up the large rocks into stones which are small enough to be worked on by women and children.	Men, often on a part time basis – for example, students or people with other jobs (e.g. drivers, carpenters, security guards).	The women engaging in subsequent stages bring large rocks from the Boss-Boss site, and 'hire' the Cut-Cut men (who work individually or in groups), i.e. pay them cash to break stones to a size that they can the work on themselves.
Three quarter: breaking down stones to large gravel. **Half inch:** breaking down stones to medium sized. **Millimetre messeh messeh:** breaking down stones to fine gravel	Mainly done by women and children (age 7-68) who have few other opportunities for support.	The women acquire rocks from Boss-Boss men or petty buyers, process the gravel to the size requested by the rock owners, and in payment are given a share of the rocks. If they are given the rocks in large Boss-Boss form, they pay the Cut-Cut men in cash to break them down to a manageable size for processing. The women then give a share of the processed gravel back to the original rock owners, and sell their own share to contractors or petty buyers. Petty buyers may also lend women money on credit, which is repaid with gravel.

Stages	Actors	Processes and relations
Load men These workers are paid (USD 0.06 per head pan) to move loads of rock/building gravel from processing or store sites to contractors trucks.	Men, normally students or people with other jobs, who do this work to supplement their income.	Load men are self-employed and paid cash by contractors. There is a load man association which is registered with Freetown City Council and only those registered with this association are allowed to work as load men in the quarry.
Petty buyers Buy, stockpile and trade the different sizes of gravel and stone to sell at a profit.	Only five petty buyers in the community, as it requires USD 910-1,040 start-up capital, which is a considerable amount for the settlement. Of the five, only one is a woman.	Petty buyers buy different sizes of gravel from women or Boss-Boss men to sell to contractors. They typically sell to contractors at a small mark-up (e.g. buying three quarter gravel at USD 0.33 per head pan and selling the same amount to contractors for USD 0.35). They may also buy large stones directly from Boss-Boss men and commission women to process it into gravel by arranging to share the processed stone with them at 70-30% or 60-40%. Petty buyers have enforced a rule that restricts women from selling gravel directly to contractors if they have been advanced stones by petty buyers.
Contractors Transport and sell stones and gravel to building companies. They visit construction sites around the city with samples of the different sizes or stone and gravel to secure contracts. They then hire vehicles to transport the building gravel to the construction sites.	Contractors range in age from 20-70 years old. They are mainly men but there are a few women. *"We do not have huge capital as people think but lean on our good relationships to get our daily income."*	Contractors buy stones and gravel from petty buyers (or, at times of high demand, they may buy direct from stone processors). They pay load men cash to load vehicles. Payment for transport is deferred until after the gravel has been sold. Contractors may give advanced payments to petty buyers.

The connections between the nodes in the chain are not arranged in a standard form, or indeed in a linear structure. In contrast, nodes may be bypassed as a result of direct local demand involving direct sales by rock breakers, or extra nodes may arise as a result of fluctuations in demand. For example, the rock extractors and breakers may at times sell directly to local builders or households involved in self-construction at a higher price rather than through middlemen or contractors. On the other hand, while rock breakers sell directly to contractors when demand for stone is high, when it is lower, they may sell rock to local middlemen who will stockpile rocks and sell when demand increases.

The main 'flows' in the value chain are of rocks, labour (e.g. the work of loaders) and of money between the different actors, though frequently money flows are delayed, or indirect via systems of trust, credit and agreed shares of processed rocks. The value chain is more complex because different nodes may be undertaken separately by different groups or, in some cases, the whole range of processing phases may be undertaken by the same person: for example, a rock extractor also breaking down rocks to fine building gravel rather than passing it on to other rock breaker groups.

While mining activities are not appropriately licensed in Moyiba, they do appear to be regulated to some extent by the authorities. In addition, while there is no formal registration of artisanal miners, several groups have occupational associations registered with Freetown City Council. These associations play a role in managing disputes across the sector and setting up mutual welfare societies. Research participants explained informal community bylaws that regulate work in the sector, generally implemented by the police and related for the main part to disputes over payment, mining in sensitive sites (such as road mining) and appropriate behaviour. Penalties for breaking such bylaws are fines, which are used by the community to fund infrastructure projects such as road maintenance. Petty buyers also appear to regulate the sales practices of women working in smaller stones processing, prohibiting them from direct sales of gravel if they have been provided stones by petty buyers.

Fishing in Portee-Rokupa

Portee-Rokupa is a coastal community of about 7,000 people, 10 km from the city centre. Due to the shortage of land and high housing costs, the incoming population reclaimed land from the seafront. The settlement is characterised by tenure insecurity and high levels of poverty. Over the years, the settlement has become one of the largest fishing communities

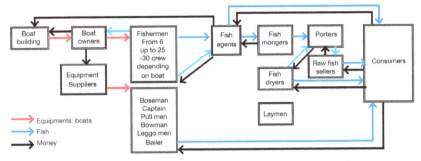

Figure 4.2 The fishing value chain in Portee-Rokupa. Source: © Authors

along the coastline in the east end of Freetown. The fishing sector includes the processing of fish through smoking, and the sale of both raw and smoked fish. People come from all over the city, and even from other provinces, to buy fish from Portee-Rokupa and the local women fish sellers also sell their fish in the main markets elsewhere in the city.

In Sierra Leone, the Ministry of Fisheries and Marine Resources has sole jurisdiction over managing and conserving fishery resources. However, the management and development of the artisanal fishery sector in Sierra Leone was devolved to local councils in 2004. Larger boats used in Portee-Rokupa are considered semi-industrial and remain regulated by the ministry. Local councils working with fishermen's associations award licences. These associations have been instrumental in enforcing fishing gear regulations to mitigate fishing of juvenile fish stock.

Discussion

Complex sectors with a gendered division of labour

The sectors we investigated presented fairly structured value chains with a complex organisation of relationships that have developed over many years and have evolved over time, often driven by the growth and expansion of the city. The actors in various chains have created their own mechanisms of cooperation, which are made possible by the high level of trust between actors who have worked in the chain for long periods of time. Such cooperation mechanisms allow the actors to fulfil larger orders, cope with difficult times of oversupply when prices collapse, and ill health.

These sectors are organised in value chains able to operate with little cash due to consolidated relationships of trust developed over long periods of time. The livelihood systems that we studied appear to

Table 4.2 Actors and processes in the fishing sector in Portee-Rokupa. Source: © Authors

Stages	Actors	Processes and relations
Boat builders Buying of materials and building of boats.	22 boat builders in the community who are mainly healthy and abled-bodied men, the majority were apprenticed into the profession through family connections.	An agreement in advance on boat price. Buyer's advance payment for some of the work and materials (timber, nails, and money for the feeding of the boat building team). They also get fish from boats that they build or repair as a way to keep a strong relationship with boat owners and fishermen.
Boat owner Commissions fishing crews. He/she must buy the boat and contract a Boseman who assembles the crew, and contract an agent for the sale of fish (often a female relative).	Around 100 boat owners. From young adults to elderly people, mainly men, though there are some women. Need to have enough money to pay for the boat.	Need to advance payments for the construction of the boat. The catch is divided, and the boat owner receives the larger share of the catch in payment, but is responsible for fuel and boat maintenance. Boat owners pass their share of the catch to an agent who will sell the fish and subsequently pay them.
Fishermen A range of roles: *Boseman:* head of the crew and responsible for all logistics and hiring the crew. *Captain:* controls the engine. *Leggo man:* responsible for the anchor and cleaning of the boat. *Bow man:* looks for fish at sea. *Pull men:* responsible for dropping and pulling the net. *Bailer:* empties water from the boat.	All men, ranging in age from around 25 to 30. They mainly come from fishing families.	Fishermen are paid by the boat owner with a share of the catch. The size of their share depends on where their role is in the hierarchy of jobs.

Stages	Actors	Processes and relations
Agents Use their social networks to find customers (including fish mongers) to sell fish to. One person can be an agent for up to ten boats.	There are over 50 agents. These are all women, most often the wives of boat owners.	Agents negotiate fish prices to fishmongers, who they attract to the boat side, and sell to them. They keep 10% of the sales value and the rest goes to the boat owner/crew.
Fish smokers (dryers) Buy fish from the agents at the boats, smoke it at their homes using a dryer with assistance from laymen, pack it for sale in markets and sell direct to wholesalers.	Fish smokers are from fishing families. They are mostly women with very few men. They need some capital to buy equipment and fish to start up.	Purchase their fish from agents, pay labourers to carry the fish to their smoking houses and laymen to lay out their fish for smoking. They sell the smoked fish to wholesalers.
Labourers Carry the loads of fish from the boats to the road junction, houses of fish smokers, or markets.	Around 60 labourers who are mainly young men, school dropouts and students.	Paid in cash by fish smokers or fish mongers, based on the distance and the weight of the load.
Laymen Wash and clean the fish and lay it out on the grid for smoking.	Young people, mainly young men and boys, often students, some women who are usually relatives of fishers.	Laymen are paid in cash by fish smokers. Sometimes, only paid once the fish is sold, or not paid because they are relatives of the fish smokers.

Stages	Actors	Processes and relations
Net menders Making and mending nets of different sizes and shapes.	Over 30 net menders in the community who are all men with skills in net-mending.	Hired by boat owners to make or mend nets. When new nets are to be made, the boat owners provide the materials (lengths of netting). They pay the net menders for their work. If the boat owners have a very big catch, they may give the net menders a share *"just to keep us close and to be flexible with them when the nets need maintenance or repairs."*
Retailers There are different types of fish sellers, including raw fish sellers (fish mongers) and wholesalers. Fish mongers also wash and prepare the fish for sale.	Raw fish sellers are mainly women. They often come from fishers' families.	Fish mongers and wholesalers buy fish directly from agents or from fish smokers to sell directly to consumers. When they sell in market they have to pay market dues for a pitch/site.

strengthen systems of trust and reciprocity within the community by establishing multiple relationships of interdependence between different actors in the value chains.

In the livelihood systems analysed, many stages are characterised by a clearly gendered division of labour. Women tend to work in stages of the sector where they can combine reproductive and productive work, but these are also the lowest paid stages and they have little power in the system.

When women do have power in livelihood systems, for example when they play key brokering roles, they tend to be women whose male family members (husbands or fathers) also have important roles in the system. For instance, when the wife of a boat owner is a prominent fish agent. Age is also important, as younger women do not generally have powerful positions in a livelihood system and often work at the lowest stages due to school dropout linked to teenage pregnancy.

Social protection of last resort

Findings demonstrates that these informal livelihoods sectors provide what the formal sector and the state are unable to do: employment and strong networks of trust and mutual assistance relationships. These sectors have two important characteristics: they are labour intensive and offer ease of entry to the very poor. The technology of production prioritises the use of labour rather than substituting it with capital-intensive productive processes. This onerous work maximises employment, offering a fundamental social function that supports the wellbeing of an expanding urban population.

Some stages of these value chains are 'open' (based on common property resources with relatively open access) and entry into the sector (based on limited tools and skills) is easy. As one stone quarrier in Moyiba observed: 'Everybody is free to use the quarry. You only need to declare yourself to the existing members and they will willingly indoctrinate you.' This means that a wide range of people can engage in these productive activities. However, competition is high and thus income levels are low, with many participants only earning enough to subsist.

In many cases, people entered the low stages of these sectors when they faced challenges in life. The sectors also involve effective systems of mutual social protection to cope with the high level of uncertainty. These can be horizontal, such as saving groups, or vertical, such as cash advances from brokers in exchange for loyalty. In this sense, these sectors contribute to building a social protection of last resort.

The contribution of these sectors goes beyond providing a livelihood to those involved. They allow 'formal' economic activities to be viable, particularly in the absence of state capacity to adequately regulate and promote economic activities. For example, these sectors provide the construction industry with materials such as stones and sand. These sectors also contribute to broader objectives by offering employment to a large number of young people. They support social cohesion, help diffuse social conflict, and prevent violence (Finn & Oldfield, 2015).

Coproduction of governance arrangements

In the context of post-civil war Sierra Leone, with the state slowly developing its capacity, different types of collective action become autonomous processes of self-governance to fill the state's gaps. The livelihoods sectors where informal settlement residents work establish self-managed informal institutions with complex and evolving regulations that contribute to coproducing effective hybrid governance systems. These institutions regulate and enable the operations of these sectors, for instance, through local by-laws on mining and fines whereby revenues are used to improve shared road infrastructures. For example, a contractor in Moyiba told us that workers were fined for fighting or using abusive language. The money collected was used for road improvement projects in the community.

These forms of autonomous collective action create horizontal bonds and trusts which is a further enabler of these sectors. They operate in a cash scarce system and therefore transactions take place on trust that people will be paid. Moreover, in these 'informal' governance arrangements, government often plays a role.

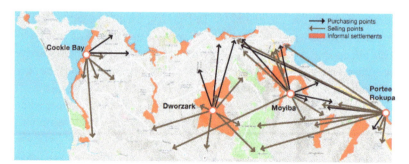

Figure 4.3 Relationships between livelihood sectors of informal settlement residents and the city. Source: © Authors based on OpenStreetMap. https://www.openstreetmap.org/copyright

The self-employment sector accounts for nearly 85% of the country's workers and the informal sector, especially the informal service sector, is the backbone of Freetown's economy. A spatial analysis of where the livelihood sectors considered in this study purchase tools and other inputs and where they sell their products attests to the strong connection of these sectors with other parts of the city (see Figure 4.3). Therefore, there are strong connections between the economy of informal settlements and the wider city economy. The analysis shows, for instance, the importance of stone supply to the construction industry and how the fish supplies wider parts of the city. Moreover, formal economic activities and the workers they employed would not be able to perform their duties without supporting services provided by workers in the informal sector. These services range from transport to lunches, trading, housekeeping and childcare. This indicates that even the most formal sectors are dependent on more informal activities. In short, these livelihoods sectors contribute to the wider city through the provision of key goods and services to formal economic activities, as well as to social security and employment to many residents. They further help make up for limited state capacity by deploying complex, hybrid forms of self-governance and self-regulation of these economic activities.

Conclusion

The livelihood activities of informal settlement residents make an important contribution to the settlements and the wider city. The sectors analysed in this research provide livelihoods to a large number of people and contribute to other key sectors of the city economy, while operating with limited capital. In stone quarrying, 70% of stone transactions take place without money being exchanged immediately, meaning that such sectors are built on trust relationships cultivated over long periods of time and on informal institutions. In a fragile and cash-scarce city economy, the sectors that develop in informal settlements where a large part of the population resides are key to the overall economy, cohesion and wellbeing. Moreover, these informal institutions regulate local economic activities by filling a governance gap left by city and central government authorities.

These sectors function as an employment of last resort for most people and have mechanisms of mutual assistance. Therefore, they help compensate for the lack of social protection services from the state.

That said, some of these livelihood sectors contribute to environmental degradation and workers may be subject to exploitative conditions. They also have little potential for expansion due to their dependency on limited natural resources.

Any disruption due to evictions, relocations or major regulatory changes may affect the supply of key goods to the city and cut the livelihoods and social protection to a large number of people. Therefore, labour-intensive livelihood alternatives must be put in place before pushing people away from livelihoods that are not sustainable in the long term. Urban planning and economic strategies should be developed through open policy dialogues with the participation of residents of informal sectors and the organisations that support them. It is important that national policy interventions in these sectors carefully consider all stakeholders to ensure the most vulnerable are not adversely affected by proposed changes. NGOs could also participate in developing alternative labour-intensive sectors that are not reliant on finite natural resources; supporting settlement-scale governance of livelihoods and the use of natural resources; and engaging informal settlements in city-scale economic planning.

This chapter also contributes to a broader body of literature that challenges dichotomic perspectives on formality and informality and calls for a change in policy towards informal livelihood activities which are currently criminalised and obstructed across cities in Africa. We question the idea that formality and informality are part of clearly defined, distinct spaces or economic activities in the city, by demonstrating the way in which informal activities are organically part of complex value chains across the entire city. We call for an understanding of the hybridity of in/formality as part of urban practices undertaken by all actors across the city as the basis of an African urbanism that acknowledges existing urban realities. The label of informality should not be politically applied to justify the elimination of 'less desirable' economic activities, which we have demonstrated to be the backbone of the city. Going beyond the in/formal divide and demonstrating the relational nature of the connections between the livelihoods of the residents of informal settlements and the broader city economy means that latent power relations can be addressed.

Note

1   This chapter draws on a research project funded by Comic Relief. Some of the data has already been published in a more extensive research report: Koroma, B., Rigon, A., Walker, J., & Sellu, A. (2018). Urban livelihoods in Freetown's Informal Settlements. Freetown. Sierra Leone: Sierra Leone Urban Research Centre. Available here: https://discovery.ucl.ac.uk/id/eprint /10062427/7/Rigon_latestversion_urban_livelihoods_in_informal_settlements_-_report _web_quality.pdf The research was conducted with the field research support of Austina Sellu, who no longer works at SLURC, but whose work we want to acknowledge.

References

Bahn, G. (2009). 'This is no longer the city I once knew': Evictions, the urban poor and the right to the city in millennial Delhi. *Environment and Urbanization*, *21*(1), 127–142.

Bhan, G. (2016). *In the Public's Interest: Evictions, citizenship and inequality in contemporary Delhi.* New Delhi: Orient Blackswan.

Boonyabancha, S. (2009). Land for housing the poor – by the poor: experiences from the Baan Mankong nationwide slum upgrading programme in Thailand. *Environment and Urbanization*, *21*(2), 309–329.

Burra, S. (2005). Towards a pro-poor framework for slum upgrading in Mumbai, India. *Environment and Urbanization*, *17*(1), 67–88.

Carney, D. (1999). *Livelihoods Approaches Compared.* London: Department for International Development (DFID).

Carney, D. (2002). Sustainable Livelihoods Approaches: Progress and possibilities for change. London: DFID.

Chambers, R., & Conway, G. (1992). Sustainable rural livelihoods: practical concepts for the 21st century. Institute for Development Studies (IDS) discussion paper 296, Brighton: IDS.

Farha, L. (2011). *Forced evictions: Global crisis, global solutions.* Nairobi: UN-HABITAT.

Farrington, J., Ramasut, T., & Walker, J. (2002). Sustainable livelihoods approaches in urban areas: general lessons with illustrations from Indian cases. Overseas Development Institute (ODI) working paper 162. London: ODI.

Finn, B., & Oldfield, S. (2015). Straining: Young men working through waithood in Freetown, Sierra Leone. *Africa Spectrum*, *50*(3), 29–48.

ILO (International Labour Organization). (2002). Resolution concerning decent work and the informal economy. 90th Session of the General Conference of the International Labour Organisation, Geneva: ILO.

Kaplinsky, R., & Morris, M. (2002). *A Handbook for Value Chain Research.* Brighton: IDS.

Meagher, K. (2007). Introduction: special issue on 'informal institutions and development in Africa'. *Africa Spectrum*, *42*(3), 405–418.

Palat Narayanan, N., & Véron, R. (2018). Informal production of the city: Momos, migrants, and an urban village in Delhi. *Environment and Planning D: Society and space, 36*(6), 1026–1044. https://doi.org/10.1177/0263775818771695

Payne, G., & Majale, M. (2004). *The Urban Housing Manual: Making regulatory frameworks work for the poor.* London: Earthscan.

Rakodi, C., & Lloyd-Jones, T. (2002). *Urban Livelihoods: A people-centred approach to reducing poverty.* London: Earthscan.

Scoones, I. (1998). Sustainable rural livelihoods: A framework for analysis. IDS Working Paper. Brighton: IDS.

Watson, V. (2009). 'The planned city sweeps the poor away…': Urban planning and 21st century urbanisation. *Progress in Planning*, *72*: 151–193.

Williams, C. C., & Lansky, M. A. (2013). Informal employment in developed and developing economies: perspectives and policy responses. *International Labour Review*, *152*(3–4), 355–380.

5

Understanding Freetown's urban health priorities and challenges: six years of health research at SLURC 2016–2022

Annie Wilkinson, Abu Conteh and Joseph M. Macarthy

Introduction

This chapter provides an overview of the health research programme developed by SLURC and partners between 2016–2022. When SLURC began, Sierra Leone was still reeling from the 2014–2016 Ebola outbreak, which was unprecedented in the way urban settings were affected, driving high rates of transmission. That experience had made it clear that the landscape and determinants of health in Freetown needed attention. Since then, Sierra Leone and the world have been rocked by the COVID-19 pandemic. In addition to these crises, the population of Freetown has faced a wide spectrum of health threats from everyday health problems – malaria, food insecurity, chronic diseases etc. – and disasters – cholera, floods, mudslides etc. – all of which result in high and often avoidable morbidity and mortality. SLURC's health research programme has explored this spectrum and seeks to generate evidence which will contribute to improved health and reduced inequality in Sierra Leone. This chapter focuses on four core challenges which have defined this work and its findings: 1) evidence gaps; 2) governance; 3) multi-sectoral interactions; and 4) capacities and relationships.

Urbanisation and health systems: start of a research agenda in Sierra Leone

When SLURC began, projections about urbanisation were, and still are, staggering. 55% of the world's population already live in urban areas and this is predicted to rise to 68% by 2050, with almost 90% of this growth happening in Asia and Africa (UN DESA, 2019). The implications for health are significant, as is the learning agenda for health systems research. In particular, there is growing recognition that a huge portion of this new urban population live in informal settlements with inadequate infrastructure and living conditions (e.g. 55% of urban populations in Sub-Saharan Africa). The rapid growth of informal settlements represented a major challenge about which existing knowledge and policies were ill-equipped (UN DESA, 2019). Multi-sectoral approaches were advocated (Weimann et al., 2016; Vearey et al., 2019), as well as those taking a holistic 'city as a system' view (Batty, 2013). Yet it was rarer to find detailed evidence of health and its determinants in informal settlements, and of how this linked to the wider policy and governance context; in particular, what shapes and perpetuates health conditions in informal settlements.

The disaster-prone nature of informal settlements means that disaster risk reduction had occupied most research and policy discussion. However, there was increasing recognition that the everyday risks and health problems of people in urban settlements are undercounted and likely to be a far greater cause of premature death than disaster (Satterthwaite & Bartlett, 2017). Meanwhile, health systems researchers had focused considerable effort on addressing the needs of vulnerable populations, including by encouraging participation in decision making and accountability in health (Nelson et al., 2019), but this had largely been with rural populations. Delivering effective health systems in informal urban settlements had been overlooked (Van de Vijver, 2015), possibly reflecting an assumption or hope that the settlements were temporary. In Freetown, from SLURC's early engagements with residents of informal settlements, it was clear that they were aware that their insecure status put them at a disadvantage in terms of health services. There is now a need to ensure that health system policy and planning addresses the needs of these informal settlements and recognises their rights to exist and to basic services. In health, as in other sectors, policy approaches have traditionally viewed informality as separate to formal systems, but informality is now being increasingly recognised as part and parcel of formal systems too (Priya et al., 2019).

Sierra Leone is becoming rapidly urbanised, with 41% of its total population already living in urban areas compared to 36.7% in 2004 (Statistics Sierra Leone, 2006; Statistics Sierra Leone, 2015). A major trend is the proliferation of precarious informal settlements, especially around the capital Freetown. The rise and spread of informal settlements became more severe during the civil war (1992 to 2002) as a result of the massive internal displacement, but it has continued rapidly since, with much road building and housing construction along the Freetown peninsula. Successive governments have perceived informal settlements to be illegal, and as a result there have not been efforts to provide them with basic services through official means. Therefore, living in informal settlements in Freetown is associated with poverty, poor housing, lack of access to water and sanitation facilities (water, toilet, waste disposal), congested or risk prone environments and inadequate health care services.

These trends in urban growth present new dimensions to the already well-documented challenges in Sierra Leone's health system. Sierra Leone's maternal and child mortality rates have reduced in the last decade but are still among the highest in the world, with maternal mortality at 717 per 100,000, and under-fives mortality 122 per 1000 (Statistics Sierra Leone, 2020). Although some free health care provision exists, for most people it is paid for privately which can be a significant barrier to access. Per capita out of pocket expenditure on health care is above the average for Sub-Saharan Africa (Government of Sierra Leone, 2019).

SLURC set out to create a programme of health research which could shed light on and address these emerging urban health dynamics. The initial exploratory work on urban health was done as part of Future Health Systems (FHS), a consortium funded by the UK Department for International Development (now the Foreign, Commonwealth and Development Office, FCDO). This early partnership was pivotal because it gave SLURC the opportunity to carry out a scoping study of the evidence base on urban health in Sierra Leone and to begin empirical research into the health conditions and priorities of residents in Freetown's informal settlements. This has informed much of its work since. Below is a list of the major health research programmes from FHS onwards:

- Future Health Systems Consortium (UK DfID): scoping study of evidence base and qualitative research into living conditions and health systems in urban Freetown.

- Shock Tactics – Urban health futures in the wake of Ebola (ESRC): ethnographic research to understand disease control practices, collective action and governance in the post-Ebola period.
- ARISE – Accountability and responsiveness in informal settlements for equity (GCRF): explores inequalities in health and wellbeing and works with marginalised people to claim their right to health and other social services through building accountability with service providers; uses participatory and interdisciplinary research and includes partners in Sierra Leone, Bangladesh, Kenya, India and the UK.
- Ebola project (IDRC): exploring socio-cultural and environmental factors in improving Ebola disease response and resilience in partnership with York University, Canada.
- TRUST 1 & 2 (NIHR/UKRI): A partnership between SLURC and London School of Hygiene and Tropical Medicine (LSHTM). The first phase explored perceptions about the government's response to COVID-19 and the factors shaping vaccine acceptance or rejection. The second phase took a gendered approach to understand the social and structural drivers of vaccine inequity and to make recommendations to policy stakeholder about improving vaccine access to all.
- Malaria (CRS SL): the urban malaria project was done jointly with the College of Medicine and Allied Health Sciences (COMAHS) to find out the prevalence of malaria in formal and informal settlements in Freetown and the social and behavioural factors influencing the spread of malaria; it was the first known study to have compared health indicators in formal and informal settlements in Freetown.

In the following sections we outline the major challenges which these projects have identified.

Evidence gaps

Data on population health is generally poor for all social and economic groups in Sierra Leone, but for residents in Freetown slums it is even more limited as their living and health conditions are rarely given attention in official health statistics (e.g. the 2013 and 2019 Sierra Leone Demographic and Health Surveys) or the census. The FHS scoping study by Macarthy and Conteh (2018) attempted to document evidence on health and health services in urban areas of Sierra Leone. The study found a patchy evidence base, representing sporadic research initiatives or NGO programmes over the years. The scoping study noted that the health risks and problems that were most frequently recorded were inaccessibility and unavailability of health services, in particular due to cost and distance related barriers; contamination of groundwater systems as a result of seepages from latrines; faecal contamination of water sources via overflowing rain water; poor waste disposal systems leading to waste accumulations in slums causing the propagation of flies, mosquitoes and rodents; vulnerability of most seaside slum communities to flooding and a variety of health risks since they suffer indiscriminately from poor sanitation; and some serious health problems faced by Ebola survivors as a consequence of the virus. Notably, most of this evidence base was focused on single diseases or topics and is likely to represent the priorities and interests of researchers rather than a comprehensive overview of the health conditions in informal settlements. Although available evidence reported that government health services were limited, there was little indication about what providers and services people used in their absence. There was also very little evidence regarding the priorities of people living in informal settlements.

These gaps in knowledge prevent a clear overview of the heath conditions and drivers in informal settlements, which in turn prevents effective policy. Without information on the priorities and problems faced in communities there is no hope of meeting people's needs and there is also a risk that differences between communities will be overlooked. SLURC research has begun to build up a more complete picture of the health challenges faced in different communities. Using participatory and in-depth qualitative methods and working with co-researchers, SLURC has begun to build up a granular understanding of people's priorities, contexts and differences. These results have shown that poor living conditions such as lack of clean water, unsuitable housing, improper sanitation etc. are indeed a major factor negatively influencing people's health – including exposing them to repeated disasters such as floods and cholera outbreaks – and has highlighted problems beyond these. The wellbeing of residents is impacted by persistent insecurities to do with livelihoods, tenancy status and relative living standards. In our more in-depth qualitative research, we have identified extensive burdens of chronic disease, including non-communicable diseases, which are often poorly diagnosed and have unclear aetiology (Wilkinson, Conteh, & Macarthy, 2020). This points to a wide spectrum of health challenges and deeply intertwined social, political and economic drivers. More recent research has begun to explore inequalities in health and to uncover the intersectional dynamics which shape these differences (Conteh, Wilkinson, & Macarthy, 2021). Having information about how social structures and differences between people influence health is crucial for developing equitable and inclusive policy.

The challenge of multi-sectoral (in)action

The research completed by SLURC on health in Freetown has consistently highlighted how many of the major determinants of health are outside of the traditional health system. People are exposed to environmental hazards through their livelihoods, for example dust in stone breaking and construction. Yet in these, often informal sectors, there are no proper occupational health standards or regulations, nor do people realistically have a choice about how they work or have the power to influence conditions, as they must do what they can to survive in the short term. Similarly with sanitation, where the lack of proper waste disposal options leads to disease risks from infectious and vector borne diseases, as well as flooding. Air pollution, caused by the burning of fuel for cookery or emissions from cars, is another major health problem which stems from the transport and energy sectors. This is by no means a unique situation; indeed, it is the picture in urban settings elsewhere (Elsey et al., 2019) and speaks to the social determinants of health more broadly.

The challenges this presents for multi-sectoral action are both intellectual and practical, and will be context specific, meaning Sierra Leone faces its own unique challenges. Intellectually, the various drivers (social, political, economic, technological) of health are hard to grapple with; they are multiple and intertwined rather than singular and discrete. Understanding these complex causal pathways is made especially difficult in rapidly urbanising settings where conditions change rapidly. These challenges are compounded by limited data (as described above).

Practically, multi-sectoral interdependencies inevitably lead to questions of responsibility and interests. Who is responsible? Where should resources to address problems come from (e.g. health, transport, waste)? This has governance implications, as each sector is structured differently and has formal and informal actors (see below). Beyond responsibility and resources, there are questions about how to build partnerships for effective cooperation and coordination. Saying that intersectoral collaboration is needed is one thing, but building the capacity and achieving it in practice is quite another. Attention is needed on how to realise co-benefits and how to negotiate politics, power, and diverse interests (Abbas, Shorten, & Rushton, 2022). Unfortunately, multi-sectoral action has a long way to go in Sierra Leone as there are limited synergies between government departments who tend to compete for resources rather than coordinate activities. Underlying multi-sectoral inaction are some stark differences in resource allocation. Spending on sectors which could contribute to the prevention of disease versus spending on curative services is imbalanced e.g. sanitation receives 0.2% of GDP compared to health's allocation of 11.1% of GDP (Government of Sierra Leone, 2019).

SLURC's position as an urban research centre working across issues of health, mobility, economy, livelihoods, infrastructure, land and housing offers great potential here as it has been able to convene sectors and stakeholders who may otherwise not interact. One SLURC initiative, the City Learning Platform (CiLP) brings public, private and community actors together to engage with SLURC research and share best practices from sectors and other cities to enhance cross-sectoral capacity as well as to address social and service-related challenges in Freetown's informal settlements. The idea is to foster shared learning and knowledge as enablers for transformative change. In addition, many of SLURC's research projects in health and more broadly have entailed setting up Steering Committees with multi-stakeholder membership relevant to the specific research problem. This approach fosters a cooperative relationship between the different sectoral actors, and joint involvement in research outputs leads to a shared understanding of the issues. However, this kind of work requires significant attention and dedication, and there are challenges in terms of how to hold stakeholders accountable. The involvement of community groups and residents is positive, but risks causing fatigue and frustration when tangible actions and impacts do not materialise.

The governance challenge

Governance is a critical, cross-cutting pillar of health systems, and good governance is imperative for addressing health inequalities and ensuring equitable participation and access for all on the pathway to universal health coverage (UHC). Yet discussions of governance in health systems are often technical, for example the WHO's 'health systems building blocks', including, for example, health workforce, finance, leadership and governance. Scholars have pointed out that health systems governance should include the wider household and community determinants of health (Sacks et al., 2018) and requires a focus on institutions (e.g. rules and norms) rather than simply facilities and structures (Abimbola et al., 2017). Urban environments create specific governance conditions which have hitherto been poorly understood in health systems research.

In Sierra Leone, SLURC's work has identified a number of governance priorities, constraints and challenges. A major concern was the historic absence of an enabling policy environment. Many foundational policies and laws are simply out of date, for example the 1960 Public Health Ordinance Act which is used to regulate public health. Meanwhile, numerous plans are drafted (often by or at the request of external funders) which have no resources attached to them and therefore exist mostly on paper e.g. One Health Plan or the Health Security Plan. Then there is the issue of 'urban blindness'. Until recently, major policy and strategy did not consider urban issues. 'Urban' is not mentioned in the National Health Sector Strategic Plan (2017–2021) or National Health Promotion Plan (2017–2021). Likewise, there is no mention of informal settlements.

Recently, there have been positive signs of change and SLURC has engaged actively in these new policy processes. Urban issues and informal settlements are very prominent in the Mid-Term National Development Plan 2019–2023 – for example, in land and housing, water and waste – and provide a coordinated overarching policy framework. SLURC has contributed an urban perspective to the National Disaster Management Policy and to an urban policy which is under preparation and aims to guide urban development in the country. Freetown City Council's (FCC) Transform Freetown agenda sets ambitious targets for health, water and sanitation based on wide consultation with Freetown residents, including those in informal settlements. However, long running tensions between central government and FCC over the extent to which responsibilities and resources are devolved to local government FCC have stymied progress on urban health and urban development more generally, meaning that FCC has limited powers.

Beyond the formal policy environment, SLURC's research has examined the norms and institutions which govern urban health in the real world. Governance on the ground is complex and plural. Multiple governance actors and structures exist across MOHS, FCC and within settlements themselves. These governance structures are often shaped by unequal power relations and exist on a spectrum of formal to informal. 'Formal' governance actors might be elected representatives such as MPs and councillors, or employees of the government; but communities also have their own elected and non-elected officials who occupy roles of authority (e.g. chiefs or chairmen), or leadership (e.g. religious leaders). In addition, some people gain influence in communities by controlling or providing resources such as water, or through having expert knowledge (e.g. health and healing), or simply through wealth and status. This influence – like all forms of influence – can be used for good or bad, for community or personal gain. A widespread perception in Freetown is that some of the people occupying the formal and apparently more powerful authority roles (e.g. MPs and councillors) are distant from the communities, while people who are closely engaged in community life have more respect and influence on day-to-day issues. This pluralistic landscape can lead to conflict and segmentation in service delivery. It also impacts on how people seek accountability for healthcare, water, and sanitation as responsibilities and pathways for redress are not clear.

Research projects such as FHS and ARISE have noted that there is limited communication between healthcare providers and that patients and providers can be mistrustful of each other. Facility management committees were formed to mediate between community members and healthcare workers. They have also witnessed the delivery of drugs to government health facilities at primary healthcare level to ensure supply chains operate correctly. However, in practice these committees are not always functional and have limited powers to mediate and monitor. SLURC projects have attempted to intervene in these governance and accountability systems. For example, in the ARISE and ESRC Shock Tactics projects, SLURC has held reflexive sessions about the nature of power relationships within communities and how these can stifle development. Projects have also sought to foster trusted relationships to support community actions and respond to local needs – for example, communities initiate actions to facilitate access to water and sanitation – but these continue to be challenged by limited sustainability and accountability beyond communities.

Relationships and capacities

While notions of community participation and co-production have been around a long time, too often there is still a troubling tendency to overlook community perspectives and capacities and bypass community institutions. In public health in particular, people and patients are often cast as ignorant or to blame for their problems, rather than as having their own valuable expertise and experience; although increasingly policy makers are striving for 'people-centred' health systems to overcome this. In Sierra Leone, as SLURC projects have repeatedly demonstrated (Osuteye et al., 2020; Ali, Macarthy, et al., 2022; Ali, Fallah, et al., 2022; Hrdličková et al., 2023), communities are extremely resourceful and have been the source of much effective local action whether it is in response to Ebola or COVID-19, or in taking steps to improve their local environments, for example organising community cleaning or building and raising funds for health centres. There is a risk that a focus on community capacity and resilience could lead to the abandonment of responsibility by authorities; hence SLURC has worked to support communities to develop and carry out their plans and towards transformative relationships and capacity. The ESRC Shock Tactics project that supported communities to develop strategies to address their problems – such as awareness raising about sanitation risks and improved sanitation – has shown that this can be effective (Conteh et al., 2021). SLURC views knowledge and capacity as essential enablers of positive change. It has also sought to foster inter-community and South–South learning with visits between settlements and further afield. Through convening platforms such as the CiLP (see above), they have also enhanced relationships between communities and government, NGOs and other service providers.

Conclusions and looking to the future

Although this chapter has focused on four challenges of urban health in Freetown, each of them represents progress that SLURC has made in building an evidence base and diagnosing problems. This is fundamental to the development of effective policy and strategy. In six years, SLURC has transformed a patchy evidence base on health into one which is nuanced, reflective of diverse people and conditions, and co-produced with communities. This work is widely respected internationally and in Sierra Leone SLURC has become the go-to centre for urban health knowledge. Working increasingly through interdisciplinary partnerships and alongside government policy processes provides opportunities to harness governance structures effectively and improve multi-sector coordination. Most importantly, throughout all this work, SLURC has built strong relationships with communities and with policy makers which provides the essential foundation for future progress.

References

Abbas, S., Shorten, T., & Rushton, J. (2022). Meanings and mechanisms of one health partnerships: insights from a critical review of literature on cross-government collaborations. *LSHTM Health Policy and Planning, 37*(3): 385–399. https://academic.oup.com/heapol/article/37/3/385/6430187

Abimbola, S., Negin, J., Martiniuk, A. L., & Jan, S. (2017). Institutional analysis of health system governance. *LSHTM Health Policy and Planning, 32*(9): 1337–1344.

Ali, S. H., Fallah, M. P., Macarthy, J. M., Keil, R., & Connolly, C. (2022). Mobilizing the social infrastructure of informal settlements in infectious disease response: the case of Ebola virus disease in West Africa. *Landscape and Urban Planning, 217*: 104256.

Ali, S. H., Macarthy, J. M., Conteh, A., Blango, V., Sesay, A., & Hrdlickova, Z. (2022). Ebola, informal settlements and the role of place in infectious disease vulnerability: evidence from the 2014–16 Ebola epidemic in Sierra Leone. *Disasters, 47*(2), 389–411. https://doi.org/10.1111/disa.12553

Batty, M. (2013). Resilient cities, networks and disruptions. *Environment and Planning B: Environment and Design, 40*(4): 571–573. https://doi.org/10.1068/b4004ed

Conteh, Y., Jones, D., Turay I., Sesay, I., Priddy, C., & Conteh, A. (2021). Inclusive sanitation: empowering marginalised urban Freetown residents. Institute of Development Studies (IDS) blog, 16 December. Accessed 25 June. https://www.ids.ac.uk/opinions/inclusive-sanitation-empowering-marginalised-urban-freetown-residents/

Conteh, A., Wilkinson, A., & Macarthy, J. M. (2021). Exploring gender, health, and intersectionality in informal settlements in Freetown. *Gender & Development 29*(1), 111–129. https://doi.org/10.1080/13552074.2021.1885215

Elsey, H., Agyepong, I., Huque, R., Quayyem, Z., Baral, S., Ebenso, B., Kharel, C., Shawon, R. A., Onwujekwe, O., Uzochukwu, B., Nonvignon, J., Aryeetey, G.C., Kane, S., Ensor, T., & Mirzoev, T. (2019). Rethinking health systems in the context of urbanisation: challenges from four rapidly urbanising low-income and middle-income countries. *BMJ Global Health* 4. https://doi.org/10.1136/bmjgh-2019-001501

Government of Sierra Leone. (2019). *Medium Term National Development Plan 2019–2023.* Accessed 25 June 2024. http://moped.gov.sl/wp-content/uploads/2022/06/sierra_leone_national_development_plan-1.pdf

Hrdličková, Z., Macarthy, J. M., Conteh, A., Ali, H. S., Blango, V., & Sesay, A. (2023). Ebola and slum dwellers: community engagement and epidemic response strategies in urban Sierra Leone. *Heliyon,* 9(7), E17425. https://doi.org/10.1016/j.heliyon.2023.e17425

Macarthy, J. M., & Conteh, A. (2018). Scoping study on the urban health situation in Sierra Leone. SLURC Publication.

Nelson, C., Sloan, J., & Chandra, A. (2019). *Examining Civic Engagement Links to Health Findings from the Literature and Implications for a Culture of Health.* Santa Monica: Rand Corporation.

Osuteye, E., Koroma, B., Macarthy, J. M., Kamara, S. F., & Conteh, A. (2020). Fighting COVID-19 in Freetown, Sierra Leone: the critical role of community organisations in a growing pandemic. *Open Health, 1*: 51–63. https://doi.org/10.1515/openhe-2020-0005

Priya, R., Singh, R., & Das, S. (2019). Health implications of diverse visions of urban spaces: bridging the formal-informal divide. *Frontiers in Public Health,* 7. https://doi:10.3389/fpubh.2019.00239

Sacks, E., Morrow, M., Story, W. T., Shelley, K. D., Shanklin, D., Rahimtoola, M., Rosales, A., Ibe, O., & Sarriot, E. (2018). Beyond the building blocks: integrating community roles into health systems frameworks to achieve health for all. *BMJ Global Health, 3*(suppl. 3), e001384. https://doi.org/10.1136/bmjgh-2018-001384

Sattertwaithe, D., & Bartlett, S. (2017). Editorial: The full spectrum of risk in urban centres: changing perceptions, changing priorities. *IIED Environment and Urbanization, 29*(1). https://doi.org/10.1177/0956247817691

Statistics Sierra Leone. (2006). Population and housing census: Analytical report on population distribution, migration and urbanisation in Sierra Leone. Freetown: Statistics Sierra Leone. Accessed 25 June 2024. http://www.statistics.sl/images/StatisticsSL/Documents/Census/2004/2004_census_report_on_population_distribution_migration_and_urbanisation.pdf

Statistics Sierra Leone. (2015). 2015 population and housing census: summary of final results. Freetown: Statistics Sierra Leone. Accessed 25 June 2024. http://www.sierra-leone.org /Census_2015.pdf

Statistics Sierra Leone. (2020). Sierra Leone: Demographic and health survey 2019. Rockville: The DHS Program, ICF. Accessed 25 June 2024. http://www.statistics.sl/images/StatisticsSL /Documents/DHS2018/SIERRA_LEONE_2019_DHS_REPORT.pdf

UN DESA (United Nations Department of Economic and Social Affairs, Population Division). (2019). World urbanization prospects 2018: Highlights. (ST/ESA/SER.A/421). New York: UN.

Van de Vijver, F. J. R. (2015). Methodological aspects of cross-cultural research. In M. Gelfand, Y. Hong, & C. Y. Chiu (Eds), *Handbook of Advances in Culture and Psychology* (volume 5, pp. 101–160). New York: Oxford University Press.

Vearey, J., Luginaah, I., Magitta, N.F. et al. (2019). Urban health in Africa: a critical global public health priority. *BMC Public Health 19*(340). https://doi.org/10.1186/s12889-019-6674-8

Weimann, A., Kabane, N., Jooste, T., Hawkridge, A., Smit, W., & Oni, T. (2016). Health through human settlements: investigating policymakers' perceptions of human settlement action for population health improvement in urban South Africa. *Habitat International, 103*, 102203. https://doi.org/10.1016/j.habitatint.2020.102203

Wilkinson, A., Conteh, A., & Macarthy, J. M. (2020). Chronic conditions and COVID-19 in informal urban settlements: a protracted emergency. *Cities & Health, 5*(sup1): S148–S151. https://doi .org/10.1080/23748834.2020.1813538

6

Freetown's development trajectory from a sustainable mobility perspective

Daniel Oviedo, Clemence Cavoli,
Alexandria Z. W. Chong, Yasmina Yusuf,
Braima Koroma and Joseph M. Macarthy

Introduction

This chapter focuses on describing the recent urban development trajectory of Freetown, the capital of Sierra Leone, from a perspective of sustainable mobility. It sits within a broader aim of understanding what specific circumstances can accelerate pathways to sustainable mobility and urban land-use. We define leapfrogging the transition to sustainable urban mobility as 'the acceleration of structural and functional transformations and the reconfiguration of urban systems towards sustainability and zero carbon emissions. These transformations must lead to systems change, at times disruptive, with a particular focus on mobility, accessibility and land-use issues at the urban level. They should lead to mobility, accessibility and land-use systems that are efficient, ecologically sustainable and socially equitable' (Chong et al., 2023, p. 6).

Understanding cities from a sustainable mobility perspective is relevant for local, national and global debates about sustainable development. Cities in Sub-Saharan Africa are currently at a critical juncture, whereby although income is increasing alongside growing levels of private car use, current motorisation rates are sufficiently low to take action to avoid a car-oriented urban development model and adopt transformative pathways to sustainable mobility and urban land-use. Within this context, expanding empirical knowledge in under-researched mid-sized cities in the region can contribute to informing the process of leapfrogging the transition towards sustainable urban mobility. Such a transition will likely contribute to localised urban development objectives and realise many of the sustainable development goals (SDGs) and other international climate agreements such as the Paris Climate Agreement. SDG 11.2 places transport as an instrumental tool in developing sustainable cities and communities by stating the goal to 'provide access to safe, affordable, accessible and sustainable transport systems for all, [...] with special attention to the needs of those in vulnerable situations, women, children, persons with disabilities and older persons' (UNGA, 2015, p. 21). Against this policy backdrop, understanding the base conditions for urban mobility and land-use in cities, where consolidating public transport is a local priority, resonates with international sustainable development discourses. It is one of the first steps in the definition of policy and practical actions that can help cities like Freetown accelerate their trajectory towards sustainable development.

Figure 6.1 Freetown from the air. Source: © David Hond (https://www.flickr.com/photos/thathondboy/1288909830) [CC BY 2.0 DEED]

Table 6.1 Urban environment area and growth rate (1974–2017). Source: © World Bank (2018b)

Year	Urban surface area (km²)*	Growth rate (%)	Approximate annual expansion rate (%)
1974	59	-	-
1986	73	+24	2
2005	83	+41	0.7
2010	116	+97	7
2017	133	+125	2

*The extent of the area of Freetown's spatial growth has been estimated from satellite image interpretation.

Freetown has a population of just over one million inhabitants. With an area of 82 km², it has a population density of 12,959 inhabitants per km² (SSL, 2016), making the city one of the densest in West Africa (World Bank, 2019). Approximately 15% of Sierra Leone's population now live in Freetown despite the city occupying 0.1% of its total land area (SSL, 2016). This population density is significantly higher than the national average of 98 inhabitants per km² (World Bank, 2019). Freetown has expanded dramatically over the last five decades despite being surrounded by hills and the ocean (Figure 6.1 and Table 6.1).

Freetown's population growth rate is estimated to be 4.2% (SSL, 2016), which will account for 36.2% of Sierra Leone's urban population by 2030 (SSL, 2017a) and translates into 'more than 535,000 residents in the next decade' (World Bank, 2019, p. 11). Demographic estimates from the local government are much higher, with the city's population reaching close to two million by 2028, which is likely to put intense pressure on Freetown's land-use system (MLCPE & FCC, 2014). Forced migrations during the civil war (1991–2002) and internally displaced people seeking economic opportunities in Freetown are major drivers of the city's population growth. These demographic dynamics are compounded by climate-related migrations from rural to urban areas (UN-Habitat, 2011).

Freetown's geography, as well as its trajectory of unstructured growth and dense population, bring significant challenges to sustainable urban development. The city's power grid has limited capacity for the generation of electricity, resulting in reduced and unequal coverage; its fragmented water and sanitation networks, as well as an inadequate provision of healthcare, are below Sub-Saharan African standards for urban areas (Ijjasz-Vasquez & Mukim, 2019). Freetown's numerous informal settlements also face significant challenges related to environmental and climate hazards, compounding some communities' vulnerability to communicable diseases. Despite the many challenges the city faces in terms of rising inequalities and social exclusion emerging from its current urban trajectory, Freetown can also leverage several opportunities to redefine its urban development pattern to improve accessibility and socioeconomic inclusion in a sustainable manner (Jones, 2016; Ortúzar, 2019; Venter et al., 2019; Cavoli, 2021). These opportunities include low-but-gradually-rising levels of private car use (compared with other cities in developing and developed contexts) and a progressive local government committed to national and global sustainable development agendas.

The chapter provides a comprehensive overview of Freetown. It first introduces the city's geography, history, socioeconomic characteristics, governance and spatial growth patterns. The issues related to transport and the implications of Freetown's current land-use dynamics on its sustainable future are subsequently discussed. The COVID-19 pandemic on the city's transport sector is briefly presented, followed by concluding reflections on leapfrogging the transition to sustainable urban mobility.

Background

Geography

Freetown, also known as Western Area Urban, is one of two districts located in the Western Area of Sierra Leone. It is situated between a long mountainous peninsula in the east, about 38 km long and 16 km wide, with peaks rising 700 m above sea level and the Atlantic Ocean in the west, where the sharply descending hills terminate (Figure 6.2). Freetown's location between these two distinct geographic features and the humid climate exposes the city to multiple disaster risks, including flooding and storm surges, which severely restrict the mobility of Freetonians whenever they occur. In August 2017, intense rainfall led to flash floods and a massive mudslide, resulting in the death of at least 1,102 people and the displacement of over 3,000 individuals (Cui et al., 2019). Additionally, it has been estimated that floods and mudslides across Sierra Leone may have led to the loss of over 1,200 individuals, with 67,000 more affected between 2000 and 2020 (EM-DAT, 2021).

Figure 6.2 Freetown, Western Urban Area. Source: © OpenStreetMap contributors, created with DataWrapper

Freetown's historical urban development trajectory

Sierra Leone's rapid urbanisation[1] has outpaced Freetown's ability to provide formal housing, which is in turn compounded by high poverty rates and accelerated expansion of informal settlements (SSL, 2017b; World Bank, 2019). These informal settlements are found close to the city's main roads and more recently, in its peripheral areas, reflecting Freetown's fragmented growth (Figure 6.3).

Land-use planning and growth of informal settlements

Freetown's land-use consists mainly of built-up areas and forests (Figure 6.4). Due to rapid population growth and the expansion of informal settlements, the city has experienced a drastic increase in built-up areas and bare land (Gbanie et al., 2015). Consequently, a marked environmental degradation is observed across the city (Mansaray et

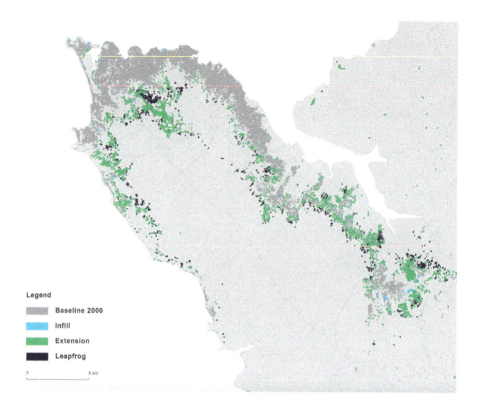

Figure 6.3 Nature of urban expansion (2000-2015). Source: © World Bank (2019)

al., 2016). For instance, the expansion of informal settlements along the coastal areas of Freetown , as well as the use of wood for productive purposes, has resulted in a pronounced decline in wetlands and mangroves (Mansaray et al., 2016).

Freetown's rapid population growth and geography limits its physical expansion[2], especially in the south, causing low-income populations to forcedly settle on marginal lands (MLCPE & FCC, 2014; Allen et al., 2017). Recent estimates indicate that 38% of the city's physical expansion has occurred in medium or high-risk areas (World Bank, 2019). At present, the city has over 68 informal settlements (CODOHSAPA & FEDURP, 2019) and slums (a constituent of informal settlements) constitute 36% of all settlements (World Bank, 2019). These informal settlements have evolved primarily along the western beaches, on the steep hills and in the estuary of the Sierra Leone River, encroaching into the city's southern forests (Figure 6.5) (Allen et al., 2017). Research into informal

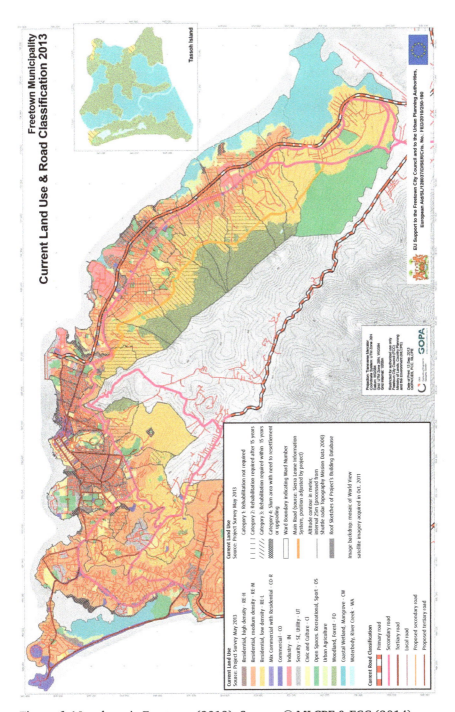

Figure 6.4 Land-use in Freetown (2013). Source: © MLCPE & FCC (2014)

settlements in Freetown has pointed at various disaster risks such as fires, landslides, flooding and the collapsing of buildings as recurrent phenomena that carry significant costs for the environment, public health and wellbeing (World Bank, 2018b). The rapid development of informal neighbourhoods in Freetown puts pressure on the limited availability of essential facilities for health and sanitation, including waste disposal facilities and clean water for consumption, which has direct effects on local mobility and accessibility patterns (Ijjasz-Vasquez & Mukim, 2019; Conteh, Jones et al., 2021).

The uncontrolled urban expansion in Freetown, coupled with the limited supply of affordable housing, has resulted in the city's unequal land-use distribution. Freetown's urban diversity, density and design reflect some of its deeply entrenched socioeconomic inequities. Specifically, informal settlements appear near the CBD (Figure 6.6), while reclaimed land and gated communities are scattered across low-lying areas of the city where transport connectivity is inadequate (World Bank, 2019). This irregular pattern of urban expansion in Freetown has led it to become a city with the worst functional utilisation of land in Sub-Saharan Africa. Estimates suggest that within five km of the city's CBD, 76% of the land area is residential, 4% is commercial/industrial, and 15% remains unbuilt (Antos et al., 2016). This land-use

Figure 6.5 Portee-Rokupa, coastal settlement in eastern Freetown.
Source: © Joseph M. Macarthy (2021)

Figure 6.6 Central Business District. Source: © OpenStreetMap contributors, created with Datawrapper

pattern further suggests an interesting trade-off between accessibility and environmental risks. Nevertheless, the proliferation of informal settlements near the CBD has potentially positive implications for low-income Freetonians in terms of gaining access to employment and essential goods and services.

Environmental and health risks

Due to its geography, Freetown regularly experiences a range of environmental disasters such as flooding, landslides, storm surges, sea level rises and coastal erosion (Figure 6.7). These environmental risks are often compounded by health crises (World Bank, 2018b). The city historically experiences outbreaks of waterborne diseases during and after the onset of a disaster. Informal settlements are particularly under-prepared for these compounded environmental and health risks due to the lack of reliable essential services (Walker et al., 2022). Further, environmental and health risks, including the more minor, everyday risks of shack fires, are progressively, with adverse effects, becoming day-to-day realities for populations living in informal settlements (Walker et al., 2022).

Sierra Leone's response to the COVID-19 pandemic was built upon its experience with the 2014–2016 Ebola Outbreak. When the Ministry of Health and Sanitation reported the city's first COVID-19 case on 31 March 2020, the Emergency Operations Centre was reactivated and a city-wide preparedness plan was already published (Grieco & Yusuf, 2020; IOM, 2020). However, despite these efforts, Mayor Yvonne Aki-Sawyerr noted

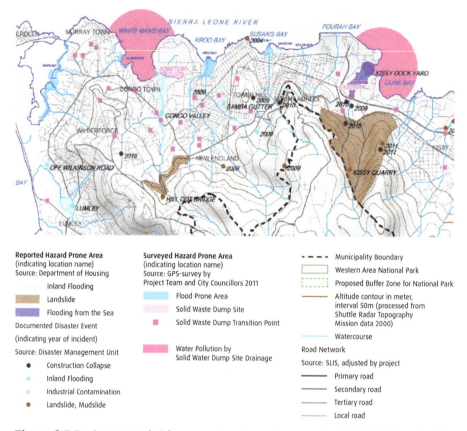

Figure 6.7 Environmental risks across Freetown. Source: © MLCPE & FCC (2014)

in an interview that the lack of widespread access to essential services was a significant challenge, making it nearly impossible to efficaciously contain the disease (WHO, 2020; Frimpong et al. 2021). This highlights that much remains to improve access to healthcare, water, sanitation and electricity in informal settlements within and around Freetown.

Additionally, the rapid population growth combined with the increased frequency and intensity of environmental and health disasters means there is a city-wide urgency for planners to allocate more land for the provision of affordable housing as well as other essential goods and services. However, to holistically address the complex factors underpinning the vulnerability of informal settlements, geographic and funding constraints remain a major planning and policy challenge (Macarthy et al., 2019).

Poverty and inequality

About 34.9% of Western Area Urban district's population is multidimensionally poor (SSL, 2017e). Although this is well below the national average of 68.3% (SSL, 2017e), Freetonians are vulnerable to multiple health risks and inequities. Communicable diseases such as malaria, cholera, tuberculosis and HIV/AIDS remain prevalent and are some of the leading causes of death among marginalised and vulnerable populations within the city (Conteh, Wilkinson & Macarthy 2021). Freetown's population density at 63.9% is the second highest of all districts in Sierra Leone (SSL, 2017e). The rapid population growth, combined with Freetown's space constraints, means that neither public nor private actors have successfully provided affordable housing, urban infrastructure or other essential social goods and services. In fact, according to the latest population census, 12% of dwellings in Freetown are categorised as impoverished homes or informal housing (SSL, 2017d). Further, access to essential services such as education, sanitation and healthcare varies significantly across the city; areas populated by informal settlements have, in general, fewer basic amenities locally (Koroma et al. 2018; Osuteye et al. 2020; Oviedo et al. 2022). These pre-existing inequalities and vulnerabilities are likely to have been exacerbated by the COVID-19 pandemic.

Urban governance

Sierra Leone is a constitutional republic. It has a unicameral legislature and three levels of government: (i) the unitary central government; (ii) local councils; and (iii) chiefdom councils. The constitution, ratified in 1991, made no provision for local government until the approval of the Local Government Act 2004, which now forms the critical legislative framework for the administration of local councils. The act re-established local councils, as they existed before 1972, and it was amended twice in 2016 and 2017 (CLGF, 2019). The sustainability of these decentralisation processes is examined within the broader context of post-conflict reconstruction as well as donor-driven institutional reforms in both scholarly and policy literature (e.g. Fanthorpe et al., 2011; Nickson & Cutting, 2016; Srivastava & Larizza, 2011).

Under Schedule 2 of the Local Government Act, the government of Sierra Leone devolved all remaining functions, including but not limited to the preparation of land-use masterplans, planning and building control[3] and issuance of building permits to local councils in March 2019 (Frediani, 2021). In principle, the devolution of planning functions should place the

Freetown City Council in a more strategic position (and within a more conducive institutional landscape) to tackle some of the aforementioned spatial growth trends and achieve sustainable development. However, Macarthy et al. (2019, pp. 13–14) observe that disparate groups of stakeholders continue to drive action on the ground with little or no coordination (nor the promotion of participatory processes), 'resulting often in chaotic development, diseconomies and negative externalities'.

Besides devolving political and administrative functions, the Local Government Act includes fiscal decentralisation by transferring administrative and development grants from the national government to local and chiefdom councils (CLGF, 2019). Councils are also given powers to raise revenue via taxes, licences, fees and charges, and receive mining revenues, interest and dividends (CLGF, 2019).

A new points-based property tax system was introduced in June 2020 to more accurately reflect the vast disparities in property values across the city, alongside its great wealth and income inequality (Kamara et al., 2020). Using satellite imagery, the reformed system introduced significantly higher tax bills for the city's most valuable properties, which increased tax revenue fivefold and, in turn, financed Freetown City Council's response to the COVID-19 pandemic (Kamara et al., 2020). The number of registered properties across the city doubled to 120,000 a year after introducing the new tax system (Knebelmann, 2022). Additionally, the government of Sierra Leone, with support from UN-Habitat, is drafting a national urban policy, which will likely have a substantial impact in increasing its direct role in shaping Freetown's future development trajectory (UN-Habitat, 2021).

Economy

As Sierra Leone's capital, Freetown has immense political and economic significance. The city contributes 28% to Sierra Leone's gross domestic product (GDP) despite housing only 14.9% of the country's total population (World Bank, 2018b). Before the COVID-19 pandemic, it was estimated that Freetown's annual economic growth rate between 2010 and 2020 would reach 4.2% (UN DESA, 2012). These figures have since been revised. With urban areas being hit significantly hard by the pandemic, the government of Sierra Leone swiftly lowered the country's GDP growth rates from 4.2% to 2.2% (SSL, 2020). GDP growth performed better in 2021, reaching 4.1% before falling to 2.8% in 2022 due to the impact of Russia's invasion of Ukraine and is projected to increase to 3.1% and 4.8% in 2023 and 2024, respectively (AfDB, 2023). At the same time, inflation rose sharply; the consumer price index (CPI) decreased slightly from 13.4% in 2020 to 11.9% in 2021 and increased to 27.2% in 2022 (AfDB, 2023). CPI reached 50.9% in 2023 (WFP, 2023), nearly double the African Development Bank's earlier estimate of 27.1% (AfDB, 2023).

Freetown's economic importance is partly due to it being the largest port city in Sierra Leone. It houses most of the country's formal and informal businesses, which benefit from urban agglomeration effects. Freetown and other urban areas, including Kenema, Bo and Makeni, supply over 70% of waged employment in Sierra Leone (Figure 6.8) (MLCPE & FCC, 2014). About 87% of jobs in the city belong to the tertiary sector (MLCPE & FCC, 2014). Additionally, Freetown's transport sector is currently the second-highest generator of employment, of which 85% are informal (World Bank, 2018a).

Formal employment in Freetown concentrates in the CBD, directly influencing the geographical distribution of street vendors and other small-scale support businesses that depend directly on pedestrian footfall. On the other hand, small-scale fisheries and stone quarries are found at the peripheries of the city and in areas inadequately served by major road corridors and public transport services, creating accessibility[4] issues for certain groups of the population employed in these sectors (Walker et al., 2022). Conversely, this unequal spatial distribution of economic activities has led Freetown to develop largely unidirectional patterns of transport connectivity. Transport services and road infrastructure connect the city's peripheries with its centre, resulting in a self-reinforcing, cyclical need to increase infrastructural capacity to accommodate the growing transport demand to and from the CBD.

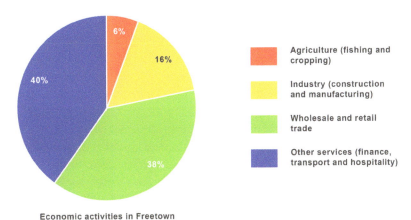

Economic activities in Freetown

Figure 6.8 Economic activities in Freetown. Source: © World Bank (2018a)

Urban transport practices and policy agenda in Freetown

This section focuses on the core issues related to transport demand and supply in Freetown. It seeks to identify relevant gaps in existing data. This section also explores accessibility issues at the mesoscale and discusses policy issues related to the city's current and future urban mobility development pathways.

Transport practices in Freetown have been affected and shaped by a range of issues, rapid urban growth, topography (hilly terrain), environmental issues (floods, storm surges and landslides) and poverty (the rapid expansion of informal settlements). Everyday mobility in Freetown is characterised by the frequent reconfiguration of informal and formal transport services and operations (Oviedo et al., 2021).

The main stakeholders involved in transport and land-use planning in Freetown are listed below (Table 6.2). However, given the wide range of stakeholders operating at different levels and, consequently, different forms of governance frameworks and institutional cultures, the efficacious formulation and implementation of transport and land-use policies remains a significant challenge.

Freetown City Council's vision to 'transform Freetown into a dynamic, efficient and clean city' is reflected in its urban development agenda[5]. At the national level, there is also a solid commitment to building resilient and sustainable transport infrastructure. It has been adopted in political rhetoric and influenced the allocation of financial and technical resources, which includes a US$250,000 investment in traffic signals and building new flyovers at critical intersections in Freetown (GoSL, 2019). Specifically, Cluster 3 of the *Medium-Term National Development Plan 2019–2023* (Infrastructure and Economic Competitiveness) highlights the strategic need to 'plan, develop, and implement infrastructure development in an integrated, holistic and cross-sectoral manner that will increase connection and safety for better utilisation and broader benefit across the country' (GoSL, 2019, p. 101). This complements the Integrated and Resilient Urban Mobility Project (IRUMP), a US$50 million project funded by the World Bank, launched in November 2019, that seeks to reform Freetown's transport sector through the implementation of formalised bus corridors and supporting infrastructure, as well as the administration of traffic management measures and the establishment of a public transport regulatory agency (World Bank, 2021). In addition, a feasibility study was launched in June 2022 (with an estimated completion date of March 2024) to plan a US$40 million mass transit cable car (MTCC) system that would address high levels of congestion along the city's eastern corridor (Thomas, 2023). The MTCC is a flagship transport

Table 6.2 Key transport stakeholders in Freetown. Source: © Adapted from Koroma et al. (2021)

Level of operation	Organisation
International	African Development Bank
	World Bank
	European Union
	United Nations Development Programme
	China International Development Cooperation Agency
	Kuwait Fund
	Islamic Development Bank
National	Ministry of Transport and Aviation
	Ministry of Lands, Housing and Country Planning
	Ministry of Planning and Economic Development
	Ministry of Works and Public Asset
	Sierra Leone Road Safety Authority
	Sierra Leone Roads Authority
	Sierra Leone Ports Authority
	Sierra Leone Road Transport Corporation
	Road Maintenance Fund Administration
	Sierra Leone Traffic Police
	Ministry of Finance
Local	Freetown City Council
Paratransit associations	Motodrivers Union
	Sierra Leone Traders Union
	Tricycle Union
	Bike Riders Association
	Indigenous Transport Owners Association
	Passenger Welfare Association
Academic and research organisations	Sierra Leone Institution of Engineers
	Sierra Leone Urban Research Centre
	Fourah Bay College

investment spearheaded by Mayor Yvonne Aki-Sawyerr. Proponents argue that the city's rugged topography and environmental risks, as well as the costly disruption period associated with the construction of other land-based mass transit systems, among other challenges and constraints, make the MTCC system a cost-effective solution with very little land acquisition and regulatory requirements required (Williams et al., 2020). It is estimated that 200 short-term construction jobs and 70 long-term jobs will be created if the project is realised (Johnson, 2021).

Transport demand and supply

Freetown experiences high levels of congestion due to a combination of factors, including rapid population growth, uncontrolled expansion of private and informal collective transport, poorly maintained roads, weak regulation of street trading and inefficient management of road traffic and parking (Oviedo et al., 2022). Uncontrolled on-street parking is often observed with a disregard for and lack of formal passenger collection points, which compounds the level of congestion observed at the city's primary transport interchanges and terminals. At the same time, pedestrians face a lack of well-designed crossings and traffic signals, as well as damaged or obstructed footpaths (Oviedo et al., 2021).

There is currently only an incomplete overview of the availability and coverage of transport services in Freetown. The limited volume of publicly available datasets on transport modes in operation results in substantial data gaps, making it a challenge for planners and policymakers to understand the actual conditions for basic access in the city (Table 6.3). There is also a lack of travel behaviour data (i.e. openly accessible travel surveys of households and individuals, as well as interception on streets and at public transport terminals and interchanges). While the local and national governments have made significant commitments to producing reliable and up-to-date datasets about demand and supply for public and

Table 6.3 Modal split in Freetown. Source: © SSL (2016)

Rate of motorisation (per 1,000 population)	Modal split
25 (total vehicles – national figure) 7 (private vehicles – national figure)	18% private car/motorcycle 23% poda-poda (minibuses) 22% shared taxis 13% okadas (motorcycle taxis) 12% kekehs (rickshaws) 12% buses

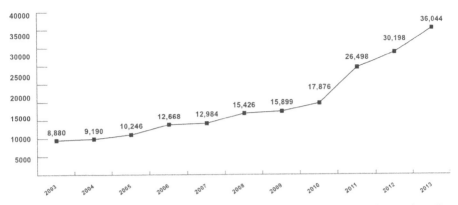

Figure 6.9 Total number of vehicles registered (2003–2013). Source: © SSL (2014)

private transport, such commitments have yet to be fully materialised (GFDRR, 2020). In addition, Sierra Leone has no import restrictions and it is estimated that used vehicles make up at least 95% of the automobiles on the road (Figure 6.9) (Ayetor et al., 2021).

The modal split in Freetown suggests that the city is uniquely positioned to vastly improve the quality of its public transport systems and restrict the future use and growth of private vehicles. Most Freetonians depend on both formal and informal forms of public transport, while private cars account for a comparatively small share of the daily travel demand. This reflects the very low car ownership rate in Sierra Leone, which is at seven vehicles per 1,000 people (IRF, 2021). In comparison, other Sub-Saharan African countries such as Ghana have 30 vehicles per 1,000 people and Senegal has 25 vehicles per 1,000 people (IRF, 2021).

Traffic counts at the busiest intersections in Freetown, which are vital in enabling access to the CBD (i.e. Lumley Roundabout, Congo Cross, Kissy Ferry and Upgun), indicate that private vehicles represent between 14% and 23% of observed traffic during the morning peak hours (Figure 6.10–6.13). Despite the limited pedestrian infrastructure, walking is the most popular mode of travel across all intersections, accounting for 31% to 54% of the observed traffic. On the other hand, cycling is rarely observed, which can, in part, be explained by topography and the lack of separated bike lanes across the city. This is in line with data on the share of passengers per mode, which shows that the proportion of passengers travelling by non-motorised/active travel modes still far exceeds that of passengers travelling by private transport at all intersections (Figure 6.14 and Table 6.4). Despite private vehicles accounting for a comparatively low share of the day-to-day travel demand in Freetown, passenger cars contribute significantly to congestion during peak hours, increasing travel time for all road users.

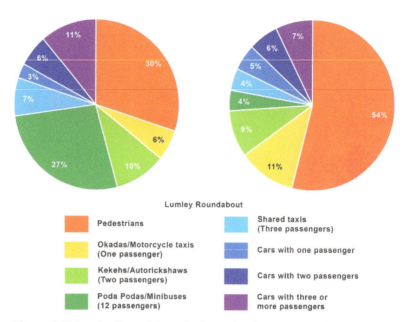

Figure 6.10 Lumley Roundabout (Left: mode of transport; right: passengers using each mode of transport). Source: © Koroma et al. (2021)

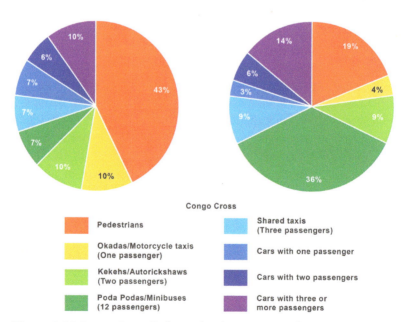

Figure 6.11 Congo Cross (Left: mode of transport; right: passengers using each mode of transport). Source: © Koroma et al. (2021)

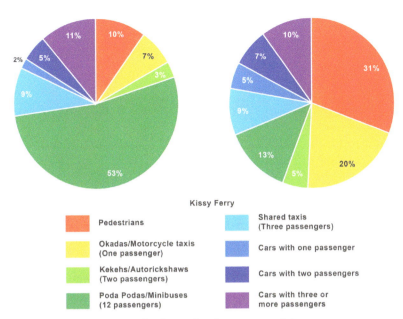

Figure 6.12 Kissy Ferry (Left: mode of transport; right: passengers using each mode of transport). Source: © Koroma et al. (2021)

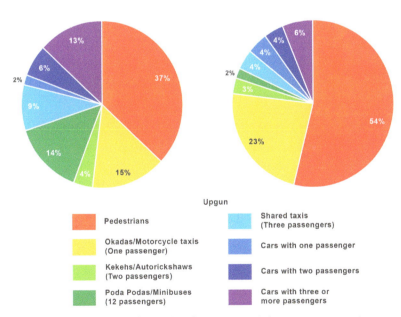

Figure 6.13 Upgun (Left: mode of transport; right: passengers using each mode of transport). Source: © Koroma et al. (2021)

Figure 6.14 Modal split of public versus private transport during evening peak hours based on passenger counts. Source: © Koroma et al. (2021)

The semi-formal sector supplies nearly 85% of the passenger transport services in Freetown (World Bank, 2019), and it primarily consists of unregulated operators running small fleets of buses[6], poda-poda (minibuses), kekehs (autorickshaws), shared taxis and okadas (motorcycle taxis). Whilst the services provided by the semi-formal sector are an essential means of everyday mobility for Freetonians (Figure 6.16), they contribute significantly to congestion due to their low capacity and irregular stops. The publicly owned Sierra Leone Road Transport Corporation (SLRTC) operates transport services on a scheduled timetable to serve various communities. SLRTC also provide on-demand services such as shared taxis and jeeps in the city. However, due to the limited institutional and technical capacity for planning public transport services that would meet existing demand, substantial gaps within the market remain best supplied by the semi-formal sector in the short term. The Ministry of Transport and Aviation is currently responsible for setting fare levels for SLRTC services as well as those provided by the semi-formal sector within Freetown and neighbouring provinces, typically in response to the adjustments in retail fuel pump prices set by the Sierra Leone Petroleum Regulatory Agency (see Table 6.5). Still, compliance among semi-formal drivers and operators remained an issue when the fares were reduced (Bah, 2022).

The modal share of kekehs (autorickshaws) has remained steady. In contrast, the modal share of buses (i.e. the city's conventional mode

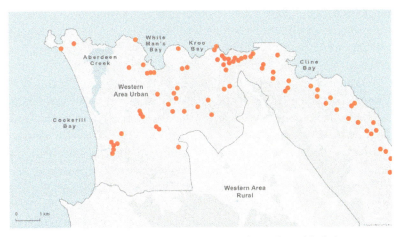

Figure 6.15 Distribution of okada (motorcycle taxi) and kekeh (autorickshaw) stops. Source: Authors using map data © OpenStreetMap contributors, created with Datawrapper

of public transport) has decreased significantly in recent years (Oviedo et al., 2022). At the same time, there has been an exponential growth of okadas (motorcycle taxis), which can be attributed to the low upfront cost and their ability to easily navigate congested roads, offering passengers concrete time-savings (Oviedo et al., 2022). Freetown's semi-formal transport operators form associations or unions to represent their specific interests (e.g. Bike Riders Association, Tricycle and Motodrivers Unions). These associations also establish branches by dividing up the network and enabling individual operators to perform their transport services role, typically based at a station (i.e. off-street parking) or a stage (i.e.

Table 6.4 Population and their access to okada (motorcycle taxi) and kekeh (autorickshaw) stops. Source: © Authors

Distance to transport stops (km)	Total population	Population with access to transport stop (%)
0.5	541,113	48
1.0	873,607	77
1.5	1,010,928	89
2.0	1,068,462	94
2.5	1,101,723	97
3.0	1,132,043	100

on-street parking). Each route operates from or between these points on the principle of fill-in-turn before departure (Figure 6.16), and branch officials are responsible for raising a departure levy and managing the process.

The highly inaccessible areas across Freetown are illustrated in Figure 6.17, where areas dotted in red are drawn by plotting a 500 m radius around poda-poda (minibus), shared taxi, and SLRTC stops. Low- and middle-income households without access to private vehicles depend on okadas (motorcycle taxis) and kekehs (autorickshaws) as their only motorised transport option to access employment and essential goods and services. For households that cannot afford motorised transport, walking long distances or staying within the vicinity of their neighbourhood remain the only viable livelihood options. The research team estimates that, for a household living on minimum wage, the ratio of average cost per okada trip to income is 18%, which is substantially higher when compared to motorised modes with fixed routes such as the poda-poda and shared taxis where the ratio is 12%.

Figure 6.16 Okadas (motorcycle taxis) waiting for passengers at a main road junction. Source: © Joseph M. Macarthy (2021)

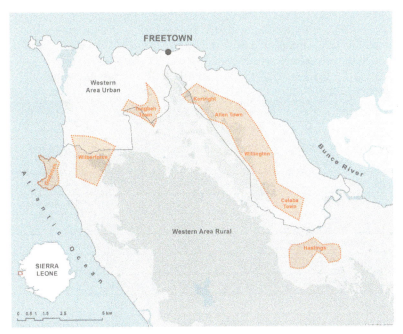

Figure 6.17 Inaccessible areas by fixed route modes. Source: Authors using map data © OpenStreetMap contributors, created with Datawrapper

Fuel price changes

Sierra Leone relies heavily on aid and loans from the International Monetary Fund, which come with strict structural adjustment conditionality, including the removal of subsidies on fossil fuel. Fossil fuel subsidies were removed in late 2019, resulting in an increase in petrol, diesel, kerosene and fuel oil prices (Table 6.5). The continual adjustments in retail pump prices since the beginning of the COVID-19 pandemic can be attributed to currency depreciation[7], a sluggish economic growth outlook and other structural factors prevalent in the international energy market.

Providing a fair distribution of space

Space is fundamentally bound up with social reality. Ever-growing literature has given rise to theories such as the right to the city (Harvey, 2008; Marcuse, 2009; Attoh, 2011; Brenner et al., 2011; Harvey, 2012; Purcell, 2013), spatial justice (Soja, 2010) and the just city (Fainstein, 2010), reflecting persistent questioning about how the use of urban space

Table 6.5 Adjustments in maximum retail fuel pump price, 2018–2023 (SLe) (US$1 = 10,000 SLe approx.). The frequency of adjustments in retail fuel prices intensified since the start of the COVID-19 pandemic. Retail fuel prices have remained at 30,000 SLe/litre at the time of writing, 12 January 2024. Source: Sierra Leone Petroleum Regulatory Agency (2024)

Dates of adjustment in maximum retail pump price	Petrol (SLe/ litre)	Diesel (SLe/ litre)	Kerosene (SLe/ litre)	Fuel Oil (SLe/ litre)
13 July 2018	8,000	8,000	8,000	7,000
7 January 2019	7,000	7,500	7,600	6,500
1 July 2019	8,500	8,500	8,500	7,500
4 November 2019	8,500	8,500	8,500	7,500
17 January 2020	9,000	9,000	9,000	9,000
6 March 2020	8,500	8,500	8,500	8,500
2 April 2020	7,000	7,000	7,000	7,000
1 September 2020	7,000	7,000	7,000	7,000
1 October 2020	7,000	7,000	7,000	7,000
1 December 2020	7,000	7,000	7,000	7,000
4 January 2021	7,000	7,000	7,000	7,000
4 February 2021	8,500	8,500	8,500	8,500
1 March 2021	8,500	8,500	8,500	8,500
1 April 2021	8,500	8,500	8,500	8,500
7 June 2021	8,500	8,500	8,500	8,500
1 July 2021	9,500	9,500	9,500	9,500
2 August 2021	10,000	10,000	10,000	10,000
10 August 2021	10,000	10,000	10,000	10,000
1 September 2021	10,000	10,000	10,000	10,000
4 January 2022	10,000	10,000	10,000	10,000
1 March 2022	12,000	12,000	12,000	12,000
16 March 2022	15,000	15,000	15,000	15,000
9 June 2022	18,000	18,000	18,000	18,000
30 June 2022	22,000	22,000	22,000	22,000
18 July 2022	20,000	20,000	20,000	20,000
29 July 2022	19,000	19,000	19,000	19,000

11 August 2022	18,000	18,000	18,000	18,000
25 August 2022	18,000	18,000	18,000	18,000
22 September 2022	18,000	18,000	18,000	18,000
6 October 2022	18,000	18,000	18,000	18,000
19 October 2022	20,000	20,000	20,000	20,000
16 November 2022	21,000	21,000	21,000	20,000
4 January 2023	19,500	19,500	19,500	19,500
2 February 2023	21,500	21,500	21,500	21,500
1 August 2023	25,000	25,000	25,000	25,000
29 August 2023	30,000	30,000	30,000	30,000

replicates existing socioeconomic inequalities and how it can be made more equitable. Understanding the everyday use of urban street space in Freetown is central to unpacking the competing rationalities between how space is thought about by built environment practitioners defining its physical configuration and the lived experiences of Freetonians negotiating it (Massingue & Oviedo, 2021). Structural asymmetries in the distribution of urban street space can signal how specific groups of the population may be reaping most benefits from public infrastructure investment while others endure a disproportionate share of their costs and externalities, leading to spatio-temporal disparities in access to opportunities (Levy, 2016; Jian et al., 2020; Guzman et al., 2021).

Despite active travel modes tending to be the primary alternative for urban mobility in rapidly developing cities, automobility infrastructure remains a central driver of transport planning (Uteng & Lucas, 2017). This means that not only is the distribution of urban street space between pedestrians, automobiles, street vendors and other competing use(r)s deeply contested, but the mainstream transport planning paradigm aggravates negative externalities associated with motorised transport (Santos et al., 2010) and makes interventions that democratise the use of street space complex (Vasconcellos, 2001; Dimitriou & Gakenheimer, 2012). The emerging debates on transport justice and mobility justice[8] reflect a broader academic inquiry about 'just transition(s)' in sustainable mobility. This chapter's working definition of transport justice builds upon Gössling's (2016) concept of transport injustice, where the distribution of space of the three key dimensions[9] determines the fair distribution of accessibility in urban areas.

The current allocation of street space in Freetown reflects various inequalities and inequities for road users. Pedestrians are faced with damaged or non-existing footpaths, as well as walkways blocked by street traders (Figure 6.18), used as on-street parking (Figure 6.19) and passenger collection points for minibuses, shared taxis and other modes of paratransit, especially where formal passenger collection points are either not clearly defined or rarely observed owing to poor enforcement (Oviedo et al., 2021). Although there are wider sidewalks in the city, they are often only found on one side of the main roads, leaving pedestrians amongst the most exposed and vulnerable group of road users despite walking being the most prevalent transport mode in Freetown (Oviedo et al., 2021). In contrast to other cities in sub-Saharan Africa, such as Accra, Kigali and Addis Ababa, Freetown has no segregated cycling infrastructure, contributing to the very low adoption of bicycles as a day-to-day transport mode. Additionally, Freetonians with disabilities have limited mobility, both on- and off-street.

A recent estimate suggests that 5% of the total land area in Freetown is allocated to roads (Figure 6.20), of which only 24% are paved compared with regional benchmarks of 10% and 50%, respectively (Tripodi et al., 2018; World Bank, 2019). In the Western Area Urban (Figure 6.20), road density per capita of 165 m per 1,000 people is about half the average (318 m per 1,000 people) of low-income African countries (World Bank, 2019). A pilot analysis of the distribution of street space for an area of 4.2 km² in a mixed land-use zone close to the main areas of economic activity in north-western Freetown illustrates the biases in existing planning

Figure 6.18 Street trading. Source: © Joseph M. Macarthy (2021)

Figure 6.19 Street parking in the CBD. Source: © Joseph M. Macarthy (2021)

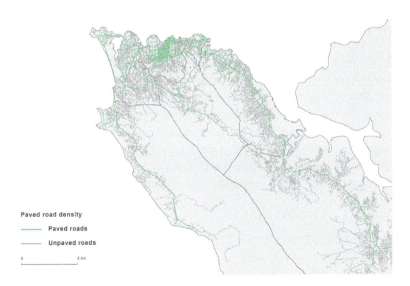

Paved road density
— Paved roads
----- Unpaved roads

0   6 km

Figure 6.20 Paved road density. Source: © World Bank (2019)

Public space distribution

———— Road network   ———— Mixed use   ———— No pavement   ███ Parking areas

Figure 6.21 Mapping public space distribution in Freetown (left: pilot study zone; right: map detail). Source: Authors using map data © OpenStreetMap contributors, created with DataWrapper

practices towards different infrastructure and public spaces for mobility (Figure 6.21). Unpaved access roads make up 14% of the study area, and the competing use(r)s of these spaces force pedestrians to the edges of the roads next to large drainage canals and as a result, they are exposed to dust and dirt during the dry season and to flooding during the rainy season. Furthermore, large tracts of space around the stadium (see detail in Figure 6.21) are devoted solely to parking, adding further to the traffic volumes and road safety issues in adjacent traffic corridors.

The poor quality of Freetown's road network and pedestrian infrastructures, inefficient traffic management and expansion of private and informal collective transport hinder accessibility within the city, contributing significantly to higher levels of road congestion (Cavoli et al., 2021). The city requires increasing infrastructure development dedicated to public and collective transport (since many Freetonians rely on motorised transport), as well as strategic investments and planning provisions for active travel modes. Yet, Freetown's historical and current development challenges stymie efforts to provide a fair allocation of street space.

Road fatalities and injuries

The rate of road accidents in Sierra Leone is one of the highest in the world. The country's average fatality rate is 27.3 per 100,000, which is far higher than that recorded throughout Africa (26.6) and Europe (9.3) (WHO, 2015). The loss of 1,661 persons for every 100,000 motor vehicles

Table 6.6 Estimated road traffic death rate across Sub-Saharan Africa per 100,000 population (2000–2019). Source: © WHO, Global Health Data Observatory (2021a)

	Sierra Leone	South Africa	Côte d'Ivoire	Senegal	Nigeria	Ghana	Ethiopia	Kenya
2000	31.2	44	25.4	24.8	29.2	25.8	24.6	26.4
2001	32.3	38.3	25.3	24.6	29.6	25.8	24.5	26.5
2002	31.3	39.9	25.4	24.7	29.8	25.9	24.7	26.5
2003	31.3	43.4	25.9	25.2	28.6	25.6	25.1	26.2
2004	31.2	41.3	26.5	24.9	27.6	25.4	24.8	25.9
2005	31.5	38.1	26.3	24.8	27	25.5	24.5	26.3
2006	31.2	41.1	25.8	25.3	26.4	24.6	23.9	25.8
2007	30.7	32.4	25.4	25.5	25.9	24	23.5	25.8
2008	30.5	29.5	25.4	25.4	25.1	23.9	23.4	25.9
2009	30.5	28.6	25.5	25.5	25.3	23.9	23.5	26.1
2010	30	28.6	25.8	25.8	25.1	23.7	23.3	25.7
2011	30	27.8	25.8	25.7	22.5	23.4	26	25.7
2012	29.3	26.5	24	24.7	22.1	23.3	26.2	26.6
2013	28.4	22.8	23.5	24.6	22.0	23.4	25.8	26.4
2014	28.7	24	23	24.1	21.9	24	25.8	26.6
2015	30.4	24.1	23.2	24.1	21.4	24.4	26	27.3
2016	30.5	25.8	23.4	24.1	21.4	24.6	26.4	27.4
2017	31.3	23.2	23.6	23.8	21.1	24.9	27	27.7
2018	32.2	22.7	23.9	23.7	20.9	25.3	27.6	28
2019	33	22.2	24.1	23.5	20.7	25.7	28.2	28.3

puts Sierra Leone's motor transport system thirteenth in terms of fatality risks in Africa (Table 6.6) (WHO, 2015), with road accidents accounting for 1.3% of its GDP loss. Yet, despite several actions by the government, including enforcing relevant regulations and public education on a range of road safety issues (e.g. speeding and non-compliance with seatbelt laws) the pace of change remains slow. Given the current growth rate of vehicle registration, these figures are expected to worsen.

It is somewhat difficult to accurately appraise the road safety situation in Sierra Leone due to poor road traffic crash data collection and management (Tripodi et al., 2018). Available figures show that approximately 70% of traffic collisions occur in Freetown and its surrounding towns compared to elsewhere in the country (Tripodi et al. 2018). The same areas also account for almost half of the fatalities and severe injury crashes in total (Tripodi et al., 2018). Available data from both the Sierra Leone Police and the Road Safety Authority attribute road traffic crashes to a range of causes. These include disregard for traffic signs, the reluctance to abide by traffic regulations and laws, poor road structure and networks and limited attention to ensuring drivers have the proper training and skills. Alarmingly, road traffic deaths tend to be under-reported, with the World Health Organization estimating actual fatalities to be nearly seven times higher (World Bank, 2019).

Impact of urban traffic on air quality and GHG emissions

Freetown is experiencing increasing levels of air and noise pollution associated with motorised road traffic, which has significant negative implications for health and wellbeing (Harrison et al., 2021). In response, local authorities have adopted traffic-reduction policies and actions such as parking, circulation control at high-demand areas and times, vehicle restriction policies associated with size, age and fuel technologies and banning old and polluting vehicles. These policies are conceived to work in tandem with recent actions geared towards improving public transport. Taylor et al. (2017) examined levels of traffic-related emissions of nitrogen dioxide (NO_2), sulphur dioxide (SO_2) and carbon monoxide (CO) at Kissy Road and Wilkinson Road, two key corridors of Freetown. The results are worrying as they show there is a higher risk of severe respiratory tract and cardiovascular diseases and infections among people, especially those already suffering from diseases such as asthma. Other vulnerable populations include children and older adults.

Recent data released by the local government as part of the C40 Cities Climate Leadership Group initiative on Freetown's greenhouse gas

Table 6.7 Emissions per capita in Freetown. Source: © C40 (2021)

Category	tCO2e (tonnes of carbon dioxide equivalent)
Stationary	0.4
Transport	0.3
Waste	0.3

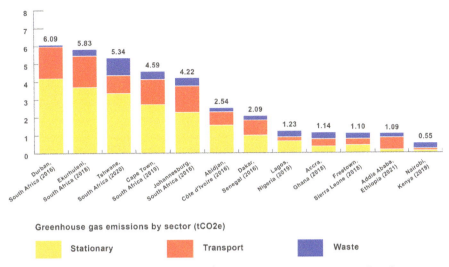

Figure 6.22 Greenhouse gas emissions per capita by sector across Sub-Saharan African cities. Source: © C40 (2024)

emissions (GHG) suggest the city is still at a considerably lower stage of carbon emissions than other African cities (Table 6.22). This data complies with the Global Protocol for Community Scale GHG Emission Inventories (GPC), recognised as an international best practice for emission inventories. However, a greater disaggregation of data within each category is necessary for informing future policy actions. Figure 6.22 illustrates that, in absolute terms, transport-related emissions in Freetown remain proportionally very low. Nonetheless, the prominence of this category as the second-highest source of emissions in wealthier cities serves as a reminder of the low-but-rising levels of motorisation in the region, which, unless addressed, is likely to worsen at a similar or faster rate in Freetown.

Data gaps

New datasets for ongoing and planned urban and transport projects in Freetown are collected as part of the planning, evaluation and monitoring process. However, these datasets respond mainly to project-specific requirements and are not always publicly accessible, even upon request. Thus, identifying and addressing critical data gaps and strengthening strategic partnerships for knowledge sharing are necessary to improve the current understanding of Freetown's transport and land-use dynamics. These dynamics play a crucial role in defining the city's future urban trajectory and are vital in enabling its sustainable urban mobility transition.

First, more publicly accessible data is required to understand the structural drivers of the city's current transport and land-use planning practices. Drawing on the results of the 2015 National Housing and Population Census, some of which are not publicly available, the latest nationwide demographic data has yet to be disaggregated by gender, age, disability and ethnic identity. This hinders the study of how various social groups use transport in the city and their broader experiences of urban mobility. There is a need to develop purpose-built socio-demographic and travel behaviour datasets that would inform both research and practice, as well as steer policy actions to address the complex travel needs and preferences of different social groups in Freetown.

There is a pressing need to document the nature and main operational attributes of existing transport services in Freetown and the information on semi-formal and informal transport. This includes a spatial description of the network (e.g. route itineraries and stopping points) information about the services (e.g. departure headway, operating hours and fares) and the performance of the system (e.g. passenger volumes, vehicle occupancy, injuries and fatalities and number of rotations per day). Equally important is consolidating knowledge of the industry structure and characteristics, including the role and organisation of unions at different geographic scales, dominant business models, relations between owners and drivers and labour conditions. Additionally, research on the experience, level of satisfaction and main challenges passengers encounter is critical to obtain a complete picture of the sector.

Second, there is sparse information about the land-use distribution in Freetown. This is further worsened by the scant understanding of complex land market dynamics and the practices of informal landholders and developers, contributing to the rapid growth of informal settlements in specific parts of the city. Satellite imagery collected by Freetown City Council as part of the reformed property tax system, alongside the creation of a land cadastre, not only informs future planning decisions but can also be used in determining land-use, land value and land tenure to understand their links to transport infrastructure and services. Furthermore, making information about the areas of planned expansion in Freetown openly available and accessible will give researchers, planners and policymakers greater insights into the spatial-temporal distribution of economic, social and cultural activities and where and how the city's urban trajectory might shift.

Third, aggregated figures on the number of road traffic incidents in Freetown, a key externality of urban transport, provide little overview of their evolution over time and space in both scale and severity. There is also limited available data on traffic infractions associated with road safety, such as drunk driving and speeding. More data on the distribution of victims of road traffic incidents will enable decision-makers to identify and introduce programmes targeting vulnerable road users and hotspots across the city. It would also inform planning and enforcement decisions, such as lowering speed limits, improving road crossings and maintenance of traffic signalling and creating pedestrian-friendly street design.

Impacts of the COVID-19 pandemic

President Julius Maada Bio suspended all international flights on 22 March 2020 and declared Sierra Leone entering a 12-month state of public emergency on 24 March 2020 (Grieco & Yusuf, 2020). While an extended lockdown was not imposed, owing to concerns over its potential impact on economic activity and the everyday lives of citizens, two three-day nationwide lockdowns were imposed in April and May 2020 and a curfew from 9 p.m. to 6 a.m. was put in place (Grieco & Yusuf, 2020). Vaccination programmes in Sierra Leone began in March 2021 (WHO, 2021b).

Despite this, like many places worldwide, the COVID-19 pandemic was more disruptive in urban areas of Sierra Leone, with the Western Area Urban district (i.e. Freetown and surrounding towns and provinces) being the epicentre (WHO, 2020). It is estimated that 82% of households in the country experienced an income drop (Egger et al., 2021). Freetonians employed in the city's informal economy were severely affected by the curfew and the restrictions on inter-district movement (Koroma et al., 2021). Freetown's population density (12,959 inhabitants per km^2), with 35% living in severely overcrowded informal settlements, made social distancing, one of the city's main COVID-19 preventative measures, incredibly challenging to implement under limited enforcement capacities (Koroma et al., 2021).

Collective transport was seen as a critical transmission vector, leading to sector-specific pandemic restrictions. The maximum number of passengers allowed for shared taxis was reduced from four to three (one in front and two at the back), while those of poda-poda (minibuses) were reduced from four to two per seat (plus one in front) (Koroma et al., 2020). The cap on maximum vehicle occupancy and restricted operating hours (to abide by the curfew) resulted in a significant loss of revenue. It also meant that operators and drivers could not accommodate persons with disabilities, especially those who require a wheelchair space (Koroma et al., 2020). Congestion and wait times for all transport services increased with the morning and evening rush hours starting earlier and extending for longer periods (Koroma et al., 2020). In addition, transport operators and drivers had to wear a facemask and carry hand sanitiser (Vincent & Peters, 2021). Some okada (motorcycle taxi) and kekeh (autorickshaw) operators responded to the pandemic preventive measures by installing hand-washing equipment in the parking lots allocated to them (Vincent & Peters, 2021).

Conclusion

This chapter unpacks urban transport and land-use development patterns in Freetown based on available evidence from a sustainable urban mobility transition perspective. We sought to illustrate the different practices and underlying drivers of recent trends in the city's urban mobility and the configuration of its urban transport system. We highlighted the areas where structural challenges can prevent the adoption of sustainable mobility practices and those areas where opportunities for leapfrogging towards clean and inclusive mobility may arise. There are five concluding reflections to be drawn from the information presented.

First, land-use distribution in Freetown is highly unequal, leading to a spatial, social and functional urban configuration that excludes a large share of the population from access to essential opportunities for social and economic development. This is compounded by the city's pivotal role in the country, which has motivated large rural-urban migrations to Freetown throughout the last 50 years. Demand for housing, opportunities and basic infrastructure has outpaced the ability of both the public and private formal sectors to supply such requirements. This limits accessibility for a large segment of the population and leads to marked centre-periphery travel and access patterns. The fragmented functional structure that the city boasts today enables easy access for a small group of wealthy, motorised elite. At the same time, most Freetonians remain bound to accessing only those opportunities available at short distances or become outright immobile.

Second, macro-level inequalities resulting from Freetown's rapid expansion and its inherent socio-spatial segregation have locked the city in a self-reinforcing cycle of spatial concentration of social, economic and cultural opportunities, along with political power and governance, which are almost invariably located in the CBD. The various degrees of inequalities across social groups at the city level also manifest at the street level regarding the distribution of road space in Freetown, leading to transport injustices. The investment in and distribution of public space investments and road infrastructure have prioritised car users while overlooking spaces for pedestrians and cyclists. The provision of spaces for cars, coupled with social and cultural conventions that allow car users to appropriate public space for parking with no penalty or enforcement, has marked a divide between those who have (a car) and those who have-not, exposing the latter to traffic-related risks such as air and noise pollution, injury and death.

Third, Freetown's public transport landscape suggests that the current public transport supply configuration – dominated by unrouted, low-capacity paratransit services – is inducing negative consequences that range from operational inefficiencies to social externalities and risks for the environment and health, such as declining air quality and higher rates of traffic fatalities and injuries. Mitigating such consequences requires purposeful and incremental actions from the public sector that range from better planning and data for decision-making to the development of new financial and legal instruments that can be leveraged to improve public transport coverage, quality and affordability, as well as its capacity to integrate with other forms of transport. Developing and implementing a short-to-medium-term strategy for developing high-capacity public transport with clearly defined governance and financial and operational parameters is, therefore, imperative.

Paratransit has apparent positive effects of improving coverage and accessibility of motorised collective transport, particularly in peripheral areas underserved by infrastructure and routed public transport. However, informal business practices and unregulated operational arrangements increase the costs of okadas (motorcycle taxis), shared taxis and kekehs (autorickshaws) for a considerable share of the population, making them unaffordable and unreliable, and pushing those in more vulnerable conditions to depend on walking for their daily mobility or, otherwise, become partially or entirely immobile. Recognising the role paratransit plays in Freetown's urban mobility system while working towards reducing their negative consequences is a priority in the transition of Freetown to a more sustainable and inclusive mobility. This means working towards integration and regulation, involving paratransit operators in dialogues and decisions about urban public transport in the city and jointly exploring ways forward.

Fourth, Freetown and many other cities at a similar stage of adoption of private must fight against the inertia in the distribution of space that has led to some of the patterns shown in Figure 6.21. Public space for walking has been heavily encroached on by private car users who appropriate it for parking. This is compounded by the rapid growth of street trading in high-traffic areas, resulting in a self-reinforcing cycle of rising congestion, pollution and deterioration of public space. The encroachment of road space is reinforced by social and cultural beliefs that place car users higher in the hierarchy of road users, with all the associated harmful consequences, including growing loss of life linked with road traffic incidents. The lack of safe space for walking and active travel disproportionately affects pedestrians and other vulnerable road users.

Finally, it is necessary to generate reliable data that can be openly shared and distributed to capitalise on some of the findings covered throughout this chapter and implement progressive actions for a sustainable transition. Developing systematic efforts for data collection underpinned by cross-sectoral partnerships is critical. The production of open access data and capacity building inside and outside of the public sector also has the potential to strengthen mobility, accessibility, and land-use research and practice. Furthermore, open information has a positive effect on levels of transparency and local production of knowledge and innovations for inclusive and sustainable transport. Setting up reliable mechanisms for data management and reproducible methods for periodic data collection will help to monitor rapidly changing urban trajectories across different parts of Freetown. Improving the capacities for planning, monitoring and evaluation will contribute to better decision-making for urban transport, enabling Freetown to accelerate its pathway towards more inclusive and sustainable mobility and urban development.

Notes

1 Urbanisation refers to 'the process by which an increasing percentage of the population comes to live in urban areas, defined as a locality of 2,000 or more people' (SSL, 2017c, p. 24).
2 The city's physical expansion has been described as leapfrog development for the 'construction on unbuilt plots not bordering existing development' (World Bank, 2019, p. 13).
3 See Lynch et al. (2020) for a historical overview of planning and Rigon et al. (2020) for the hybridity of (in)formality in Freetown.
4 Accessibility refers to 'the ease of reaching desired destinations given a number of available opportunities and intrinsic impedance to the resources used to travel from the origin to the destination' (Bocarejo & Oviedo, 2012, p. 143).
5 For further information see: https://fcc.gov.sl/transform-freetown/transform-freetown-clusters/.
6 The city had 66 buses as of 2019 (World Bank, 2019).
7 The Sierra Leonean Leone (SLe) depreciated from approximately USD$1 = SLe8,850 in July 2018 to USD$1 = SLe22,900 in January 2024. In particular, between September 2022 and September 2023, the Sierra Leonean Leone depreciated against the United States Dollar by nearly 60%, marking one of the steepest declines in a country's domestic currency against foreign currencies in West Africa.
8 See Verlinghieri and Schwanen, 2020.
9 The other dimensions of transport injustice are exposure and time.

References

AfDB. (2023). *Sierra Leone economic outlook*. African Development Bank. Accessed 25 June 2024. https://www.afdb.org/en/countries-west-africa-sierra-leone/sierra-leone-economic-outlook

Allen, A., Koroma, B., Osuteye, E., & Rigon, A. (2017, April). Urban risk in Freetown's informal settlements: making the invisible visible. *Urban Africa Risk Knowledge*, briefing no. 6. London: International Institute for Environment and Development. Accessed 25 June 2024. https://www.slurc.org/uploads/1/0/9/7/109761391/urbanark_briefing_6_web_1_.pdf

Antos, S. E., Lall, S. V., & Lozano-Gracia, N. (2016). *The morphology of African cities*. Policy Research Working Paper, No. 7911. Washington, DC: World Bank Group. Accessed 25 June 2024. http://hdl.handle.net/10986/25810

Attoh, K. A. (2011). What kind of right is the right to the city? *Progress in Human Geography*, *35*(5), 669–685.

Ayetor, G. K., Mbonigaba, I., Sackey, M. N., & Andoh, P. Y. (2021). Vehicle regulations in Africa: impact on used vehicle import and new vehicle sales. *Transportation Research Interdisciplinary Perspectives*, 10, 100384. https://doi.org/10.1016/J.TRIP.2021.100384

Bah, M. J. (2022, August 16). *Drivers reluctant to adhere to new transportation fares*. Freetown: Sierraloaded. Accessed 25 June 2024. https://sierraloaded.sl/news/drivers-adhere-transportation-fares/

Bocarejo S. J. P., & Oviedo H, D. R. (2012). Transport accessibility and social inequities: A tool for identification of mobility needs and evaluation of transport investments. *Journal of Transport Geography*, *24*, 142-154.

Brenner, N., Marcuse, P., & Mayer, M. (Eds). (2011). *Cities for People, Not for Profit: Critical Urban Theory and the Right to the City*. Abingdon & New York: Routledge.

C40. (2021, November). *Greenhouse gas emissions interactive dashboard*. C40 Knowledge Hub. Accessed 25 June 2024. https://www.c40knowledgehub.org/s/article/C40-cities-greenhouse-gas-emissions-interactive-dashboard?language=en_US

C40. (2024). *A Clean and Inclusive Energy Future for African C40 Member Cities*. London: C40. Accessed 9 August 2024. https://sustainable.org.za/wp-content/uploads/2023/11/C40-cities-report-FINAL-digital.pdf

Cavoli, C. (2021). Accelerating sustainable mobility and land-use transitions in rapidly growing cities: Identifying common patterns and enabling factors. *Journal of Transport Geography*, 94, 103093.

Cavoli, C., Yusuf, Y., Oviedo, D., Mella Lira, B., Koroma, B., & Jones, P. (2021). *Transitions to Sustainable Urban Mobility: Participatory policy planning*. London: T-SUM, UCL.

Chong, A., Saha, S., Cavoli, C., Oviedo, D., & Yusuf, Y. (2023). *T-SUM Lexicon*. Accessed 25 June 2024. https://www.t-sum.org/_files/ugd/b4aba8_f9b8641235d040b79e247fb7a74d4828.pdf

CLGF. (2019). *Country Profile: The local government system in Sierra Leone*. London: Commonwealth Local Government Forum.

CODOHSAPA, & FEDURP. (2019). *Community Profiling Enumeration Report 2019*. Freetown: Centre of Dialogue on Human Settlement and Poverty Alleviation.

Conteh, Y. O., Jones, D. B., Turay, I., Sesay, I. J., Priddy, C., & Conteh, A. (2021, December 16). *Inclusive sanitation: Empowering marginalised urban Freetown residents*. Institute of Development Studies. Accessed 25 June 2024. https://www.ids.ac.uk/opinions/inclusive-sanitation-empowering-marginalised-urban-freetown-residents/

Conteh, A., Wilkinson, A., & Macarthy, J. M. (2021). Exploring gender, health, and intersectionality in informal settlements in Freetown. *Gender and Development*, *29*(1), 111–129.

Cui, Y., Cheng, D., Choi, C. E., Jin, W., Lei, Y., & Kargel, J. S. (2019). The cost of rapid and haphazard urbanization: Lessons learned from the Freetown landslide disaster. *Landslides*, *16*, 1167–1176.

Dimitriou, H. T., & Gakenheimer, R. (Eds). (2012). *Urban Transport in the Developing World: A handbook of policy and practice*. Edward Elgar.

Egger, D., Miguel, E., Warren, S. S., Shenoy, A., Collins, E., Karlan, D., Parkerson, D., Mobarak, A. M., Fink, G., Udry, C., Walker, M., ... & Vernot, C. (2021). Falling living standards during the COVID-19 crisis: Quantitative evidence from nine developing countries. *Science Advances*, *7*(6), eabe0997.

EM-DAT. (2021). *Mapping Tool*. Centre for Research on the Epidemiology of Disasters. Accessed 15 July 2024. https://public.emdat.be/

Fainstein, S. S. (2010). *The Just City*. Ithaca, NY: Cornell University Press.

Fanthorpe, R., Lavali, A., & Sesay, M. G. (2011). *Decentralization in Sierra Leone: Impact, constraints and prospects*. London: Fanthorpe Consultancy Limited for Department for International Development.

Frediani, A. A. (2021). *Freetown: City scoping study*. Manchester: African Cities Research Consortium.

Frimpong, L. K., Okyere, S. A., Diko, S. K., Abunyewah, M., Erdiaw-Kwasie, M. O., Commodore, T. S., Oviedo Hernandez, D., & Kita, M. (2021). Actor-network analysis of community-based organisations in health pandemics: Evidence from Covid-19 response in Freetown, Sierra Leone. *Disasters*. https://doi.org/10.1111/disa.12508

Gbanie, S. P., Thornton, A., & Griffin, A. (2015). 'The diamond of Western Area is land': Narratives of land use and land cover change in post-conflict Sierra Leone. *The Australasian Review of African Studies*, 36(2), 51–73.

GFDRR. (2020, January). Results in Resilience: Making transportation climate resilient in Freetown. Global Facility for Disaster Reduction and Recovery. Accessed 25 June 2024. https://www.gfdrr.org/en/feature-story/results-resilience-making-transportation-climate-resilient-freetown

GoSL. (2019). *Sierra Leone's Medium-Term National Development Plan 2019–2023: A new direction for improving people's lives through education, inclusive growth, and building a resilient economy*. Freetown: Government of Sierra Leone.

Gössling, S. (2016). Urban transport justice. *Journal of Transport Geography*, *54*, 1–9.

Grieco, K., & Yusuf, Y. (2020). COVID-19 Series: Working Paper – Sierra Leone's response to COVID-19. Oxford: Oxford Policy Management.

Guzman, L. A., Oviedo, D., Arellana, J., & Cantillo-García, V. (2021). Buying a car and the street: Transport justice and urban space distribution. *Transportation Research Part D: Transport and environment*, *95*, 102860.

Harrison, R. M., Vu, T. van, Jafar, H., & Shi, Z. (2021). More mileage in reducing urban air pollution from road traffic. *Environment International*, *149*, 106329.

Harvey, D. (2008). The right to the city. *New Left Review*, *53*.

Harvey, D. (2012). *Rebel Cities: From the Right to the City to the Urban Revolution*. London: Verso.

Ijjasz-Vasquez, E., & Mukim, M. (2019, February 14). The 3 challenges in building urban resilience in Freetown. World Bank Blogs. Accessed 25 June 2024. https://blogs.worldbank.org/sustainablecities/3-challenges-building-urban-resilience-freetown

IOM. (2020, May 8). Learning from the Ebola outbreak to fight COVID-19 in IOM Sierra Leone. International Organization for Migration. Accessed 25 June 2024. https://www.iom.int/news/learning-ebola-outbreak-fight-covid-19-iom-sierra-leone

IRF. (2021). *World Road Statistics 2021*. Geneva: International Road Federation.

Jian, I. Y., Luo, J., & Chan, E. H. W. (2020). Spatial justice in public open space planning: Accessibility and inclusivity. *Habitat International*, *97*, 102122.

Johnson, S. (2021). Developing a cable car mass transit network to connect the city. C40 Cities Finance Facility. Accessed 25 June 2024. https://c40cff.org/projects/connecting-the-city-with-a-cable-car-mass-transit-network

Jones, P. M. (2016, July). The evolution of urban transport policy from car-based to people-based cities: Is this development path universally applicable? 14th World Conference on Transport Research, Shanghai, China.

Knebelmann, J. (2022, June). Digitalisation of property taxation in developing countries: Recent advances and remaining challenges. London: Overseas Development Institute. Accessed 25 June 2024. https://cdn.odi.org/media/documents/Digitalisation_of_property_taxation_in_developing_countries.pdf

Koroma, B., Macarthy, J., Yusuf, Y., Cavoli, C., & Oviedo, D. (2020). Policy Brief: Freetown: urban mobility, accessibility & COVID-19. London: T-SUM, UCL.

Koroma, B., Oviedo, D., Yusuf, Y., Macarthy, J. M., Cavoli, C., Jones, P. M., Levy, C., & Sellu S. A. (2021). City Profile: Freetown, base conditions of mobility, accessibility and land use. London: T-SUM, UCL.

Koroma, B., Rigon, A., Walker, J., & Sellu, S. A. (2018). Urban Livelihoods in Freetown's Informal Settlements. Freetown: Sierra Leone Urban Research Centre.

Levy, C. (2016). Routes to the just city: Towards gender equality in transport planning. In Moser, C. O. N. (Ed.), *Gender, Asset Accumulation and Just Cities: Pathways to transformation* (pp. 135–149). Abingdon & New York: Routledge.

Lynch, K., Nel, E., & Binns, T. (2020). 'Transforming Freetown': Dilemmas of planning and development in a west African city. *Cities*, *101*, 102694.

Macarthy, J. M., Frediani, A. A., & Kamara, S. F. (2019). *Report on the Role of Community Action Area Planning in Expanding the Participatory Capabilities of the Urban Poor*. Freetown: Sierra Leone Urban Research Centre.

Mansaray, L. R., Huang, J., & Kamara, A. A. (2016). Mapping deforestation and urban expansion in Freetown, Sierra Leone, from pre- to post-war economic recovery. *Environmental Monitoring and Assessment*, 188(8), 470.

Marcuse, P. (2009). From critical urban theory to the right to the city. *City*, 13(2-3), 185-197.

Massingue, S. A., & Oviedo, D. (2021). Walkability and the Right to the City: A snapshot critique of pedestrian space in Maputo, Mozambique. *Research in Transportation Economics*, 86, 101049.

MLCPE, & FCC. (2014). Preparatory Components and Studies for the Freetown Development Plan 'The Urban Planning Project.' Freetown: Freetown City Council.

Nickson, A., & Cutting, J. (2016). The role of decentralisation in post-conflict reconstruction in Sierra Leone. *Third World Thematics: A TWQ Journal*, 1(6), 799–816.

Ortúzar, J. D. (2019). Sustainable urban mobility: What can be done to achieve it? *Journal of the Indian Institute of Science*, 99, 683–693.

Osuteye, E., Koroma, B., Macarthy, J. M., Kamara, S. F., & Conteh, A. (2020). Fighting COVID-19 in Freetown, Sierra Leone: The critical role of community organisations in a growing pandemic. *Open Health*, 1(1), 51-63.

Oviedo, D., Cavoli, C., Levy, C., Koroma, B., Macarthy, J., Sabogal, O., Arroyo, F., & Jones, P. (2022). Accessibility and sustainable mobility transitions in Sub-Saharan Africa: Insights from Freetown. *Journal of Transport Geography*, 105, 103464.

Oviedo, D., Okyere, S. A., Nieto, M., Kita, M., Kusi, L. F., Yusuf, Y., & Koroma, B. (2021). Walking off the beaten path: Everyday walking environment and practices in informal settlements in Freetown. *Research in Transportation Business & Management*, 40, 100630.

Prichard, W., Kamara, A. B., & Meriggi, N. (2020, May 22). Freetown just implemented a new property tax system that could quintuple revenue. International Centre for Tax and Development. Accessed 25 June 2024. https://www.ictd.ac/blog/freetown-new-property-tax-system-quintuple-revenue/

Purcell, M. (2013). Possible worlds: Henri Lefebvre and the right to the city. *Journal of Urban Affairs*, 36(1), 141–154.

Rigon, A., Walker, J., & Koroma, B. (2020). Beyond formal and informal: Understanding urban informalities from Freetown. *Cities*, 105, 102848.

Santos, G., Behrendt, H., Maconi, L., Shirvani, T., & Teytelboym, A. (2010). Part I: Externalities and economic policies in road transport. *Research in Transportation Economics*, 28(1), 2–45.

Soja, E. W. (2010). *Seeking Spatial Justice*. Minneapolis, MN: University of Minnesota Press.

Srivastava, V., & Larizza, M. (2011). Decentralization in postconflict Sierra Leone: The genie is out of the bottle. In P. Chuhan-Pole & M. Angwafo (Eds), *Yes, Africa Can: Success stories from a dynamic continent* (pp. 141–154). World Bank Group.

SSL. (2014). Transport sector statistics bulletin 2013. Freetown: Statistics Sierra Leone. https://www.statistics.sl/images/StatisticsSL/Documents/Publications/2013/2013_transport_sector_statistics_bulletin.pdf

SSL. (2016). 2015 Population and housing census: Summary of final results. Freetown: Statistics Sierra Leone.

SSL. (2017a). Sierra Leone 2015 population and housing census: National analytical report. Freetown: Statistics Sierra Leone.

SSL. (2017b). Sierra Leone 2015 population and housing census: Thematic report on housing conditions. Freetown: Statistics Sierra Leone.

SSL. (2017c). Sierra Leone 2015 population and housing census: Thematic report on migration and urbanization. Freetown: Statistics Sierra Leone.

SSL. (2017d). Sierra Leone 2015 population and housing census: Thematic report on population projections. Freetown: Statistics Sierra Leone.

SSL. (2017e). Sierra Leone 2015 population and housing census: Thematic report on poverty and durables. Freetown: Statistics Sierra Leone.

SSL. (2020). COVID-19 quick action economic response programme (QAERP). Freetown: Statistics Sierra Leone.

Taylor, E. T., Jalloh, A. D., & Jallow, H. (2017). Gaseous air quality indicators along traffic routes in Greater Freetown, Sierra Leone. *International Journal of Geography and Geology*, 6(2), 32-39.

Thomas, A. R. (2023, April 5). Cable car transport system for Freetown makes sense economically, socially and environmentally. The Sierra Leone Telegraph. Accessed 25 June 2024. https://www.thesierraleonetelegraph.com/cable-car-transport-system-for-freetown -makes-sense-economically-socially-and-environmentally/

Tripodi A., Wurie N., Robibaro M., Centro di ricerca per il Trasporto e la Logistica – FRED Engineering S.r.l. (2018). *Pilot study to collect more robust accident data for Sierra Leone: Final Report*. London: ReCAP for Department for International Development.

UN DESA. (2012). *World Urbanization Prospects: The 2011 revision*. New York: United Nations Department of Economic and Social Affairs.

UNGA. (2015, October 21). Transforming Our World: The 2030 agenda for sustainable development. seventieth session (agenda items 15 and 116). New York: United Nations General Assembly. Accessed 25 June 2024. https://www.un.org/en/development/desa/population/migration /generalassembly/docs/globalcompact/A_RES_70_1_E.pdf

UN-Habitat. (2011). *Global Report on Human Settlements 2011: Cities and climate change*. Nairobi: United Nations Human Settlement Programme.

UN-Habitat. (2021, August 23). UN-Habitat supports Sierra Leone urban planning capacity building. UN-Habitat. Accessed 25 June 2024. https://unhabitat.org/un-habitat-supports -sierra-leone-urban-planning-capacity-building

Uteng, T. P., & Lucas, K. (Eds). (2017). *Urban Mobilities in the Global South*. Abingdon & New York: Routledge.

Vasconcellos, E. A. (2001). *Urban Transport, Environment and Equity: The case for developing countries*. London: Earthscan.

Venter, C., Mahendra, A., & Hidalgo, D. (2019). *From Mobility to Access for All: Expanding urban transportation choices in the Global South*. Washington, DC: World Resources Institute.

Verlinghieri, E., & Schwanen, T. (2020). Transport and mobility justice: Evolving discussions. *Journal of Transport Geography, 87*, 102798.

Vincent, J. B. M., & Peters, K. (2021). Accelerating COVID-19 related 'best practice' in the urban motorcycle taxi sector in Sub-Saharan Africa – Sierra Leone Country Report. London: UK Aid Direct. Accessed 25 June 2024. https://www.gov.uk/research-for-development-outputs /accelerating-covid-19-related-best-practice-in-the-urban-motorcycle-taxi-sector-in-sub -saharan-africa-country-report-sierra-leone

Walker, J., Koroma, B., Sellu, S. A., & Rigon, A. (2022). The social regulation of livelihoods in unplanned settlements in Freetown: Implications for strategies of formalisation. *International Development Planning Review, 44*(1), 33–54.

WFP. (2023). WFP RAM Sierra Leone Market Prices Bulletin | Quarter 3, 2023. Rome: UN World Food Programme. Accessed 25 June 2024. https://docs.wfp.org/api/documents/WFP -0000154666/download/

WHO. (2015). *Global Status Report on Road Safety 2015*. Geneva: World Health Organisation.

WHO. (2020, October 23). Freetown tackles a dual challenge to protect its citizens from COVID-19 amidst food insecurity. World Health Organization. Accessed 25 June 2024. https://www .who.int/news-room/feature-stories/detail/freetown-tackles-a-dual-challenge-to-protect-its -citizens-from-covid-19-amidst-food-insecurity

WHO. (2021, August 26). *Sierra Leone steps up countrywide COVID-19 vaccination*. World Health Organization Regional Office for Africa, 26 August. Accessed 25 June 2024. https://www.afro .who.int/news/sierra-leone-steps-up-countrywide-covid-19-vaccination

WHO. (2024). Road traffic injuries, age-standardized death rates (15+), per 100,000 population. Accessed 15 August 2024. https://www.who.int/data/gho/data/indicators/indicator-details/ GHO/road-traffic-injuries-age-standardized-death-rates-(15-)-per-100-000-population

Williams, M., Ito, R., & Li, C. (2020, September). *The cable car as a cost effective mode of public transport for the city of Freetown*. 48th European Transport Conference.

World Bank. (2018a). Reviving Urban Development: The Importance of Freetown for the National Development. Washington, DC: World Bank Group.

World Bank. (2018b). Sierra Leone Multi-City Hazard Review and Risk Assessment. Final Report (Volume 2 of 5): Freetown city hazard and risk assessment. Washington, DC: World Bank Group.

World Bank. (2019). Freetown Urban Sector Review: Options for growth and resilience. Washington, DC: World Bank Group.

World Bank. (2021, November 7). Integrated and Resilient Urban Mobility Project. World Bank Group. Accessed 25 June 2024. https://projects.worldbank.org/en/projects-operations /project-detail/P164353

7

The strategic importance of knowledge production on assistive technology, disability and informality: The rATA survey in Thompson Bay and Dworzark

Hawanatu Bangura, Braima Koroma, Ignacia Ossul Vermehren and Julian Walker

This chapter[1] presents a research initiative focused on the need for and access to assistive technology (AT) in two slum communities in Freetown. The research demonstrated the strategic importance of knowledge production in relation to two topics which are often misrepresented, stereotyped, or rendered invisible due to their association with stigma and institutional marginalisation: disability and the informal sector.

The main research component discussed in this chapter was a quantitative survey into the need for and access to AT in two mainstream settlements of the urban poor in Freetown: Dworzark and Thompson Bay. We argue that this research was strategically relevant at the city level in influencing the orientation of the representative organisation of the urban poor towards disability; and provided knowledge resources for disabled people's organisations (DPOs) at the national level by feeding into the Technical Working Groups on AT that were set up in 2020. At the international level, the research influenced the Global Cooperation on Assistive Technology (GATE) initiative on AT led by the WHO. Across these different levels, our research attempted to address the lack of knowledge and work around AT in Freetown, caused in part due to disability related stigma. Equally as important, the research addresses the failure to acknowledge and engage with the informal sector as a key AT actor. This is due to both political and institutional hostility towards working with informality, and the unfamiliarity of the concepts and debates related to informality among the health institutions leading on AT globally.

Disability, AT and informality

Assistive technology (AT) is an umbrella term encompassing assistive products (AP), and the related systems and services that support the delivery and use of AP. According to the World Health Organization (WHO), an assistive product is 'Any external product (including devices, equipment, instruments or software), especially produced or generally available, the primary purpose of which is to maintain or improve an individual's functioning and independence, and thereby promote their well-being' (WHO et al., 2016). Commonly known examples of APs are wheelchairs, hearing aids, spectacles, white canes, or prosthetics; but there are many more. The WHO has a list of 50 priority APs.

Increasing access to AT is a key global challenge. According to the WHO, 15% of the global population has a disability and more than a billion people need one or more assistive products; but only one in ten people have access to the devices they need. The WHO further projects that the need for AP will increase rapidly with ageing populations and growth in non-communicable disease, so that more than two billion people will need at least one AP by 2030 (WHO, 2021).

However, while the prevalence of disability and need for AT has been documented in general terms, there is little data on low-income settlements in the global South. This is an important gap, given the high association between disability and poverty (Groce & Kett, 2013), and the reality that in the global South many AT users need to pay for (often expensive) access to AT. Therefore, it is to be expected that residents of low-income settlements in the global South face challenges accessing AT.

Furthermore, given limited capacity, the lack of substantiated policy commitments to ensuring access to AT in many countries, the insufficient budgets for state health and social care institutions and the expensive and poorly developed formal private sector AT provision, the reality is that many people on low incomes in the global South access their AT from informal providers.

Substantial literature exists on the informal economy and its definition remains a subject of much debate (Bunell & Harris, 2012; Boanada-Fuchs & Boanada-Fuchs, 2018). However, 'the prevailing definition accepted across disciplinary and ideological boundaries is that the informal economy refers to income generating activities that operate outside the regulatory framework of the state' (Meagher, 2013, p. 2). If, in line with this definition, informal AT providers are those that operate outside of the regulatory ambit of the state, this can imply both problems and opportunities for efforts to ensure access to appropriate AT at scale. Understanding the informal economy in terms of lack of regulation is important when we consider informal enterprises as a source of AT; as this implies there is limited regulatory intervention to ensure the adequacy and safety of AT for users (in addition to other forms of regulation around tax, or intellectual property). This is a particular concern as inadequate AT can be associated with increased morbidity and mortality for users (Øderud, 2014). However, informal providers of AT are often more accessible to people on low incomes, providing more affordable products and services. Furthermore, AT enterprises developed by persons with disabilities/AT users are often positively associated with AT innovation and may be evaluated more positively by users than formally provided AT. Such enterprises often remain informal due to barriers to formal registration for small, user-led enterprises (Walker et al., 2020).

The contradictory value of informal providers for AT users therefore presents a key policy research gap: the need to better understand 'how can the benefits of informal AT providers in providing broader and less expensive access to otherwise unserved populations be promoted whilst protecting AT users from unsafe products and services?' (Walker & Tebbutt, 2022, p. 9). To support such policy research, there is a need for more data on the role of informal enterprises in AT provision and its merits and weaknesses vis-a-vis other providers.

This research therefore responded to two key knowledge gaps. Firstly, it addressed the lack of data on AT need and access in low-income communities in Freetown, which is a critical resource for advocacy by disabled people on their rights, as well as for planning public policy on disability and AT access more generally. Secondly, it aimed to make visible the role of informal AT providers and explore both the positive and negative implications of informal provision for users.

AT2030 and the rATA survey

The research discussed in this chapter takes the form of a quantitative survey, with a parallel qualitative study. The research was undertaken by a team from SLURC in partnership with national partners the Sierra Leone Federation of the Urban And Rural Poor (FEDURP) and the Centre of

Dialogue on Human Settlement and Poverty Alleviation (CODOHSAPA); and international partners the Bartlett Development Planning Unit of University College London (DPU), the international disability NGO Leonard Cheshire and the Global Disability Innovation Hub (GDI Hub) as part of the AT2030 research project on Community Led-Solutions.

Given the strong association of disability with poverty and the challenges faced by people in need of AT living in contexts of poverty in the global South, the wider AT2030 project that this research contributed to aimed to better understand the experiences of AT users, or those in need of AT, amongst low-income urban residents.

The quantitative survey was undertaken using the WHO Rapid Assistive Technology Assessment (rATA) tool.[2] The WHO developed this survey tool because other surveys about health or disability rarely include questions about assistive products, or do not provide enough information to inform decision-making. The rATA aims to address that gap by providing a simple tool to determine answers to the most basic yet important questions about AT (Nossal Institute for Global Health, 2019). The survey is composed of five parts. The first collects demographic information about the individual and is followed by three core data collection sections: need for AT, demand and supply, and satisfaction. There is a final optional section on recommendations. The survey includes a poster produced by the WHO GATE programme, which includes images of 26 assistive products. The APs depicted relate to the areas of hearing, mobility, seeing, remembering or concentrating, self-caring, and speaking or communication.

It is important to note that the rATA survey draws on respondents' self-reported perceptions of AT need and their experiences of AT access and use. This is unlike other population survey tools for AT that are based on clinical assessment. The advantages of a self-reported survey like rATA are that it is quick and low cost, uses consistent and comparable survey elements, and involves AT users' own perspectives and experiences. However, research suggests that self-reported surveys often fail to correspond well to clinical assessments, featuring significant elements of both under- and over-reporting of the need for AT (Boggs et al., 2021). Despite this caveat, in the absence of population-based clinical assessments of AT need in Sierra Leone, the rATA has an important contribution to make in highlighting locally perceived patterns of AT need and access.

Two 'mainstream' communities were selected in Freetown, Dworzark and Thompson Bay (i.e. communities of urban poor in Freetown which have residents who are disabled people and AT users, but which do not have any unusual concentration of disabled residents or disability related facilities). The rATA survey was also conducted in one other disability specific settlement in Freetown – a land occupation by a group of wheelchair users, Help Empower Polio People, HEPPO – and two settlements in Banjarmasin, Indonesia; but these are not the focus of this chapter.

The data was collected and stored using KoBoToolbox, a suite of tools for data collection and analysis for use on a smartphone, especially within challenging environments. Using a population survey approach, the rATA was conducted in a specific area of each of the communities selected during four weeks in September 2019. The aim was to survey 1,000 individuals within a defined area of the settlement using a population survey approach, hence everyone in a specific area. In Dworzark and Thompson Bay (Sierra Leone) 2,076 individuals were surveyed. A team of twelve enumerators from FEDURP participated in three-day training conducted by DPU and SLURC that was evaluated by the Nossal Institute for Global Health for the WHO. The survey was conducted during the day (9 a.m.–4 p.m.) and data collectors only went back to houses once during the same day to pick up residents who had been absent during the first visit.[3]

The rATA survey, which was implemented through the AT2030 project, included some small adaptations to the original WHO survey. A specific change related to the focus of this chapter was the addition of informal providers as an option for AT source, which was not included as an option in the original rATA survey. This option was added based on initial field observations that low-income urban residents in the areas surveyed by the project access many of their devices from the informal market. Data collectors defined 'informal providers' as second-hand shops, street markets and street hawkers.

Context: disability and assistive technology in Sierra Leone

The primary source of information on the prevalence of disability in Sierra Leone is the 2015 Population and Housing Census, conducted by Statistics Sierra Leone. According to the accompanying thematic report, (Kabia & Tarawally, 2017), 93,129 people in the country, or 1.3% of the population, have a disability. Compared to global data, this is an unusually low disability prevalence and though the census represents the most comprehensive overview of disability, national disability stakeholders involved in the AT2030 research project, including DPO representatives, have argued that it underestimates the true prevalence of disability in the country. This finding justifies the implementation of the rATA in low-income communities in Sierra Leone, as, in addition to charting need for and access to AT, it also gives a fresh indication of disability prevalence. Conversely to the census, in which disability is asked about directly, the rATA only asks about a person's functioning, which may avoid some of the stigma associated with a person self-defining as 'disabled'.

According to the census, more males than females have a disability (male 54%, female 46%), with a large portion between the ages of 20 and 50 (45%). More reside in rural than in urban areas (67% to 33%) and many are neither educated nor employed (63% and 44%, respectively). The distribution of disability types picked up in the census indicates that the most common disability type is physical (mobility) impairment, followed by visual impairments. Disease or illness is the major cause of disability among the country's disabled population, accounting for 40.5% of cases.

In Sierra Leone, there is no comprehensive source of data about the availability of AP. The Sierra Leone Disability Act of 2011 defines AT as 'assistive devices and services' such as 'carers, implements, tools and specialised services provided by people to persons with disability to assist them in education, employment or other activities.' As our research showed, some of the main providers of AT are non-state actors, and databases are often maintained on an organisational basis and rarely shared externally (as is the case with NGOs).

The case study settlements

The settlements of Dworzark and Thompson Bay were selected as 'mainstream' settlements of the urban poor, having no specific disability related features, facilities or unusually high levels of disabled residents. The intention was to understand the experiences of AT users and those in need of AT, living in ordinary settlements where they are less likely to be a highly visible group, or to have an unusual level of access to AT, disability related infrastructure or services.

Dworzark is a hillside settlement, located 5 km from Freetown's city centre. It is divided into twelve sections and has been populated since the 1940s. There has been rapid urbanisation in the area since the 1980s, leading to the expansion of the uphill parts of the settlement. The 313-acre settlement contains 5,236 households (CODOHSAPA and FEDURP, 2011). Land in the settlement is composed of a steep hillside and features large rocks or boulders over-hanging buildings. Housing is built of mud bricks and corrugated iron sheets, connected by unpaved road networks. The drainage system is poor and many households fetch water from beneath boulders. The community has about twelve public toilets used every day by more than 2,500 people. There is no connection to the main city water pipeline and there are only 20 public water points which serve more than 4,000 residents every day. Residents depend on the George Brook Stream, wells and spring water for their daily water needs. The community has one formal market, twelve schools and one health centre.

Thompson Bay is a seaside settlement approximately 10 km from Freetown city centre which has been populated since the late 1990s. The density of households has been increasing, and the settlement now contains about 1,624 households (CODOHSAPA and FEDURP, 2011). The community is situated in a wetland (a mangrove swamp) that has been banked up over the years for the construction of homes. Most of the land area is used for residential purposes, and the settlement is characterised by a mix of well-designed concrete and poorly constructed, housing, with reasonably good road networks. Water is rationed with almost no home receiving a 24-hour supply and consequently there is limited access to safe drinking water. Sanitation is poor and there are no council-designated waste dumps. The community has a food market, mosque, school and a health centre which was previously demolished following a land dispute.

The rATA survey findings

The 2,076 individuals surveyed using the rATA tool were distributed across 815 households. The household composition ranged from one to 16 members and the average number of household members was five. From the total number of respondents, 55.7% were women and girls and 44.3% were men and boys. The population surveyed in Thompson Bay and Dworzark was young; 23.71% of the population was below 29 years old and only 4% of the population was older than 60 years.

In using the rATA survey data to assess disability prevalence, we defined those people reporting 'some difficulty' or more in any one of the functioning domains (hearing, mobility, seeing, remembering or concentrating, self-caring, and speaking or communication) as having a disability, and a severe disability as those reporting 'significant difficult' or 'cannot do at all'. Based on this, one fifth (20.6%) of the population of the two settlements had a disability and 4.3% had a severe disability (see Figure 7.1).

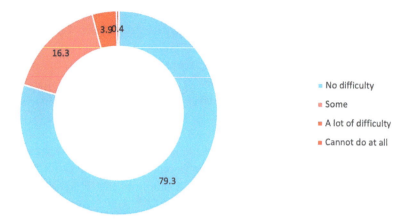

Figure 7.1 Disability prevalence in Thompson Bay and Dworzark.
Source: © Authors

Of the respondents that reported having a difficulty, around one third (35.3%) had difficulties in seeing/vision and one third (33.9%) had difficulties with mobility. Most people that had a severe disability acquired it as an adult. Difficulty in seeing/vision was acquired on average (median) at the age of 22 and mobility at the age of 38.

There was a higher prevalence of disability among older people, but they also had the highest AP coverage. 62.5% of people over 60 had a disability, this was three times more than the working age population (23.5%). Men and women over 70 had a very high prevalence of difficulty in seeing/vision (males 84.6%, 50% females) and in mobility (males 69.2%, 45% females). Respondents over 60 years old had the best AP coverage (34%), although this coverage is still very low.

Females had higher disability prevalence than males, lower AP coverage and self-reported more need for AP. Females have a slightly higher disability prevalence than males (females 21.6%, males 19.5%). They also had less AP coverage (females 12.8%, males 17.9%) and the AP they have was less sophisticated. Males had six types of APs, while females only had three types (spectacles, auxiliary/elbow crutches and cane/sticks, tripods or quadripods). No female had a wheelchair, despite there being females with severe mobility impairments. Self-reported AP need was also higher in females (41.2%) than in males (38.5%).

Looking more specifically at access to AT, AP coverage was extremely low and the variety of APs was limited. Only 14.9% of the disabled population had access to at least one device they needed, while 85.1% had no AP. Respondents that had 'some difficulty' had the least coverage (only 9.8%). Even among those with 'a lot of difficulty' that had the best coverage (35.4%), coverage remains very low. Interestingly, a smaller proportion of people who 'cannot do at all' (22.2%) have access to AP than people with 'a lot of difficulty'. By age, older people had the best coverage (34%), while children had the least coverage (6.6%). APs used by males' are more sophisticated and more varied than those used by females: Males had six types of APs listed on the WHO GATE list of priority AP (spectacles, auxiliary/elbow crutches, canes/sticks, tripod and/or quadripod, push and basic type wheelchairs, therapeutic footwear and rollators/walking frame), while females only had three types (spectacles, auxiliary/elbow crutches and cane/sticks, tripods or quadripods). No female had a wheelchair, despite there being females with severe mobility impairments.

The variety of devices was very low: the survey found only seven different types of APs (spectacles, auxiliary/elbow crutches, canes/sticks, tripod and/or quadripod, manual wheelchairs basic and push, and therapeutic footwear). All the devices relate to a mobility and seeing/vision impairment, despite there being people that have impairments in all the domains. 81.0% of the devices found were spectacles.

Finally and germane to the focus of this chapter, most of the APs owned in Thompson Bay and Dworzark came from the informal market (see Figure 7.2). One third (30.8%) of AT users obtained their AP, mostly spectacles, from the informal sector, such as second-hand shops, street

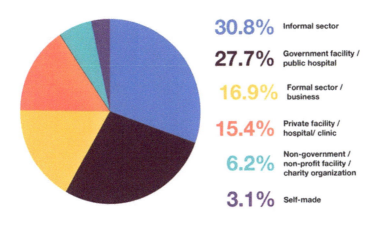

Figure 7.2 Sources of AP owned by respondents in Thompson Bay and Dworzark. Source: © Authors

markets and street hawkers. This was followed by government facilities or public hospitals (27.7%). Most users had to pay for their AP (70.7%), which were mostly spectacles bought in the informal market. The only APs not paid for were those received from NGOs/charities (100%, four people), or those which were home-made (50%, two people). Respondents were generally satisfied with the quality of their AP and the maintenance and follow-up services.

Almost half the people with a disability do not currently have the AP they think they need (40.1% or 172 people). Affordability is the main reason for not having an AP (80.5%). Of the 172 individuals who self-reported AP need but did not have AP, the most common reason given was 'lack of affordability' (80.5% or 140 answers), followed by 'not being aware' (8.0% or 14 answers), and 'not available' (5.0% or four answers). The least common answer was 'lack of transport' (0.5% or one answer).

Strategic importance of the rATA survey

The findings of the rATA survey, as presented in brief above, have several important policy and advocacy implications. Firstly, the level of self-declared disability prevalence. 20.6% of the population surveyed is significantly higher than the figure derived from the national census survey of 1.3% (Kabia & Tarawally, 2017) and much closer to the global estimate (15%) specified in the World Report on Disability (WHO, 2011). There are a number of possible explanations for the big difference in the figures from the two surveys. It could be explained by the respondents to the census being unwilling to self-define as 'disabled' in response to the census survey, given the high levels of disability stigma in Sierra Leone. In contrast, the rATA survey refers to difficulties across the functioning domains but does not use the term 'disability'. Alternatively, it may be that, given the association of disability with poverty, disability prevalence is far higher in urban slums than the national average. However, regardless of the reason, the difference between the prevalence suggested by the national census and the rATA survey is striking. The higher figure gives rise to policy implications in terms of highlighting the scale of relevance of disability in urban settlements of the poor, both directly and indirectly (given the impact of disability on the incomes and responsibilities of families and households containing disabled people).

Secondly, the survey highlighted the very low access to AT for those who need it: only 14.9% of those who indicated that they had a disability had access to an AP. As the vast majority of the AP that people did have access to were spectacles, the extremely limited range of AT available is also noteworthy as an indicator of poor coverage across types of disability other than vision. An associated factor is that affordability was given as the main reason for a lack of access to AP, meaning that people need affordable ways to access AT. In this context, the biggest source of AT that people did have access to was from informal markets. This is significant both in terms of highlighting the very limited reach of formal AT providers in mainstream slum settlements, as well as the need to better understand how informal markets for AT function, and how they can be better regulated or supported, as relevant.

In an effort to take these lessons forward, short factsheets summarising the rATA findings were created to disseminate to key policy actors and disability advocacy organisations. Using these resources and the wider rATA report, SLURC have been able to influence key policy and strategy development in the Ministry of Health and Sanitation. This includes, for instance, joining the technical working groups established by the Ministry of Health and Sanitation (National Disability, Assistive Technology and Rehabilitation (NDAR) and CHAI-SL under AT 2030). As part of the technical working groups, we have made technical inputs based on the rATA survey data, and provided policy recommendations that were incorporated into the Sierra Leone Assistive Technology Policy and Strategic Plan (2021–2025) and Priority Assistive Technology Product List of Sierra Leone. Working closely with the Ministry of Health and Sanitation (MoHS), the World Health Organisation (WHO), CHAI-SL and disability-related actors and institutions have created opportunities for engaging with the concerns, service delivery and ultimately the improvement of quality of life and wellbeing for persons with disabilities in the country.

In addition to the relevance and use of the core findings of the rATA survey, the process of data collection and analysis with local partners has also been a space through which the team worked to address the stigma related to disability, increase awareness of AT, and promote an uptake of focus on disability issues and AT demands by mainstream organisations of the urban poor.

At the community level, the process of the rATA survey gave space for residents in Dworzark and Thompson Bay to share their experiences of disability and AT need, which aided in assessing the need, use, supply and impact of assistive technology in the overall AT2030 research project. Demonstrating that AT was a shared need cutting across disabled and older people promoted 'access to AT' as a common demands for communities. The survey also opened a discussion on the relevance of AT and disability which aimed to challenge disability stigma. This included the use of a short video to inform people about the project as part of the consent process, which also tried to address language about and attitudes to disability. Through participating in this research, the SLURC and FEDURP teams observed that many people who before did not want to talk about themselves as disabled, started to see being disabled as a normal lived experience in the community. Many participants said that they had overcome part of their shame to go out into a public space due to this research.

What did not work so well, in terms of allowing people to directly express themselves, was the presence of caregivers. While the survey was also designed for caregivers to share their own experiences as carers, they still wanted to share the experience of the person they were caring for. This was a concern as we noticed that disabled participants who needed assistance from their caregivers due to the level of difficulty they faced did not express themselves in the survey; instead their carers did. Also, some residents were not surveyed because data collectors only went back to houses once to assess residents who had been absent during the first visit. The FEDURP data collectors felt that those with hearing impairments would be excluded because there was no sign language interpreter amongst them, and they may not be able to understand the language of a hearing-impaired person. However, with some changes and cooperation, this problem was solved.

The rATA survey also served to influence participating community organisations. Working on the survey, FEDURP members reflected on the relevance of disability in their communities. A poster with 26 images of AP that was used by FEDURP team members to introduce AP to survey respondents also helped FEDURP raise awareness in their communities, where the concept of AT and the variety of AP available was unfamiliar. Before the rATA survey training, some FEDURP members felt they lacked the skills to participate in programmes related to disability and AT. The FEDURP Chairperson, who was also part of the survey exercise, reflected that the survey was a space for gradually changing language and attitudes around disability. They committed to not use the harsh terms most residents in their communities usually used to describe disabled people (i.e. cripple, blindman etc.).

Working with FEDURP to conduct the survey in their own communities was also a unique opportunity to contribute to their wider strategies of community development, while bringing a disability focus. We noticed a change in perception with the FEDURP data collectors (who were all non-disabled) after participating in three-day training and implementing the survey in the settlements for one month. This has helped them to mainstream disability in other urban projects and in advocacy. The FEDURP team, including the Chairperson, who had previously been unused to working with disabled people in the core activities of the grassroots federation (for example savings groups), started to change their perspectives and have now included commitments to mainstreaming disability in key activities such as the savings groups, their community led data collection work, media and advocacy, as well as in the other urban projects they are involved with. During the International Day of Disabled People 2020 the FEDURP chairperson noted how the research had helped FEDURP change their attitude towards disability and how they want to mainstream disability in the planning of the informal settlements of Freetown going forward.

Finally, conducting the rATA survey in urban poor communities, both in Freetown and Banjarmasin in Indonesia, and its findings have had implications at an international level. They push for methodological reflection by the team leading globally on promoting the rATA data collection tool, as part of the GATE initiative led by the WHO. The original rATA survey tool being used by the WHO GATE team included the question: 'From where did you get your assistive product?' with the following response options:

- gov. facility/public hospital
- non-govt, non-profit facility/charity
- private facility/hospital/clinic
- friends/family members/relatives
- online, and
- self-made.

Based on an initial scoping discussion with local team and community members, we changed this list of options to omit 'friends and family', focusing instead of the ultimate source of the AP. We removed 'online', which was not a relevant source in the case study communities and changed 'self-made' to 'home-made' to recognise that much locally produced AP in our case study settlements are not made by the user themselves, but by other households or community members. Crucially, we also added 'informal markets' as an option following feedback that this was an important source of AP in the case study communities. When we applied the survey tool across the four mainstream urban poor communities in Sierra Leone and Indonesia, this change revealed that informal markets were the most common source of AP. This included unregistered shops, second hand markets, and untrained artisans (such as auto-mechanics in Freetown who fashion and repair products such as crutches).

Highlighting the importance of such informal sources of AT in urban poor communities was a point of reflection for the strategic focus of the GATE initiative, which to date has primarily focused on formal private and public health care institutions as AT providers, as well as disability NGOs. Given the importance of informal markets as sources of AT, this research has fostered a discussion on how to work with informal AT providers to ensure broader access to life-changing and vital AT, at the same time as guarding against sub-standard and dangerous AT which may be provided through unregulated providers.

Based on the rATA surveys and a subsequent qualitative study that we initiated to further explore the role of informal markets for AT in Sierra Leone (Walker et al., 2020) we have used interactions with the GATE team, through the wider AT2030 programme, to explore how to engage with informal providers of AT in wider global AT strategies. The over-arching concern is how the benefits of informal AT providers in providing broader and less expensive access to otherwise unserved populations can be promoted, whilst protecting AT users from unsafe products and services. In Sierra Leone, some key policy implications to this end include the need to understand that AT market regulations can be introduced to improve the quality of products and services without pushing providers into increasing costs or reducing accessibility, as well as to consider how to better promote knowledge about what constitutes good quality and safe assistive products and services amongst informal AT providers and their clients. We anticipate that such investigations would have wider relevance in other contexts where those in need of AT rely on informal markets.

In conclusion, this research has aimed to make two 'grey' areas more visible, thereby trying to make them more prominent in policy advocacy debates. Firstly, we have highlighted that the scale of AT need in urban poor communities in Freetown appears to be much higher than that suggested by formal data collection sources, such as the national census, meaning that disability continues to be marginalised from national policy agendas. Secondly, we have been able to reveal that, in practice, official providers of AT have very limited reach in settlements of the urban poor in Freetown, while informal markets play a key role. While professionals tasked with extending access to AT rightly are strongly concerned with ensuring that AT users have access to safe and appropriate products and services, this may lead to mistrust of informal (unregulated) sources.

However, the findings of the rATA survey show that official AT sources remain largely out of reach for residents in the settlements surveyed. The implication is that, in addition to focusing on the extension of official AT sources, there is an immediate and pressing need to engage with the de facto providers, currently dominated by informal actors, and their clients, to improve their knowledge and delivery of safe and appropriate products and services.

Notes

1 This chapter draws on the research report by Ossul-Vermehren et al. (2021).
2 See: https://www.who.int/publications/i/item/WHO-MHP-HPS-ATM-2021.1
3 In Dworzark and Thompson Bay, the rate of people answering the survey was 84%. Non-respondents included people who declined to provide consent and incidences where no adult carers were present to interview children.

References

Boanada-Fuchs, A., & Boanada-Fuchs, V. (2018). Towards a taxonomic understanding of informality. *International Development Planning Review*, *40*(4), 397–420.

Boggs, D., Hydara, A., Faal, Y., Atta Okoh, J., Olaniyan, S. I., et al. (2021). Estimating need for glasses and hearing aids in the Gambia: Results from a national survey and comparison of clinical impairment and self-report assessment approaches. *International Journal of Environmental Research and Public Health*, *18*(12), 6302. https://doi.org/10.3390/ijerph18126302

Bunnell, T., & Harris, A. (2012). Re-viewing informality: perspectives from urban Asia, *International Development Planning Review*, *34*(4), 339–348.

CODOHSAPA & FEDURP. (2011). Community-Led Enumeration and Profiling: The state of 11 coastal slums in Freetown, Sierra Leone. CODOHSAPA-FEDURP. Accessed 25 June 2024. https://sdinet.org/wp-content/uploads/2015/04/State_of_11_Coastal_Slum_in_Freetown _Sierra_Leone.pdf

Groce, N., & Kett, M. (2013). The disability and development gap. Working paper no. 21. Leonard Cheshire Disability. https://www.ucl.ac.uk/epidemiology-health-care/sites/epidemiology-health-care/files/wp-21.pdf

Kabia, F., & Tarawally, U. (2017). Sierra Leone 2015 population and housing census. Thematic report on disability, Freetown: Statistics Sierra Leone.

Meagher, K. (2013). Unlocking the informal economy: A literature review on linkages between formal and informal economies in developing countries. Women in Informal Employment Globalizing and Organizing (WIEGO) working paper no. 27. Accessed 25 June 2024. Unlocking the Informal Economy: A Literature Review on Linkages Between Formal and Informal Economies in Developing Countries (wiego.org)

Øderud, T. (2014). Surviving spinal cord injury in low income countries. *African Journal of Disability*, *3*(2).

Ossul-Vermehren, I., Carew, M. T., & Walker, J. (2021). Assistive Technology in urban low-income communities in Sierra Leone and Indonesia: Rapid assistive technology assessment (rATA) survey results. Bartlett Development Planning Unit, Global Disability Innovation Hub, London.

Pryor, W., & Nguyen, L. (2019). Measuring need and unmet need for assistive technology: The rapid Assistive Technology Assessment (rATA) tool for national representative survey enumeration: a manual. WHO resource. Accessed 23 January 2023. https://cdn.who.int/media/docs/default-source/assistive-technology-2/rata-master-training/20201021-rata-enumerator-manual-final.pdf?sfvrsn=3864b5f8_12 Walker, J., Rifai, A., Jamil, F., & Kurniawan, V. (2020). Country capacity assessment for assistive technologies: informal markets study, Indonesia. Global Disability Innovation Hub Report, AT 2030 Programmer, GDI Hub, London.

Walker, J., & Tebbutt, E. (2022). The informal economy as a provider of assistive technology: lessons from Indonesia and Sierra Leone. *Health Promotion International, 38*(3). https://doi.org/10.1093/heapro/daac005

WHO (World Health Organization). (2021). Assistive Technology fact sheet. Accessed 25 June 2024. https://www.who.int/en/news-room/fact-sheets/detail/assistive-technology

WHO, USAID, & International Disability Alliance. (2016). Priority assistive products list: improving access to assistive technology for everyone, everywhere. Accessed 25 June 2024. https://apps.who.int/iris/bitstream/handle/10665/207694/WHO_EMP_PHI_2016.01_eng.pdf?sequence=1&isAllowed=y

WHO & WB. (2011). World Report on Disability. Geneva: WHO. Accessed 8 August 2024. https://www.who.int/teams/noncommunicable-diseases/sensory-functions-disability-and-rehabilitation/world-report-on-disability

8

Resilient or just city-making? Exploring the political space to tackle risk traps in Freetown[1]

Adriana Allen, Braima Koroma, Emmanuel Osuteye and Rita Lambert

Reframing urban resilience

Urbanisation in Sub-Saharan Africa is increasingly associated with endless risk accumulation cycles or urban 'risk traps', which are still poorly understood and tackled. This framing encapsulates both the cumulative impacts of 'extensive risks' – everyday hazards such as infectious disease, and small disasters such as localised floods and fire outbreaks – and 'intensive risks'; larger, less frequent disaster events such as tropical storms and earthquakes.

While intensive risks are receiving increasing attention in disaster risk management (DRM), climate resilience debates and policymaking, in most African cities the accumulation of preventable extensive risks remains unattended, while accounting for a high proportion of all disaster-related injuries, impoverishment, damage and destruction of social and physical infrastructure. As a result, risk accumulation is often normalised as part of life and quietly confronted through a combination of individual and collective coping strategies by those most affected. Overtime, these cumulative impacts erode the capacity to act of poor women and men who find themselves locked in risk traps.

We define risk traps as the vicious cycle through which various environmental hazards and episodic, but repetitive and often unrecorded, disasters accumulate in particular localities and grow exponentially over time (Bull-Kamanga et al., 2003; Allen et al., 2015). Just as urban poverty traps are produced through combined aspects of urban deprivation that over time undermine the potential benefits offered by cities, we argue that urban risk traps undermine the multiple resilience-seeking efforts and investments made by the urban poor and state agencies to disrupt risk accumulation (Allen et al., 2017).

While the slow-burn effects often lock urban systems and dwellers into intractable risk trajectories, '...path dependency need not be path determinacy' (Coaffee & Lee, 2016, p. 243). Understanding how resilience-seeking strategies work across space and time is crucial to disrupt risk traps. This requires engendering grassroots-led processes to assess not only how, where, and why risk accumulates, but also what and whose responses are adopted and with what consequences. We therefore argue that it is not enough to look at the question of resilience of what and for whom, but also by whom.

Risk resilience has been the subject of multiple contributions but also critics over the last decade. The latter point to the tendency in resilience debates and advocacy to dilute political questions of rights and entitlements and the risk of displacing responsibility onto ordinary citizens individuals and away from the State. For instance, the promotion of self-reliance and self-organisation practices adopted by the urban poor by growing their own food is often celebrated as a resilience-seeking practice. Yet, it could also be read as of way of ignoring the unjust conditions that perpetuate not just their access but lack of control over increasingly commodified food systems and the role that the state needs to play in regulating the commodification and increasingly hyper-financialisation of urban life.

Throughout the discussion, we take a critical approach to resilience by emphasising the relational and fundamentally political nature and tensions between what we define as resilient-seeking practices by those women and men already bearing the brunt of risk accumulation cycles and those driven by governmental and external actors' interventions. We argue that the critical question is not just to bounce back or forward from shocks – whether related to intensive or extensive risks – but rather to elucidate how and why the production and reproduction of risk accumulation traps calls for engaging with structural injustices. An emphasis on just resilience calls for an active engagement in tackling not only unevenly distributed impacts on people and places, or the recognition of ordinary women and men's capacities to manage risk, but fundamentally the conditions that enable or undermine their parity of political participation in decision-making (Allen et al., 2017; Ziervogel et al., 2017).

Following the above considerations, the discussion focuses on what and whose capacities to act are embedded in resilience-seeking practices and explores the processes and relations that expand or constrain the political space in which they are conceived and implemented. Over time, the notion of 'political space' has been developed with different but interconnected meanings and aims. Webster and Engberg-Petersen (2002) define political spaces as the institutional channels, political discourses and social and political practices through which the poor and their supporting organisations can pursue poverty reduction. McGee (2004) adopts this notion to examine the transformative potential arising from specific junctures, where citizens and policymakers come together. Cornwall and Coelho (2006) conceptualise such spaces as opportunities to advance democratising effects, enabling ordinary women and men to claim citizenship and affect governance processes. Building upon these conceptualisations, we use the notion of 'political space' to explore the whereabouts of the nexus between power, space and the networked boundaries that delineate fields of possible action (Hayward, 2000). This entails an interrogation of how the resilience-seeking discursive and material practices adopted by national and local governments, external support agencies (ESAs) and local communities converge into specific geographies and with what intended and unintended consequences.

Interrogating how DRM practices work spatially and at different scales unveils the real scope of decentralised approaches not only to reach those most vulnerable to risk, but also to include their experience, learning, voice, and capacity to act. This involves travelling across the scales that delineate (a) the policy 'boundaries' of decentralised DRM bodies; (b) the actual 'boundaries' under which institutional, collective, and individual resilience-seeking practices are pursued; and (c) the micro scale at which risk is experienced. Travelling across these three scales is crucial to understand why certain risk accumulation processes remain more invisible than others – socially and spatially – therefore restricting the capacity of institutional and grassroots efforts to tackle risk traps.

Furthermore, understanding risk trajectories requires historical perspective to shed light on who tends to become trapped in risk accumulation cycles, and on the factors and processes shaping their mobility in and out of risk. Such an approach allows us to understand how risk is perceived and experienced, what learning is acquired and applied to act, and how such learning travels from individual to collective and city-wide resilience-seeking practices. Examining how specific risk-prone areas have been intervened in over time reveals the actual drivers of risk accumulation and the way in which ongoing resilience-seeking practices need to be reworked.

This discussion draws on two streams of work devoted to co-producing actionable knowledge on how risk traps work and can be disrupted in collaboration with local communities in Freetown. The underpinning research was conducted by the authors under the Urban Africa Risk Knowledge (Urban ARK)[2] project, in collaboration with a city-wide network of collectives of the urban poor, NGOs and local authorities. This body of work was further developed under the DPU MSc ESD/SLURC Learning Alliance[3] implemented between 2017–2020, which sought to co-produce meaningful strategies to tackle risk traps across the city, while strengthening in-situ resilience to build a better Freetown for all (DPU MSc ESD/SLURC Learning Alliance, 2019).

The next section examines how risk accumulation works in Freetown, followed by a discussion of policy trajectories seeking to decentralise DRM. Section 2 offers a critical examination of the junctures and disjunctures for transformative change, while section 3 explores the potential of several strategies co-developed with local communities to disrupt risk traps. We conclude by reflecting on the opportunities and challenges faced to widen the political space between institutional DRM and grassroots resilience-seeking practices, in a relational and inclusive way.

Risk Experiences and Policy Trajectories: what and who is to be made resilient?

While our understanding of urbanisation in risk across Africa has been significantly expanded in recent years, the bulk of the knowledge produced in this field centres on mega-cities at the expense of small and medium cities (Jaglin et al., 2011; Resnick, 2014; Satterthwaite, 2016; Dodman et al., 2017). We focus on Freetown to address the under-investigated political, social and environmental specificities of non-metropolitan African contexts.

The city has experienced rapid urbanisation and a population growth rate of about 3% per annum since 1985, in a country with the highest annual rainfall in Africa. Freetown's origins date back to the end of the eighteenth century, as the outcome of British philanthropists, abolitionists, and entrepreneurs to establish a slave-free settlement in Africa (Banton, 1969; Adderley, 2006). Throughout the nineteenth century, the city grew through the settlement of released slaves from across West Africa by the Royal British Navy's West African Squadron, which explains the foundations of today's largest segment, the Christian Creole population. After Sierra Leone's independence in 1961, Freetown became home to further migrants from West Africa, most of whom were Muslim. In 1991 a civil war that lasted 11 years destroyed much of its infrastructure and economy and forced mass migration from the countryside into the city (Lynch et al., 2020).

With just over one-million residents (approximately 21.1% of the national population), Freetown is the most populous and dense city in the country and contributes approximately 30% of national GDP (Frediani, 2021). Rapid urbanisation has contributed to the proliferation and expansion of informal settlements across the city, a process that today is underpinned by a growing unmet demand for proximal living to livelihood opportunities, coupled with unaffordable land and housing in formalised areas.

The topography of Freetown, a narrow peninsula constrained between the sea and the hills, limits its spatial expansion, forcing low-income groups to settle mostly on marginal lands. As a result, the urban poor are predominantly settled in three distinct geographic areas: dense coastal settlements on the western side, sprawling inland settlements along the Sierra Leone River estuary and hillside settlements in the steep hills surrounding the city. In these settlements, flooding, fires, rock-falls, building collapse and landslides are common, with significant impacts ranging from the destruction of property and infrastructure to injuries, diseases, and fatalities. The incidence of disease epidemics, especially those that are water borne, is also significantly high. The geographic location and spatial distribution of informal settlements translate into significant urban health and sanitation challenges. Freetown is home to at least 68 informal settlements, comprising approximately 36% of all settlements, many perched on artificially banked land along the sea, while others sprawl over the hillsides (Allen, Koroma et al., 2020).

African cities have notoriously outdated planning and bureaucratic governance structures, which are often unresponsive to the needs and demands of poor and impoverished dwellers (Simone & Abouhani, 2005; Myers, 2011; Pieterse & Parnell, 2014; Parnell, 2016). In recent years the resilience agenda has been pushed forward into a prominent role in urban governance across the region. Internationally endorsed by the SDGs and the UN-Habitat Urban Agenda, a political discourse calling for 'inclusive, safe, resilient and sustainable' cities is galvanising across many African countries, reframing risk management and climate adaptation as part of integrated development planning.

The Government of Sierra Leone (GoSL) has subscribed to the Sendai Framework for disaster risk reduction (DRR) (2015–2030) and adopted new policies and institutional channels advocating for the integration of DRM into wider development strategies. While seeking societal resilience through decentralised governance features highly in policy rhetoric, in practice, these efforts have been highly reactionary in nature and activated in response to large scale disasters. Since 2002, responsibility for coordinating DRM has rested with the Office of National Security (ONS) (GoSL, 2002). In 2004, a disaster management department (DMD) was created within ONS to coordinate responses to natural and man-made disasters and to build 'safe and resilient' societies. A national disaster management policy (NDPM) was introduced in 2006, providing strategic directives on the steps to be taken before, during and after disasters, while a national disaster preparedness and response plan mapped out the roles of different stakeholders in its implementation. These documents highlight that community leaders are mandated to play a key role in coordinating local responses prior, during and after disaster events. In practice, however, these instruments have not been fully operationalised, despite the country's commitment to the resilience building agenda.

More recently, the enactment of the 2020 National Disaster Management Act sought to enhance GoSL's planning and coordination capacity and better align with the UN Sendai Framework commitments. This legislation sets out the current DRM institutional framework and provides the legal basis for the operations of the new National Disaster Management Agency (NDMA). This decision marks a shift from previous institutional arrangements, which conflated disasters with other security concerns in the country and by extension prioritised large-scale disaster events. The NDMA aims to develop more proactive and integrated disaster management processes that align with and support the country's developmental goals. In addition, the 2020 act establishes a multisectoral body called the 'National Platform for Disaster Risk Reduction'. Comprising 33 representatives from ministries, departments, agencies, civil society, and local communities, this body has primary responsibility for generating coherence across DRR, adaptation and development interventions. Furthermore, the act mandates regional, district and chiefdom level coordination, and enacts the establishment of a national disaster management fund. A new multi-hazard national integrated emergency plan maps out the roles of different stakeholders: government officials, UN Agencies, international organisations, NGOs, volunteer organisations and all other disaster management key stakeholders. In addition, local government councils now have DRM legal responsibility and budget allocations. It is expected that these instruments and dispositions will enable government agencies to mainstream resilience-seeking activities into their cross-sectoral development strategies, plans, and programmes (see Figure 8.1).

Nevertheless, there is still significant scope to bridge DRM decentralisation efforts with the resilience-seeking practices of the urban poor. For instance, a multistakeholder national platform (NPF) for DRM and climate change adaptation was launched in 2011. The aim was to promote the integration of resilience-seeking strategies into national development policies, plans and strategies, yet implementation on the ground remained patchy. In 2013, the GoSL commissioned a further study to assess DRM capacities to act in three districts, including Freetown (IFRC, 2012). Yet, plans to pilot capacity-building and to expand the initiative to the rest of the country are still to be implemented. The effective inclusion of informal settlements in DRM policy formulation and implementation calls for bolder actions in decentralisation efforts.

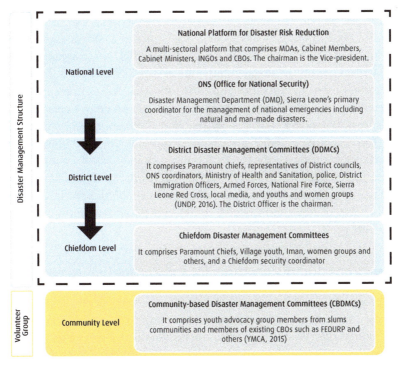

Figure 8.1 Disaster risk management (DRM) structure. Source: A. Allen, B. Koroma et al (2020), © Routledge with permission.

The residents of informal settlements still respond to extensive risks on their own and through their collectives, notably the Freetown Federation of the Urban Poor (FEDURP) and through grassroots DRM structures, such as community-based disaster management committees (CDMCs) and Community Health Workers (CHWs). These local networks – which include traditional authorities and community stakeholders – are acknowledged in the institutional DRM structure but considered voluntary groups and ad-hoc structures. However, local communities account for the bulk of resilience-seeking efforts and investments in Freetown, often pursued through non-financial contributions (labour and manpower) and one-off investments to meet identified shared needs through household contributions. These grassroots practices fill the critical gap left by government structures, while straddling formalised-informalised spaces. CDMCs play a key role in sharing DRM knowledge, reporting disaster events and building localised responses, but they operate without legal acknowledgement and support by DRM official bodies.

Local resilience-seeking practices are often supported by the Freetown City Council, Catholic Relief Services (CRS), Young Men's Christian Association (YMCA), Sierra Leone Red Cross, United Nations World Food Programme (WFP) and the Centre of Dialogue on Human Settlement and Poverty Alleviation (CODOHSAPA). These organisations are also engaged in shaping national DRM policy models and ideals. Informal networks established by ESAs mostly operate in response to disaster events, but also play an important role in assessing damages and conducting scoping activities, feeding their findings to ONS and other NGOs to coordinate relief/recovery efforts. While the 2020 DRM policy framework recognises the crucial role of community-based organisations and their leadership in supporting the NDMA in resilience-building, it remains to be seen how this translates into enabling powers and the allocation of resources to these community-based structures over the coming years.

Junctures and disjunctures for transformative change

The previous section reveals why and how certain resilience-seeking policy narratives and practices have matured over time. We now scrutinise specific junctures when discursive and material practices have changed, expanding the political space to tackle risk traps. Such moments could be seen as what Capoccia and Kelemen (2007) define as 'critical junctures' encompassing accelerated moments of decision-making with potential impacts for transformative change. The action-research work conducted by the authors in Freetown sought to expand the room for manoeuvre opened by policy commitments at the national level towards the decentralisation of DRM and a shift from risk mitigation to resilience-building. The rest of this section reflects on key moments from within this process.

Grounding political spaces

Carving political spaces to advance the decentralisation of DRM governance involved building upon the apparent fragilities of the institutional channels in place to ground a more proactive approach incorporating the experience, voice and learning of those most at risk.

As discussed, DRM decentralisation has been ubiquitous on paper but vaguely operationalised in practice. While community-based disaster risk management committees (CBDRMCs) were identified as the lowest DRM governance level in policy documents, on the ground they operated to implement ad-hoc awareness-raising and post-disaster relief in response to specific disaster events, such as the Ebola crisis. In 2014, a new city-wide platform emerged called the Pull Slum Pan Pipul (PSPP) or Freetown Urban Slum Initiative. Initially funded by Comic Relief (a UK-based international charity organisation), this platform brought together five non-governmental organisations (Restless Development, Youth Development Movement, BRAC Sierra Leone, CODOHSAPA, and YMCA) with SLURC and FEDURP. This development offered a fruitful juncture to invigorate the CBDRMCs, to expand their scope, and articulate their role with other collectives of the urban poor.

In discussion with the PSPP platform, communities from 15 informal settlements across the Western, Central and Eastern districts of Freetown joined Urban ARK to understand risk accumulation and to seek new ways to respond to their problems. Through this process, participant organisations acquired new capacities to act and became recognised as legitimate local structures in the wider architecture of DRM governance in Freetown. The pivotal role of organisations such as SLURC was essential to carve and sustain active interfaces between grassroots and decentralised bodies, and various government levels. The strategic action plans developed through these structures led to their recognition by the Mayor of Freetown City Council and were cemented via an agreement to develop settlement-wide strategic action plans as part of the updated Freetown Structural Plan.

Reframing what is to be made resilient

Creating political spaces to improve the scope and impact of resilience-seeking practices requires more than DRM decentralised structures. As argued above, risk accumulation is highly invisible, even to those who are directly caught in risk traps (Osuteye et al., 2016). Thus, activating new capacities to capture risk traps across time and space is essential to break the normalisation of such processes. Working through existing grassroots DRM structures, a bold attempt at co-producing relevant and community-led knowledge was adopted in 15 informal settlements. Workshops led by the Urban ARK team brought together community residents and other stakeholders involved in urban planning and risk governance, and fieldwork was led by the communities and their collectives over a six-month period. The findings were fed into collective discussions and exchange visits across settlements and into action plans co-designed with governmental and non-governmental organisations. To prioritise the community-voice and experience, three participatory methods were adopted to capture risk accumulation across time and space, and to identify what capacities to act and practices converge in efforts to tackle risk traps (Allen, Osuteye et al., 2020).

Figure 8.2 Research team mapping risks. Source: A. Allen, B. Koroma et al (2020), © Routledge with permission.

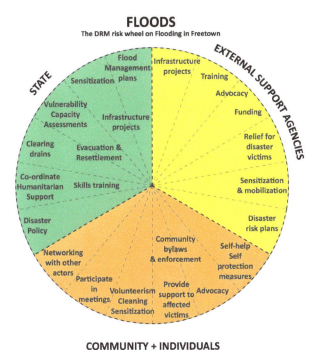

FLOODS
The DRM risk wheel on Flooding in Freetown

STATE

Flood Management plans
Sensitization
Vulnerability Capacity Assessments
Infrastructure projects
Clearing drains
Evacuation & Resettlement
Co-ordinate Humanitarian Support
Skills training
Disaster Policy
Networking with other actors
Participate in meetings
Volunteerism Cleaning Sensitization

Infrastructure projects
Training
Advocacy
Funding
Relief for disaster victims
Sensitization & mobilization
Disaster risk plans
Self-help Self protection measures
Advocacy

EXTERNAL SUPPORT AGENCIES

Community bylaws & enforcement
Provide support to affected victims

COMMUNITY + INDIVIDUALS

Figure 8.3 The DRM risk wheel on flooding in Freetown. Source: A. Allen, B. Koroma et al (2020), © Routledge with permission.

First, settlement timelines were used to plot risk events over time, outlining socio-demographic changes and the actions adopted to improve adequate housing, protective services, and infrastructures. These timelines revealed landmark events that shaped local risk perceptions and experiences. A forensic approach to these turning points helped to understand when and why these changes triggered different ways of acting. For example, eviction threats were often found as junctures that activated collective action towards risk prevention. Second, community-led mapping built upon the previous methods to produce geo-referenced information and a risk profile of each covered settlement in Freetown through transect walks, observation and collective discussions. The information collected was fed into 'ReMapRisk', an online platform created by the authors to document and monitor how risk accumulation cycles materialise over time, where and why. Hazards, vulnerabilities, and capacities to act were captured using co-designed surveys through open-source mobile phone applications, which community dwellers were trained to use (see Figures 8.2 and 8.3).

This tool allows the visualisation of multi-variable enquiries into maps, as well as an interactive assessment of the capacity to act of residents, authorities, and support organisations in relation to specific or multiple hazards and vulnerabilities. It records the type of interventions implemented to reduce risk threats and their spatial distribution. The mapping process was essential to render visible the ongoing internalisation of various hazards that over time consolidate risk traps. As previously discussed, while shock events are tackled through the different means available within existing DRM structures, slow-burn risks tend to be internalised by local dwellers as something that is part of their everyday life and must be tackled through individual efforts.

Third, DRM 'wheels' were used to map out the universe of resilience-seeking practices converging around a particular challenge and to assess their scope and impact. As an example, Figure 8.4 shows all the practices adopted to deal with flooding risk across different informal settlements in Freetown. The wheel highlights the role of ESAs and the implicit dependency on intermittent projects and donor funding. Attributing weight to the resources devoted to each practice revealed gaps between what is planned and done. It also revealed overlapping efforts concentrated on awareness-raising and disaster-relief actions. By discussing what could be done differently, how and with whom, the wheel provided a relational map of practices, enabling the identification of alternative options and what they would entail.

Figure 8.4 Screenshot of ReMapRisk Freetown. Source: © Authors

Doing things differently

Strategic action-planning was instrumental in inducing ways of 'doing things differently', expanding the scope of existing resilience-seeking practices to tackle ongoing injustices. The reframed diagnosis built by local communities fed into the design and implementation of specific projects to tackle risk accumulation. These included 14 strategic action plans produced by local community organisations from 15 informal settlements, roughly just under a quarter of all informal settlements in the city, which benefitted around 120,000 people.

The PSPP platform established governance arrangements to support the implementation of the pilot initiatives co-designed by local communities, while FEDURP managed the funds disbursal, monitoring and reporting progress on implementation and challenges. This process helped to build a shared vision based on local needs and promoted local discussions on equally shared responsibilities and benefits. Iterative planning and exchange across all settlements enabled a shift from reactive interventions to more strategic resilience-seeking actions. The latter included slope stabilisation and tree planting to reduce the risk of landslides and rock falls, improved drainage infrastructure to reduce flooding risk, and a combination of actions to improve solid waste handling, safe sanitation, and water access to tackle the incidence of water borne diseases, among others. Some initiatives focused on developing 'soft' embedded collective actions to address multiple critical challenges, such as the development of a co-managed mechanism to enforce zero-banking, prevent eviction threats and enable environmental rehabilitation along coastal settlements, which we explore in the next section. The process set up valuable precedents for collective interventions across settlements and raised awareness of the wider actions required at the city level, for instance, by identifying hot spots where poor waste disposal or infrastructural works obstruct the flow of water into the sea.

Overall, the action planning process paved the way for the PSPP platform to play a key role in a new city-wide initiative led by the Office of the Mayor, dubbed Transform Freetown. This expanded the political space for collectives of the urban poor to engage strategically with urban resilience planning. The outcomes are indicative of how to shape more inclusive and sensitive interventions to tackle risk accumulation at scale. They mark a juncture in urban governance and planning discourse in the city with potential scope to articulate informed grassroots demands into city-wide institutional responses.

Forging co-produced strategies

Beyond concrete interventions, the following key strategies were identified in partnership with local communities to tackle structural responses to risk accumulation, while strengthening in-situ resilience.

Environmental coastal rehabilitation

Communities settled in fragile and risk-prone areas can play an active role in safeguarding vital ecosystems that support the life and economy of Freetown now and into the future. Over the last year, progress has been made in some coastal communities towards zero-banking pacts to ensure that expansion over flood-prone areas is limited and that mangroves and creeks are preserved. These efforts require active alliances between local community organisations and municipal and national authorities. For example, in the coastal settlements of Cockle Bay, a co-management committee has been established with representatives from the community, FEDURP and National Protection Environmental Agency (NPEA) and tasked with the responsibility of enforcing community by-laws for the protection/wise use of the mangrove ecosystem. Setting a valuable precedent for other coastal settlements, the pact requires equal support and recognition of tenants and landlords to participate. While not free of challenges, this initiative demonstrates how a juncture has been productively exploited by linking local practices and community bylaws with governmental bodies to articulate social and environmental objectives and ultimately the reproduction of risk mitigation along the coast.

Cooperative disaster risk reduction (DRR)

Cooperative DRR involves strengthening the capacity of informal settlements' residents to deal with risk through collective responses that are responsive to heterogeneous realities and experiences shaped by the intersection of gender, tenure security and location within each settlement. For example, for people who live in dense compound housing and are seasonally displaced by flood events within and outside the settlement, their ability to act depends on social networks, including family members and friends, CBOs and savings groups. Strengthening these networks can help to prepare, prevent, and recover from flood events, providing an alternative to relocation, which disrupts social networks.

As another example, while institutions and dwellers are fully aware of the contribution of poor solid waste management to the incidence of flooding, the lack of waste management options still leads to waste disposal into drains and waterways. By increasing cooperative efforts between the various CBOs, community volunteers and authorities, the settlements could enhance their community waste management systems, for instance, by implementing regular cleaning days of communal areas and targeted areas that are underserved by existing initiatives.

Tenure security and collaborative upgrading

A sizeable portion of Freetown's dwellers in informal settlements live under highly uncertain tenure conditions. Many of them are tenants, who are often off the radar of government and even community-based collectives. Furthermore, tenants face contrasting outcomes depending on whether they are on short-term or longer-term agreements. While the former find little incentive to invest time in the collective life of the settlement, those enjoying a higher degree of tenure certainty are more likely to play an active role in collective organisation and community-led upgrading efforts.

In many settlements, landlord-tenant agreements are in place to recognise individual investments made at the household level through rental deductions. Such arrangements incentivise tenants to undertake improvements in housing and basic services, that in turn have positive impacts on the health of children and the elderly, and of the community as a whole. After fire episodes, in many cases reconstruction is led by tenants who contribute materials and labour to rebuild their structures; while landlords agreed to rent-free periods to compensate for their investments. Beyond this example, tenure security can be enhanced by protecting land and housing rights through collective usufruct entitlements.

In community-led upgrading, inclusivity is essential to help address issues of access, location, affordability and management in the provision of vital services. This requires working together with local authorities and utility providers to ensure more flexible payment options that match the needs of different local dwellers. Co-managed services also need to develop more transparent and effective mechanisms to redirect collected fees to additional development initiatives, where they are most needed.

Resource mobilisation

As mentioned previously, local communities contribute the bulk of the resources deployed to abate risk. However, external support is required not just in the form of one-off interventions, but also to leverage efforts and scale-up community-led interventions in a responsive and inclusive manner. The experience of Colbot settlement sets a valuable precedent on how to enhance community funding capacity while leveraging external resources. In 2017, after a serious flood that affected 7,000 individuals and caused mass displacement, the Cline Town Community Disaster Management Committee (CDMC) was created to strengthen community responses to environmental risk. The CDMC embarked on an ambitious initiative which consisted of hiring an excavator to clear the main drainage channel. This was paid for through household contributions which amounted to 40 million Leones, with an additional 23 million leveraged from the Red Cross. The project was unique as it was planned, carried out and largely funded by the community and it greatly reduced the impact of flooding in 2018. The experience has demonstrated that communities can successfully mobilise resources, but also highlights the need to devise funding and savings mechanisms that pull together community resources as well as external funds in a sustainable manner. Despite limited governmental and private resources, there is scope for developing resilient financing systems to improve the living conditions in informal settlements across the city. Central to these financing systems is the ability to capture the existing financial, technical, and organisational capacities of local dwellers, government institutions and civil society organisations at the local to city-wide scales.

Expanded political spaces for bridged resilience?

Throughout the chapter we have explored how risk traps become solidified over time in specific locations, often with disproportional impacts upon the most vulnerable groups. This reinforces the need to re-evaluate the actual impact of resilience-seeking practices across time and space, as it is through such analytical perspectives that risk trajectories become visible and therefore amenable to more transformative approaches.

Looking at risk accumulation reveals that the question of 'resilience to what' typically points to a wide risk continuum, where large hazards represent only tipping points and yet attract the bulk of governmental and ESAs' resources and efforts. This confronts us not only with slow-onset disasters but, more significantly, with slow-onset risk cumulative trajectories. Exploring the question of 'resilience by whom', reveals that while typically the urban poor account for the bulk of collective and individual resilience-seeking efforts and investments, over time such efforts often erode their capacity to act, particularly when assuming the form of individual coping strategies. Furthermore, even collective resilience-seeking efforts may unwillingly reinforce patterns of risk consolidation, externalisation, and inclusion.

The analysis reveals that the political space within which urban resilience-seeking practices operate in Freetown and other African cities might be bounded in several ways. The first and most obvious refers to the adoption of what could be defined as an 'instrumental' approach to DRM decentralisation, by which local community collectives are faced with additional implementation responsibilities, but often without the required recognition and resources to feed into wider city resilience-seeking visions and planning strategies.

A second challenge refers to the way in which power dynamics might reproduce patterns of exclusion even within what might be externally regarded as decentralised local community structures. In Freetown, a large proportion of those living in informal settlements are tenants. Contrary to widespread perception, many tenants are not recent migrants but have lived in the city for a long time. They typically live in precarious and overcrowded structures and are at the mercy of sudden price increases due to the high demand for rental accommodation, particularly in the most central informal settlements. This means that many often move from one settlement to another over short periods, in turn making it difficult to consolidate their affiliation with local community organisations. Thus, tenants remain the weakest link in the grounded networks working to address risk accumulation. This is the case even for grassroots platforms such as FEDURP. While the federation continues to make concerted efforts to include tenants, federated members report the difficulty of engaging tenants in self-enumerations and collective savings.

A third challenge refers to the boundaries of decentralised bodies or, in other words, the evolving architecture of these political spaces. Often, efforts to decentralise DRM rely on highly centralised bureaucratic agencies that bypass local government authorities. One assumption embedded in DRM governance is that technically well-functioning bureaucratic arrangements need to be in place to deliver resilient outcomes. However, such arrangements often have little relation to the lived practices adopted on the ground by state actors, ESAs, and ordinary citizens. This points to the need to further understand the disjuncture between Western idealisations of what states should be and do, and to consider the multiple histories, trajectories and practices through which state actors go about DRM practices in relation to other actors of civil society, particularly those deemed to be more vulnerable to risk. It also points to the need to acknowledge that statutory and customary systems are deeply imbricate in the running of everyday affairs in African cities – DRM included – and the influence of external support agencies engaged in development aid in shaping both the national adoption and ground implementation of DRM policy models and ideals.

To conclude, the analysis suggests that the ability of emerging, decentralised DRM structures and ongoing grassroots responses to tackle risk accumulation cannot be disassociated from a critical reading of the extent to which the political space in which resilience-seeking practices operates. Articulating an active call for justice across urban resilience readings and interventions is critical to challenge the internalisation and normalisation of risk, as yet another dimension to be endured by the urban poor. The State continues to have a key responsibility in enabling their right to the city in a relational way and across multiples scales, by engaging more progressively with the actual conditions that structure risk and injustices as inherent conditions of incremental urbanisation and urban development.

Notes

1   This chapter is based on a slightly modified version of a previous publication by the authors (Allen, Koroma et al., 2020).
2   For more information see https://www.urbanark.org/.
3   The DPU MSc ESD/SLURC Learning Alliance was established to support transformative action towards a socially and environmentally just Freetown, bringing together staff and postgraduate students at the DPU practice module of the MSc Environment and Sustainable Development (MSc ESD), the Sierra Leone Urban Research Centre (SLURC), the Federation of Rural and Urban Poor (FEDURP) and Centre of Dialogue on Human Settlement and Poverty Alleviation (CODOHSAPA). For more information visit: https://www.esdlearningalliance.net.

References

Adderley, R. M. (2006). 'New Negroes from Afric': Slave trade abolition and free African settlement in the nineteenth-century Caribbean. Bloomington: Indiana University Press.

Allen, A., Belkow, T., de los Rios, S., Escalante Estrada, C., Lambert, R., Poblet, R., & Zilbert Zoto, L. (2015). Urban Risk: In search of new perspectives. Clima sin Riesgo, Policy Brief No 1. Accessed 2 December 2021. http://www.climasinriesgo.net/wp-content/uploads/2015/07/CSR_Policy_Doc_August-2015_ENG_WEB.pdf

Allen, A. Griffin, L., & Johnson, C. (Eds). (2017). Environmental Justice and Resilience in the Global South. New York: Palgrave McMillan.

Allen, A., Koroma, B., Manda, M., Osuteye, E., & Lambert, R. (2020). Urban risk readdressed: bridging resilience-seeking practices in African cities. In M. A. Burayidi, A. Allen, J. Twigg & C. Wamsler (Eds), The Routledge Handbook of Urban Resilience (pp. 331–348). London: Routledge.

Allen, A., Osuteye, E., Koroma, B., & Lambert, R. (2020). Unlocking urban risk trajectories in Freetown's informal settlements. In M. Pelling (Ed.), Breaking Cycles of Risk Accumulation in African Cities (pp. 55–61). Nairobi: UN-Habitat.

Allen, A., Zilbert Soto, L., Wesely, J., in collaboration with Belkow, T., Ferro, V., Lambert, R., Langdown, I., & Samanamú, A. (2017). From state agencies to ordinary citizens: reframing risk-mitigation investments and their impact to disrupt urban risk traps in Lima, Peru, *Environment and Urbanization*, *29*(2): 477–502. https://doi.org/10.1177/0956247817706061

Banton, M. (1969). *A Western African City: A study of tribal life in Freetown*. London: Oxford University Press.

Bull-Kamanga, L., Diagne, K., Lavell, A., Leon, E., Lerise, F., MacGregor, H., Maskrey, A., Meshack, M., Pelling, M., Reid, H., Satterthwaite, D., Songsore, J., Westgate, K., & Yitambe, A. (2003). From everyday hazards to disasters: the accumulation of risk in urban areas. *Environment and Urbanization*, *15*(1): 193–204.

Capoccia, G., & Kelemen, R. D. (2007). The Study of critical junctures: theory, narrative, and counterfactuals in historical institutionalism. *World Politics*, *59*(3): 341–369.

Coaffee, J., & Lee, P. (2016). *Urban Resilience: Planning for risk, crisis and uncertainty*. London: Palgrave.

Cornwall, A., & Coehlo, V. S. (2006). *Spaces for Change? The politics of citizen participation in new democratic arenas*. Chicago: University of Chicago Press.

Dodman, D., Leck, H., Rusca, M., & Colenbrander, S. (2017). African urbanisation and urbanism: implications for risk accumulation and reduction. *International Journal of Disaster Risk Reduction*, *26*: 7–15.

DPU MSc ESD & SLURC Learning Alliance. (2019). Co-learning for Action to Transform Freetown. Brief. Accessed 25 June 2024. https://www.slurc.org/uploads/1/0/9/7/109761391/pb _introduction.pdf

Frediani, A. A. (2021). Freetown: City scoping study. Manchester: African Cities Research Consortium, University of Manchester.

GoSL. (2002). National Security and Central Intelligence Act No.10 of 2002. Accessed 18 December 2021. http://www.sierra-leone.org/Laws/2002-10.pdf

Hayward, C. R. (2000) *De-Facing Power*. Cambridge: Cambridge University Press.

IFRC. (2012). International Disaster Response Laws (IDRL) in Sierra Leone. Accessed 17 December 2021. https://disasterlaw.ifrc.org/sites/default/files/media/disaster_law/2020-09/1213700 -IDRL-Sierra %20Leone-EN-LR %20 %281 %29.pdf

Jaglin, S., Repussard, C., & Belbéoc'h, A. (2011). Decentralisation and governance of drinking water services in small West African towns and villages (Benin, Mali, Senegal): the arduous process of building local governments. *Canadian Journal of Development Studies / Revue Canadienne d'études Du Développement*, *32*(2), 119–138. https://doi.org/10.1080/02255189.2011.596021

Lynch, K., Nel, E., & Binns, T. (2020). 'Transforming Freetown': Dilemmas of planning and development in a West African city. *Cities*, 101, 102694.

McGee, R. (2004). Unpacking policy: actors, knowledge and spaces. In K. Brock, R. McGee, & J. Gaventa (Eds), *Unpacking Policy: Actors, knowledge and spaces in poverty reduction* (pp. 1–26). Kampala: Fountain Press.

Myers, G. (2011). African Cities: Alternative visions of urban theory and practice. London, New York: Zed Books.

Osuteye, E., Johnson, C., & Brown, D. (2016). The data gap: An analysis of data availability on disaster losses in sub-Saharan African cities. Urban Africa Risk Knowledge Working Paper No. 11.

Parnell, S., & Pieterse, E. A. (2014). *Africa's Urban Revolution*. London: Zed.

Parnell, S. (2016). Defining a global urban development agenda. *World Development, 78*, 529–540. doi:http://dx.doi.org/10.1016/j.worlddev.2015.10.028

Resnick, D. (2014). Urban governance and service delivery in African cities: The role of politics and policies. *Development Policy Review*, *32*, s3–s17.

Satterthwaite, D. (2016). Background paper: small and intermediate urban centres in sub-Saharan Africa. Urban ARK Working Paper No 6. London: IIED.

Simone, A & Abouhani, A (2005) *Urban Africa: Changing contours of survival in the city*. Dakar: CODESERIA.

Webster, N., & Engberg-Petersen, L. (2002). *In the Name of the Poor: Contesting political space for poverty*. London: Zed Books.

Ziervogel, G., Pelling, M., Cartwright, A., Chu, E., Deshpande, T., Harris, L., Hyams, K., Kaunda, J., Klaus, B., Michael, K., Pasquini, L., Pharoah, R., Rodina, L., Scott, D., & Zweig, P. (2017). Inserting rights and justice into urban resilience: a focus on everyday risk. *Environment and Urbanization*, *29*(1), 123–138. https://doi.org/10.1177/0956247816686905

9
Community-led planning in Freetown
Beatrice De Carli, Alexandre Apsan Frediani,
Braima Koroma and Joseph M. Macarthy

Introduction

This chapter[1] discusses the process and outcomes of three community area action plans (CAAPs) undertaken in Freetown over the period 2017–2021. CAAPs were first developed in response to the introduction of action area plans in the Freetown Structure Plan 2013–2028, as mechanisms that can enable planning processes focused on the improvement of local areas in Freetown. In practice, CAAP is a proactive planning tool for transforming local areas through a bottom-up process that both complements and challenges, formal policy frameworks.

A key aspect of action area plans is that they should 'indicate the precise private and public use of all land and transport systems, parcel numbers, eventual reservation or protection lines, as well as development and building regulations to be followed when using parcels included in the plan' (Government of Sierra Leone, 2014, p. 16). The underlying assumption is that area action plans can synchronise development in local areas with citywide planning principles and processes. However, the current policy does not indicate how these plans should be implemented and by whom. This limits space for local participation (Macarthy et al., 2019).

The idea of creating community area action plans in Freetown first emerged within this context as a means of complementing existing planning procedures and supporting the implementation of area action plans through a localised, community-led approach. The CAAP process was first designed and tested through a collaboration between the Sierra Leone Urban Research Centre (SLURC), The Bartlett Development Planning Unit of University College London (DPU), Architecture Sans Frontières-UK

(ASF-UK), and the Federation of Urban and Rural Poor of Sierra Leone (FEDURP-SL). The process draws from ASF-UK Change by Design (CbD) methodology. In 2018–2019, two CAAPs were developed in the settlements of Dworzark and Cockle Bay, with a third CAAP produced in Portee-Rokupa in 2021–2022. Each of these CAAPs captures residents' needs and desires for their local area and outlines possibilities for its future transformation.

This chapter describes the collaborative planning process that underpinned each CAAP and analyses the findings from these experiences; focusing on residents' aspirations and their desired pathways to change. Following this introduction, the paper includes three sections. Section 2 outlines the story of the CAAPs and discusses aspects of the methodology used. Section 3 discloses key findings from each CAAP. Finally, section 4 examines future possibilities for the CAAP and for community-led planning in Freetown.

Story of the CAAP

The CAAP process so far has been jointly facilitated by SLURC and ASF-UK, using and adapting the ASF-UK Change by Design methodology for participatory design and planning. In 2018, the methodology was applied in parallel in two settlements – Cockle Bay and Dworzark – where SLURC had strong community ties and had developed in-depth knowledge of their social and physical makeup. In 2021, a similar methodology was used to develop a CAAP for Portee-Rokupa, where SLURC and their partners had also built strong relationships with residents and their organisations and had participated in other action-research initiatives before the CAAP commencing.

The name Change by Design describes both a methodology and a knowledge-sharing programme. The programme was initiated by ASF-UK in 2011 as a platform for developing planning and design methodologies that can support community-led informal settlement upgrading (Frediani, 2016). Change by Design positions participation beyond formal planning systems and highlights everyday life as a key site for the creation of planning frameworks and procedures (De Carli and Frediani, 2021). As such it connects to other approaches elevating everyday acts of city making (Frediani and Cociña, 2019), through an emphasis on self-help housing (Turner, 1976), the social production of habitat (Ortíz Flores, 2007) and insurgent practices (Holston, 2008). It also focuses on devising open-ended scenarios and options for change, rather than on determining set courses of action (Hamdi, 2004; Hamdi, 2010).

The practical Change by Design methodology has four stages: diagnosis, dreaming, developing, and defining. The diagnosis stage assesses local patterns and situations. The dreaming stage explores the needs and aspirations of residents. The developing stage sketches out potential pathways to change. The defining stage sets out concrete plans for action. The initial stages facilitate co-design activities at three scales: micro (dwelling/home), meso (community/neighbourhood) and macro (city); and include participatory research around urban policy and planning systems. In the later stages, the findings from scale-specific activities are brought together into a collaborative planning exercise, called the portfolio of options, that explores cross-scale interactions and assesses trade-offs between scales (Figure 9.1).

The Change by Design methodology places a strong emphasis on initiating discussions about personal and collective dreams and aspirations for the future. However, in a context where significant structural barriers exist, this approach can pose risks. Participants may feel frustrated or disillusioned if they perceive their aspirations as unattainable due to the challenges they face, leading to a decrease in motivation and engagement. Nevertheless, discussing aspirations also plays an important role in supporting mobilisation processes. Grounded in a collaborative, reflective process, they can serve as a catalyst for identifying strategies to overcome barriers and inspire collective action.

The adaptation of this methodology for the context of Freetown began with a pilot workshop held in 2017 in Cockle Bay, testing how the Change by Design process could link to the ongoing mobilisation and enumeration work carried out jointly by FEDURP and CODOHSAPA

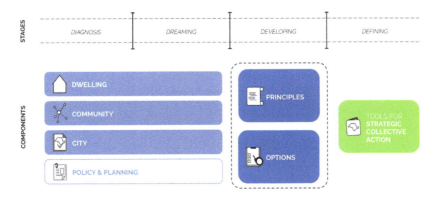

Figure 9.1 The Change by Design methodology: key stages and components. Source: © B. De Carli for ASF-UK (2018)

(Frediani et al., 2018). Following the pilot workshop, the first two CAAPs in Cockle Bay and Dworzark were developed in 2018 over one year, including nine months of field-based research and three months of data processing.

In each settlement, fieldwork was divided into four phases, according to the scales and stages of the Change by Design methodology. The first phase focused on the Policy and Planning aspects of informal settlement upgrading in Freetown. This phase aimed to examine the context of upgrading processes in Freetown, and to define how the CAAP would fit within the local and national urban policy environment. The following three phases each focused on one scale of design: home, community and city. Within each scale, activities followed the Change by Design cycle, from diagnosis to developing. The Home phase sought to understand the current housing conditions in each settlement, and to imagine with residents what upgraded housing could be like. The Community phase focused on social dynamics surrounding collective spaces (such as streets and community facilities) and infrastructures (transport, water, sanitation, energy and information). The City scale focused on citywide processes, conditions and experiences, with the aim to explore spaces in the city that are relevant to the lives of local residents and that identify residents' values and aspirations for the city as a whole. Findings from these four phases were distilled into a set of design principles and options for informal settlement upgrading. These formed the basis for the fifth and last phase of fieldwork which consisted of a portfolio of options exercise. The exercise brought together the four streams of work and explored the kind of negotiation needed between different scales and priorities to achieve a cohesive set of guidelines for the upgrading of each settlement. By the end of the session, participants had created an action plan consisting of a modelled and a drawn layout of the upgraded settlement, alongside a set of organisational strategies.

The practical activities carried out during the CAAP process included a variety of creative methods such as drawing-elicited interviews, participatory modelling, group mapping activities, and participatory photography (Figures 9.2 and 9.3). These drew from the broader traditions of participatory rural appraisal (Chambers, 1994) and community action planning (Hamdi, 2010) and specifically, from the repertoire of participatory design methods and tools developed by ASF-UK (French et al., 2011; Frediani et al., 2014; Frediani et al., 2015; Bainbridge et al., 2016; Frediani, 2016; Bennett et al., 2018; Frediani et al., 2018; De Carli, 2020; De Carli and Frediani, 2021). All the activities

Figure 9.2 Participatory modelling at the home scale. Source: © SLURC

had a strong focus on social diversity, with the aim to reveal and recognise the diverse range of experiences, needs and aspirations present within each settlement.

Outputs from the first CAAP processes in Cockle Bay and Dworzark included two reports (SLURC & ASF-UK, 2019a, 2019b); a set of illustrated, foldable pamphlets in English summarising both the process and key recommendations of the CAAPs; a series of illustrated posters in Krio for dissemination within the local communities; and a two-minute jingle (audio recording) also in Krio, for distribution via social media and messaging apps. A third set of similar documents is currently in the making for Portee-Rokupa (SLURC & ASF-UK, 2023). Parallel to the place-based outputs, ASF-UK led the production of a two-part Freetown Community Planning Toolkit, with the first volume focusing on settlement profiling (ASF-UK & SLURC, 2022) and the second illustrating the community action planning (ASF-UK & SLURC, 2023).

After the completion of the CAAPs, the institutions involved also agreed that a more detailed evidence base was needed, to substantiate the principles, options and guidelines included in the plans and support advocacy. For this reason, two in-depth community profiles were produced for Cockle Bay and Dworzark over the course of 2019, drawing from both previous research by SLURC and new participatory data collection processes (SLURC, 2022a; SLURC, 2023). When starting the process in Portee-Rokupa, the community profile was carried out as a first step in 2020 and informed the development of a CAAP in 2021 (SLURC, 2022b).

Due to the experimental nature of the process, the development of the first two CAAPs in Cockle Bay and Dwozarck was led by ASF-UK in collaboration with SLURC. Co-design activities were coordinated by an ASF-UK field volunteer who was based in Freetown for the duration of the project. Day-to-day data collection and analysis were aided locally by researchers at SLURC and remotely by the ASF-UK project team. Later in Portee-Rokupa, co-design activities were led by SLURC, with remote methodological support from ASF-UK. In each of the neighbourhoods where this process took place, the co-design activity included approximately thirty residents, providing representation across identity groups and different areas of the settlements.

The development of the CAAPs also involved designing a grassroots-based governance system, ensuring that the process would remain accountable to residents and their organisations. For this reason, in 2018 SLURC and FEDURP facilitated the forming of two community-based Steering Committees, one in Cockle Bay and one in Dworzark; and a city-wide advisory committee with oversight of the CAAP process across the two sites.

Figure 9.3 Participatory mapping exercise at the community scale.
Source: © SLURC

The aim of the advisory committee was to provide strategic advice and link the CAAPs to other urban processes relevant to informal settlement upgrading. This committee comprised representatives from local and national governments: Freetown City Council, Sierra Leone Ministry of Lands and Housing, and the Office of National Security; from non-governmental organisations involved in supporting residents in informal settlements: the Young Men's Christian Association – Sierra Leone (YMCA-SL), and the Centre of Dialogue on Human Settlement and Poverty Alleviation (CODOHSAPA); from city-wide grassroots groups such as FEDURP; and from each of the settlements involved in the planning process. For each CAAP, the Advisory Committee met the ASF-UK/SLURC team at the beginning of the planning process to discuss the strategic value and audience of the initiative, during the participatory process to monitor direction, and at the end of it to provide feedback on what had been done and help identify future steps.

Secondly, a local steering committee was set up in each of the settlements with two primary aims: to inform the development and application of the CAAP methodology step-by-step; and to ensure that all planning activities would meaningfully involve a representative sample of the settlement's residents. This included supporting the process of community mobilisation and organisation that underpinned the CAAP and linking this novel planning process to other community-led practices such as enumerations. The steering committee met the ASF-UK/SLURC team at the end of each phase of fieldwork, to provide feedback on the process thus far and give advice as to the best ways forward. The steering committee also met the team at the end of the whole process to provide feedback on its development and review the draft outputs before they were finalised.

With the support of SLURC and their research partners, in the years following the first two CAAPs, these two committees consolidated into a network of locally based community learning platforms and a city learning platform. The latter is a city-wide initiative that operates through periodic meetings and represents a variety of voices and organisations to discuss experiences, coordinate and develop proposals for the upgrading of informal settlements in Freetown. To date, these institutions remain one of the key legacies of the CAAP process, as established mechanisms for community-led urban governance.

Table 9.1 The CAAP process in Cockle Bay and Dworzark: workshops with residents and key stakeholder meetings. Source: © ASF-UK (2019)

01–02/2018	Mobilisation	Setting up of Advisory Committee / City Learning Platform	Meeting – Introduction to the process
		Setting up of Steering Committee / Community Learning Platform	Meeting – Introduction to the process
02–03/2018	Policy and Planning	Diagnosis	Interviews with key stakeholders
			Land workshop with Development Action Group (DAG)
03–04/2018	Home	Diagnosis	1 day workshop x 30 community participants
		Dreaming	1 day workshop x 30 community participants
		Developing	1 day workshop x 30 community participants
		Advisory Committee / City Learning Platform – Review findings	
		Steering Committee / Community Learning Platform – Review findings	

04–05/ 2018	Community	Diagnosis	1 day workshop x 30 community participants
		Dreaming	1 day workshop x 30 community participants
		Developing	1 day workshop x 30 community participants
		Advisory Committee / City Learning Platform – Review findings	
		Steering Committee / Community Learning Platform – Review findings	
06–07/ 2018	City	Diagnosis	1 day workshop x 30 community participants
		Dreaming	1 day workshop x 30 community participants
		Developing	1 day workshop x 30 community participants
		Advisory Committee / City Learning Platform – Review findings	
		Steering Committee / Community Learning Platform – Review findings	
08/ 2018	Portfolio of Options	Defining	1 day workshop x 30 community participants
		Advisory Committee / City Learning Platform – Review findings	
		Steering Committee / Community Learning Platform – Review findings	

Place based findings

Community area action plans stemmed from an understanding that conventional forms of planning do not always meet the needs of informal settlement residents. By contrast, the CAAP process was designed to meaningfully involve residents in shaping the planning decisions that affect them. This was based on the recognition that the knowledge and creativity of residents is valuable and important, and that their needs and aspirations should be the key drivers of local development processes. Therefore, any planning processes aiming to understand and address the challenges facing their local areas should be developed with residents' active involvement. The following section outlines the key findings that emerged from the CAAP across the three localities involved, by exploring the concerns, aspirations and priorities articulated by residents during the process.

Home

The Home scale sought to understand the current housing conditions in each settlement, and to imagine with residents what upgraded housing could be like. The aim was to explore a definition of 'home' and to capture residents' diverse values and aspirations for this fundamental component of their living environment. To this end, the team engaged residents through a variety of participatory tools aimed at developing principles and options that could guide future homemaking and housing interventions.

Building materials and typologies

The most common housing typology in Cockle Bay, Dworzark and Portee-Rokupa is a one-storey, one-room structure built with mud blocks (dirt blocks) or corrugated iron sheets (normally referred to as panbody). Incremental improvements have also led to some structures being made of concrete blocks, or a mix of these materials. Interior spaces are usually free of internal walls and most homes are organised around two key spaces: an indoor living space and an outdoor veranda. Most participants expressed concerns over the lack of privacy at home, due to the internal lack of space and overcrowding, coupled with the settlements' high density, and the proximity of other structures. Most residents also indicated the lack of protection from climate conditions as a key issue affecting them, as their homes do not protect them from either hot weather or heavy rainfalls. Panbody houses, which are the most common structures found in the three areas, are the most vulnerable to extreme weather conditions.

Safety at home

Concerns for safety featured prominently in conversations and, in many cases, residents emphasised the importance of doors, fences, and walls, as mechanisms for protecting themselves against the threat of burglary or violence. When discussing housing typologies to be built in the future, a recurring theme particularly in Cockle Bay and Dworzark was the development of clusters, including several homes organised around a shared open space. This was seen as a way of addressing safety issues, while also creating space to grow food and conduct livelihood activities.

Accessing water and sanitation

Participants often reported that their homes were not well provisioned with basic infrastructure. The CAAPs highlighted very clearly residents' need and desire to improve their access to water and sanitation facilities, as well as to electricity. Lack of safety in accessing water and sanitation was consistently voiced as a major concern for residents, and one that affects young girls most of all, as the burden of fetching water falls disproportionately on them. The CAAPs revealed a deep preoccupation with cleanness and hygiene, and throughout our engagements, participants voiced the urgent need to improve the number, quality and accessibility of toilets and water points in their local areas.

Denser, taller buildings

When thinking of their future home, most participants focused on a detached house, often two storeys high. Most aspirations were for a housing layout based on the existing one, with a parlour as the main room, linking and providing access to all other spaces. At the same time, when questioned about the future of the wider area, participants across the three sites recognised the advantages of building taller, multi-storey buildings, to provide a greater variety of housing options. Denser and taller typologies were linked to greater quality of construction, greater variety in layouts, the creation of affordable rental housing opportunities and the preservation of open space in the settlement. In a few cases, the diversification and densification of buildings was also seen as a means of increasing tenure security, to collectively avoid evictions and resist market-led displacement.

Scarcity of space and housing finance

When asked about the major barriers to upgrading their settlements, the lack of land and space to build new homes was consistently mentioned as a key challenge both to incremental upgrading and to the construction of new housing developments. For instance, in Dworzark, residents highlighted the difficulty of dealing with the area's steep topography: in Cockle Bay and Portee-Rokupa, the proximity to the coast constitutes a challenge. Alongside the physical conditions of the settlements, the lack of housing finance was perceived as a key barrier that hinders the improvement of housing conditions at scale.

Community

The community scale focused on social dynamics surrounding collective spaces (such as streets and open spaces) and infrastructures (including transport, water, sanitation, energy, and information). The aim was to understand the current conditions of shared spaces and infrastructure in each settlement and the meanings and aspirations that residents attach to them. Residents were engaged in a variety of participatory mapping and modelling activities aimed at developing principles and options for the future of their shared spaces. Options referred to both concrete interventions and ways of building partnerships and alliances for change.

Shared space in short supply

Cockle Bay, Dworzark and Portee-Rokupa are densely populated settlements, with few spaces available for recreation and collective use, including buildings (for instance community halls and religious buildings) and open spaces. Residents' assessment of the quality of these spaces varied from place to place, but the common experience is that shared buildings are usually better maintained and safer than shared open spaces. Because of the scarcity of shared spaces, most of these need to accommodate multiple uses. This can provide value (for instance, the football field in Dworzark doubles as a parking space at night) but can also generate conflict between competing and even incompatible uses, for example when recreational spaces for children are also used as waste disposal sites. These conditions affect certain groups more than others. Across the three areas, women are less likely to feel welcome in social spaces, such as restaurants and religious buildings; and many open spaces are unsuitable for children because of either their location (steep slopes, risk of fast tides) or the exposure to crime and violence. At this intersection, young girls are disproportionately less likely to have access to a safe place where they can meet with other young people outside their home.

Negotiating environmental conditions

Residents consistently reported flooding as a key issue affecting their communities. This is mostly related to the combination of heavy rainfalls and the lack of adequate stormwater drainage systems. In Dworzark, because of the steep slopes, consequences can range from minor localised flooding to major floods accompanied by land and rockslides, which can destroy buildings as well as roads and footpaths, blocking residents' access to other parts of the settlement and key spaces like mosques. In Cockle Bay and Portee-Rokupa, the risk of flooding is increased by the proximity to the sea. In Cockle Bay in particular, the wharf and other parts of the settlement are regularly overtaken by tidal waves. The destruction of the mangrove ecosystem has played a role in the coastal settlements' exposure to flooding, with increasing effects in terms of coastal erosion and soil instability. Participants across the three areas demonstrated great awareness of these issues and highlighted improvements to water drainage as key priorities for upgrading, to let water flow through their settlements without causing damage.

Safe drinking water

Access to safe drinking water emerged as another key concern of residents. This was felt strongly in Dworzark where access to water points is very difficult, as the steep terrain constrains well-digging, aggravating challenges that are common to other settlements. Child water carriers bear a disproportionate burden, travelling long distances to reach the few available wells and taps. Then, time taken to fill buckets is determined by the existing queue and velocity of the water, commonly extending into night-time. This exposes girls particularly to increased risks of harassment, both at water collection points and on the way home, with many in constant fear. In the dry season, when water scarcity is greater, girls are subjected to worse violence, enticed into selling their bodies in exchange for water. Water scarcity can be exacerbated by residents cutting the water mains or obstructing flow and it triggers tension within homes over the amounts available, who uses it, and for what. At the dreaming stage of the CAAP, residents of the three areas spent a wealth of time exploring practical solutions to water shortages, considering options such as the instalment of water tanks and the improvement of the roads and footpaths network, so that water points become safely accessible to more people.

Accessibility, connectivity and inclusion

Residents across the three settlements discussed questions of accessibility, connectivity, mobility, and transport as central concerns. They generally felt that in different ways, the three areas are not well connected to the main transport network, and that mobility within each area is difficult due to the terrain. At the dreaming stage, strong emphasis was placed on the use of more durable materials so that roads are not eroded by stormwater and flooding, and on improving the network of footpaths, stairs, and footbridges specially to deal with steep slopes and water streams. This is particularly important to ensure that spaces within the community are made accessible for children, the elderly, and people with disabilities; and mainly when it comes to vital infrastructure such as water points and toilets, as well as access to the city's wider transport network.

City

The city scale focused on citywide processes, conditions, and experiences. Activities included the exploration of spaces in the wider Freetown area that are relevant to the lives of residents, and the identification of residents' values and aspirations for the city. Participants were then asked to develop city-level interventions that could have a positive impact on their settlement, spanning issues of transport, public services, and livelihood opportunities. The resulting principles and options explored ways to improve residents' experience of Freetown.

Affordable homes to rent

Across the three settlements, participants highlighted the shortage of affordable homes to rent in Freetown. Rental housing options are only available in a few parts of the city and to a few groups: for instance, unmarried women are regularly denied apartments to rent. Discussions highlighted that residents often live in informal settlements because they do not have alternatives, and at the dreaming stage of the CAAP, participants stressed that the creation of affordable formal accommodation in well-located areas is a key issue to be addressed to make Freetown a more inclusive city. In Portee-Rokupa in particular, some of the workshop participants described their accommodation in the settlement as transitional and expressed the aspiration to move elsewhere in the future. This was an important discussion point, highlighting that upgrading processes should offer a variety of tenure options, in consideration of both long-term and transitional residents.

Basic infrastructure networks

Participants in the three sites identified the quality of urban infrastructure as a priority. In continuity with conversations held at the community scale, the issues mentioned the most were the quality of water and sanitation infrastructure and the quality of the drainage and wastewater systems. It was reported that many parts of the city lack adequate access to water and sanitation and that the drainage network is in poor condition and is often used for waste disposal. Residents voiced specific concern for how the drainage and wastewater network impacts on public health and the transmission of diseases across the city, with consequences particularly for those living in informal settlements.

Mobility and accessibility

Questions of accessibility and connectivity were also identified as a key priority, with reference to both the physical road network and the traffic management and transport systems. Participants suggested that public transport should be improved and made cheaper, and that the road network should be repaired and extended, particularly to better connect informal settlements to other parts of the city. This last point was felt strongly across the three sites, as physical improvements to the road network are seen as paramount for residents to gain access to key urban services like hospitals and to employment and livelihood opportunities.

Introducing environmental protection

Environmental protection was not highlighted as a priority at the city scale, but questions concerning the quality of the environment and the balance between urban and natural systems emerged through conversations focussing on a variety of other topics. For instance, participants highlighted the importance of tourism for local livelihoods (which led to discussing beach pollution and plastic waste management); challenges to fishing activities (leading to conversations on marine pollution); the risks associated with tidal flooding (highlighting the ongoing destruction of mangrove ecosystems) and landslides (leading to conversations around hillside deforestation). Although residents would not use this wording, the ASF-UK/SLURC team felt that environmental protection is an area that deserves specific attention in future discussions around upgrading.

Policy and planning

The policy and planning focus of the first CAAPs included two lines of work. At the beginning of the process, activities sought to explore current and emerging urban and environmental policies that could provide context both to the development of the CAAP as a novel planning tool, and to the transformation of each local area. Initial activities also included a detailed stakeholder analysis, which supported the creation of the steering and advisory committees described above. Later in the process, considerations around governance were made integral to activities concerning the home, community and city scales, and to the final portfolio of options exercise. This exercise explicitly asked residents to consider who should lead and manage the changes they had prioritised and which groups and institutions should be involved on different issues or at different stages of the upgrading process.

The policy and planning context

When the CAAP process started in 2018, there were two officially recognised documents setting out planning policies for Freetown: Town and Country Planning Act (TCPA) and Freetown Improvement Act (FIA), both published in 1960. The TCPA is not widely used as a planning document; the FIA is more commonly used but its relevance is limited, because most informal settlements emerged after its publication. More relevant to the current context is the National Land Policy of Sierra Leone (NLPSL). Created in 2014 and finally approved in 2021, the NLPSL sets out the national priorities and conditions that should guide local policy and planning processes. The Freetown Structural Plan (FSP) was also created in 2014 to provide planning direction for the municipality of Freetown. As of now, the FSP has yet to be officially adopted by the government. However, it remains the most comprehensive planning document available in Freetown to date and includes important policies that address the reality of informal settlements. For this reason, the CAAP as an instrument was designed to fulfil the policy conditions set in this document as well as in the NLPSL Simultaneously, it acknowledges international policy obligations, such as those defined by the New Urban Agenda and establishes connections with existing grassroots planning initiatives, such as community-led self-enumerations.

A rich local governance system

Against this background, the CAAP process aimed to also uncover the variety of decision-making practices and governance systems that exist in each local area. When asked about key stakeholders in their community, participants in the three settlements mapped out several leadership figures, including traditional leaders or chiefs, religious leaders, and elected councillors. Additionally, they emphasised the role played by citywide community-based organisations, namely the Federation of the Urban and Rural Poor in Cockle Bay and Dworzark, and the Freetown Eastern Slum Dwellers Association in Portee-Rokupa; and by local groups such as community disaster management committees and community health workers. This set of stakeholders was also recognised as central to the future of the three sites and during the final phases of the CAAP, residents explored various options for collectively managing change in their local areas. For example, one group from Dworzark agreed that future actions should be decided by community vote and that upgraded homes should be under shared ownership. This was recognised by other residents as an interesting way of approaching upgrading, and there was general agreement that with adequate support from local and national governments, similar arrangements could allow the community to be more sustainable in the future.

Pathways for community-led development

Debates held at the portfolio of options stage suggested that residents are eager and ready to drive change in their areas. They have sophisticated ideas about potential forms of community representation and can deal with issues concerning the inclusion of diverse voices in decision-making. Participants in the three areas also agreed that upgrading depends on the creation of partnerships involving different stakeholders, with nuanced reflections on the roles and responsibilities of different institutions. They specifically suggested that government authorities should play a significant role in several areas, from creating the conditions that would enable community groups to lead local development, to delivering affordable housing and improving mobility and transport infrastructures within local areas and in the city. Amongst the enabling factors that were discussed, access to appropriate finance was often identified as a priority. Participants agreed that access to finance is currently an obstacle to community-led development and discussed the need for grants and loans with favourable conditions for residents and community-based organisations. In Cockle Bay, participants' choices demonstrated heavy reliance on support from both national government and international NGOs, as currently there are no community finance schemes available.

Future possibilities

The CAAP was conceived as an experience of advocacy planning, as it enabled communities in informal settlements to engage in participatory planning outside official and statutory frameworks. Given that all the CAAPs were grounded in existing community-led processes, both their development and outputs played a significant role in shaping residents' city-making practices. For instance, residents of both Cockle Bay and Dworzark reported that collective decisions taken during the CAAP meetings directly informed their plans and actions for improving shared buildings and infrastructure. Therefore, the knowledge and plans generated through the

CAAPs have been used by communities not only to capture and amplify their needs and aspirations, but also to prioritise resource allocation, to plan improvements and to enforce collective norms.

At the same time, the CAAP process was also meant to influence formal planning mechanisms, providing a methodology for localising the implementation of area action plans. By emphasising the 'community scale' of area action plans, SLURC and their partners aimed to demonstrate that informal settlements residents can meaningfully participate in decision making processes that concern their city and local areas, and thus set a precedent for community-led planning in Freetown. Our ambition was that if the first CAAPs could demonstrate the feasibility and usefulness of such a process, then local and national governments would be motivated to find ways not only to endorse the CAAP but also to support its replication and institutionalisation.

Already, both Freetown City Council (FCC) and the Government of Sierra Leone have explicitly expressed support for the CAAP. FCC has recognised the CAAP as an important framework to guide the development of informal settlement upgrading initiatives in Freetown and recently adapted the methodology to carry out an action area plan in Moyiba. As of 2024, this plan remains in draft. Meanwhile, the Ministry of Planning and Economic Development has recognised the usefulness of the CAAP in situating and localising participatory methodologies, in line with the objectives and approach of the country's national strategic planning process. International development organisations like the World Bank have also demonstrated interest in learning from the CAAP experience, with the CAAP already becoming a valuable reference for the development sector both in Freetown and in Sierra Leone. In fact, the CAAPs' embeddedness within the city learning platform has been fundamental for disseminating this experience beyond Cockle Bay, Dworzark and Portee-Rokupa.

However, there are persisting challenges to the replication and institutionalisation of the CAAP methodology. As of the date of writing this contribution, formal policy and planning frameworks have not yet established the conditions for integrating a community-led approach into area action plans. Area-based planning approaches are being tested by the current municipal administration but are not integral to the council's planning practice, which tends to foreground issue- rather than place-based decision-making, as seen in the Transform Freetown agenda. As a result, informal settlement upgrading initiatives led by the local government have not taken a systematic approach to community-led spatial planning. At the same time, national ministries, while demonstrating support for the CAAP, have not yet created the policy mechanisms that would allow for financial and human resources to be allocated to its implementation.

Many factors have contributed to this slow uptake. Bureaucratic inefficiencies, complex rules and procedures, and a lack of willingness or capacity within local authorities are all contributing factors. Conflicting interests and priorities may also divert attention from the need to push the transformation process forward, resulting in slow and interrupted implementation. Power dynamics within institutions further complicate matters, making it difficult for emerging initiatives such as the CAAPs to have a tangible institutional impact in the short term.

In response to these conditions, SLURC has adopted a two-pronged strategy for scaling community-led planning in Freetown. On the one hand the organisation advocates for institutional reforms by pushing for streamlined processes and improved coordination between different government departments. Simultaneously, SLURC's approach also includes fostering participatory decision-making from the ground up and working closely with local communities to amplify their voice in shaping policies and practices.

The CAAP has played an important role in this regard. In addition to introducing changes in the policy and planning landscape, it created a space for meaningful dialogue that connects residents and their organisations to government and development actors. This approach ensures that the aspirations of the community are heard and builds ownership and accountability among stakeholders. Moving forward, a key challenge is to preserve this space of dialogue as one that is community-led and addresses the diverse needs and aspirations of informal settlement residents. One way to achieve this would be to directly connect the CAAPs with local council wards and their representative structures while also linking them with participatory budgeting instruments.

So far, the network of stakeholders involved in both the city learning platform and the relevant community learning platforms has played a key role in shaping, supporting and sustaining the CAAP as a tool for advancing community-led planning in Freetown. On the one hand, the future of the CAAP as an instrument now depends on the extent to which national and local policy will create a more supportive environment for its implementation. On the other, the CAAP will be taken forward if residents and their organisations continue valuing the process and are able to mobilise around it. At the time of the first pilot plans in Cockle Bay and Dworzark, the making of the CAAPs offered a strategic entry point to bring together a diverse set of stakeholders to jointly call for the democratisation of urban planning. Moving forward, the future of CAAP will be interlinked with the opportunities it offers to affect the politics of imagining and planning urban development in Sierra Leone.

Note

1   The collaborative processes discussed in this chapter involve a broader network of individuals who contributed to the work over the years. In addition to the authors, the team that developed, managed, and produced the CAAPs and relevant settlement profiles included Andrea Klingel, Sulaiman Kamara, Ibrahim Bangurra, and Ansumana Tarawally at SLURC, as well as Sophie Morley, Charles Wright, Francesco Pasta, and Niki Sole at ASF-UK. The project also received support from Lucia Caistor-Arendar, Tamara Khan, and Louisa Orchard. The authors would also like to extend their appreciation to the many community facilitators, as well as the residents of Cockle Bay, Dworzark, and Portee Rokupa for their time and insights.

References

ASF-UK. (2018). Change by Design. Dworzark Community Action Area Plan. Freetown: ASF-UK & SLURC.

ASF-UK & SLURC. (2022). *Freetown community planning toolkit: Settlement profiling*. London: Architecture Sans Frontières UK.

ASF-UK & SLURC. (2023). *Freetown community planning toolkit: Community action planning*. London: Architecture Sans Frontières UK.

Bainbridge, E., Bennett, J., Campkin, B., De Carli, B., Frediani, A. A., French, M., Macedo, C., Walker, J., Macgregor-Rourke, H., Issadeen, A., Matiashe, W., & du Trevou, C. (2016). Change by Design: Reimagining regeneration through participatory design in Cape Town. Workshop report (2015). London: ASF-UK.

Bennett, Jhono, du Trevou, Claire, Morley, Sophie, & Wong, Katherine. (2018). Change by Design: Tools and methods to support grassroots neighbourhood development in Cape Town. Workshop report (2017). London: ASF-UK.

Chambers, Robert. (1994). The origins and practice of Participatory Rural Appraisal. *World Development, 22*(7), 953–969.

De Carli, Beatrice. (2020). Change by Design: Imagining equitable cities. AAD Practice Research Portfolios. London: London Metropolitan Architecture.

De Carli, Beatrice, & Frediani, Alexandre A. (2021). Situated perspectives on the city: A reflection on scaling participation through design. *Environment and Urbanization, 33*(2), 376–395.

Frediani, Alexandre A. (2016). Re-imagining participatory design: Reflecting on the ASF-UK Change by Design methodology. *Design Issues, 32*(3), 98–111.

Frediani, Alexandre A., & Cociña, Camila. (2019). 'Participation as planning': strategies from the South to challenge the limits of planning. *Built Environment, 45*(2), 143–161.

Frediani, Alexandre A., De Carli, Beatrice, Nuñez Ferrera, Isis, & Shinkins, Naomi. (2014). Change by Design: New spatial imaginations for Los Pinos. Workshop report (2013). Oxford: ASF-UK.

Frediani, Alexandre A., De Carli, Beatrice, Shinkins, Naomi, Kinnear, Melissa, Morley, Sophie, & Powis, Anthony. (2015). Change by Design: Collective imaginations for contested sites in Euston. Workshop report (2014). Oxford: ASF-UK.

Frediani, Alexandre A., Morley, Sophie, & Wright, Emily. (2018). Change by Design: How can neighbourhood planning bring about inclusive city-making in Freetown? Workshop report (2017). London: ASF-UK.

French, Matthew A., Frediani, Alexandre A., & Nuñez Ferrera, Isis. (2011). *Change by Design: Building communities through participatory design*. Napier, NZ: Urban Culture Press.

Government of Sierra Leone. (2014). *Freetown Structure Plan 2013–2028. Main development issues and analysis. Sierra Leone Preparatory Components and Studies for the Freetown Development Plan Support to Freetown City Council and to the Urban Planning Authorities*. EuropeAid /SL. Cris. No.: FED/2010/250–190.

Hamdi, Nabeel. (2004). *Small Change: About the art of practice and the limits of planning in cities*. London: Earthscan.

Hamdi, Nabeel. (2010). *The Placemaker's Guide to Building Community*. London: Earthscan.

Holston, J. (2008). *Insurgent Citizenship: Disjunctions of democracy and modernity in Brazil*. Princeton: Princeton University Press.

Macarthy, Joseph. M., Frediani, Alexandre A., & Kamara, Sulaiman F. (2019). Report on the Role of Community Action Area Planning in expanding the participatory capabilities of the urban poor. Freetown: SLURC.

Ortíz Flores, Enrique. (2007). *Integración de un Sistema de Instrumentos de Apoyo a la Producción Social de Vivienda*. Mexico City: Coalición Internacional para el Hábitat (HIC-AL).

SLURC. (2022a). Cockle Bay: Settlement profile. Freetown: SLURC.

SLURC. (2022b). Portee-Rokupa: Settlement profile. Freetown: SLURC.

SLURC. (2023). Dworzark: Settlement profile. Freetown: SLURC.

SLURC & ASF-UK. (2019a). Change by Design: Cockle Bay community action area plan. Freetown: SLURC.

SLURC & ASF-UK. (2019b). Change by Design: Dworzark community action area plan. Freetown: SLURC.

SLURC & ASF-UK. (2024). Change by Design: Portee-Rokupa community action area plan. Freetown: SLURC.

Turner, John F. C. (1976). *Housing by People: Towards autonomy in building environments*. London: Marion Boyars.

10
Exploring the role of empowerment in urban humanitarian responses in Freetown

Joseph M. Macarthy, Alexandre Apsan Frediani and Milimer Morgado

Introduction

In Sierra Leone, international and national humanitarian actors have been involved in a series of initiatives addressing humanitarian emergencies caused separately by the civil war, cholera outbreaks, the Ebola crisis and the recent flooding in Freetown (and a few other places within Sierra Leone) due to torrential rains. In each case, there has been a variety of response approaches, from community-led (such as the community-led Ebola response), to top-down relocation (such as the temporary site at the national stadium). While there has been documentation of these processes, there has been little work attempting to bring studies and perspectives together to generate a reflection for the wider humanitarian community of practice.

To explore these issues in more detail, this research narrowed down its focus to the humanitarian responses in the Portee-Rokupa neighbourhood of Freetown.[1] This location was identified because of its variety of approaches to humanitarian responses, from community-led to state-driven. Also, it is an area with which the Sierra Leone Urban Research Centre (SLURC) has an ongoing relationship; working closely with local community groups and attempting to support their activities through action research projects.

The term empowerment has been widely defined and used by scholars and policymakers. As the meaning has changed over time, its application by governments and development agencies has also been altered to the point that the term is now deemed to be vague. Despite the controversy, empowerment is broadly seen as a participatory process through which people/local community residents are made to become more productive and ultimately contribute to the development of their society (Naguib, 2024). Empowerment becomes only meaningful when the process goes beyond making people feel empowered to using the new skills and knowledge to make actual improvements in the lives of the people and their living conditions. Empowerment matters for how we think about humanitarianism because while people and locally based organisations work to pursue the collective self-interest of urban communities, they normally operate on low budgets with limited skills and understanding to mobilise international assistance to effectively respond to the needs of people in emergencies. The population of Sierra Leone is growing and with an increase of young people and urban residents. With little economic opportunities for young people and poor infrastructure and housing in cites, this process is leading to rising inequalities making more people vulnerable to a growing number of disasters particularly in Freetown. Individuals and small community groups are slowly rising to the challenge by providing support to others within and outside their communities. Fechter (2023) has described this 'everyday humanitarianism' act by ordinary people who are busy filling gaps left by established formal humanitarian organisations as 'vernacular' to reflect the informality of the service which tend to be sidelined by the more important actors.

By focusing on the empowerment implication of humanitarian responses, this research explores the extent to which approaches have been able to build the capacities of informal dwellers' groups, foster collaboration among different stakeholders, enable critical learning, and open opportunities for the recognition of the diverse needs and aspirations of vulnerable groups within the wider policy and planning environment. Furthermore, we hope to elicit the conditions in the humanitarian sector that have enabled or compromised the achievement of empowerment outcomes. As an output, the research has generated a specific set of recommendations to the humanitarian sector on how empowerment can be supported through urban humanitarian responses.

As Sierra Leone has experienced various forms of disasters in recent years, with the frequency expected to increase and the scale often exceeding the coping capacity of the government, it is reasoned that unless the different stakeholders (international, national, local, non-state, etc.) prepare for events by putting appropriate mechanisms in place, there is the risk of response failure. With disasters expected to extend to more new areas, especially in informal settlements, there is the danger that most slum dwellers living in 'at risk' locations will be displaced if sufficient, suitable precautions are not taken in advance. Porter (2003) identifies the main factors underlying humanitarian response failures and includes the absence of a clear lead agency to drive the process: inadequate knowledge of the nature and scale of the humanitarian need, improper monitoring of response activities and the impacts, the lack of a clear strategy, and the fragmented approaches of the different actors involved in the response. To a large extent, the current approach to humanitarian response in Sierra Leone bears all these hallmarks, which makes it more prone to abuse. Thus, having an understanding of the existing procedures, identifying the different skills and capacities of the different actors, and empowering the role of actors at different levels, are all necessary actions for enabling responses now and in the future. Moreover, exploring the role of empowerment in urban humanitarian response is critical in view of the seemingly increasing engagement of informal settlements by the humanitarian community in response to the drawbacks associated with urbanisation in Sierra Leone. The resultant unplanned development of urban space to accommodate population growth is causing fresh vulnerabilities while intensifying existing ones, thereby increasing the scale of exposure of poor urban households to disasters, with implications for humanitarian response (Dickson et al., 2012; McCallin & Scherer, 2015).

Humanitarian crises have always occurred in both urban and rural areas, but it is clear that the nature and scale of the crises for each have always differed, with urban areas in Sierra Leone experiencing more severe outcomes. As Mohiddin and Smith (2016) argue, this is due largely to the high population densities which are mostly mobile, the prevalence of informal settlements – often in unstable locations – and the diverse trades and lifestyles undertaken. All of which increase vulnerability to disasters. As the humanitarian community increasingly seeks to empower groups to respond to disasters in more effective ways, exploring the role of empowerment presents an unparalleled opportunity to understand not only the current state of preparedness of the country to respond to disasters, but also to understand the accountability mechanisms for the response. It will also allow the government to build more effective emergency preparedness and response mechanisms, as well as to shape existing policies to fittingly support the response strategies. By doing so, this chapter calls for dwellers of urban informal settlements to be recognised as key humanitarian actors, playing a key role to respond to increasing urban shocks and stresses (for more on this, see Ley & Ssorin-Chaikov, 2023).

Methodology

The research methodology applies Amartya Sen's capability approach to facilitate the examination of the linkages between empowerment and humanitarian responses. This research approach sheds light on three main analytical domains: stakeholder's perceptions of the potential and actual empowerment outcomes generated by urban humanitarian responses; the role that humanitarian response plays in drawing, strengthening or weakening assets available to Portee Rokupa's community groups to pursue empowerment outcomes and the ways in which the policy and planning environment affects the relationship between humanitarian responses and the empowerment of urban poor groups in Freetown.

The research methods used in this study include literature review; policy document analysis; ten interviews with informants from different, key government and civil society humanitarian institutions; interviews with eight different community-based organisations involving 24 representatives and two focus group discussions involving 22 participants representing ten different community based organisations from Portee-Rokupa.

Introducing Portee-Rokupa

The study area is Portee-Rokupa, a community located in the eastern part of Freetown. Portee-Rokupa shares boundaries with Kuntolor to the south, Congo water to the east and Grassfield to the west. To the north is the mouth of the Rokel river where it empties into the Atlantic Ocean. Situated politically within two separate wards (Portee in Ward 355 and Rokupa in Ward 354) in Constituency 99, Portee-Rokupa has been affected by all the major humanitarian crises Freetown has experienced in recent times. These include cholera in 2012, flooding in 2015 and the Ebola viral disease (EVD) in 2014–2015. Politically, the community is run by a parliamentarian, a councillor, and various tribal chiefs, and it has a ward development committee set up by the FCC.

According to the local tribal chiefs that participated in the focus group discussions, Portee-Rokupa was first settled in the early 1940s. The first known settlers were *Pa Rokupr* and *Pa Kapr*.[2] They named the community 'Ro-Poti'; the name of the village they came from in Port Loko district in northern Sierra Leone. Owing largely to the growth and boom in the economy of Freetown in the 1950s, many residents from Port Loko district came by sea to trade in Ro-Poti. Since then, the settlement has grown into a vibrant fishing community.

After Sierra Leone gained independence in 1961, the inhabitants of Portee-Rokupa increased significantly, but people initially resided only in the area known today as Portee. At the time, the area known as Rokupa was merely a forest which was later acquired by the Sierra Leone Prisons Department for use as a cemetery to bury prisoners who died in custody. The relocation of the cemetery in the mid-1970s witnessed the overall transformation of Rokupa, as private individuals started occupying and converting the land into a human settlement.

Up until 2004, when decentralisation and local governance were reintroduced into Sierra Leone, Portee-Rokupa existed as a single settlement. However, the boundary delimitation for the first local elections in 2004 caused the settlement to be officially divided into two. Thus, whereas the entire area known today as the wharf was previously part of Portee, the new boundary divided it into two halves by way of the drainage running through to the wharf, with one half situated in Portee and the other in Rokupa (Kargbo, 2015). For that reason, the wharf settlement is now commonly referred to as Portee-Rokupa. Over the years, this wharf has developed to become one of the largest fishing communities in the east of Freetown with the two settlements (Portee and Rokupa) currently named after it.

A key feature of Portee-Rokupa is its high population density. While the community previously drew much of its population from Port Loko district, a major turning point came during the civil war when a significant proportion of displaced persons from conflict-ridden areas in the provinces were forced to move into Freetown. With nowhere else to go, Portee-Rokupa became one of the main areas where people chose to settle, mainly because of its relatively cheap housing rents. The projected populations for 2012 by Statistics Sierra Leone showed that Rokupa (Ward 354) and Portee (Ward 355) had populations of 18,763 and 24,855 respectively. Among these, a recent study by the YMCA and CODOHSAPA (2015) found that in 2015, 6,059 people lived in the poorest part of the area, in a locality frequently described as 'informal'.

Two distinct settlements can be identified in Portee-Rokupa: the formal and the informal. The informal settlement, which comprises much of the lower area by the seafront, is characterised by poverty, with major challenges being unemployment, illiteracy, poor hygiene, inadequate skills, and low political participation. From our observations, inequality can be shown in the differences in the standard of living for different places or categories of people. This can also be seen in the varying levels of access to certain essential services for the residents in different parts of the community. Whereas essential services like electricity and water are easily accessible to residents of places widely described as 'formal settlements', there is limited or rarely any access to those same services for residents in the 'informal settlement'. Service provision is limited because residents generally lack formal land titles to allow for formal provision. This unequal access to services suggests the degree of spatial inequality to which residents in informal settlements are often subjected. Coupled with the acute lack of infrastructural protection, residents here are disproportionately affected whenever there is a disaster, with many sustaining injuries or losing relatives and their dwellings and other possessions liable to flooding.

In Portee-Rokupa, the high population density and lack of space create substantial challenges for residents in pursuing their livelihood strategies. They have little or no space for social infrastructure facilities like schools, health centres, and markets. However, even within the formal and informal settlements, our observations and interviews with residents show that social inequalities among households and people from different social categories (sex, age and ethnic groups) mean unequal access to available social goods such as education, health care, electricity and water standpoints. Nonetheless, residents argued that social and spatial inequality are more prominent in the informal settlement part of the neighbourhood, where most residents do not have easy access to essential services, and they must often walk long distances or climb steep slopes in order to access them.

Apart from the areas referred to as informal settlements by the seafront, there has been local investments and improvements of basic amenities in Portee-Rokupa. This is due to the growing informal economic activities in the community, partly explained by its strategic location along the main transport route linking the east end of Freetown to the central business district; and partly, by its proximity to the sea where different kinds of trade (e.g. fishing and fuelwood), and activities (e.g. transport and boat making) are carried out. These different trades and activities have allowed residents in informal areas, particularly those living along the shoreline, to benefit from fishing and the growing boat transport trade, while those along the main transport route (formal areas) benefit from the thriving petty trade and associated support services. Over the years, these advantages have not only improved the wellbeing of residents but have also attracted rural-urban migration into the community (Government of Sierra Leone, 1996). However, when new residents arrive, they usually have nowhere to reside in the already overpopulated formal settlement. Coupled with the marked poverty and the shortage of land for settlement expansion, most new arrivals are forced to live in the depressed and overcrowded informal settlement area by the seafront, where they reclaim land by making sea defences to put up their dwelling shacks. The poor living conditions, the high population density and the lack of improvement in services and infrastructure, have coalesced into worsening socioeconomic conditions in the community.

As Portee-Rokupa is primarily a fishing community, the various informal economic activities carried out (especially petty trading) support and sustain the fishing industry. This is necessary since the fishing trade does not only ensure the constant supply of fresh fish to nearby markets, but it also serves as a vital source of income for a number of households in the community. Portee-Rokupa has excellent business relations with the Port Loko district, including the riverine communities situated along the Rokel river. The community serves as the first port of entry for fresh vegetables, fruits, and woodfuel from the nearby villages in Port Loko district into Freetown. However, the importance of the wharf is slowly declining because there is no access road from the main highway, and this makes it difficult to transport goods elsewhere. In addition, there are no cold storage facilities for residents to preserve the daily catch of fish. The economic conditions of those engaged in the fishing industry are further challenged with competition from a few Chinese fishing companies in Freetown and this has often resulted in declining fish prices.

Humanitarian crises in Sierra Leone and Portee-Rokupa

Portee-Rokupa has been affected by most of the humanitarian crises that have affected Freetown since independence. The foremost of these crises in the recent past are the civil war (1991–2002), cholera (2012), Ebola (2014–2016) and the flooding that occurs annually.

The civil war (1991–2002)

The civil war, which lasted for nearly 11 years and ravaged much of Sierra Leone, triggered the most severe humanitarian crisis ever in the country. Reports show that by January 2002 when the war ended, nearly two-thirds (2.6 million) of the country's population was displaced, with almost 70,000 fatalities. Portee-Rokupa was among the areas that a significant proportion of the displaced population from the rural areas moved to. Even though relatively safe, these areas were already heavily congested. This increased the concentration of underprivileged people in depressed and unstable locations.

Cholera outbreak (2012)

The 2012 cholera outbreak was perhaps the largest cholera epidemic in Sierra Leone's since first reported in 1970. It caused extensive numbers of deaths amongst people living in informal settlements. By December 2012, when the outbreak was nearly over, the total reported cases were 22,973 with 299 deaths countrywide (Oxfam, 2013). Urban poor areas have always suffered disproportionately whenever there is a cholera crisis in the country. Portee-Rokupa is no exception and is exposed to cholera due to poor sanitation, contaminated water sources, limited access to clean and safe drinking water and high population density. Added to that, the difficult economic situation residents are faced with also creates a situation wherein the activities they engage in makes them prone to a more unhygienic situation, which increases the likelihood of cholera. There is no sewerage system in Portee-Rokupa and all sewage from the upper and better planned areas in the east end of Freetown empties near to the cliff situated in the informal settlement. There is also a high rate of coastal pollution due to solid waste. The residents interact with this in their daily activities when fishing, with children swimming, or when carrying out domestic and economic activities along the coast.

Annual flooding

Flooding has now become a regular feature in Portee-Rokupa during the rainy season. Torrential rains, poor drainage, indiscriminate dumping of waste in drains which reduces the surface flow of water, stone mining, deforestation of the peninsular forest, clearing of the mangroves and poor planning are largely responsible. According to ReliefWeb (2015), the September 2015 flooding, for instance, was one of the worst flooding crises Freetown had seen, with over 3,000 people displaced. According to the councillor of Ward 355, the community is affected every rainy season when there is a heavy downpour. In the September 2015 flooding, Portee-Rokupa's unpaved roads turned into streams of fast flowing water. The houses along the roads and drainage could not withstand the pressure of the water and it flowed into many houses. About 27 houses were affected, including nine that were extensively damaged and three that were completed demolished. There were two recorded deaths and some minor injuries and fractures. One notable fatality was a child who was swept away and drowned. Affected households suffered major economic setbacks, and these impacted on the timely return of their children back to school after the summer holidays. Community groups, volunteers, and relatives were the first respondents and they provided shelter and warm clothing, while others sought refuge in the mosque. The councillor and various community groups helped with the search and rescue, diversion of the waterways, and protection of residents' properties from looters.

Ebola viral disease (2014–2016)

The first cases of Ebola were detected in Sierra Leone on 28 March 2014 and remained until 17 March 2016, before the country was declared Ebola-free. This Ebola outbreak, which reached a few countries in West Africa, was the largest such outbreak in the world and was the first Sierra Leone had experienced. The country registered 14,122 confirmed cases (WHO, 2015). The first confirmed case of Ebola in Freetown was reported on 23 June 2014; the victim came from the Port Loko district and the virus entered through the wharfs of one of the informal settlements in Freetown. The Ebola virus thrived mainly in the informal settlements, partly because of overcrowding, poor hygiene and no access to essential services. Portee-Rokupa is one of the most densely populated communities in the east of Freetown and was also amongst the worst hit by Ebola. The squalor, mainly in the informal side of the settlement, outstripped sanitation, and that created the unfortunate conditions allowing for the easy spread of the virus. According to a tribal chief, many residents of the informal settlement were propagating the rumour that the spread of the virus was a ploy by the government to solicit foreign donor money and to regulate birth control. The consensus from some of the community-based organisations interviewed was that Portee-Rokupa recorded more Ebola confirmed cases than neighbouring communities. According to the community records available from the councillor, there were 23 deaths: 18 from the informal settlement, and five from the formal side. The informal settlement had 25 quarantined houses and the formal side had nine quarantined houses.

Policy context and stakeholders involved in humanitarian response in Sierra Leone

At the time of this research in 2017, Sierra Leone did not have a comprehensive disaster response law to facilitate and guide international humanitarian response operations in the country. The main legal instrument dealing with disaster management was the National Security and Central Intelligence Act No. 10 (2002) (Government of Sierra Leone, 2002), which established the Office of National Security (ONS) as the central body for the coordination of all security and intelligence issues of the state at policy level. The Act also declared the Disaster Management Department (DMD) to be one of the eleven departments within the ONS (Morgado, 2016). This department has responsibility for the coordination of all issues relating to disaster by bringing together all stakeholders (public, private, civil society, etc.) which have disaster risk reduction (DRR) as their mandate or as part of their mandate. The department also has responsibility for monitoring all the different actors involved in humanitarian response to ensure that they comply with the existing rules and policies, and to reduce fraud and the misappropriation of relief supplies.

The DMD's response to disaster and the kinds of stakeholders it involves is usually determined by the type of disaster event, with the relevant sectoral ministry taking lead in the response. To ensure its nationwide representation, the ONS has offices in all 14 administrative districts in Sierra Leone. The disaster management committees (DMCs) in all these districts constitute the national platform for DRR which is led by the office of the vice president. The platform brings together stakeholders, not only from the central and local government, but also from civil society and the private sector, to work collectively on humanitarian crises. In addition, Sierra Leone has several other legal provisions on humanitarian crises which are scattered among a variety of general laws. Some of these isolated legal instruments, while not dealing directly with disaster, have clauses that influence the role and activities of international humanitarian actors (relating specifically to customs clearance and taxation procedures).

Whereas the DMD has chiefdom disaster management communities (CDMCs) as the lowest tier of its management structure in the districts, in Freetown, the lowest level of the DMD is constituted by the community based disaster management committees (CBDMCs). Apart from being the first responders since they are already resident in the community, CBDMCs serve as the main points of contact for the DMD in the respective communities. However, since the CBDMC is comprised mostly of volunteer groups drawn mainly from the communities, it is usually not recognised in national decisions on disaster risk reduction (DRR). Therefore, only the 14 disaster management committees constitute the national platform for DRR, which is led by the office of the vice president.

While at the national level humanitarian relief is usually provided by UN agencies through the appropriate sectoral ministry, delivery is often based on a partnership involving a variety of other government ministries, agencies and NGOs. Partnership is required because no individual organisation has the resources to deal with all the challenges caused by a crisis. However, while different spaces/structures exist at the community level, only a few local actors (in particular community based organisations; CBOs) are recognised in the response. For the most part, humanitarian agencies prefer to work separately, because to them the CBOs do not seem to be properly registered with the government, and hence have no clear 'legal entity' and capacity. Therefore, the efforts of many CBOs which had hitherto intervened in the community are easily overwhelmed by the emergent international humanitarian agencies, especially when they do not have a reliable source of funding. Only the CBDMCs and a few parallel community structures set up by some INGOs are actively involved. Nevertheless, CBOs were observed to be very active in humanitarian response in the community. To a large extent, the active role of CBOs at this level suggests that only a few crisis-affected people benefit from international humanitarian interventions, with the vast majority left to either cope with or recover from the crisis by themselves.

Although the resident councillor is the political head of the ward, he is often not recognised in humanitarian response. During the Ebola crisis in particular, even if there was a general recognition of the need to involve community leaders in humanitarian response, the lack of active and sustained involvement of communities and their structures led to a feeling of rejection towards the work of NGOs and to fear and distrust in their interventions. A similar case was pointed out by the FCC, which even though broadly recognised as a major stakeholder in humanitarian crises, was only involved in the Ebola response mid-way into the implementation process, thereby missing out on the design and planning phases. Therefore, from the perspective of the councillor and FCC representative, communities, as well as municipal authorities, are undermined by NGO responses.

These tensions emerge as a result of lack of coordination as well as equitable conditions for community groups to be recognised and supported in humanitarian responses and reflects wider debates and criticism of associated to community engagement in humanitarianism. Given the condition of emergency, humanitarian practitioners at times have perceived community engagement as an impediment for prompt action. Furthermore, a lack of understanding of local dynamics could also result in the reproduction of unequal power asymmetries within communities, as well as devolving burdens and exposure to further risks to community groups. Therefore, assumptions such as those associated to the value of community engagement in humanitarian responses have played an important role in the way CBOs were ended up being involved in more institutionalised and formal urban humanitarian responses in Freetown.

Empowerment outcomes

The review of the humanitarian crisis and responses in Portee-Rokupa reveals that there are interventions and activities led by different stakeholders which have different types of impact on the empowerment assets of community groups.

1) Government-led (national): One of the national interventions reviewed in this research was the implementation of quarantines. These were tools used in the Ebola response and quite particular to the public health emergency facing the country. Nevertheless, they had a substantial negative impact on the empowerment assets of local residents and groups (especially social and financial).

2) Government-led (council): Registration and support of relief activities had some positive impact on the recognition of local groups and their capacity to act locally. But this is limited, without substantial implications for the enhancement of political empowerment assets.

3) NGO-led: Relief activities and targeted infrastructural projects have been successful in working with CBOs and strengthening some empowerment assets. However, limited resources and lack of coordination has compromised a more substantial impact of NGO efforts.

4) CBO-led: This has been the most substantial mechanism to enhance the empowerment assets of local communities. The research reveals several community-led activities that have been sustained mainly by community efforts and with limited support from external actors.

In terms of policy and planning, the research reveals that there are productive entry points in current policy frameworks for community participation and the recognition of approaching humanitarian crises as an opportunity for empowering communities. However, in practice there are limitations in addressing this: a) stakeholders have an instrumental perception of community actors, at times blaming local residents for risks and recognising them as a labour force for implementing mitigation and response activities; and b) this leads to a substantial institutional gap between the CBDMC and other DRR structures. Nevertheless, new platforms, such as the Portee Ebola Response Alliance Volunteers (PERAV; see Box 10.1), have been identified as key initiatives with the potential to address these limitations (see also Morgado, 2016).

Box 10.1 Portee Ebola Response Alliance Volunteers (PERAV)

Portee Ebola Response Alliance Volunteers (PERAV) was formed in September 2014. It was the idea of the ward councillor who is also a resident of the community. The alliance was created to bring credible, hardworking and respected community groups together to accomplish a specific goal, which was to fight the spread and stop the Ebola viral disease, which would not only benefit the individuals in the groups, but the community and the country as a whole. The alliance was mainly involved in social mobilisation and awareness-raising campaigns, as well as environmental and sanitation activities such as community cleaning, clearing of drains, and house-to-house garbage collection. They also provided support to INGOs and MDAs, such as the MoHS, SLP, and WHO, with contact tracing, quarantine processes and the distribution of relief items.

With regard to empowerment assets and outcomes, the exploration of stakeholders' claims of empowerment outcomes from humanitarian responses revealed two main tensions. The first tension emerged in the relationship between NGOs and CBOs. While NGOs claim to support CBOs, they also argue that there is low capacity within communities to involve them in humanitarian responses. Meanwhile CBOs argue that the main challenge is not the lack of capacity, but lack of support. As a result, NGOs' narratives end up reproducing the lack of recognition of CBOs and potentially compromising the possibility of them being involved in other development or humanitarian initiatives.

The second tension emerged regarding the empowerment claims between government authorities (FCC and ONS) and CBOs. While the FCC and the ONS claim to have empowered communities to become self-reliant, CBOs argue that FCC rarely intervened during emergencies and that ONS did not usually recognise local leaders when delivering humanitarian responses in communities.

This research reveals that the humanitarian responses studied have drawn on and strengthened, but also hindered, empowerment assets. Community groups' skills and existing community facilities, strong social networks, existing partnerships between international non-governmental organisations (INGOs) and government institutions, as well as the informal livelihoods of local residents, were key empowerment assets drawn from various humanitarian responses. Humanitarian responses have also strengthened empowerment assets by building the capacities of local leaders and groups to work on risk prevention, triggering social mobilisation, fostering collaboration among different city stakeholders, providing a platform for communities to display their capacities to implement projects on the ground and generating funds for the implementation of initiatives which allowed CBOs to manage and carry out activities.

However, humanitarian responses have also hindered empowerment assets, by occasionally restricting human rights and freedom of movement, and hampering livelihood opportunities. Lack of coordination has fostered communities' mistrust of government and NGOs in the humanitarian sector and fractured the social cohesion of communities.

This study has explored how humanitarian organisations seize the spaces offered by emergencies as an opening to build the capacity of communities and their groups to meaningfully take part in urban decision-making processes. It has shown that while the complexity of cities exposes the urban poor to a variety of risks and threats given their vulnerability, it also presents opportunities, not only for a shared understanding of the existing problems, but also for collective action. As a result, there is the potential to change the perception of different actors of each other's capacities to respond and mitigate risks. Placing the needs of the residents at the heart of this process and getting them actively involved in the identification, prioritisation, planning and delivery of the responses offers great prospects for building empowerment assets with implications for community empowerment outcomes. Despite the challenge of dealing with the eminent power imbalances, this study offers a few useful lessons which can inform future humanitarian response activities either in Sierra Leone or elsewhere. These are presented as follows.

- When the existing national policy on humanitarian response does not explicitly recognise community participation as a core requirement for international/national humanitarian actors, the possibility of including community actors in the response will be low, despite their recognition as the first responders to the crisis. This is particularly the case when the process of monitoring response activities and impacts is inadequate, and also when the approaches of the different actors involved in the response are fragmented.

- The existence of a clear lead agency to drive humanitarian response in the country (in this case, the DMD) and a governance framework (in this case, the national platform for DRR) is an effective means to bring together the different stakeholders (from central and local government, civil society, the private sector, NGOs, community actors and international organisations) to bear collectively on humanitarian crises. However, the existence of the lead agency (DMD) within a superstructure (ONS) sometimes limits the timeliness of its decisions and actions.

- While community actors and local NGOs can make significant contributions to humanitarian responses during emergencies, the lack of funding (stand-by emergency funds) sometimes prevents them from doing so. Therefore, it is INGOs that are more likely to be active at the start of the crisis. Furthermore, in contexts where UN agencies only have mandate to provide support through relevant central government ministries and agencies, local NGOs and CBOs are only able to take part in humanitarian emergencies long after the response has begun. Therefore, the efforts of many CBOs that are more active in the community can easily be overwhelmed by the emergent international humanitarian agencies.

- The dominant approach by most international humanitarian organisations is the provision of immediate food relief. As the study shows, organisations that provide responses beyond the mere provision of relief supplies (with implications for empowerment outcomes) are mostly NGOs and CBOs that are more directly engaged in community development work and therefore may have pre-existing relationships with community stakeholders.

- Different sets of empowerment outcomes were ensured by humanitarian organisations acting either separately or through partnerships with other organisations (including CBOs). Several of the empowerment outcomes relate to the human and social dimensions, with fewer in terms of the physical dimension owing to the limited priority given by the humanitarian community to improvements in community infrastructure and services. For most community actors, empowerment outcomes are low because most of the funds they used in their response were contributed by the members, thereby depriving themselves from meeting their own needs.

- The range of humanitarian responses over the years has enabled the building of a diverse set of assets (human, physical, social, political, etc.) available to the Portee-Rokupa community. This has helped the implementation of humanitarian responses within the community. Humanitarian responses also enabled state institutions and other humanitarian organisations to build their capacities, knowledge and skills for the implementation of responses.

Conclusion

The urban poor in Freetown have been affected by the cumulative impacts of a series of humanitarian emergencies, which include civil war, cholera outbreaks, flooding and the Ebola crisis. International and national humanitarian actors as well as community groups have been involved in a variety of approaches to responses, from community-led to top-down relocation. This research focuses on the humanitarian responses in the Portee-Rokupa neighbourhood. It explores the role of humanitarian responses in building capacities of informal dwellers' groups, fostering collaboration among different stakeholders, enabling critical learning, and creating opportunities for the recognition of the diverse needs and aspirations of vulnerable groups within the wider policy and planning environment.

Firstly, this research reveals that community-based humanitarian practices have been the most substantial mechanism to enhance empowerment assets of residents of Portee-Rokupa. Community practices responding to humanitarian crises led to the strengthening of social networks within and among informal settlements, it enabled processes to share skills and build capacities, and it mobilised collective resources. These practices were mostly sustained by community efforts, but they also draw on the limited opportunities generated by humanitarian agencies to support and expand communities' access to empowerment assets. In the meantime, the study shows that humanitarian responses can hinder communities' access to empowerment assets, as was the case with the quarantines implemented by the national government in Portee-Rokupa, restricting human rights and freedom of movement, fostering government mistrust and fracturing social cohesion within communities.

Secondly, while the current policy frameworks mention that humanitarian responses can create opportunities for community empowerment, in practice this is still far from becoming institutionalised. Community based disaster management committees are referred to as a means to achieve this, however, they are set up with the scope of information dissemination and at best, coordinate efforts locally, rather than creating meaningful spaces for dialogue and participation.

Thirdly, this study reveals that NGOs' approach to urban humanitarian response in Freetown risks compromising the political empowerment of community groups. While NGOs claim to aim to support CBOs, they also argue that there is low capacity within communities to involve them in humanitarian responses. Meanwhile CBOs argue that the main challenge is not the lack of capacity, but lack of support. As a result,

NGOs' narratives end up reproducing the lack of recognition of CBOs and potentially compromising the possibility of them being involved in other development or humanitarian initiatives.

Based on these findings, this research generated a series of recommendations for the national and international humanitarian sector, which fundamentally calls for a reframing of the role of community participation in urban humanitarian response. If crises are to be seen as moments of opportunities to renegotiate power imbalances, then community participation in humanitarian responses needs to be framed not merely as a mechanism of implementation of pre-defined initiatives, but as a process of supporting and strengthening community empowerment.

Notes

1   This chapter is based on the research 'Exploring the role of empowerment in urban humanitarian responses in Freetown' which was made possible by a grant provided by the International Institute for Environment and Development (IIED) through the Urban Crises Learning Fund. The authors wish to acknowledge input from Sulaiman Kamara who was part of the research team at the time of the research. For a full report outlining the methodology, evidence and findings of the research, please access: https://www.iied.org/sites/default/files /pdfs/migrate/10845IIED.pdf
2   *Pa Kapr* means a chief in the Temne language, which is one of the most widely spoken languages in Sierra Leone.

References

Dickson, E., Baker, J. L., Hoornweg, D., & Tiwari, A. (2012). Urban risk assessments: understanding disaster and climate risk in cities. Urban Development Series. Washington, DC: World Bank. http://documents.worldbank.org/curated/en/659161468182066104/Urban-risk -assessments-understanding-disaster-and-climate-risk-in-cities.

Fechter, A (2023) 'Every person counts': The problem of scale in everyday humanitarianism. *Social Anthropology/Anthropologie Sociale, 31*(1), 14–29.

Government of Sierra Leone. (1996). The National Plan of Action for Habitat II Conference. Ministry of Lands, Housing, Town and Country Planning. Accessed 25 June 2024. http://habitat3.org /wp-content/uploads/Habitat-II-NR-1996-Sierra-Leone.pdf

Government of Sierra Leone. (2002). The National Security and Central Intelligence Act 2002.

Kargbo, A. H. (2015). Governance Processes in Sierra Leone 1799–2014. AuthorHouse.

Ley, L., & Ssorin-Chaikov, N. (2023) Editorial. *Social Anthropology/Anthropologie Sociale, 31*(1), v–vii. https://doi.org/10.3167/saas.2023.310101

McCallin, B., & Scherer, I. (2015) Urban informal settlers displaced by disasters: Challenges to housing responses. Internal Displacement Monitoring Centre (iDMC) report. Accessed 25 June 2024. https://api.internal-displacement.org/sites/default/files/publications/documents /201506-global-urban-informal-settlers.pdf

Mohiddin, L., & Smith, G. (2016). A review of needs assessment tools, response analysis frameworks, and targeting guidance for urban humanitarian response. International Institute for Environment and Development (IIED) Working Paper. IIED, London. Accessed 25 June 2024. http://pubs.iied.org/10796IIED

Morgado, M. M. (2016). Social learning for building resilience: the case of youth community-based organisations in informal settlements of Freetown, Sierra Leone. MSc Thesis, Development Planning Unit, UCL.

Naguib, R. (2024). Grounded approach to women's empowerment: Understanding the complexities. In R. Naguib (Ed.), *Women's Empowerment and Public Policy in the Arab Gulf States* (pp. 13–53). Gulf Studies, vol 11. Singapore: Springer. https://doi.org/10.1007/978-981-99-6006-4_2

Oxfam. (2013). Evaluation of Sierra Leone cholera response 2012: Effectiveness review. Accessed 25 June 2024. http://reliefweb.int/sites/reliefweb.int/files/resources/er-cholera-response -sierra-leone-effectiveness-review-061213-en.pdf

Porter, T. (2003). The interaction between political and humanitarian action in Sierra Leone, 1995 to 2002. Accessed 25 June 2024. https://reliefweb.int/report/sierra-leone/ interaction-between-political-and-humanitarian-action-sierra-leone-1995-2002

ReliefWeb. (2015). Sierra Leone: Floods – Sep. 2015. ReliefWeb. Accessed 25 June 2024. http:// reliefweb.int/disaster/fl-2015-000131-sle

WHO (World Health Organization). (2015). Ebola in Sierra Leone: A slow start to an outbreak that eventually outpaced all others. Accessed 25 June 2024. https://www.who.int/news -room/spotlight/one-year-into-the-ebola-epidemic/ebola-in-sierra-leone-a-slow-start-to-an -outbreak-that-eventually-outpaced-all-others

YMCA SL (Young Men's Christian Association) & CODOHSAPA (Centre of Dialogue on Human Settlement and Poverty Alleviation). (2015). Community profiling, enumeration, vulnerability and capacity assessment report. Freetown: YMCA SL & CODOHSAPA.

Part III
Learning and action

11
Research-based training

Andrea Rigon, Joseph M. Macarthy, Braima Koroma and Alexandre Apsan Frediani

Capacity building has lain at the centre of SLURC since its conception. In 2012, Comic Relief commissioned a preliminary study on the knowledge available about the needs of the residents of Freetown's informal settlements (see Chapter 3). This was conducted by current SLURC Executive Director Joseph M. Macarthy and Alexandre Apsan Frediani, at the time a lecturer at the Bartlett Development Planning Unit (DPU). Comic Relief soon realised the need for hiring international researchers alongside Sierra Leonean ones to provide the knowledge base needed by international and national development actors intervening in the informal settlements. As a result, they looked to set up a larger consultancy contract with the DPU. However, such an approach would not have built in-country capacity, thus reproducing dependency on international labour. Therefore, the counterproposal made to Comic Relief was to set up a centre that could generate the knowledge needed by urban actors in informal settlements, while at the same time building the capacity in Sierra Leone to produce such knowledge.

This chapter reflects on SLURC's approach to capacity building and research by exploring how SLURC responded to the demand for new skills and knowledge by embedding training in research processes. As this aim is so central to SLURC, there are many other activities that developed capacity and learning, some of which are covered in other chapters. In this chapter, we adopt a narrower focus on the research-based training. In the first three years (2016–2018), SLURC trained 225 individuals, but there were many more in total attendance given that many people attended more than one training session. Forty per cent of our trainees were female. While this is still far from equal participation, we consider it to be a tremendous achievement in the context of Sierra Leone, one of the countries with the highest gender inequality indexes, where there was a low presence of women amongst the urban actors, including university graduates.

In Box 11.1 below, we list the main research-based training undertaken by SLURC. These all share the characteristic of being held on multiple, consecutive full days, in most cases five or six, including days in the field for practical activities. We have excluded from the analysis a number of more technical training sessions, mostly aimed at building the capacity of SLURC staff and close partners. For example, financial management (September 2017), mobilising resources (October 2018), geographic information systems (2017) and coding and data analysis (2017). We also excluded training sessions that were part of some research projects where only the researchers involved in that project benefitted.

Box 11.1 Main SLURC Research-based training (2016–2019)
Co-learning the city through the lens of risk (July 2016)
Gender and livelihoods (February 2017)
Urban risk mapping and profiling (March 2017)
Participatory design and planning change by design (September 2017)
Participatory photography (February 2018)
Pro-poor land rights and informality (February 2018)
Development and planning in African cities (June 2018)
Participatory spatial research methods (January 2019)
Community led data collection for informal settlement profiling (April 2019)
Rapid assistive technology assessment (September 2019)

In the first three years we planned to deliver two major training sessions on research methods for urban development focusing on more traditional research approaches, and two major training sessions on innovative research methods. The contents were to be decided after a deeper needs assessment and consultations with key stakeholders. Soon, we realised the importance of connecting the training to actual research and the problematic dichotomy of innovative/traditional methods. On this basis, we developed our model for research-based training.

Research in a particular area would start with intense one-week training session bringing together a very diverse range of actors that would rarely find themselves in the same environment as equals. These included staff of local and central government and other public bodies, early career academics, staff of non-governmental organisations and members of communities affected by the research issues, generally informal settlements.

These training sessions were facilitated by a team of Sierra Leonean and international academics and practitioners. The concept was that of reciprocal learning whereby international trainers would share specific methodologies or conceptual approaches to a problem, for example urban risk, and local trainers would share their knowledge of the local context and practice around that theme. Initially, this model was thought to enable the Sierra Leonean trainers to rerun further editions of the training in future without international input and potentially, in the long-term, embed it into university education. For this reason, a lot of care was put into developing training manuals and jointly assessing the learning objectives after each course. While the formal replication of the training by the local team has not yet been done, the training succeeded in creating strong bonds amongst the trainers, which in many cases led to additional activities, often research projects. For example, inviting an international trainer from our partner university, UCL, or elsewhere would help us explore together during the training how their knowledge and approach could develop into joint research or other collaborations. At the same time, it made SLURC work known in other contexts. For example, the first training was a route for Adriana Allen to test the ground and then to bring in her project, Urban ARK and subsequently a wide range of other projects and initiatives that are so central to what SLURC is today. Similarly, after a training session on gender and livelihoods and a related research project, Julian Walker worked with SLURC on a much larger project on assistive technologies. Architects Sans Frontiers UK was initially invited to work with the SLURC team on a training course on participatory development and planning, and later worked closely with SLURC on other training and research activities linked to the Urban KNOW project.

At the same time, the training allowed SLURC to consolidate its relationship with a number of urban actors in Sierra Leone, whose members were impressed by the training which also built a common language for discussing urban challenges. These actors included the Freetown City Council, other government bodies, the Sierra Leone Federation of the Rural and Urban Poor and a network of NGOs operating in the informal settlements of Freetown, among others.

Our initial thinking about the training was that eventually they could, at least partly, become commercial and generate revenues to sustain SLURC. However, a more detailed scoping study indicated that, while demand for the skills we could offer was very high, there was little willingness to pay for such training and beyond our initial start-up grant, we did not find other donors willing to fund such training. What we did not expect was that the training also contributed to developing strategic relationships for SLURC both internationally and nationally, and in turn, these relationships enabled research contracts which sustained the organisation.

All these courses involved at least two days of field practice in poor communities to pilot some of the research methodologies. These were important to ensure the learning was informed by the city, and to respond to the need for practical knowledge that participants could apply and use straight after the course.

This approach had several outcomes which shaped both the research process outputs as well as the impact of such research.

A network of relations across different sectors

We were particularly impressed by the different layers of understanding of the issues and struck by the dismissive understanding of the capacity and context of the residents of informal settlements by other actors, for example, academics and local and central government staff. In some cases, there have been challenges in encouraging some actors to accept the presence of residents of informal settlements as peers on training courses.

The days in the field were particularly effective at generating strong relationships. A significant number of participants had never stepped into informal settlements before, despite being such significant parts of the city. For some of the government, academics and NGO actors, field research was also counter to the expectations of what training is: sometimes being perceived or associated with comfortable hotel conference rooms and a nice breakfast and lunch. In one instance, during a rainy week, we received requests to cancel the field visits because it could be 'slippery and dangerous' and a trainer almost accepted the request. In the end we completed the field visit. A resident of an informal settlement and a government officer teamed up under the same umbrella trying to avoid muddy puddles to carry out the exercise. Lots of laughter and conversations emerged from the pair and the day ended with the government officer promising to visit the church of the other participant located in an informal settlement with the members of his own church. Our initial scoping study demonstrated a social fabric of actors who distrusted each other without space for dialogue. These training provided this space to build relationships and provided participants with common concepts and a language to talk about difficult issues, thus helping to deal with their differences.

Grounding research in local understanding

These training weeks helped ground the subsequent research in the knowledge and understanding of key local actors who shaped research plans. The model allowed for pilot fieldwork embedded in the training and for a collective reflection and analysis of the preliminary data and the research process with feedback from a wide range of actors. This process helped to fine tune the research following suggestions from residents on how best to approach certain issues, and on important aspects that had so far been ignored, while taking on board suggestions by government on how the research could be made more useful to the policy making process.

Local research capacity

The model built the long-term capacity to generate and analyse knowledge of Sierra Leonean urban actors. At the end of the week, the process left about 25–30 people able to carry out research with some supervision. Several training participants were also recruited as research assistants and these had already gained a conceptual understanding of the research issues. Therefore, they became more effective researchers and able to contribute to the analysis. The process also allowed for the identification and recruitment of some researchers then employed by SLURC, creating a process through which young graduates and community leaders could start work as research interns and then move up into a research career.

Communities understanding the research

We trained some members from the researched communities. This meant that we had a number of people within the informal settlements who had a good understanding of the research that was to be conducted and could explain it to other community members or help the research team. Moreover, the approach of SLURC to include slum dwellers in research and training activities has increased their capacities to assess needs within their communities, become aware of risks and equip themselves with skills and knowledge to advocate for their needs. This is being demonstrated in the Urban ARK project in which 15 communities developed action plans for project funding, with the community co-funding part of the activities. Data and knowledge from community action area plans developed with trained residents have been used to advocate for interventions and guide NGOs when they come to communities.

This approach was also central to the ethos of SLURC, as an organisation working for the wellbeing of the residents of informal settlements. It has helped to achieve the objective of working with residents rather than for them, thereby going beyond the idea of academics producing research benefiting informal settlement residents and instead creating the conditions for co-producing knowledge.

Expanding the capacity of local academics

An important set of participants were local academics, who were involved both as participants and sometimes as part of the extended pool of local trainers. Involvement in these training expanded their repertoire of research methods, often offering tools to conduct research in informal settlements that they were not previously well-equipped to carry out. The training also provided inspiration for their teaching practice.

Generate understanding of the research process and demand

Researchers are often blamed for not understanding what policymakers need, especially when foreign researchers are involved in the Global South. This is an important theme and we explained how this approach enables local actors, including policy makers, to influence the research agenda. However, it is also important the other way around: institutional actors understanding key concepts, the complexity of the research process, and what research can offer to them. We believe that the training contributed to generating demand for evidence. Moreover, as a result of the value they gained in training, SLURC has been increasingly recognised as an important player and its expertise requested by government.

Actionable knowledge

Most importantly, the training provided participants with both conceptual and concrete tools to continue exploring the course's issues through their work in a variety of settings from the municipality to NGOs. This allowed for a rapid deployment of new skills in the city. For example, the participatory planning and design training gave attendees the tools with which to lobby for change.

Here are some quotes from a range of training participants across different sectors, about what they considered most useful about the training and how it would influence their practice.

'This training has been an eye opener. We participants will serve as change agents by educating our colleagues and institutions, particularly regarding the importance of citizen participation.' – Training participant from academia

'Learning from examples of other countries, to think how to apply this in Sierra Leone.' – Anonymous

'Participatory planning using the lens of spatial justice and diversity. This will strongly help in identifying the target group we will be working with.' – Civil engineer and humanitarian professional

'Every topic was important but the most important was the diversity in planning and development. Participatory planning, the way in which marginalised people contribute to planning. We sit in the office and plan for them, and this is a problem.' – Anonymous

'This training helped me a lot. I learnt the difference between formal and informal and how to engage through a participatory process. I learnt that it is not just about giving them [informal communities] something but help communities leveraging their own resources to address issues.' – NGO practitioner

'1. Participatory planning: I plan to mainstream it in my work and institution as a whole. 2. urban value capture: I plan to work with line MDA's and the management of my institution for its full implementation. 3. Urban infrastructure: I plan to network and partner with the line MDA's to implement the best practices learnt.' – Environmentalist

'The aspect of participatory planning and governance. We train students on development in my institution. And most of these students end up working in advocacy groups/NGOs and some in governance. I will use this knowledge to properly prepare them on how to face issues discussed here [more] appropriately than before.' – Lecturer, training participant

Give back

SLURC was designed to change the extractive model of academic research, whereby foreign investigators extract data for their research agendas. We found that having researchers building the capacity of a larger pool of people, before or alongside their research projects, was an effective way to give something back and build lasting capacity. We embedded in the research protocol that every SLURC partner was meant to sign, the need to plan the time to build local capacity.

Conclusion

This chapter illustrated the potential of a combined training/research approach to generate more actionable knowledge and capacities to improve the wellbeing of urban residents. What SLURC did was to go beyond research-based teaching (Fung, 2017) and almost reverse the process by initiating research with training activities. These training sessions were aimed at delivering the knowledge of the issues and methodologies to a set of important local stakeholders, with whom we reflected about the issues in the specific context and together piloted some initial research. These initial pilots produced feedback from a wide range of different stakeholders who fully understood the conceptual, practical issues, the motivation of the research and the potential of the methodologies. Crucially, these training sessions enabled the creation of strategic relationships that ensured the success of SLURC while creating a platform for dialogue between urban actors that is fundamental to ensure a just urban development that prioritises the wellbeing of slum-dwellers.

References

Fung, D. (2017). *A Connected Curriculum for Higher Education*. London: UCL Press.

12
Crafting environmental justice through co-learning
Rita Lambert, Pascale Hofmann, Julia Wesely, Adriana Allen and Amadu Labor

Introduction

Conventional planning education within higher education institutions, both across the Global South and North, has long been called out for predominantly framing African cities as objects of study (Watson & Odendaal, 2013), as well as for using pre-established theoretical lenses that negate the possibility of theory building from the ground up (Parnell & Pieterse, 2016). It thus fails to engage with the experiences, practices and aspirations of women and men who, despite contributing to building, managing and running cities, are systematically excluded from planning processes and policies. We therefore ask: How do we shift from learning and writing *about* African cities to instead learning *from* them? And how do we learn with others to become urban development practitioners that activate and strengthen pathways towards environmental justice?

In tackling these questions, the Bartlett Development Planning Unit (DPU) at UCL is committed to developing pedagogical approaches based on embedded co-learning to build the sensibilities and capacities of practitioners that strive towards just and sustainable cities. Over the years, these approaches across the DPU's seven MSc programmes have been delivered through so-called 'learning alliances', which in a nutshell are platforms through which action-research is conducted from a transdisciplinary approach and through the participation of community members, and MSc staff and students. These alliances are built upon long-standing partnerships between the DPU and institutional actors and local communities in cities across Latin America, Africa, Asia and Europe.

In this chapter, we draw from a learning alliance established in 2017 between the DPU MSc in Environment and Sustainable Development (ESD), the Sierra Leone Urban Research Centre (SLURC), the Federation of the Rural and Urban Poor, and the Centre of Dialogue on Human Settlement and Poverty Alleviation (CODOHSAPA). This chapter is based on the dialogical reflections of five members of the learning alliance: four researchers based at the time at the DPU in the UK and one based in Sierra Leone. We explore how the principles of the learning alliance have been practised over four years between 2017 and 2021. The first two years included DPU ESD staff and students travelling to conduct fieldwork with local partners in Freetown, whilst the last two years were based on remote collaboration, due to the impact and travel restrictions imposed by the COVID-19 pandemic.

More specifically, we reflect on two aspects that support practice-based co-learning: 1) the principles that guide learning with others to generate reciprocal and meaningful encounters with the lived realities of African women and men; and 2) the pedagogic practices that support reflexive learning to foment key insights or 'new' ways of seeing and understanding Freetown. After elaborating on the pedagogical principles of the learning alliance, the following sections examine four key modes for co-learning applied in Freetown: learning spatially, embedded learning, reflexive learning, and strategic networking of urban knowledges.

Pedagogic principles of co-learning in the MSc ESD/ SLURC Learning Alliance

Between 2017 and 2021, the MSc ESD/SLURC Learning Alliance provided a shared platform to co-produce knowledge. It included UK-based international students, researchers at the DPU and SLURC, as well as local interns, practitioners, inhabitants and community representatives in Freetown. Transdisciplinary teams worked over four years to diagnose environmental injustices and co-develop concrete strategies to tackle them. Over the years, these teams conducted research on nine themes (including land and housing, waste management, sanitation, mobility, energy amongst others) in eight settlements across Freetown (Cockle Bay, Moyiba, Dworzark, Susan's Bay, Portee-Rokupa, Crab Town/Kolleh Town/Grey Bush (CKG), Colbot, Kroo Bay), and produced fifteen policy briefs, 17 videos and three reports[1]. Taken together, insights from these themes and locations are entry points to develop strategic pathways towards environmentally just urban futures in Freetown.

To understand the principles and practices involved, it is important to recognise that the notion of a learning alliance evokes that learning is not conceptualised as a theoretical and individualised process that precedes action, but rather as happening in action and interaction with others. The focus is not so much on learning about Freetown, but learning with, from and for the city and its actors. The pedagogic goal encapsulated in the notion of an alliance is thus to cultivate the sensibilities and capacities required for all participants to engage in co-learning towards environmentally just cities. As with previous learning alliances, '[w]e approach such a pedagogical undertaking as a fundamentally political process that opens, in our view, multiple opportunities to explore new ways of conceiving, perceiving and living the city; to contrast and interrogate preconceptions and ultimately, to oxygenate the ways in which we connect urban theory and planning praxis, within a world made of differences' (Allen et al., 2018, p. 356). Hence, learning in alliance and as an alliance requires recognising the political nature of learning, unlearning and re-learning relationally; acknowledging, problematising and working with and against the tacit and explicit inequalities upon which research processes and partnerships with equivalence are built.

The juxtaposition of diverse learners and geographies – and of their worldviews, experiences, aspirations, and knowledges – makes collectively learning Freetown neither a straightforward nor a predictable process. Rather, the drafting of our terms of reference, group formation, the design and implementation of data gathering and analysis, and the production and dissemination of outputs, are complex processes of encounters, detours, and circumventions.

The compass to navigate these complex processes is a set of principles which have been developed across the DPU's MSc programmes and continuously refined through each learning alliance (Allen et al., 2015). In the MSc in Environment and Sustainable Development, these principles relate to learning spatially, embedded learning, reflexive learning, and strategic networking of urban knowledges. Put into practice, these principles aspire to strengthen the individual and collective capacities of transdisciplinary teams to:

1. Read, produce and audience maps as a mode of investigation and communication to grasp the spatiality of environmental (in)justices in all their complexity, while revealing the multitude of actors and how different parts of the city are governed
2. Embed themselves in local contexts and understand the power dynamics and agency of different actors to influence urban processes

towards environmental justice at multiple scales. 'Embedding' here is understood as rooting oneself in a wider network of urban practitioners based on social attachments such as friendships and professional relationships. Closely related to this principle is the process of situated learning, which refers to the positionality we take in interpreting and practising within this network

3.   Develop a reflexive praxis individually and collectively, while challenging our assumptions and biases throughout the action-learning process

4.   Recognise the ecosystem of urban knowledges at work, in the way a city is perceived and experienced and what part they play in theory and practice, with the aim of foregrounding marginalised knowledges as well as creating spaces for constructive dialogue and advocacy.

While these principles are interconnected, in the following sections we take each as an entry point to elaborate on their application in Freetown.

Learning spatially – revealing 'hidden' governance structures

The pedagogical approach of the ESD learning alliances is based on shifting modes and spaces as participants move between theory and practice, between desk and ground, and between local and trans-local connections. These movements, in their iterative form, help precipitate collective 'aha' moments that promote a different way of learning and acting upon the city. To begin with, for each new cohort of ESD students, the research and learning kicks off from afar. Many months are dedicated to desktop research in preparation for fieldwork, often relying on scarce academic sources and grey material that is difficult to verify in a context with an information lacuna like Sierra Leone. This time is used to grasp key concepts and set the boundaries for enquiry in dialogue with local partners. An important step before all parties meet face to face in the field, is to find productive ways to acknowledge and make explicit assumptions that would otherwise remain unchallenged, if not captured in concrete ways.

Critically engaging with spatial information and mapping collectively has been crucial for all those involved in the alliance to better understand what is happening in Freetown. For months, we scanned satellite maps, travelling across rooftops and reading geographic signifiers to establish relations between things we thought could be known authoritatively, like infrastructure, topography, community functions, place names, and boundaries amongst others. On the ground, the ESD cohorts are joined by local interns, researchers and community representatives to work on the ground through transdisciplinary teams. This mapping helps guide the conversation with others, confronts pre-conceptions and provokes new readings of the urban. In so doing, it makes visible otherwise hidden processes and the myriad of relations that constitute the city. The mapping work that was undertaken by the teams in Colbot and Dworzark, two informal settlements in Freetown, are here illustrative of the new readings that emerged through the process.

Situated on a hillside and home to approximately 30,000 people, Dworzark has twelve clusters defined by the local community and named after the countries that have played in the FIFA World Cup, with Germany, England, Brazil, Italy and Ethiopia among them. Colbot, located in a low-lying area between the sea and the second largest dumpsite in the city, is divided into six zones also locally defined: Rockfall, Crown Base, Camp No Strain, Headquarter, Central and Last Banking. These zones and clusters appear to approximately correlate with different waves of arrivals in each settlement over time and they also reflect the territorial divisions used by external support agencies to coordinate risk responses.

Team members plotted the boundaries on their maps prior to the fieldwork, expecting that they would translate into clear governance structures within the settlements. However, the lines on paper did not reflect the complexity of reality. Dworzark is governed through a multitude of networked actors, many embedded in the customary system, with eighteen traditional chiefs from various clans, mammy queens (key women leaders), religious leaders and various civil society organisations. Mapping revealed that these key actors had no evident territorial anchors linked to the toponomy of our maps, as their roles and responsibility were spatially diffused. The cultural and spiritual affiliations, imperceptible to outsiders at first sight, were the very fabric driving development in Dworzark.

In Colbot, it was impossible to ignore the influence of religion on the lived space and lives of inhabitants as we encountered numerous Imams supervising the building of their mosques; veiled girls walking to Islamic schools; and regular calls for prayer from different megaphones and turrets within the settlement. Although transect walks were important to draw attention to the importance of religion in this settlement, it was not until the map was unfolded and community representatives and local inhabitants placed on it all the dots that mark religious organisations that a new interpretation of reality emerged. It became evident that Colbot has a very large number of religious organisations in relation to its population size.

While invisible from the initial desktop studies, religion emerged as a key driver of development and social organisation within the settlement. Most puzzling for those coming from outside Sierra Leone was how Islam, the prevailing religion in Colbot, manifested through not one but numerous mosques, some within the same street. Different mosques had different joining fees and compulsory donation practices. Each therefore catered for different groups of dwellers within the settlement, while taking differential social, spiritual, and economic functions.

As the team's immersion in Colbot progressed, participatory mapping (Figure 12.1) revealed the myriad of separate organisations under the umbrella of Islam, as well as numerous civil society organisations and savings groups, often overlapping in function and scope. Faced with this complexity, discussions within the team revolved around the need to streamline governance arrangements, and a consolidation of efforts and resources to get rid of redundancy. However, through further reflection and debates with community representatives, 'redundancy' was reframed, not as a hindrance, but a positive feature that sustains many inhabitants that might otherwise fall through the net. The agential response of local organisations to adverse social, political, and economic environments is backed by their invisible structures, overlap and interconnectivity. Recognising these structures, without over-glorifying them, provided all learners with a critical lens that acknowledged the quiet encroachment of otherwise overlooked systems in development and people's lives. Such a reading of place cannot simply be plotted on a map, but rather begs an examination beyond the settlement and the mapping of wider sets of relations within Freetown and beyond that reveal where the power of these structures comes from and how they acquire legitimacy under the broader umbrella of religion or customary tradition. These realisations also demanded the adoption of an intersectional perspective to better understand why so many organisations emerged and survived. They also gave us a chance to analyse more profoundly how diversity and exclusion are manifested in/through space and urban governance.

Using tools like mapping across various settlements in Freetown enabled the co-learning teams to capture the spatial manifestation of critical issues at various scales, to learn about otherwise invisible processes and to foster critical reflection and awareness for all involved.

Figure 12.1 Participatory mapping with inhabitants to better understand the organisations on the ground and their territorial reach. Source: © DPU MSc ESD (2019)

Embedded learning – challenging misconceptions and foregrounding marginalised voices

A central aspiration of the learning alliance is to embed action-research processes so they generate reciprocal and meaningful encounters with the lived realities of women and men in Freetown. That is, to co-produce knowledge that recognises the experiences and aspirations of local dwellers, whose city-making practices often remain overlooked in spaces of decision-making and therefore are unsupported by development policies and programmes.

The process of immersing the transdisciplinary teams in the context of selected settlements triggered many opportunities for staff, students, interns, community representatives and local dwellers to challenge assumptions and re-problematise misconceptions commonly held in relation to local experiences, practices and aspirations. Pedagogically, this process was curated through multiple steps, starting with a joint and careful selection of the settlements willing and interested in participating in the learning alliance. In some instances, our work deepened previous research and SLURC's local partnerships in specific localities. While in others, they created opportunities for engagements in previously under-researched communities. An example of the former is research in the settlement of Cockle Bay, which received significant attention through action-research projects, such as Urban Africa Risk Knowledge (Urban ARK) and Knowledge in Action for Urban Equality (KNOW), both analysed in other chapters of this book.

In Cockle Bay, the learning alliance sought to shed light on perspectives that remained hidden despite multiple previous research engagements. We used methods which included household surveys to investigate the intersectional aspects of environmental injustices, as well as the existing local capacities to tackle them. For instance, in 2019 participants in the learning alliance conducted a survey which revealed that almost 80% of Cockle Bay's households were tenants, with female-headed households representing almost half of the total. Timelines (Figure 12.2) further revealed that many tenants were not a transient group, but long-term residents of the settlement. These findings stood in contrast to common perceptions, by outsiders as well as Freetonians, of tenants being a predominantly single and male fluctuating group, which spends short periods in Cockle Bay while engaging in casual labour and petty trade in the city centre. This misconception implied that female, long-term, tenants were typically disregarded by local community structures as potential or active contributors to community-led improvements. They were also not considered and supported by the government and other urban actors.

Challenging this misconception required in-depth qualitative methodologies which allowed for processes of individual and collective unlearning and relearning, embedded within a network of social relations. In Cockle Bay, the learning alliance engaged in several in-depth conversations, which offered further insights into the complex social relations of female tenants, and their ways of navigating their invisibility within the settlement. For instance, 'Amina' migrated from the countryside three decades ago. Thanks to her lineage connection with one of the local Chiefs, she settled in Hillet View, the oldest and most consolidated part of Cockle Bay. In contrast, 'Fatima' moved in 2017 from a nearby rented dwelling that became unaffordable, to settle with her three children as a tenant in a predominantly Muslim area known as Mafengbeh. For both, Cockle Bay is not a provisional 'shelter' solution, but rather 'home'. Yet, their experiences talk about the struggle to be included and recognised as part of the local community in their capacity of engaging and leading individual and collective improvements and upgrading efforts.

Women like Amina and Fatima carve different ways to be part of collective action efforts. For Amina, working with SLURC as a community facilitator enabled her to realise and then show others that not all tenants in Cockle Bay are men seeking a temporary place to sleep at night: 'I have been in this community for decades, but I only realised recently that if you are a woman and a tenant, you are not part of the story, you don't know who to talk to. Since then, I have been fighting to open the eyes of our community leaders and explain that ALL women have a right to join the local saving groups, regardless of whether or not we are tenants.'

Fatima is not yet part of any saving group. Since her arrival in Cockle Bay, the local Imam has been her main support to navigate through local social dynamics and relations. She recalls: 'For some time I didn't even know that there were any women's groups in Cockle Bay, my Imam told me to work hard, and he mediated with my landlord to accept some of the improvements I made as part of my rent.' Fatima's shack is next to the coast, in a spot where several hanging toilets are located, an area that gets flooded with human waste every time it rains. Six months after settling in Cockle Bay, she started to build a defence made of sandbags to protect her home from the floods and soon after joined forces with another three households to install a water tap and to build a shared latrine. 'At the time, people told me I was crazy to pay for things that were going to benefit my landlord and even perhaps increase my rent, but this is our home now and worth every effort, even if I don't know how long I will be able to stay here.'

These two contrasting trajectories tell us about some of the many challenges and opportunities of women who are and might always be tenants. More widely, they highlight why their tenure security status is often not just overlooked by researchers and decision-makers, but also by local community structures. Embedded (un)learning that engages with typically marginalised dwellers, has the power to shed light on gender inequalities and often-overlooked dimensions of urban research, planning and practice. In this instance, embedded learning opened new ways of 'seeing the city like a woman and a tenant'. This, in turn, enabled participants in the learning alliance to 'see' a whole web of relations that shape how people go about gaining access to and control over water, sanitation, energy and so on. It allowed us to challenge firm misconceptions on how and under what conditions they produce and invest in cities like Freetown. Practising the principle of embeddedness means nurturing the capacity of local dwellers and communities and of (future) urban practitioners through methodological skills as well as relational sensibilities. This allows the development of strategies that challenge blind spots and marginalising political processes, and hence have further capacity to advance gender equality and inclusive urban development.

Figure 12.2 Focus group discussion to populate the settlement timeline and capture the arrival date of residents. Source: © DPU MSc ESD (2019)

Reflexive learning – confronting normalised roles, practices and traditions

An important aspect of the learning alliance is its composition, which allows collaboration between so-called 'insiders' and 'outsiders', i.e. between researchers, practitioners, interns, community representatives and local dwellers who have lived and worked in Freetown, and ESD staff and students. The long-standing partnership between DPU and SLURC and its affiliated organisations provided everyone in the alliance with a safe space to engage with difficult and uncomfortable questions to make sense of the realities encountered through a process of individual and collective reflection. Regular dialogue and exchange between 'insiders' and 'outsiders' offered a fresh perspective on the situations and developments observed on the ground and enabled all involved to challenge and reconsider what seems to be taken for granted and perceived as unchangeable. This can be illustrated through research conducted in Portee-Rokupa, a peri-urban coastal settlement in Freetown, where we focused on a critical examination of water gathering practices from a gendered perspective.

Sierra Leone remains, by and large, a patriarchal society that normalises the subordination of women and girls and the roles and identities prescribed for them (Borishansky, n.d.). Social norms and persisting cultural ideas actively shape practices within local communities whereby women and children (especially girls) are responsible within their households for managing and procuring access to water (Figure 12.3). The reproduction of patriarchal relations and the assumption that women and girls are naturally best placed to meet the water needs of their households, translate into well-documented gender inequalities that manifest in time poverty and differential access to education, among other negative impacts.

Portee-Rokupa has experienced a steady influx of people since the Civil War, which has increased the demand for basic services, such as clean water and good sanitation facilities. Over time, this community has been reported as one of the hotspots for diseases such as cholera and Ebola. Participatory research in the field through mapping, transect walks, focus group discussions and individual interviews confirmed gender disparities and highlighted not only how most women and girls carry an extra burden when it comes to accessing drinking water sources, but also shed light on their coping strategies and a degree of resilience to deal with the challenges they face. 'Abdulai' and 'Sallay' have lived in this community for over twenty years and experienced increasing challenges related to water supply. In one of our discussions with them about gender roles to secure water access, Abdulai was aware of the burden on women and girls, which he describes as follows: 'Women and girls are more vulnerable when it comes to accessing water. They are more involved than men who sometimes only return home in the evening from work.' To substantiate his point, he drew attention to the water sources within the community, as well as beyond it, that predominantly show women and girls queuing for water. He further emphasised the heightened risk of sexual violence, particularly for the younger women and girls. Sallay confirmed that accessing water is difficult for her and her children, age nine and twelve, stressing her dependence on local water providers for meeting her family's water needs: 'I sometimes have to wake up very early in the morning together with my children to access the water source closer to my house [but] (d)espite waking up so early in the morning to queue, there are times when the owners of local water facilities refuse to grant us access especially during the dry season.'

Sallay further talked about the risk of gender-based violence when relying on water sources outside her compound. She remembered that when she was about 15 or 20 years old, she and her friends were often harassed by young men on their way to access water late in the evenings: 'This didn't stop me from going to fetch water. I tried my best to resist them although most of my friends gave in and they got pregnant leading to their drop out from school.'

The vulnerability of women and girls towards gender-based violence linked to water access is not limited to Portee-Rokupa. The research in Dworzark provided insights into how gangs monopolise water sources and grant access in exchange for sex. Corporeal violence on women and girls is one of the most acute yet not only consequence of their subordinated position within the patriarchal society.

Someone growing up in the city within these communities may be accustomed to the experiences recalled by Abdulai and Sallay, as the 'way life is' While many are aware of the gender inequalities that persist within their communities and society at large, a shift from patriarchal practices towards gender equality often seems unattainable. It is therefore assumed that it is up to individuals to find a way to cope, as put by Sallay: 'We should learn to be resilient because the change and strife to these norms seems impossible and therefore, we should always use the beauty of no-choice and love to outweigh the pains.'

While the structural changes required to address gender equalities are by no means easy, the learning alliance nurtured a critical and ethical engagement among its members to unsettle routine practices and customs that normalise unequal gender roles, as well as inaction towards such injustices. This has created a consciousness among members of the alliance to challenge the taken-for-granted as a basis to imagine transformative change (Katz, 2004). The methodologies and processes of

Figure 12.3 Image showing how the burden of carrying water for daily use falls on women and children. Source: © Rita Lambert (2019)

critical exchange and reflection on underlying worldviews, assumptions and beliefs can better prepare urban practitioners with the capacities needed for more inclusive urban futures.

Strategic networking of urban knowledges – trans-local learning across innovative practices

Learning spatially, reflexively, and collectively within the learning alliance enables participants to confront assumptions and provoke new framings of urban change. The accounts in the previous sections above all demonstrate the importance of situating and embedding ourselves in the field to trigger important insights. However, the onset of the COVID-19 pandemic in December 2019, with strict global travel restrictions, meant enforced physical remoteness from the field throughout 2020 and 2021. Since transdisciplinary learning relies heavily on immersion in context, having contact with people and being able to closely collaborate, what happens when physical distancing is the new reality? Here, embeddedness is deeply cast into question.

The team members of the learning alliance were challenged to curate a relational inquiry into lived experiences of concrete social groups in a context where physical fieldwork was made impossible for ESD staff and students. Many of the latter lacked prior experience of living and/or working in African cities.

Confronted with the new reality of the pandemic, many students reflected on their 'outsider' positionality, asking how to contribute to the production of embedded, rigorous, and relevant knowledge from afar. Local interns in Freetown became the groups' eyes, ears and voices on the ground, which raised difficult questions around mediating and negotiating multiple expectations especially between community members and students. At the same time, this approach affirmed the critical role of interns as integral team members throughout the design and analysis of each group's research.

With the advent of the COVID-19 pandemic, it became clear that practising the principle of embeddedness had to go beyond basic considerations in the shift from in-person to online co-learning. Pedagogically, practising embeddedness remotely required a fundamental realignment of the different roles, responsibilities, aspirations and practices assumed within the learning alliance. Setting aside any anxiety related to the lack of 'fieldwork' as commonly understood and practiced, the pandemic opened new opportunities for co-learning, for situated practices and for understanding 'the field'. Local interns and SLURC staff in Freetown engaged much earlier and worked regularly alongside students and staff in London. Moreover, this brought about the possibility of reaching out to other 'elsewheres' to broaden knowledge and stakeholder networks. As we moved online, 'the field' changed, no longer conjuring a determined geographic space, but rather relating to a set of wider relations developed on the basis of overlapping concerns, interests and agendas.

Learning alliances are set up over several years so that cohorts can build on, and expand, the work done in previous years. As teams could draw on research undertaken by the learning alliance over two years prior to the pandemic, including fieldwork in various settlements, they already had context-specific insights from previous cohorts. Their focus then shifted to learning from a diverse range of progressive initiatives worldwide that could provide valuable insights for supporting environmental justice in Freetown. They interviewed several international organisations, as well as local institutions and civil society groups engaged in these initiatives, drawing key lessons for just and sustainable urban development. Through this process, 'the field' was re-imagined and widened with the possibilities of networking stakeholders globally and supporting South–South knowledge exchanges.

The work of the team working on food security illustrates this well. They focused on understanding the workings of community kitchens in light of the COVID-19 pandemic, since it aggravated pressures on food security in Freetown and elsewhere. Households suffered from falling purchase power due to a loss in daily income and remittances, exacerbated by rising food prices. Moreover, human mobility restrictions and market closures severely curtailed the ability of people to access food sources. Global and regional food production, food logistics, and food supply chains were significantly disrupted. In this context, community-driven responses played a pivotal role in tackling the emergency, both for their capacity to efficiently act at the local level and for strengthening community resilience.

As the learning alliance interviewed different stakeholders from community kitchens around the globe, including those in Freetown, it became apparent that participants would benefit from, and were interested in, a space to exchange experiences and ideas. Several spin-offs from the research were generated in this way. For the team working on food security, this meant organising an online workshop entitled 'Cooking together: Sharing knowledge for sustainable community kitchens' with participants from Santiago, Lima, Cape Town, and Freetown. This

Figure 12.4 Map showing the location of initiatives that were examined under the 2021 Learning Alliance. Source: © DPU MSc ESD (2021)

exchange explored the opportunities and challenges of engaging in community kitchens in response to the COVID-19 crisis and how to make these sustainable beyond the pandemic. Given the renewed importance of, and interest in, community kitchens brought about by the pandemic, this interaction supported a network of community kitchen initiatives across the four cities with an emphasis on South–South exchanges.

The example of community kitchens clearly hints that, as geographies of learning shift, so does the configuration of learning flows within and between local and global scales; hence, issue-based comparative research across cities of the Global South became an important strategy for co-producing relevant knowledge from and for Freetown and beyond. In 2021 alone, eight working groups reached out to representatives from almost 70 initiatives across the globe (Figure 12.4) to learn trans-locally about progressive and transformative actions to tackle environmental injustices. This is not to deny the importance of deeply contextual diagnoses and strategies, but rather to demonstrate the scope of remote engagement and co-learning. Specifically, this remote engagement allowed groups to take inspiration from transformative approaches elsewhere, previously invisible, not considered or intentionally nurtured, to further just and sustainable agendas in the context of Freetown.

Re-learning Freetown collectively

The pedagogic approach applied by our learning alliance invited those participating to think and see differently; to challenge pre-established conceptions, advancing the possibility of building theory from the ground, and adopting an unsettling collective inquiry to reveal deeply ingrained blind spots. Reframing existing narratives and diagnoses to produce actionable knowledge for just and sustainable futures requires going beyond the usual suspects, paying attention to the knowledge and capacities of marginalised dwellers, and putting the spotlight on overlooked dimensions of urban research, planning and practice.

The organisation of the learning alliance by its very nature dismantles formal structures of learning, opening new avenues for understanding the city collectively. At the same time, Freetown as a learning environment is profoundly generative as it provokes learners to confront assumptions about how the city works. It also forces learners to engage with the aspirations, practices, and experiences of those often referred to as the 'urban poor'; an ambiguous notion that hides the full complexity and diversity of the social identities and relations through which a large majority of women and men claim and carve their right to the city.

Shifting from learning and writing about African cities to, instead, learning from and with them means making learning with others an embedded unlearning and relearning process based on trust and care. Worth highlighting is how the experience of the learning alliance over the last two years, which overlapped with the COVID-19 pandemic, provides further lessons for how we might practise and cultivate remote instead of distant learning. The experience has made us appreciate multiple new ways of doing research and conceiving the 'field', to work with different forms of embeddedness, inhabiting a wider field of relations that do not depend on physical, but rather social, proximity. Although these reflections were by no means conclusive in producing 'how to' solutions for remote co-learning, they nevertheless opened up different imaginaries of its possibilities. This matters profoundly for constructing a shared and inclusive vision for how 'we', as a wider collective of urban thinkers and practitioners, can work towards transformative change and more inclusive urban planning and development. Given the complex global challenges we face, everyday city-makers and professional practitioners require capacities to detect opportunities within what might seem dire situations, to embrace different physicalities and relations, to navigate different scales and disciplines, as well as to actively network diverse geographies.

As argued by Bayat in his 2013 book *Life as Politics*, the transformative power of everyday actions by ordinary citizens is often overlooked and somehow silenced in accounts of how injustices are counteracted through practices of quiet encroachment. Allen (2022) raises a similar point when exploring the counter-stigmatisation strategies practiced by poor women and men in the context of Lima's peripheral urbanisation processes. These authors, among others, point to the importance of interrogating differently the dynamics of social and spatial change. In relation to this point, co-learning is a critical means to generate new accounts and insights which are not just articulated by a third party but by ordinary citizens themselves retaining the power of deciding what needs to come to the fore to negotiate and ultimately advance more just urban trajectories.

Approached as a fundamentally political activity, situated co-learning can promote a sense of political confidence equitably among those whose voices are typically excluded. This does not simply imply their involvement in the thick description of their experiences and practices but relies on crafting spaces for collective reflection, interpretation and action that, in turn, nurture a process of 'conscientisation', or critical awareness of the social and material world (Freire, 1969). In the case of Freetown, the political agency of local communities participating in the learning alliance develop through the iterative nature of the process and through its practice – through and beyond the alliance – in the community action area plan (CAAP), an ongoing interface for local communities to meaningfully participate in the planning of Freetown (Koroma & Macarthy, 2022).

Yet, the political is always personal as much as the personal is always political. Thus, the capacity of this learning engagement to dive deeper into overlooked questions, also comes with the responsibility to engage sensitively with instances of recalling traumatising experiences, for instance of sexual violence. This in turn calls for developing the capacity of all participants to engage actively with the ethics of research practice, which go far beyond protocols and adhering to questions of anonymity, no harm and confidentiality. Doing so entails anticipating the potential consequences of an open learning environment for its participants and developing a strong sensibility and sense of care to draw the line between what can lead to either their empowerment or disempowerment.

Note

1 The outputs can be accessed through the ESD Learning Alliance website: www.esdlearningalliance.net

References

Allen, A. (2022). Navigating stigma through everyday city-making: gendered trajectories, politics and outcomes in the periphery of Lima. *Urban Studies, 59*(3), 490–508. https://doi.org/10.1177/00420980211044409

Allen, A., Boano, C., Frediani, A. A., Levy, C., Lipietz, B., & Walker, J. (2015). Five principles for de-centered urban learning. Urban Pamphleteer #5: Global Education for Urban Futures. Accessed 16 January 2022. http://www.urbanpamphleteer.org/global-education-for-urban-futures

Allen, A., Lambert, R., & Yap, C. (2018). Co-learning the city – towards a pedagogy of poly-learning and planning praxis. In V. Watson, B. Bhan, & Srinivas, S. (Eds), *Companion to Planning in the Global South* (pp. 355–367). London: Routledge.

Bayat, A. (2013). *Life as Politics: How ordinary people change the Middle East.* Amsterdam: Amsterdam University Press.

Borishansky, M. (n.d.). Examining gender inequality in the post-conflict peacebuilding efforts of Sierra Leone. In G. Burgess and H. Burgess (Eds), Beyond Intractability. Conflict Research Consortium, University of Colorado, Boulder, Colorado, USA. Accessed 10 March 2022. https://www.beyondintractability.org/casestudy/borishansky-gender-sierra-leone

Freire, P. (1969). *Education for Critical Consciousness.* New York: Continuum.

Katz, C. (2004). *Growing up Global: Restructuring and children's everyday lives.* Minneapolis: University of Minnesota Press.

Koroma, B., & Macarthy, J. (2022). Participatory planning: the role of community and city learning platforms in Freetown. GOLD VI Pathways to Urban and Territorial Equality, Cases Repository: Democratizing. United Cities and Local Governments. Accessed 15 January 2024. https://gold.uclg.org/sites/default/files/2022-06/ch9_democratizing_57.pdf

Lambert, R. and Hofmann, P. (Eds). (2021). Students Reports MScESD/SLURC Learning Alliance. Transformative Strategies for a just Freetown. London: DPU. Accessed 9 August 2024. https://www.ucl.ac.uk/bartlett/development/sites/bartlett_development/files/report_transformativestrategiesfreetown.pdf

Parnell, S., & Pieterse, E. (2016). Translational global praxis: rethinking methods and modes of African urban research. *International Journal of Urban and Regional Research, 40*(1), 236–246.

Watson, V., & Odendaal, N. (2013). Changing planning education in Africa: the role of the association of African planning schools. *Journal of Planning Education and Research, 33*(1), 96–107.

13

Freetown through a citizens' media lens: participatory photography for inclusive neighbourhood planning and beyond

Alexander Macfarlane and Alexander Stone

Introduction

The proliferation of digital technology has resulted in citizens from even the most remote parts of the globe enjoying the ability to capture high-resolution images and share them instantaneously, with the potential of going 'viral'. It is becoming increasingly common to see such citizen-produced digital outputs on traditional media platforms. We have witnessed the power of citizens' news sources on social media to change how people see the world, how they treat themselves, and each other. Despite this improved access to powerful technology – bringing with it unparalleled access to information – and the means to share and consume it, old issues remain. Growing inequality, lack of access to essential services, inadequate housing and poor planning remains a reality for many living in the Global South.

This chapter critically engages with communication for development and social change, situating participatory photography within this broader field. It considers how photography can be used to produce grassroots, or citizens' media, in a way that can challenge mainstream media discourse. In the Sierra Leonean context, this typically depicts informal settlements and their residents in a negative and stigmatising manner.

The core of this chapter is based on a week-long collaborative workshop held at SLURC that brought together a group of ten participants from two Freetown informal settlements, Cockle Bay and Dworzark.

This workshop, undertaken by the authors of this chapter, was based on the DPU's previous engagements in the field of civic urban media, also drawing heavily on the ASF-UK's Change by Design methodology (see Chapter 9).

This chapter concludes by looking forward. Using analysis from the workshop, the views of its participants and the wider Freetown community, the authors will examine the opportunities for photography as a participatory visual technology to be used in the Freetown context. Specifically, this chapter explores its potential to build upon existing residents' networks to challenge dominant representations within mainstream media and contribute towards inclusive urban planning.

Media landscape

The workshop that forms the basis of this chapter emerged from a consideration of the role that citizens' media could play in urban planning, and how groups of citizen journalists could use photography as a tool to self-represent, tell their own narratives, recodify collective identities and interact with mainstream media discourses. A long-term intention for the legacy of the workshop was to begin developing a network of potential citizen journalists who could continue to produce audio-visual outputs for SLURC.

Much of the literature on mass media production highlights the power imbalances inherent in the top-down process of news production. The mass media can be understood as narrative-makers that can influence public perception (Macdonald, 2003, p. 1). The media act discursively, producing representations that play an active constitutive role in constructing a particular 'reality' (Hall, cited in Macdonald, 2003, p. 12) rather than just reflecting and reporting on events that have happened in the past.

If the media plays an active role in cultural construction, then this can be argued to reflect the ideological interests of those who own the media, often society's elites (Herman & Chomsky, 1994). As a result, the representation of individuals or groups in society (whether positive or negative) is rooted in structural systems.

Sierra Leone has an increasingly diversified media landscape, though radio remains the most common form of mass communication (BBC, 2016). However, since 2002 there has been a proliferation of TV stations, mobile phone usage and internet access (BBC, 2016). According to the Freedom of the Press Index 2020 (RSF, 2020), mainstream media in the country is considered pluralist and independent, with measures being taken to guarantee the protection of journalists to operate freely. Most notably, legislation that criminalised press offences was repealed in 2020, which makes steps towards ending the arbitrary arrests of journalists.

Radio remains the most common form of mass communication (BBC, 2016), with print media remaining relatively niche (Wittels & Maybanks, 2016, p. 17). Despite the growth of the number of newspapers available, barriers such as national literacy rates have resulted in readership remaining low. The majority of the consumers of print media are located in urban areas such as Freetown (Wittels & Maybanks, 2016, p. 17), where there are over a dozen newspapers printed (Mediabuzz.org, 2020).

Although somewhat diverse and with a degree of freedom, the mainstream media in Sierra Leone can still be understood as typically top-down. Media such as newspapers are generally privately owned, though must be registered with the Ministry of Information (Wittels & Maybanks, 2016, p. 17). Applying Herman and Chomsky's *political economy of the mass media* model we can understand how representations of informal settlements manufactured through the mass media reflect the interests of media producers and also shape the perceptions of media consumers. Residents of informal settlements are largely excluded from being able to portray themselves through the mass media.

The informal settlements of Freetown are usually framed by the media as places characterised primarily by what they lack in terms of services, rather than by the inventiveness of residents and their capacity to act. A dominant representation of residents of informal settlements is that they struggle with widespread poverty and deprivation. While some residents do not dismiss the insanitary conditions in which they and their neighbours live, they resent being defined by it. This view was vividly expressed by a Development Committee Member, Abu Sesay in Cockle Bay as follows:

> You tell me about any part of Freetown that does not require improvement. We accept that our places are bad but there are also a lot of good things happening here. Why do they always have to report [only] the negative aspects?

In particular, residents observe a significant disconnect between their life experiences and the prevailing media discourses. They maintain that journalists continuously portray exaggerated messages regarding deplorable and at-risk conditions in the settlements, while disregarding the valued features that residents celebrate. Residents agree that there are both good and bad things about living in informal settlements but feel frustrated when people who live outside of those places only report on the negative aspects.

Workshop context and background

The one-week collaborative workshop held in Freetown in February 2018 aimed to contribute towards the ongoing communication action area planning project that was being undertaken at the time through a collaborative alliance between ASF-UK, SLURC and the DPU: 'The Role of Action Area Plans for Inclusive City-Making in Freetown' (for more information on the project, see Chapter 15).

Through a week of photography training and practice, a group of ten participants from two of Freetown's informal settlements, Cockle Bay and Dworzark, were brought together to consider issues of their choosing faced by their communities, to explain the context of these issues and their impact on residents; consider both current and potential solutions and finally to include any barriers to these solutions.

The workshop was based on the ASF-UK CbD methodology of diagnosis, dreaming, developing and defining (for more on this see Frediani, 2016). It was designed to explore the extent to which participatory photography (PP) as a methodology could be utilised in the information gathering stages of the above research project, whilst simultaneously remaining true to the PP methodology, including placing importance on storytelling and narrative.

The consideration of issues at the different scales of home, neighbourhood and city is also a feature of both this workshop and the Change by Design methodology. This methodology and its significance in shaping this particular PP engagement will be detailed in the methodology section.

Communication for development and social change, citizens' media and civic urban media

The workshop was rooted in the theoretical traditions of participatory action research (PAR) and communication for development and social change (CfDSSC).

PAR forms part of the action research tradition, an integral part of which is the inclusion of participants as co-researchers who engage in cycles of action and reflection. With PAR also aiming to encourage dialogue through the creation of new 'communicative spaces' (Reason & Bradbury, 2008, p. 3), there is considerable overlap between the literature on PAR and on participatory approaches to communications for development (Gumucio-Dagron, 2006). Fraser and Restrepo-Estrada (cited in Quarry & Ramirez, 2009, p. 9) define CfDSSC as

> the use of communicating process, techniques and media to help people toward a full awareness of their situation and their options for change, to resolve conflicts, to work towards consensus, to help people plan actions for change and sustainable development, to help people acquire the knowledge and skills they need to improve their condition and that of society, and to improve the effectiveness of institutions.

Storytelling methodologies that use digital media as part of the research process form part of the body of literature on participatory communication for development. PP is one such methodology that falls within the scope of PAR.

However, alternative forms of communication practices have emerged in response to these imbalances, providing the possibility to challenge the dominant representations produced, known as citizens' media. Citizens' media can be understood as occurring when 'the people are responsible for gathering content, visioning, producing and publishing the news product,' wherein 'professionals are not involved at all' (Nip, 2006, p. 218). Citizens' media is when those that are traditionally the audience or consumers of media become the content producers (Rosen, 2008). It is an alternative to mainstream media, allowing people to construct their own knowledge and tell their own narratives which manifests as an alternative source of power (Pettit et al., 2009, p. 444). Citizens' media can be used to directly influence content in mainstream media, for advocacy, to build an independent media in which a new media discourse can be constructed, or to empower audiences to be more critical of media representations (Carroll & Hackett, 2006, p. 88–89).

The workshop also aimed at contributing to the growing portfolio of work being undertaken by the DPU that has been termed 'civic urban media'. Civic urban media aims to explore the nexus between digital media, civic participation and urban planning. Civic urban media additionally takes the communication methodology as the object of analysis in itself (UCL, 2018). Drawing on the body of literature on media discourse and citizens' media, the workshop was used as a way to:

1) Consider the extent to which photography could be used as a communications tool that, when in the hands of members of the public, could constitute a form of citizens' media.

2) Explore how photography could be used by residents of informal settlements to challenge dominant representations and discourses produced through the mainstream media, to tell their own story and to consider the type of home, community and city in which they would like to live.

3) Build on the DPU's work around civic urban media and consider the extent to which this grassroots media could be a tool to influence urban planning, in particular the ASF-UK CbD process.

Participatory photography

Emerging from the theoretical background outlined in the section above, the workshop utilised PP as a PAR and CfDSSC methodology. PP draws on PAR and CfDSSC in that it encourages individuals and communities to utilise a visual methodology in order to tell their own story. It can be defined as

> a process by which people can identify, represent, and enhance their community through a specific photographic technique. It entrusts cameras to the hands of people to enable them to act as recorders, and potential catalysts for social action and change, in their own communities. It uses the immediacy of the visual image and accompanying stories to furnish evidence and to promote an effective, participatory means of sharing expertise to create healthful public policy. (Wang & Burris, cited in Blackman & Fairey, 2014, p. 10)

The Change by Design methodology is made up of four stages. Diagnosis, concerned with understanding and analysing the nature of issues faced by the community. Dreaming, where different design methods are used to unlock creative aspirations. Developing, aimed at developing and assessing a number of potential planning and design options and defining, which includes discussing priorities for action and revealing challenges and opportunities for implementing action. These stages are undertaken at three different scales: home, neighbourhood, and city. Groups work separately at their scale until coming together for the final stage, where shared challenges and opportunities are identified (ASF-UK et al., 2017).

Challenges and limitations of PP methodology

Before undertaking the engagement, it was important to understand the challenges and limitations of PP as a methodology, and then to take steps to mitigate them. This begins with photography as a medium for communication in itself. Photographs are never neutral, rather they are subjective representations of reality created by the photographer (Berger, 2013, p. 18–21). They are therefore discursive, reflecting the 'aesthetic, polemical, political or ideological' viewpoint of the photographer (Clarke, 1997, p. 28–29), and are embedded with their codes, values and beliefs, as well as those of their broader culture and community. What the photographer chooses to include, as well as what they exclude, is inherently biased. Images are also never viewed passively, instead they are 'read' by the viewer (Clarke, 1997), who will reinterpret their meaning with their own subjective cultural viewpoint.

There are other related practical and ethical limitations for PP as a methodology, with cameras likely to be less welcome in locations with a '…history of political repression, surveillance, use of retaliation to settle conflicts, or betrayal by neighbours' (Prins, 2010, p. 440). Some risks, such as that posed to participants taking images of people, places or processes without fully informed consent are easy to predict, whilst unanticipated impacts for those involved are detailed in Gotschi et al. (2009). Cameras can also be seen as an invasion of privacy, or associated as a technology of surveillance (Prins, 2010, p. 440). There is the question of 'access' to spaces that outsiders cannot visit or record images of. These could be sensitive, showing images of situations, processes, or individuals that could be used against those involved.

Taking part in a PP workshop is potentially triggering, especially if the aim is for participants to explore challenging experiences. Similarly, the ability for participatory processes such as PP to empower can be oversold. Strack et al. (2004, p. 57) describe how undertaking a PP workshop can leave participants 'more hopeless and unempowered' than they were prior to taking part.

There are also considerations regarding the role of the facilitators. One of the core tenets in PAR is for the methodology to blur traditional power imbalances between those leading the process and those taking part. Zhu (2019, p. 64) sees a potential disconnect between PAR's theory and practise, suggesting that 'privileged, highly educated and professionally trained' facilitators might 'fail to practise the principles of PAR' and so: 'Reproduce unequal social and power relations, such as race, gender, and class relations between them- selves and participants within the social institution and a larger global and neo-liberal context.'

Those leading the sessions have a degree of influence over the images taken and selected. As such, there are some arguments for little to no teaching to take place in order to reduce this potential impact. A further consideration is what happens to the images after the button is pressed to release the shutter. Photography is much more than capturing an image. Who decides where it is shared, digitally or in a physical space?

Workshop structure

Participants were asked to consider the issues from their respective neighbourhoods at the three scales noted; think about the changes they might like to see; include either something they would like to see happening or something that was already happening to combat the issue identified; and show any potential barriers to this change.

The workshop was designed with activities that fit into five stages, namely:

1. Diagnosis
2. Planning
3. Production
4. Curation
5. Sharing

The workshop began with an introduction to the main aims and intentions of the workshop, which included explaining the ideas of mainstream and citizens' media, before building some basic visual literacy and camera skills through a series of activities. The participants had possession of the cameras from the start of the week, a core philosophy of PP. From the first afternoon, participants were set photo tasks in the area around the SLURC office, which were then shared and discussed as a group.

The **diagnosis** phase involved a collective exploration of the main issues that participants could identify in their communities, which was joined by Joseph Macarthy, SLURC Executive Director and one of the leaders of the action plan research. The **planning** phase required participants to consider how photography and visual imagery could be used to tell a narrative. They were then tasked with planning their own photo stories, initially in groups, and then individually.

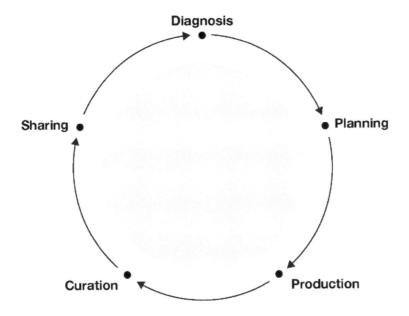

Figure 13.1 Workshop structure. Source: © Authors

The importance of understanding the challenges of photography as a medium featured in all stages of the workshop, which also included a specific session on ethics during the planning stage. This covered the issues associated with the photographic representation of people and communities, and how the context of a photograph can be ambiguous (using examples of how photo manipulation or cropping can change the meaning of a photograph). This session also emphasised the importance of informed consent.

The **production** phase involved producing the photographs, which participants took themselves independently in their communities. It was decided that facilitators should not attend in order to limit their influence on the process. The **curation** stage was based around exercises that emphasised the importance of editing photo series in order to most effectively tell a story and also considered the ways in which text can complement the story.

Finally, the **sharing** stage involved an exhibition of participants' photographs. Members of the pubic and the media were invited to view the photographs and take part in a discussion to interrogate the ways in which informal settlements of Freetown are portrayed by the mainstream media, and the extent to which citizen media photography initiatives could be used to challenge these representations, create new knowledge, and feed into planning processes. While the location was selected by the facilitators, the photos were selected by participants, who wrote their captions and decided how to present their images in the space. All members of the group were present in order to lead discussions around their photo stories with attendees.

Analysis

The ten workshop participants selected issues in their communities, mostly identified during a collective discussion session, that they wished to document. The intention was to unpack the issues through a clear narrative, and to finish the story on a more positive note through a consideration of what a solution or way forward could, or does currently, look like.

The photo stories provided a compelling diagnosis by considering the associated impacts that result as a consequence of the chosen issue. Many of the photo stories were quite explicit in their acknowledgement of the interconnection between issues. This analysis section evaluates the linkages between the workshop, PP, and citizens' media, with the aims set out at the beginning of the chapter. Specifically, this was to consider the extent to which photography could be used as a communications tool that, when in the hands of members of the Freetown public, could constitute a form of citizens' media.

Sierra Leone has an adult literacy rate of 41%, while 'illiteracy remains a persistent challenge' (UNDP, 2021). These figures are likely to drop further in the country's informal settlements. One of the strengths of photography as a media practice is its ability to tell a story and communicate information in a way that does not require the ability to read and write to a high standard – and so is more accessible – and a more feasible way for residents of informal settlements to document and share their reality than traditional print journalism.

The growing availability of digital technology, including the proliferation of smartphones, makes it increasingly common for residents to have almost constant access to a digital camera. This ease of access allows residents the ability to capture images that document their reality at all times.

Abu Sesay's quote demonstrates that residents are acutely aware of a significant disconnect between their life experiences and the prevailing media discourse. This shows an appetite by residents to share their story and to include both the positive and negative aspects of their life and their neighbourhood. It is important to emphasise again that photography is embedded with the subjective viewpoint of the photographer, so it should not be assumed that community photography is automatically representative of the lived experiences or perspectives of every resident of Freetown's informal settlements. However, photography is a communication tool that can be powerful in revealing other, less represented perspectives.

Applying Nip's (2006, p. 218) definition of citizens' media, the photography undertaken during this workshop can be classified as citizens' media. In order to help counteract the power imbalance between participant and facilitator that is inherent within PAR methodologies, the latter were not present when the content was gathered, and thus not involved in the process of production. The photographs were gathered, produced and published by residents of two of Freetown's informal settlements within this workshop, with an exhibition held at the end of the week in the SLURC offices. These photo stories represented an alternative to mainstream media representations, where participants in the workshop, the usual consumers of mainstream media content, became the producers, crafting their own narratives about their neighbourhoods.

Charlie Wright, of ASF-UK, who planned and facilitated various urban planning workshops with informal community members in Freetown commented that the narrative structure to the photo stories was really helpful as participants '…learned that they needed to tell the full story and that they really had to think creatively to do that. Also, giving them the camera from the first day allowed them to tell the whole story themselves about themselves, which challenges power as they are then controlling their own narrative.'

The definition of PP previously quoted in this chapter identifies it as '…a process by which people can identify, represent, and enhance their community through a specific photographic technique.' Running training workshops in this way, where residents are encouraged to tell their own stories, provides a solid foundation for challenging the dominant negative representations perpetuated through the mainstream media.

Furthermore, residents and the organisations that represent them are aware that media representations present the settlements and their residents negatively, both to the wider public and the city authorities who ultimately make decisions on urban development. This view was summed up by FEDURP member Abu Sesay:

If they [the mainstream media] really want to help us, let them come and meet us. Most of them pretend to know about our settlements but they have never come here. We challenge them to come and hear our own side. Let them come and see all the good works we have done. Just because you're a journalist does not mean that you should report anyhow. We too are slowly now becoming our own journalists.

The final sentence demonstrates Freetown residents' enthusiasm to produce their own media narratives to challenge the negative representations of them and the communities they call home. In the last two years, there has been an emergence of a strong citizens' media team, with residents working directly with FEDURP and CODOHSAPA to support other community residents in collecting and analysing data to report on their settlements and to engage city authorities on ways to make the city more inclusive. The approach, dubbed 'Know Your City Campaign', was introduced by Slum Dwellers International with support from Cities Alliance.

However, there is a long way to go before citizens' media can meaningfully challenge mainstream media discourse around informal settlements in Freetown. There would need to be significant improvements in the quality and quantity of the outputs, establishment of connections with those currently working in and producing mass media in Sierra Leone, as well as a willingness from those in power to accept, share and publish citizens' media narratives that challenge the prevailing discourse. Despite these barriers, there are precedents for achieving this across the growing global networks of citizens' media initiatives.

In Brazil, there is a strong tradition of grassroots media initiatives successfully confronting the stigmatisation of their communities and residents through photography, providing residents with the skills required to generate more accurate representations. In Rio de Janeiro, Viva Favela was established as the first Internet photography portal by and about the residents of Rio de Janeiro's informal settlements, or 'favelas' (Jucá & Nazareth, 2008). Viva Favela comprises favela residents who produce reportage and photography from within the favela (Jucá & Nazareth, 2008). Brazilian media often picks up on stories first broken by Viva Favela, who visualise themselves as being part of an 'international movement of visual inclusion to change dominant media' (Lucas, 2008).

Closer to Sierra Leone, the Lagos-based NGO, Justice & Empowerment Initiatives (JEI), has facilitated the creation of the Nigerian Slum/Informal Settlements Federation's Media4Change Teams in Nigeria and Benin. Through the use of a range of digital media practices, the teams use storytelling to '...counter negative representations of informal settlements by media channels which fail to include community voices, perspectives, and realities' (JEI, n.d.), and are working '...to challenge dominant discourse about their communities and reframe their relationship to their city's identity and development plans'. Through public screenings and a strong social media presence, the work of the teams has reached a wide audience. Films produced have been shown at the Eko Atlantic hotel, the *Tiwan Tiwa Festival* and the *Lagos Theatre Festival*.

In both instances, the success of the initiatives in creating active networks of community-based media-makers initially required focussed and sustained guidance and training from experienced professionals. This helped develop and sharpen the required skill sets, as well as creating confidence and establishing a habitat for the growth of the networks, and for the continued and active storytelling and dissemination.

A final aim of the workshop was to evaluate how PP in general could be an effective tool that can contribute to the ASF-UK Change by Design methodology. The workshop design drew heavily on this methodology, in particular at the diagnosis stage, by aiming to create an open space where there were no correct answers and where residents were free to discuss issues. The stories produced include information on various pressing issues, and their impacts on different groups living in the communities in question.

For example, Fatmata Koroma described the population density of Cockle Bay and how it had an impact on families at the home level, with large families living in one room. She then described the problems at community level, explaining how a lack of space for roads meant there was poor emergency vehicle access. There were also multiple photo stories that described possible solutions and next steps, which can potentially be used to contribute towards the dreaming and designing stages.

Another example comes from Joana Kaine, who diagnosed the issue of lack of good toilet facilities in the community and the sanitation issues this caused. However, through the example of a well-built toilet in the community, Joana was able to dream of a scenario where further, similar, well-constructed facilities were spread through the community. Charlie Wright of ASF-UK added,

> the PP workshop really helped prepare participants for later community profiling activities in Cockle Bay and Dworzark. I think the exercise encouraged them to be critical about how they told their

Figure 13.2 'The area is densely populated, with houses in Cockle Bay clustered too close together.' Source: © Fatmata Koroma/SLURC

Figure 13.3 'Because of the housing density, many families live together in only one room, meaning that they lack space.' Source: © Fatmata Koroma/SLURC

Figure 13.4 'There is a lack of good quality toilet facilities in the community. As a result, long queues are evident where there are better facilities.' Source: © Joana Kaine/SLURC

Figure 13.5 'However, there is a high-quality toilet that has been constructed in Cockle Bay by FEDURP with support from the YMCA. Local resident Abdulai G. Barrie, said "We would like more NGO and government support to build more of these toilets to create a better sanitary environment and reduce our exposure to disease."' Source: © Joana Kaine/SLURC

story. This is important for Freetown and wider contexts because there are so many problems that it is often hard as an outsider to know what the most important ones are until someone is able to show you what really matters to them.

In processes such as Change by Design, which are usually time pressured, participants who have some prior experience are invaluable. PP seems to marry most effectively with the diagnosis stage. However, when considering the other three stages – dreaming, developing, and defining – showing 'outsiders' one's reality, the ability to tell a story effectively, and to be critical in how this story is told, are relevant to all and play important roles in the exploratory process.

Conclusion

In terms of next steps, primarily and perhaps most importantly, there was a unanimous, strong commitment from the participants to continue their training and activities as community photographers after the workshop. During the evaluation and reflection session, their expectations for the week were met and all expressed a desire to continue learning. Potentially key to ensuring this happens is capitalising on the energy and positivity generated by this workshop as soon as possible. At the end of the final day, participants had already begun to plan their next stories and projects, some intending to work alone and others to work together, using the cameras left at SLURC after the project.

Regarding the future use of PP, there was also considerable enthusiasm from SLURC and the DPU, not just in terms of continuing to work with this group of participants, but also for going on to train other residents from Freetown's various informal settlements. SLURC have established strong connections with many of these communities and with various residents' associations; creating a strong community of photographers from settlements across Freetown is an exciting possibility. The previously mentioned projects already underway at FEDURP and CODOHSAPA are examples of the current community uptake. This shows the appetite and potential in Freetown's informal settlements for using photography to challenge dominant representations and discourses produced through mainstream media, to tell their own story, and to consider the type of home, community and city in which they would like to live.

There is potential for SLURC, the DPU and community photographers to work together to produce mutually beneficial outputs. Workshops like the one detailed in this chapter help prepare participants to gain control and tell their own stories through building their own narrative. These skills can then be applied to other workshops and processes, potentially contributing to their success.

Despite the obstacles, there is an exciting opportunity in Freetown to build a network of citizen journalists to contribute to the production of grassroots media content that could feed into or contrast the mainstream media, producing a more well-rounded and balanced narrative. As previously noted, it would require time, resources and expertise, but there is an important and often under-acknowledged need to challenge discourses that stigmatise and criminalise. There is also a clear appetite from residents to produce their own media, which organisations with dedicated members have already started to do. This is a process that will hopefully be allocated resources to build a narrative around informal settlements and their residents, that better reflects the lived experiences and knowledge of those who live there.

References

ASF-UK (Architecture Sans Frontieres), SLURC (Sierra Leone Urban Research Centre) & UCL. (2017). Innovative research methods. Participatory planning and design: can neighbourhood planning bring about inclusive city making? SLURC workshop training pack.

BBC. (2016). 'Sierra Leone's changing media landscape offers fresh opportunities for development communications'. Accessed 22 June 2021. https://www.bbc.com/mediaaction/publications -and-resources/research/summaries/africa/sierra-leone/media-landscape

Berger, J. (2013). *Understanding a Photograph*. London: Penguin.

Blackman, A., & Fairey, T. (2014). *The PhotoVoice Manual: A guide to designing and running participatory photography projects*. London: PhotoVoice.

Carroll, W. K., & Hackett, R. A. (2006). Democratic media activism through the lens of social movement theory. *Media, Culture and Society*, 28(1), 83–104. https://doi.org/10.1177 /0163443706059289

Clarke, G. (1997). *The Photograph*. Oxford: Oxford University Press.

Frediani, A. A. (2016). Re-imagining participatory design: reflections on the ASF-UK Change by Design methodology. *Design Issues*, 32(3), 98–111.

Gotschi, E., Delve, R., & Freyer, B. (2009). Participatory photography as a qualitative approach to obtain insights in farmer groups. *Field Methods*, 21(3), 290–308. https://doi.org/10.1177 /1525822X08325980

Gumucio-Dagron, A., & Tufte, T. (Eds). (2006). *Communication for Social Change. Anthology: Historical contemporary readings*. New Jersey: Communication for Social Change Consortium.

Herman, E. S., & Chomsky, N. (1994). *Manufacturing Consent: The political economy of the mass media*. London: Random House.

JEI (Just Empower International). (n.d.). Nigeria and Benin Federation Media4Change. Accessed 24 October 2021. https://www.justempower.org/media4change

Jucá, M., & Nazareth, O. (2008). *Viva Favela*. Rio de Janeiro: Olhares.

Lucas, P. (2008). Viva favela: photojournalism, visual inclusion, and human rights. In Mayra Jucá and Otávio Nazareth (Eds), *Viva Favela*. Rio de Janeiro: Olhares.

Macdonald, M. (2003). *Exploring Media Discourse*. New York: Arnold.

MediaBuzz.org. (2020). Sierra Leone newspapers and Sierra Leone newspaper list. Accessed 25 June 2021. https://www.mediabuzz.org/newspapers/sierra-leone/

Nip, J. Y. M. (2006). Exploring the second phase of public journalism. *Journalism Studies*, *7*(2), 212–236. https://doi.org/10.1080/14616700500533528

Pettit, J., Salazar, J. F., & Gumucio-Dagron, A. (2009). Citizens' media and communication. *Development in Practice*, *11*(4/5), 443–452. http://www.jstor.org/stable/27752085

Prins, E. (2010). Participatory photography: a tool for empowerment or surveillance. *Action Research*, *8*(4), 426–443. https://doi.org/10.1177/1476750310374502

Quarry, W., & Ramirez, R. (2009). *Communicating for Another Development: Listening before telling*. London: Zed Books.

Reason, P., & Bradbury, H. (2008). Introduction. In P. Reason & H. Bradbury (Eds), *The Sage Handbook of Action Research: Participative inquiry and practice*, second edition (pp. 1–10). London: Sage.

Rosen, J. (2008). A most useful definition of citizen journalism. Pressthink. Accessed 9 August 2024. http://archive.pressthink.org/2008/07/14/a_most_useful_d.html

RSF (Reporters without Borders). (2020). Sierra Leone. Accessed 22 June 2021. https://rsf.org /en/sierra-leone

Strack, R., Magill, C., & McDonagh, K. (2004). Engaging youth through photovoice. *Health Promotion Practice*, *5*(1), 49–58. https://doi.org/10.1177/1524839903258015

UCL. (2018). Civic urban media. Accessed 22 October 2022. https://www.ucl.ac.uk/bartlett /development/research-projects/2021/oct/civic-urban-media

UNDP. (2021). Sierra Leone country information. Accessed 21 October 2021. https://www.sl.undp .org/content/sierraleone/en/home/countryinfo.html

Wittels, A., & Maybanks. N. (2016). Communication in Sierra Leone: An analysis of media and mobile audiences. Accessed 22 June 2021. https://assets.publishing.service.gov.uk/media /57a0896040f0b6497400004a/mobile-media-landscape-sierra-leone-report.pdf

Zhu, Y. (2019). Can participatory action research empower participants in adult education studies? *Canadian Journal for the Study of Adult Education*, *31*(1): 63–73.

14

The development and running of the massive open online course in development and planning in African cities

Andrea Rigon, Joseph M. Macarthy, Joanna Stroud and Alexander Stone

Introduction

This chapter reflects on the development and running of the massive open online course (MOOC) Development and Planning in African Cities, running since 2018 with 6,900 learners. The course was developed as a partnership between SLURC and the Bartlett Development Planning Unit (DPU). It outlines the ways in which a MOOC can be part of a strategy to meet some educational and professional development needs, as well as contributing to creating a community of practice.

After a brief introduction on what MOOCs are and a brief description of what we have done, we engage in an analysis of what was achieved. Put simply, a MOOC is an online course which puts together freely accessible resources, facilitated and curated by acknowledged experts in a specific field, on a social digital platform that offers a learning experience which enables connecting with peers with the ease of most social networks. MOOCs enable active engagement amongst hundreds or even thousands of learners who come together around shared learning objectives. The courses are generally short (three to six weeks) and involve a few hours per week (although in some instances, learners can learn at their own pace, taking longer or skipping some parts). They are usually completely asynchronous, which means that learners can connect and learn at different times that are convenient for them. MOOCs can be facilitated by educators who input into the thread of comments, although this is not necessary. A MOOC is generally free (although learners, depending on the platform, may pay for unlimited access or a certificate) and has no prerequisites, except for internet access. Over the last 15 years, MOOCs have become very popular, with all major global universities offering them.

Changing learning landscapes and the needs of urban professionals

MOOCs respond to an increased demand for learning, but also to a professional landscape where lifelong or continuous learning is necessary. In the field of urban development and planning in the Global South there is a huge skill gap amongst the professionals involved, especially in the public sector, combined with a rapidly changing urban context and evolving concepts and approaches. This requires urban professionals to acquire up-to-date knowledge and learn from the challenges and solutions identified by peers elsewhere.

In the African context, this need is more acute. With over 50 disparate countries and huge diversity within individual countries (in particular federal countries like Nigeria which has 36 states) there is a richness of approaches and solutions to urban problems. While these urban contexts are very different, there are some commonalities which make critical comparative learning from each other's experiences useful. For example, some countries share a similar colonial legacy and inherited similar urban planning approaches. Moreover, comparable geographies and patterns of urban growth raise common challenges and vulnerabilities.

Many university degrees in Africa are often based on urban theories centred on the urban experience of the Global North (Watson, 2009; Pieterse & Simone, 2013), because when urban professionals study abroad they often learn theories about the region where they study. It is not uncommon to find planning lecturers trained in the Global North teaching the same planning theory and practice about Europe they learned in 1970s and 1980s. This theory is inappropriate for African cities. Moreover, the visions of current urban leaders and managers are often linked to 'urban fantasies' and problematic views of modernity that are not rooted in the reality of their cities and residents (Watson, 2014). Despite efforts from the African Association of Planning Schools to develop a new curriculum relevant to the present urban context, the process of transforming existing courses and then training a new generation of professionals to replace current urban professionals, will take decades.

This highlights a need for training of existing and aspiring urban professionals. The founding of SLURC was the result of a needs assessment that revealed the demand for skills and capacity building of existing professionals. The initial grant from Comic Relief to set up SLURC included the funding for several short training courses. Since the beginning, these training courses were conceived with international and Sierra Leonean academics working together to build a course that included days in the field exploring Freetown, ground learning in local practices and making theories relevant to the city context. Each of these training courses (see Chapter 11) brought together a different range of urban stakeholders. The founding grant also sponsored multiple international exchanges to Tanzania, Uganda, South Africa and Malawi. Soon, the team realised the importance of learning from each other's contexts. However, the financial cost of such exchanges was very high, and involved major resources for preparation. Very few people could participate at such a high cost for SLURC, and it also required significant time from participants. As an example, a group of Sierra Leonean professionals due to participate in an exchange in South Africa had to travel to Ghana and remain there for almost a week to process their South African visas, which could not be processed in Sierra Leone and could not be obtained by post. This meant that several key professionals had to forfeit two weeks of work for a five-day exchange with South Africa. Some of these professionals are the only people working in the municipality on specific tasks, thus paralysing important and urgent work.

Developing and implementing the MOOC

By the time we organised our last Comic Relief-funded training, we had become attracted to the idea of producing a MOOC after hearing how it had been used for the professional development of teachers in humanitarian contexts (Kennedy & Laurillard, 2020). On top of solving some of the issues described above, we could bring together the best international scholars on every topic. Moreover, while SLURC had given priority to the short-term training of existing professionals, we were devising a long-term plan of developing an MSc course in development and planning in African cities to respond to a lack of planning education in Sierra Leone. We thought that the preparation of the MOOC could help us discuss the key elements of such a programme.

The process started with the SLURC team writing a joint academic piece to identify and discuss what we considered to be the key issues in urban planning in Africa and how they related to the urban development context (Rigon et al., 2018). Then, we triangulated these issues with the curriculum developed by the African Association of Planning Schools (AAPS, 2010) and presented an initial proposal to the MOOC's advisory committee. The committee was created to refine the curriculum and allocate each topic to an international expert that was paired with an expert based in Freetown. By that time, we were already in touch with the Digital Education Team at UCL which provided technical advice.

The course targeted urban professionals, including academics, in Sub-Saharan Africa who wanted to increase their understanding of how cities are made and work and to explore the tensions between urban processes, conceptual issues and their spatial manifestations in a specific context. The academic level was aimed at people with a degree in any subject from any country in the world with a desire to learn about urban development and planning in African cities and potentially to those who would like to pursue a career in development/urban planning. The course was designed to provide a master's degree level content in a variety of accessible formats without assuming prior knowledge of the issues discussed. More advanced students could deepen their knowledge through optional materials.

Before building the MOOC, we used the prospective MOOC contents to run a one-week face-to-face course in Freetown (June 2018) and asked participants to carefully evaluate it in order to improve the material. The course involved 28 participants from local and central government, NGO and private sector staff, and university lecturers.

Two additional considerations impacted on course design. First, we wanted to attract a strong presence of all urban actors, including a range of urban professionals: planning officials, government workers, NGO staff; as well as residents of informal settlements and their leaders. Second, given the centrality of the practice and field component in all our trainings, we wanted the course to relate all the theories covered to specific sites and examples, and to generate a common knowledge base and vocabulary from which participants would be able to debate the issues from the position of different actors. Moreover, we wanted to avoid the silos of understanding of different issues affecting African cities by showing how these issues interacted in a specific place. Therefore, we decided that the main character of the course was the city of Freetown, from where all topics and sessions had to draw their examples. The immersive experience was produced through interviews, pictures, interactive maps, short videos, including videos of crossing the city on public transport that showed how the city changed. For each topic, starting from the case of Freetown, participants were asked to compare and share their experience and examples from other cities in Africa and elsewhere. The pedagogical approach coupled theoretical inputs at African level with inputs showing how theories apply to Freetown, making a complex case study of the city.

The team disseminated the MOOC through all our networks, in particular the African Association of Planning Schools and African Urban Research Initiative, and provided an incentive of free unlimited access and a certificate for Africans based in Africa who completed the course. For later editions, the course was included in a British Council programme offering free unlimited access and a certificate to participants from all developing countries who applied. United Cities and Local Government Africa (UCLG Africa) was impressed by the contents and so promoted the course as part of their academy for urban managers and leaders.

The first run of the MOOC in October 2018 attracted 1,731 learners from 123 countries with four African countries amongst the top six (Sierra Leone, South Africa, Nigeria, Kenya, as well as the USA and UK), which is a radically different cohort to what other courses on the platform normally attract. With the second cohort, we had smaller numbers (736) from 93 countries, but still with a prominent participation of African learners. The third run had 2,411 participants from 128 countries again with four African countries in the top six, (11% of learners from Sierra Leone and 10% from Nigeria, 5% from South Africa), meaning that hundreds of African urban professionals were taking the course. Since August 2021, after five runs with discussions facilitated by DPU and SLURC staff, the course has been open continuously without an active input from educators and, in total, has seen the participation of 6,900 learners.

Discussion

MOOC as social learning

The open comparative ethos of online conversations on the MOOC platform created a sense of community where participants could see how other cities faced and dealt with similar challenges. Hundreds and hundreds of African residents were able to connect with each other to discuss urban planning and development issues across the region. The MOOC was particularly effective as a professional development tool through knowledge sharing for professionals who struggle to gain international exposure and can contribute to changing mainstream urban discourse through reflection on experience. The MOOC was an effective pedagogical tool targeting particular educational problems, specifically the difficulties of reaching learners across a broad geographical area and with a range of time/finance constraints, that prevent them from attending face-to-face courses.

Transforming urban development and planning education

In our very first SLURC face-to-face training, we were shocked when academics participating in the training started to say that the residents of those settlements were illegal, had to be evicted and represented a risk and a nuisance. They also complained that the training was open to some residents of these settlements without the degrees needed to understand the course.

This cemented the need for targeting academics in our trainings and activities, confirming the problematic assumptions about urban planning reproduced in local academia. Academics in Sierra Leone were very eager to participate, valued that the training was run in partnership with an international university (UCL) and enjoyed the learning. We also realised that it is sometimes difficult for local academics in under-resourced environments (when we started the process, our partner university had almost no Internet connection on their main campus) to access case studies from other African countries or gain access to up-to-date academic papers. Therefore, we made all the MOOC materials available on the UCL Open Education Repository to create open educational resources (OER) with a creative commons license so that any educators in the world could easily download all the materials. OER are digital and reusable learning/instructional objects produced through teaching and training activities. They need not be a full course but can be individual items created by staff to aid teaching and learning, or student-generated content which showcases teaching output. Anything that can be reused for teaching and training is an OER.

To further facilitate the download process, we provided all the materials on 100 USB memory sticks which were provided for free to university staff.[1] We saw this as an opportunity to provide valuable up-to-date teaching resources that academics could use to support their work. The open repository also allowed people with limited internet connection to study all the course materials offline.

A relevant number of MOOC participants were academics or aspiring academics who valued the opportunity of learning directly from leaders in the field. For example, a Nigerian certified town planner looking to move into academia said:

> All the aspects of the course were enriching and insightful to me. Notable among these were the lessons on informality, infrastructure, land value capture, spatial injustice, social diversity, etc. to mention a few. The course delivery and technologies was [sic] also impressive. I look forward to using these knowledge and skills to undertake a PhD in urban planning.

Another South-African graduate student said:

> I think the teaching method of this course was excellent and [I] appreciated the variety of voices that you were able to bring into the content. There is a lot to discuss on development in Africa but I think you have managed to take a great snapshot of the context.

Opening up education

A significant proportion of contributors to this MOOC were academics based in top universities where postgraduate education is often expensive and very selective. The MOOC provided a tool offering free access to their knowledge, otherwise marketed at those able to afford very high fees and a year abroad. It was a tool to practise *epistemic justice* – albeit with a limited scope – and to give back to counter an extractive approach, as the learning comes from African cities but many expensively sell this knowledge through universities in the Global North. This is in line with an approach of democratising and decolonising higher education through the co-design of learning (Czerniewicz & Naidoo, 2013; Balaji & Kanwar, 2015; Bali & Sharma, 2017; Rambe & Moeti, 2017).

Crowdsourcing data through MOOCs

As lead educators, through the MOOC we have found ourselves in possession of rich examples from dozens of small, medium and large cities across Africa. These are examples of problems, policies, and solutions. Participants went a long way to explain and even research their own issue to present it clearly to other participants in several discussions. We also had a final, longer course assignment that was peer-reviewed by other participants. Here, participants had to analyse an issue that is negatively affecting the lives of the residents of an African city of their choice in a thousand words. This provided even deeper real time data from many different African cities. Although we knew of colleagues (Kennedy & Laurillard, 2019b) who used MOOCs to crowdsource research data, we did not expect to generate such useful data and did not plan accordingly to reuse learner-generated content for research on urban Africa. However, there is certainly a lot of potential and Andrea Rigon has planned to crowdsource data from a MOOC in a forthcoming project.

Assessing a MOOC's impact

There is wide literature clarifying that MOOCs should not be evaluated using the same framework as other courses, particularly in terms of their impact in developing countries (Liyanagunawardena et al., 2013). Their open nature means that completion rates are significantly lower than traditional courses, and that participants choose what sections they like and need, with only a smaller number of participants taking the full course and participating actively and regularly in the discussions.

For this reason, Kennedy and Laurillard (2019a) argue that we need a new way to assess the value that participants get from these courses. For them, most evaluation methods focus on quantitative analysis of platform data which does not capture this value. Moreover, many MOOC participants are professionals, such as teachers or healthcare workers, and are undertaking continual professional development in MOOCs. Therefore, what matters is how they use their learning to impact the lives of others, such as students or patients, or in their own professional development activities. This reflection was highly relevant for this MOOC because we were particularly interested in understanding what people have accomplished with their new knowledge. Ideally, this means getting back to users long after the end of the course. This was not possible because of a number of data issues and permissions. However, the FutureLearn platform hosting the course offered to add additional questions to their evaluation survey sent shortly after the completion of the course. This allowed us an idea of how people intended to use what they learned. Following the first edition, 98% of participants in the survey said they gained new knowledge or skills by taking the course, and 68% said they had already applied what they learned, while 87% said they had shared what they learned with other people.

Some excerpts from their feedback included:

What was most useful to me were the definitions, explanations and illustrations of the concepts of social diversity and spatial injustice; and how these concepts relate to city planning. I particularly loved the use of real-life-experience videos and Google Maps to supplement the readings, thus making the course to be both practical and theoretical. I will use this course to reinforce my training in urban management; and would also recommend it to my colleagues at the local government training centre. Kudos to the course developers and facilitators. – Head of training at the local government of Buea, Cameroon.

The course content was very useful and informative to me. This course should target city and urban planners as well. I will utilise this information in my ongoing Environmental Impact assessment and audit work. It will help me engage effectively with city and urban planners. – Kenyan Environment impact assessment and audit expert.

Every topic discussed was very useful to me. I learnt a lot about participatory planning, decentralisation, city planning and waste management with insights from slums in Freetown which is a lot similar to what we have in Nigeria. On the long run, I aim for a career in Africa and International Development and I strongly believe that insights gathered from this course would help shape my career path. – Lagos, Youth Development Officer in a local NGO.

I really enjoyed this course, and the in-depth insight into Freetown. I found the additional links useful for getting fuller picture of what the city is like and what challenges it faces. I also enjoyed the interaction that the comments provide, and learning from my peers based on their experiences. I look forward to applying what I learnt. – Intern with NGO focusing on informality, Durban, South Africa.

Understanding the workings of the informal sector was very important. Getting to know that there is a lot of potential in the informal sector and economy in African cities was an eye-opener. In my career as a transport manager, I would look to include the informal sector in planning, rather than disregard them as this is often the case in Nigeria. – Nigerian Transport Manager.

This course has broadened my horizon on planning and development issues in African cities. Urban governance is a very striking tool for effective and sustainable urban development. In the course of this programme I have earned greater insight on urban governance and its workings, urban infrastructure and sanitation, participatory Planning, etc. This will be of great use and importance in my consultancy/private practice career as a Registered Town Planner. – Port Harcourt Nigerian, Registered Town Planner and Secretary of his state's chapter of the Nigerian Institute of Town Planners (NITP).

In four years 2018–2022, the course generated £9,111 net revenue from the paid upgrades for unlimited access and certification. A part of this was reinvested in providing free upgrades to Sierra Leonean and African participants. This income, however, represents only a fraction of the cost of producing such a course, and probably is not even sufficient to cover the staff time for the online facilitation. This is a low revenue figure for MOOCs, partly due to the choice to pitch the course at the lowest price point to accommodate its audience. At the same time, it is not an insignificant amount. SLURC and the DPU also benefited from the exposure to thousands of people in this niche area. As the DPU has something to sell, this is likely to have brought new students as well as promoting the DPU brand to global urban professionals. For SLURC, this has not brought an economic benefit but we think that at least within Sierra Leone, it has helped gain visibility and position SLURC at the centre of urban knowledge production.

Conclusion

This MOOC constitutes a process of professional development with a strong component of facilitating peer learning amongst urban professionals who are unlikely to get similar opportunities elsewhere. The course generated conversations which would otherwise be unthinkable in order to change the dominant discourse around key development and planning issues in African cities. The value of this approach cannot be assessed through metrics used for other types of academic courses. A MOOC represents a light intervention with potentially greater impact through trans-sectoral, international dialogue. It allows for important low-carbon global participation in learning from different geographies with potential for crowdsourcing key cutting edge data from multiple, otherwise difficult to reach, locations. Finally, the MOOC provides academics a way to offer free access to their knowledge, otherwise marketed only at those able to afford very high fees and thus represents one strategy to democratise knowledge.

Note

1   People wanting to take the course in Freetown who did not have access to the internet were provided with a memory stick containing all the materials and allowed to use a computer in the SLURC office to participate in the interactive elements.

References

AAPS. (2010, 22 April 2022). AAPS curriculum development toolkits. https://africanplanningschools.org.za/resources/curriculum-resources/

Balaji, V., & Kanwar, A. (2015). Changing the tune: MOOCs for human development – A case study. In C. J. Bonk, M. M. Lee, T. C. Reeves, & T. H. Reynolds (Eds), *MOOCs and Open Education Around the World*. New York: Routledge.

Bali, M., & Sharma, S. (2017). Envisioning post-colonial MOOCs: Critiques and ways forward. In R. Bennett & M. Kent (Eds), *Massive Open Online Courses: What went right, what went wrong, and where next?* (pp. 26–44). New York: Routledge.

Czerniewicz, L., & Naidoo, U. (Producer). (2013). MOOCless in Africa. OpenUCT.

Kennedy, E., & Laurillard, D. (2019a). A MOOC value creation methodology. Paper presented at the Centre for Global Higher Education Seminar 102. Accessed 25 June 2024. https://www.researchcghe.org/events/cghe-seminar/a-mooc-value-creation-methodology/

Kennedy, E., & Laurillard, D. (2019b). The potential of MOOCs for large-scale teacher professional development in contexts of mass displacement. *London Review of Education*, *17*(2), 141–158. https://doi.org/10.18546/LRE.17.2.04

Kennedy, E., & Laurillard, D. (2020). MOOCs and professional development: the global potential of online collaboration. In C. Callender, W. Locke, & S. Marginson (Eds), *Changing Higher Education for a Changing World* (pp. 157–171). London: Bloomsbury.

Liyanagunawardena, T., Williams, S., & Adams, A. (2013). The impact and reach of MOOCs: a developing countries' perspective. eLearning Papers(33). Accessed 25 June 2024. https://centaur.reading.ac.uk/32452/

Pieterse, E. A., & Simone, A. M. (2013). *Rogue Urbanism: Emergent African cities*. Johannesburg: Jacana Media.

Rambe, P., & Moeti, M. (2017). Disrupting and democratising higher education provision or entrenching academic elitism: towards a model of MOOCs adoption at African universities. *Educational Technology Research and Development*, *65*(3), 631–651. https://doi.org/10.1007/s11423-016-9500-3

Rigon, A., Koroma, B., Macarthy, J., & Frediani, A. A. (2018). The politics of urban management and planning in African cities. In T. Binns, K. Lynch, & E. Nel (Eds), *The Routledge Handbook of African Development* (pp. 415–425). New York: Routledge.

Watson, V. (2009). Seeing from the south: refocusing urban planning on the globe's central urban issues. *Urban Studies*, *46*(11), 2259–2275. https://doi.org/10.1177/0042098009342598

Watson, V. (2014). African urban fantasies: dreams or nightmares? *Environment and Urbanization*, *26*(1), 215–231. https://doi.org/10.1177/0956247813513705

15

The role of community action area planning in expanding the participatory capabilities of the urban poor

Joseph M. Macarthy and Alexandre Apsan Frediani

Introduction

The Freetown Structure Plan 2013–2028 recognises the role of action area plans as a mechanism to enable planning processes to bring about improvements to neighbourhoods in Freetown. A key aspect of these plans is that they should '...indicate the precise private and public use of all land and parcels within the "action planning area" and indicate areas reserved for utility services, roads and transport system, parcel numbers, eventual reservation or protection lines, as well as development and building regulations to be followed when using the parcels included in the plan' (Bloch, 2014, p. 16). The underlying assumption of the Freetown Structure Plan is that this planning instrument can be used as a mechanism to synchronise local developments with city-wide planning principles and processes. However, in the current policy, the processes through which these plans are supposed to be implemented and by whom are not indicated.

In the meantime, the Federation of the Urban Poor in Sierra Leone together with their support NGOs (CODOHSAPA and YMCA) have been developing their own informal settlement profiles to make visible the needs and aspirations of the urban poor. For them, such settlement profiles are not a means to implement city-wide visions, but instead to advocate for their rights to a more just and inclusive city.

While representing important achievements of the urban poor and their support network to gather information about urban dwellers, these profiles have had limited recognition and impact into policy and planning processes.

These two contexts present a typical condition of the dichotomy between potential invited spaces of participation in the city led by governmental authorities with the objective to implement programmes and projects; against the claimed spaces led by grassroots actors attempting to contest and influence planning processes from the bottom up. In this research, SLURC investigates the potentials of an in-between space of participation in the city, where socially just agendas can be advanced through localised plans drawing on the initiatives by grassroots actors, while at the same time aiming to achieve recognition from key urban stakeholders to unlock opportunities for the production of a more equitable city.

This chapter draws on findings from action research which involved elaboration, implementation and reflection about community action area plans (CAAP) in the informal settlements of Dworzark and Cockle Bay (Macarthy et al., 2019). The CAAP processes were designed as a method to complement current planning procedures, supporting the implementation of action area plans through a participatory and localised approach. The CAAP methodology was developed and implemented in partnership with Architecture Sans Frontières-UK, by drawing on their Change by Design methodology (Frediani et al., 2011, 2014, 2015; Frediani, 2016; Bainbridge et al., 2016). The main focus of this chapter is to examine the role of this CAAP process in expanding the capabilities of informal settlement dwellers to participate in city-making processes. To respond to this focus, the research addresses the following research questions:

1.   What are the challenges and opportunities within the current policy and planning context in Sierra Leone for participatory forms of city-making? How does the CAPP process respond to these policy and planning conditions?
2.   How does the CAAP process recognise the diverse needs and aspirations of city-making in Freetown?
3.   In what ways do informal settlement dwellers involved in the process enhance their agency, ability and opportunity to affect decision making processes towards more equitable city-making?

This chapter outlines the methodology used in this research project, and then unpacks its findings in the following four sections. Firstly, the policy and planning context is examined, through the analysis of policies relevant to setting the context for participation in government-led processes affecting city-making. Then, the chapter unpacks the aspirations and motivations of different stakeholders that participated in the CAAP process, revealing some synergies as well as differences in relation to the role of participation in city-making processes. Thirdly, the chapter delves in more detail into the participatory practices implemented by the CAAP process, exploring its methods and instruments. This section elaborates on the power relations shaping the practice of participation and compares it with previous participatory engagements that local informal settlement dwellers have engaged in in the past. Finally, the chapter reflects on how the CAAP process drew on, expanded or compromised participants' assets to participate in decision making processes. In its concluding section, key lessons learned are outlined, particularly in relation to how the CAAP process can be applied in the future to build pathways for equitable city-making.

Methodology

This research has an action-oriented character, as it enables a process of designing and implementing 'community action area planning' in two informal settlements (Dworzark and Cockle Bay). It conducts a series of research activities to explore people's experiences of participating in this process. These two settlements were prioritised for this study due to three main reasons. First, they are localities where SLURC have been building long term collaborations; secondly, the CAAP process would be a helpful exercise to bring together findings from different past studies to inform planning processes and finally, they would allow the study to explore the role of CAAP in two settlements of very different sizes and topographies. Dworzark is a larger settlement, in an area size of 313 acres, with an estimated 2,003 structures, accommodating 5,236 households at the time of this study, located by the hill sides, whereas Cockle Bay is a smaller settlement located by the coast, with an estimated 520 structures, accommodating 1,350 households in an area size of 45 acres at the time of this study (CODOHSAPA & FEDURP, 2019).

The CAAP process was facilitated by Architecture Sans Frontières-UK and it involved conducting participatory design activities divided inzto four different stages: diagnosis, dreaming, developing and defining. These stages were used to facilitate activities that were associated with different scales of design: home, community and city. In its developing stage, the methodology involved conducting an exercise in each settlement entitled 'portfolio of options', which interrogates the different principles for community action area planning and development options that came up from previous participatory design activities. In the defining stage, the main findings of the 'developing' process were systematised in the community action area plans (see Chapter 15 for more details on this methodology).

The research component of this initiative focused on documenting the experience of those that took part in this process. To allow the CAAP process to take place as well as its monitoring, the research set up a city-wide advisory group, which involved key urban stakeholders, including representatives from government, NGOs and community groups. In each settlement, the research set up a community steering committee, which was also consulted throughout the process. The meetings with the advisory group and the community steering committees were key to defining the purpose and methodological aspects of the CAAP, as well as for monitoring its progress and achievements. At the settlement level, activities were run in three or four day workshop formats, associated to scales of design (home, community and city) and then culminating in the 'portfolio of options' exercises. In the beginning and at the end, focus group discussions and interviews with a selective number of participants captured their expectations and experiences of the process. Finally, interviews with key informants aimed to understand the wider role that the CAAP could have in democratising urban governance in Freetown. A total of 154 people participated in the CAAP processes from both settlements and 145 people participated in the research activities that led to this chapter through 21 focus group activities and 83 semi-structured interviews.

All interviews and focus group discussions were translated (from Krio) where necessary and then transcribed. These transcriptions were then analysed through the 'participatory capabilities' framework. The following sections outline the main findings of this analysis. This research methodology was informed by a commitment to inclusion as well as to bring about benefits and no harm to those participating in this process. Therefore, the research team was particularly attentive to involve diverse residents in the research process, as well as to manage participants expectations associated to their engagement in the CAAP process. By asking for their aspirations and motivations for engaging in this CAAP process, facilitators and research officers were able to continuously explain the scope of this action research to research participants. Furthermore, expectations were also managed by discussing with participants about the obstacles and opportunities that would affect the realisation of these aspirations. In this sense, the integration of this research process in the action planning process played an important role to discuss and manage expectations collectively.

Policy and planning analysis

The CAAP aimed to complement localised planning, by supplementing the existing tools for spatial planning in Freetown. At the time of the research, the key spatial planning frameworks for Freetown were outlined in the Freetown Improvement Act and Rules (FIAR), Chapter 66 of 1960, which provides the technical rules guiding housing development in Freetown and the 2014 Freetown Structure Plan (FSP). In particular, the FSP proposes a range of actions to enable Freetown to adequately deal with its rapid and uncontrolled growth. One of these propositions involves actions to ensure the better distribution of the population within the Freetown City Council (FCC) area, with intensified urban development to be promoted in some specific places. A Spatial Development Strategy developed alongside the FSP also seeks to generate discussions around the spatial transformation of Sierra Leone, including agreeing on a national spatial development plan.

A supplementary document to the FSP – 'Strengthening Land-Use Planning in Local Councils' – provides guidelines that require all local councils to produce action area plans (AAP) for neighbourhoods, following consultation with local residents and other relevant key stakeholders. Accordingly, the AAP should set out the strategic vision for a place and should seek to provide the framework for actions to address the local challenges and priorities of people relating mainly to their current and future development aspirations. In the design of the plan, city authorities are required to collaborate actively with a wide range of stakeholders and agencies that help to shape and bring about transformations in local areas. Moreover, AAPs should be designed in line not only with the neighbourhood and city plans, but also with the national priorities set out in national policies and plans. Arguably, the current CAAP has been conceptualised within the framework of AAP. This work favours CAAP because in Freetown, it is often difficult to define exactly what an area is, given the varied nature of places including the differences in physical and social make up. Since most people identify themselves with 'bounded communities', the concept of CAAP has been preferred here.

Key findings

Analysis of the varied aspirations/motivations/expectations among the different stakeholders

Stakeholders expressed a range of expectations and aspirations from the CAAP process. As understood throughout the CAAP process, expectations are 'desirables, motivating factors or gains from the process' which would help shape stakeholder (community, civil society, state etc.) aspirations within the timeframe of the project. Aspirations, on the other hand, were understood as what stakeholders hoped to achieve as a result of the CAAP process and what the process may lead to in the long term. For ease of comprehension, the different aspirations are summarised into nine main types as follows.

i.   a sense of community and citizenship
ii.   a sense of identity and voice by local residents
iii.   a sense of inclusivity/connectivity with citywide processes
iv.   recognition of the community's agency and role
v.   relevant planning skills to make participants employable and self-independent
vi.   relevant skills as an important means for changing lives in the community
vii.   building confidence of local residents and trust
viii. building/strengthening relationship between the community and government (local and national)/NGOs/donors
ix.   networking and relationship building with other residents and community groups involved in development activities in the community

The associated explanation for each aspiration and the communities where they were expressed are shown in Table 15.1.

The aspirations of stakeholders were met in different ways by the CAAP process and outputs. For example, NGO workers consider that the CAAP process ensured the active participation of the residents thereby creating feelings of ownership. They consider that the skills learned by the residents may go well beyond the CAAP process and may help to improve the community over the long term. Participants from government agencies also consider that by bringing a wide range of participants to the process, the CAAP provided access to a broader range of perspectives and ideas, creating space for often-disenfranchised groups to be heard.

It additionally helped to build strong relationships amongst community residents. All stakeholders agreed that the process built trust between SLURC and the communities, with the participants exposed to new skills such as the design of community plans, taking photos, community mapping, interview and presentation skills, including procedures to run meetings.

On the other hand, community residents held different impressions about how the CAAP process matched their aspirations, which it did in five main ways: it allowed them to acquire knowledge and skills in community mapping and planning practices and to learn how their locality is connected to citywide activities; it imparted knowledge about the risks of living in chaotic settings and the skills to work creatively with others to identify ways to transform the community; it exposed residents to an updated map of the community which was used to identify places and other areas of interest for the research; it enabled them to make new friends especially with others they had not known or worked with before and it allowed them to continue to apply some CAAP key principles in their usual work as a way to ensure its sustainability. This view was highlighted by a community representative in Dworzark:

> The process has helped us to understand some of the disaster risks faced in our community and how planning can help us deal with it. It also helped us to identify the shared spaces in our community, define their current uses (and categories) and agree on ways to preserve them.

A few aspirations were not met. These include the hope to be provided with learning materials with sufficient capacity and a certificate to allow them to secure planning jobs, and to be provided with copies of a plan of the community to use for lobbying the government and other development actors. Most residents are still hopeful of attaining these aspirations.

The nature of participatory spaces created in the CAAP process

The CAAP process brought together people from all sections of each community to discuss and plan for the future development of the community.

During the CAAP process, different participatory spaces were provided spanning the home stage to the community, city and unto the portfolio of options stages. Since the process involved working mostly

Table 15.1 Aspirations associated with the CAAP. Source: SLURC

	Aspiration type	Meaning	Place where expressed
	Desire for:		
1.	A sense of community and citizenship	To work with other local residents involved in the CAAP process to improve their community. The CAAP output to ensure the recognition of their right to the city	Cockle Bay & Dworzark
2.	A sense of identity and voice by local residents	To work jointly on the CAAP to showcase to government/NGOs the uniqueness of problems in informal settlements, including advocating for the issues to be mirrored in the city's development agenda	Cockle Bay & Dworzark
3.	A sense of inclusiveness/ connectivity with citywide processes	Planning through the CAAP process to improve links/ flows (especially goods) between the community and the city centre	Dworzark
4.	Recognition of the community's agency and role	The CAAP output to highlight to government/NGOs about the central role residents play in transforming their own communities; to guide government/NGOs in the design of plans to develop their (residents) community	Cockle Bay & Dworzark

No.			
5.	Relevant planning skills to make participants employable and self-independent	CAAP output to include a physical plan of the community that can be used to guide its current and future growth processes; to be giving a certificate of participation which can be used to help secure a job	Dworzark
6.	Relevant skills as an important means for changing lives in the community	CAAP process to empower community residents by providing them with innovative skills, knowledge and practices to inspire local community actions	Cockle Bay & Dworzark
7.	Building confidence of local residents and trust	The CAAP to ensure the active participation of the community residents, foster relationships and trust amongst community residents	Cockle Bay & Dworzark
8.	Building/strengthening relationship between the community and government (local and national) /NGOs /donors	The CAAP to build unique collaboration/ alliances between the local residents, NGOs and the government in dealing with community problems	Cockle Bay & Dworzark
9.	Networking and relationship building with other residents and community groups involved in development activities in the community	The CAAP to create a platform for collective engagement of local residents and their groups in dealing with common concerns in the community	Cockle Bay & Dworzark

with community people, messages were delivered using Krio (a broadly spoken local language) throughout the facilitation process. This was to ensure clarity and a better understanding of the ideas and procedures. Each stage involved such activities as dreaming, mapping, discussing and determining the options that should be prioritised for action in each of the communities. Most participants were excited by the mapping process which involved pinpointing their houses and other important structures on an aerial photograph taken of their community. For many participants, the mapping exercise was their first experience of this type. Throughout the process, participants were able to socially connect with others, make new friends and exchange their thoughts. This inspired everyone to continue working together on the project. The process also involved a continual shaping of community expectations about the project from an initial prioritisation of jobs, services and infrastructure, to a focus on community planning and research.

Several participants claimed that they had participated in other forms of community development work which were either community-led initiatives or initiatives led and funded by NGOs. These initiatives consisted of different types involving the construction of a football pitch, community centre, water wells, health centre and market etc. Whereas participatory practices concerning community-led initiatives involve community members taking initiative and more control (e.g. financing, self-help labour etc.) in the implementation of actions in their community, participatory practices by NGOs often involve limited participation by the people in identifying their needs/priorities and in working with them to proffer solutions. The local residents' role is sometimes limited to the provision of manual labour, with meagre incentives (money, food etc.) given in return. During one of the evaluation sessions, the Chairlady of Dworzark commented as follows:

> We have had some NGOs that have intervened in this community. Their approach is more about telling us what they have come to do so, they actually impose everything on us...we are rarely allowed to make inputs.

According to the participants, the participatory practices created by the CAAP process were different since they involved community residents more as agents than clients. The CAAP did not only allow participants to take more control over the process, but it also created space for the participants to interact with others thereby enriching their knowledge and capabilities. The shared space allowed for pertinent issues to be discussed about the communities with some action points identified. These were scrutinised by the participants along with some feedback/reflections on the issues provided by the SLURC team.

In effect, the participatory practices of the CAAP were largely bottom-up with many of the ideas coming from the community participants themselves. So, while the process is led by SLURC, the ideas and practices were shaped by the participants to reflect their shared visions and aspirations. Instead of focusing purely on consensus building, the process was facilitated in a way that enabled different visions and experiences to be shared, while also putting into place mechanisms that allowed concrete actions to be prioritised. A CBO member in Cockle Bay expressed this as follows:

> We argued a lot and also disagreed a lot but at the end of the day we were able to come up with solid solutions…that brought out the best in us and also helped those who initially lagged behind.

An important aspect throughout the entire process was about giving voice to the people, which involved listening to their concerns, aspirations and priorities. These were later fed back into discussions in subsequent stages. As described by a steering committee member in Dworzark:

> The CAAP process was always about hanging heads together, sharing ideas and testing the prospect of the different development options suggested for our community. I really like it.

The process was mainly bottom up, with many of the ideas sought from the residents reflecting their main concerns, experiences and priorities. The process not only tapped into community knowledge and experiences, but also worked to build their existing capabilities. Most participants cherish the opportunity of taking part in putting together a document which will be used to guide the development of their community. A major highlight of the CAAP was the notable role of the steering committee members who not only guided the research process, but also worked to organise the community participants. Also notable was the role of the citywide advisory group who, apart from helping to set the wider research agenda, were also very supportive of the CAAP process. Nevertheless, when the steering committee of Cockle Bay reviewed the final CAAP produced from this process, they argued that the document was good enough to help them to advocate for benefits in their settlement with other stakeholders, but difficult for local residents to fully understand its content.

The CAAP report in itself can be something we can show case to the authorities, about the how far the community has gone with ideas and the community's willingness to transform (...) We just want a version of the output that we can relate to better (...) Once we have other outputs that are easy to read and use we can easily align our community laws with them, as we are going to make rules and regulations that will help put the work or the output into practise (...) We recommend that the Freetown City Council makes the CAAP mandatory for all settlements. (...) A CAAP should be done in all settlements across Freetown, this can be done by either the FCC or any other donor or NGOs and this should now be the development bible for every community. So, when people come and want to work in the community, they should go by the CAAP.

Some key successes attributed to the CAAP process were that it ensured the broad and active participation of residents, and that it created feelings of ownership of the process with strong community ties built among the residents. In Cockle Bay, the FEDURP leader noted as follows:

We have never had a session in this community that has gone to the level of depth like this and there has never been this level of community participation.

In particular, bringing a wide range of participants to the CAAP process allowed for a broader range of perspectives/ideas to be shared while also creating space for often-disenfranchised groups to be heard. The challenge, however, was that the sessions were usually too long and often required the CAAP team (facilitators and participants) to spend all day in the field in order to collect the desired information and to meet deadlines. This recurrently exerted a lot of pressure on the team who had no option but to continually keep a few sessions longer since the short timeline for the project did not allow sufficient time for the data collection process. Moreover, the tight project timeframe meant that at times it was difficult to gain agreements on how to proceed on particular issues. It was also difficult to maintain the commitment of some participants for the entirety of the CAAP process. Additionally, a few participants found the activity plans difficult to understand. Often, extra time had to be taken to explain the ideas in ways that would allow participants to have a clear understanding of the concepts. This tended to consume more time, thereby limiting the amount of information gathered.

The CAAP and communities' assets to participate in decision making processes

The CAAP process focused on developing the human capabilities of participants through providing them with the requisite knowledge, as well as exposing them to a variety of skills. According to the participants, the different approaches used to deliver the sessions allowed them to learn new ideas, skills, and experiences and to also interpret basic features on the map. Participants also learnt to do group presentations and to ask questions. Most participants were delighted at the opportunity to discuss the issues affecting their community and to suggest options on how to deal with them. Participants were also allowed to share their own knowledge and experiences with others, while respecting differing perspectives. This allowed a shared understanding of community problems and a joint commitment to plan and work together to improve their communities. As a result, participants now feel more confident to build on the CAAP process. Many participants consider that the process has worked to change the mindset of residents from being merely clients to agents of change in their communities. This view was pointed out by a youth representative in Cockle Bay as follows:

'This process has brought us all together not only to discuss but to learn more about our community. To me that is one big change...it has changed my life forever.'

Participants also consider that the relationships they formed with other stakeholders (NGOs, government workers etc.) during the CAAP process has increased trust and mutual understanding amongst the groups, since it has opened up spaces for interaction and dialogue and for the views and aspirations of each person to be respected and recognised by the others. In particular, the process has now created avenues whereby community representatives are now involved in making decisions about the city, and so can now freely discuss their communities with the Freetown City Council. As explained by a CBO member in Dworzark:

The CAAP process has created opportunities for us to build relationship with the city authorities. It has helped us to be included in the city's decision-making processes. We now have the opportunity to talk about the issues affecting our community.

Participants additionally feel that the CAAP process has successfully built a trusted relationship between the communities and SLURC. Many describe this as a major asset given the incessant effort by SLURC to broker relationships for them through its varied activities and to also work with them to draw the attention of policy makers to the realities of informal settlements. Participants further claim that they have built on the relationships formed during the CAAP process to create networks around specific issues about their community, and to lobby the government for recognition. Moreover, with the knowledge gained from the CAAP, participants are now well placed to advocate for support and to engage government and other development actors to improve their communities, since they already know the core community priorities and what to request.

The CAAP process did not only deepen the interest of residents in planning, it also increased their awareness about the merits of living in well-planned areas. Therefore, most participants are eager to have plans for their own communities. Participants are particularly excited by the knowledge from the mapping exercises which allowed them to identify the different shared spaces in the community including their usefulness. This exercise allowed them to imagine the kind of future they wished for their community. As explained by a steering committee member in an evaluation session in Cockle Bay:

> The discussions and activities/tasks have greatly improved our knowledge and skills in community planning. We were trained to do community mapping, identify points on a map, draw plans and a lot of other basics things. We will use these ideas and skills to make our community a better place to be.

Since the CAAP process was carried out in places that are generally considered to be illegal, the participants consider that they now have a better understanding of their communities especially in terms of the problems, the response actions to take and the prospects that the CAAP final output will offer in guiding them to reorganise the future growth of their communities. This will include decisions on where best to locate water points, markets, health centres or to pass access roads. In this regard, participants would want to have a well-structured physical plan of the community with a clear layout of where to pass the roads, waste and drainage systems, water lines – including the sites for water points – and a health centre. A few other participants consider that the CAAP offers prospect to address the service deficits in their communities and the challenges related to flooding. It has also made people to appreciate their communities rather than lament over the conditions. Most people can now identify proudly with their localities.

Conclusion: main findings on how the CAAP expanded participatory capabilities

The research outlines that the CAAP process has the potential to ensure the active participation of local residents in ways that will not only increase their understanding about the challenges associated with the unplanned growth of their community, but also provide them with the practical skills needed to respond to the challenge. The shared aspiration among stakeholders involved in this research was for the CAAP process to highlight the gains to communities of putting local residents at the heart of their own development and to showcase this to state/development agencies as an innovative practice, including guiding them on how to promote participatory practices at the community level.

Most stakeholders felt that their aspirations were met by the CAAP process in diverse ways. These include the active involvement of residents who introduced a range of pioneering ideas, thereby aiding the learning of new skills and the feelings of ownership. To many community residents, the CAAP process allowed them to learn more about their locality and how it is connected to citywide activities. It also allowed them to work creatively with others to identify ways to transform living conditions in the community (for more details about the issues addressed by the CAAPs and their recommendations, see Chapter 15). The CAAP process did not only focus on developing the human capabilities of participants, it opened up spaces to make new bonds and to interact and dialogue with other stakeholders (NGOs, government workers etc.). This has created prospects for the views and aspirations of the local residents to be considered in decision making processes about the city. A key finding of this research is that participants expanded their 'planning literacy': enhancing the ability of marginalised urban groups to engage with built environmental professionals, development practitioners and government officials on issues related to city-making.

Most participants claim that they are now well placed to advocate for support and to engage with the FCC and other development actors involved with the Freetown transformation plan. A few participants, however, consider that their ability to act would have been further advanced if they were provided with a more accessible product which could be more easily used to disseminate the findings of the engagement with diverse stakeholders.

The research also shows that to improve the participatory capabilities of poor and marginalised participants in the CAAP process, it is critical to not only limit representations to recognised community groups, but to also seek representations from other socio-demographic categories (gender, age, marital status, literacy status etc.). The CAAP process would also need to prioritise providing community champions with extra skill sets – such as modelling, mapping etc. – so they will be better equipped to support the facilitators in carrying out the exercises and to continue with the process after the close of the project. Linking community actors with relevant development/government agencies as well as setting up an implementation strategy for the plan should also be part of this process.

This chapter concludes by arguing that the CAAP has the potential to play a crucial role in expanding the participatory capabilities of the urban poor in Freetown as well as in democratising urban governance more widely in Sierra Leone. For this potential to be realised, further work is needed to make this planning instrument more responsive to local needs in ways that makes its process, as well as its product, more accessible to a wider set of stakeholders.

References

Bainbridge, E., Bennett, J., Campkin, B., De Carli, B., Frediani, A. A., French, M., Macedo, C. & Walker, J. (2016). *Change by design: reimagining regeneration through participatory design in Cape Town*. London: Architecture Sans Frontières-UK.

Bloch, R. & Sesay, M. I. (2014). A spatial development strategy for Sierra Leone, urban planning project 2011–2014. Preparatory components and studies of the Freetown development plan: Support to Freetown City Council and to the urban planning authorities EuropeAid/128037/D/SER/SL. Cris. No.:FED/2010/250–190.

CODOHSAPA & FEDURP. (2019). Community Profiling Enumeration Report 2019. Freetown: Centre of Dialogue on Human Settlement and Poverty Alleviation. Frediani, A. A. (2016). Re-imagining participatory design: Reflecting on the ASF-UK Change by Design methodology. *Design Issues, 32*(3), 98–111.

Frediani, A. A., De Carli, B., Shinkins, N., Kinnear, M., Morley, S., & Powis, A. (2015). *Change by Design: Collective imaginations for contested sites in Euston.* London: Architecture Sans Frontieres

Frediani, A. A., De Carli, B., Nuñez-Ferrera, I., & Shinkins, N. (2014). *Change by Design: New spatial imaginations for Los Pinos,*. London: Architecture Sans Frontières-UK.

Frediani, A. A., Fench, M. A., & Ferrera, I. N. (2011). *Change by Design: Building communities through participatory design.* Napier, New Zealand: Urban Culture Press.

Macarthy, J. M., Frediani, A. A., Kamara, S. F. (2019). Report on the role of community action area planning in expanding the participatory capabilities of the urban poor. SLURC Publication.

Sierra Leone, (2014). A spatial development strategy for Sierra Leone, urban planning project 2011–2014. Preparatory components and studies of the Freetown development plan: Support to Freetown City Council and to the urban planning authorities EuropeAid/128037/D/SER/SL. Cris. No.:FED/2010/250–190.

16
City and community learning platforms: institutionalising knowledge spaces towards inclusive informal settlement upgrading

Camila Cociña, Stephanie Butcher, Joseph M. Macarthy, Braima Koroma, Alexandre Apsan Frediani and Andrea Klingel

Introduction

Over the last decade, Freetown has witnessed the consolidation of collaborative efforts towards improving conditions and recognising the rights of residents of informal settlements in urban policy and planning. Through the establishment of community-based organisations such as the Federation of the Urban and Rural Poor (FEDURP-SL) in 2008, the formation of community disaster risk management committees (CDMCs) and efforts in community action area planning (CAAPs), informal settlement residents have engaged in collective organising, mapping and upgrading to respond to their urban environments. Likewise, civil society organisations, NGOs, research institutions such as SLURC and governmental authorities at the national and local level have increasingly adopted multi-sectoral and multi-stakeholder partnerships, aiming to improve the wellbeing of an estimated 35% of city inhabitants residing in informal settlements (SLURC, 2019, p. 9). These collaborative partnerships acknowledge that it is only through nurturing inclusive and collective processes that recognise multiple knowledges and experiences that Freetown can be 'transformed' towards more sustainable and just futures.

As a part of these efforts, SLURC has led the establishment of a city learning platform (CiLP) and a series of community learning platforms (CoLPs) in several informal settlements (Koroma & Macarthy, 2022). The CiLP is a space for learning and sharing, which provides a forum to discuss issues around informal settlement upgrading, with a strong focus on participatory and inclusive practices. This city-wide initiative operates through periodic meetings representing a variety of voices, organisations and authorities, and in close collaboration with community learning platforms at the settlement level. Such interconnected platforms support the aims of identifying solutions, coordinating, and developing proposals for the upgrading of informal settlements in Freetown. Together, these platforms aim to respond to and influence policy and practice linked with the Transform Freetown Framework, the National Development Plan and other planning instruments.

The main objective of this chapter is to reflect on the structure and principles of the CiLP and CoLPs, how they engage diverse knowledge sources and the potentials and challenges of these learning spaces to advance an inclusive informal settlement upgrading agenda in Freetown. It proceeds by, firstly, outlining the wider planning trajectories within the city, highlighting the legacy of institutional efforts that have shaped and informed these platforms. The chapter then outlines the structure and activities of the platforms, including a discussion of their multi-stakeholder and sectoral approach, how they support a politics of representation and recognition, and the activities and principles through which diverse forms of knowledge are recognised and mobilised. Finally, this chapter explores the main institutional challenges and opportunities of the CiLP and CoLPs to establish durable structures of representation, propose concrete solutions for developmental challenges in Freetown and scale-up practices that can respond to local and national frameworks. In particular, it reflects on the role of the platforms in generating and mobilising diverse knowledge(s) to build pathways towards greater urban equality.

Historical precedents: urban planning trajectories in Freetown

The CiLPs and CoLPs represent one part of an ecosystem of partnerships aimed at improving the quality of life in informal settlements in Freetown, with efforts growing particularly over the last two decades. As such, this chapter starts by briefly outlining some of the broader urban development trajectories through which these platforms have come into being. These trajectories are rooted in historical processes linked with the wider political economy of Sierra Leone, its history of coloniality, conflict and urban development (Macarthy et al., 2022).

Freetown is marked by deep legacies of socio-spatial segregation, emergent as in many African cities from the colonial era of planning. Since the nineteenth century, public health and hygiene narratives – particularly linked with threats of malaria – were used to reinforce urban colonial order, implemented through restrictive laws to ensure racial segregation (Bockarie et al., 1999; Njoh, 2008; Beeckmans, 2013; Lynch et al., 2020). This segregated order was reinforced by physical planning efforts during the first half of the twentieth century. Colonial narratives framed by the UK-based Slum Clearance Committee (1939–1961) led to the first attempts at codification of formal and informal areas during the 1940s, reinforcing processes of urban exclusion, which '...maintain[ed] the class and racial distinctions in the town's residential structure' (Doherty, 1985, p. 154).

These deep inequalities were inherited in the post-independence era after 1961, while modernist ideals of planning proliferated around the globe. This period in Freetown saw the rise of urban planning aimed at harnessing the 'growth' potential of cities, in line with 'utopian' ideals, as part of the formation of the independent state. However, the continued reliance on zoning and planning education based upon Western standards was largely inappropriate for the city and geared towards city competitiveness (i.e. Borys Plan of 1961), leaving behind both rural areas and informal settlements in planning initiatives (Lynch et al., 2020).

Undoubtedly, the urban trajectory of Freetown was marked by the armed conflict that took place during the decade-long civil war, from 1991–2002. This period not only saw the disruption of planning initiatives, but also major urban transformation as the result of the arrival of nearly 500,000 internally displaced people to Freetown from the provinces. The existing informal settlements in the city rapidly increased as a direct result of the conflict in rural areas, while the city simultaneously experienced major disruption in planning and development.

Following the end of the war in 2002, Sierra Leone faced several challenges related to human and infrastructure losses, but also to the weakening of institutions: what has been termed by the international community as 'a fragile state' (Gberie, 2009). This period was marked by the deep economic shock left by the conflict, in a city where the informal economy is estimated to provide jobs for as many as 70% of the population (Macarthy & Koroma, 2016). It was also in this context, however, that social organisations increased their actions and strategies to improve the living conditions of the country's impoverished population, particularly those inhabiting informal settlements. It is therefore in the post-war period that Freetown has seen a rebirth of planning in the city, and with it, a newfound recognition of the intensity and specificity of planning requirements for informal areas. At this time, a number of key initiatives facilitated the formation of collaborative planning, including the 2004 Local Government Act (which emphasised participation and inclusion), a rising international engagement and discourse linked with 'slum upgrading' and an increased authority, in principle, devolved to local councils.

Perhaps most significant in this regard was the establishment of the Federation of the Urban and Rural Poor (FEDURP-SL) in 2008. This network of informal settlement dwellers has engaged in advocacy, mapping, and planning, working together with NGOs, and drawing on the methodologies, approaches and ethos of Slum Dwellers International (SDI) in the Sierra Leonean context. The first Federation-led enumerations mark the emergence of alternative forms of engagement, supporting a shift towards new forms of data and knowledge from the grassroots aimed at informing city planning. These enumerations allowed informal settlements' dwellers to use '…this data as a critical resource to engage [with planning and policy]. From that point on, the authorities started realizing that we… have certain resources that they don't have'.[1]

From its inception, the Federation aimed to collaborate with other actors within the city. In 2014, in an important effort to formalise existing collaborations, the 'Pull Slum Pan Pipul' consortium (PSPP) was established, linking local and international NGOs and research institutions working in Freetown's informal settlements. PSPP partnered with the Federation, following the '…desire to strengthen collaboration of the six Comic Relief Grantees/Organizations in their efforts to improve the living conditions of slum dwellers in Freetown' (SLURC, 2016, p. 5). During the same period, Freetown City Council increased its efforts to develop a spatial strategy to systematise available urban knowledge through the Urban Planning Project (2011–2014) supported by the European Union. In this context, PSPP was key to bringing together urban actors interested in advancing a progressive vision of informal settlement upgrading, supporting coordinated advocacy, research and action. These diverse efforts took place during a decade in which the city faced new challenges related to crises such as the Ebola epidemic, persistent flooding, the 2017 mudslide and more recently the COVID-19 pandemic (Frediani, 2021b).

The establishment of the Sierra Leone Urban Research Centre (SLURC) in 2015 played a key role in building capacities, mobilising knowledge, and supporting the already ongoing works of the Federation in certain informal settlements '…both empowering and building capacity within these communities' (Lynch et al., 2020, p. 12). Importantly, from the beginning SLURC has focused on connecting the knowledge and claims from informal settlements to city-wide actors and institutions (Frediani, 2021a; Butcher et al. 2022).

Setting up city and community learning platforms in Freetown

The city learning platform (CiLP) and community learning platforms (CoLPs) were established by SLURC in 2019, in collaboration with FEDURP-SL and a network of government and civil society organisations and as part of the Knowledge and Action for Urban Equality (KNOW) programme. Building on the long legacy of engagements between SLURC and organisations such as CODOHSAPA, FEDURP-SL and YMCA, the mandate of these platforms was to move beyond siloed approaches to urban planning and build a collective agenda for the city, to better address challenges impacting informal settlement residents. The platforms add a learning and exchange infrastructure from the practice-based knowledge of NGOs and civil society organisations, to the policy and planning knowledge of local and national government officials.

The CiLP is an open consortium that has met five times between 2019 and 2022,[2] drawing together representatives across the city from local and national government, civil society groups, private sector actors, professional bodies, researchers, a few faith-based organisations and social groups (e.g. women, youth and religious groups) and informal settlement dwellers represented by members of the CoLPs. There have been about 36 participants in CiLP meetings with the biggest group representing Community Based Organisations and CoLPs (31%). This is followed by I/NGO (20%) and other participants including SLURC staff and media (22%). Central government and ministries, departments, and agencies (MDAs) represent just under 10% on average, followed by academics (8%) and local council representatives (7%). The smallest participating sector is the private sector with 3%. To date, the CiLP has been structured according to different thematic focuses (i.e. issues of urban livelihoods and urban health), with meetings entailing presentations from key stakeholders and experts, discussions of the main

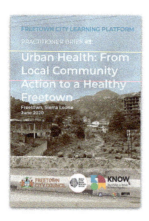 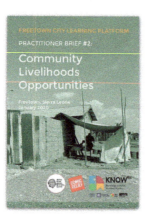 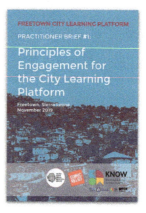

Figure 16.1 Covers of Practitioner Briefs published in 2020. Source: © SLURC

challenges and propositions for future collaborations. The production of practitioner briefs linked with each meeting supports the consolidation and dissemination of knowledge produced in these spaces (CiLP, 2019, 2020a, 2020b). After a year of work, the CiLP was formally endorsed by Freetown City Council as an important learning and exchange space in the city.

At the settlement level, the community learning platforms are a forum to discuss the concerns and aspirations of informal settlements' dwellers, and link with the city level through representation at CiLP meetings. The CoLPs emerged in 2019 as an expanded version of the Steering Committees set up in the settlements of Cockle Bay and Dworzark as part of the community area action planning (CAAP) process, in direct collaboration with FEDURP-SL at the local level. The establishment of the CoLPs sought to expand upon previous structures, ensuring representation across crucial identity dimensions such as gender, tenure, ethnicity, age and ability. Currently, CoLPs exist in ten informal settlements across Freetown, each with 10–15 participants. The presence of the two levels generates a dynamic feedback loop, bringing the voices, concerns, and knowledge of the community to the city level, while feeding learning, action, and commitments established in the city platform back to the community.

Crucially, CILP activities are informed by a set of core principles, discussed and agreed in the first meeting of the CiLP (CiLP, 2019). These are:

- A shared vision, a common purpose: with a commitment to inclusivity in terms of urban stakeholders, identities, geographic features, settlements, and issues
- Sharing knowledge and information: acknowledging that solutions are not within the mandate of a single actor or institution, and that knowledge-sharing partnerships and collective thinking are key to effective action
- Sustainable and knowledge-based solutions: seeking to inform decision-making which is built on co-produced evidence. This also entails accountability around aspects such as prompt attendance, regular meetings, and committing to time-bound and defined outputs
- Collaboration, participation and communication: while drawing on the interests, knowledges, and capacities of a broad range of stakeholders, the platform should put the concerns and aspirations of the urban poor at the forefront of all discussions, adopting innovative methodologies in participatory and community-led approaches
- Mutual respect and trusted relationship: acknowledging the diversity of approaches and partners in this platform, adopting discussion and facilitation which ensures non-judgemental participation, respect, and confidentiality.

Alongside these principles, members of the CiLP set three main objectives.

1. Creating a democratic platform for policy dialogue, debate and discussions.
2. Providing concrete solutions conducive to enabling actions at different scales.
3. Creating a feedback chain from community to the city level and vice versa, allowing the institutionalisation and dissemination of participatory planning methodologies (CiLP, 2019).

In what follows, we discuss critical questions around these three objectives, highlighting their main opportunities and challenges.

Consolidating institutional spaces for inclusive urban development: opportunities and challenges

Creating a democratic platform for policy dialogue, debate and discussions

The platform seeks to create an enabling environment where diverse stakeholders can work collaboratively, based on high levels of dialogue and networking. This involves promoting and fostering tolerance at the community level, creating a common platform for sharing information, and building networks with the different community groups. This has engendered frank discussions on actions to address development challenges, helped empower community residents, and addressed gaps or invisibilised issues. For example, in February 2020, the CiLP convened a meeting focused on urban health. This meeting highlighted that health issues pertaining to urban areas, including within informal settlements, have historically not been considered in major health policies, highlighting the lack of engagement with residents of informal settlements about their health-related priorities, beliefs and experiences. The sharing of research and programming experiences revealed the necessity and value of working with local and informal providers of health-related services, including local and traditional healers, and the use of participatory approaches to move 'from local community action to a healthier Freetown' (CiLP, 2020b).

Establishing a multi-scalar, democratic and participatory platform has likewise fostered greater civic and political participation, with impacts beyond the platform itself. For instance, FEDURP-SL is gradually now being included by the FCC and other MDAs in other decision-making committees regarding issues such as slum upgrading, emergency COVID-19 response, and disaster management. This can be seen, for example, in urban policy preparation, where there is an active representation of FEDURP-SL, SLURC, and CODOHSAPA in shaping processes such as the development of the Transform Freetown Framework and participating in the 'Western Area Planning Committee' by the Ministry of Lands, Housing and Country Planning.

Despite supporting the development of equitable partnerships and building relationships, there have been some key challenges in the creation of durable spaces for dialogue. The first challenge relates to moving beyond rhetoric to setting up concrete actions that build on the CiLP/CoLP engagements with the aspirations of community residents as the key focus. For example, while CiLP meetings focus on the review of policies and plans across different thematic areas, opportunities and barriers towards action, and outline concrete suggestions (from skills trainings, to loan, grant or subsidy schemes, suggested policy changes, or investment in existing community-based structures, such as community health workers), ensuring the implementation of these recommendations is beyond the scope of the platforms. Other enduring challenges relate to managing power relations between actors, including setting a common agenda and building consensus around issues. For example, while representatives from settlements such as CKG and Colbot identified disaster risk management as their key priority as a result of recurrent experiences with flooding, areas such as Dworzark, Moyiba and Cockle Bay were keener to promote the agenda around livelihood opportunities. As such, specific issues across diverse communities can vary a lot, which also shapes the priorities of different NGOs in the settlements. Finally, there remain some challenges around inclusive representation. For instance, while garnering female representation from CSOs and the communities has been easier in platform meetings, it was harder to secure the same from MDAs, universities, and the private sector. This suggests a lack of gender parity in middle management positions for most organisations.

Generating concrete solutions for participatory processes that can shape and solve developmental challenges in Freetown

The platform was set up based on a clear methodology which involved meetings and other forms of participatory engagements, aimed at supporting knowledge co-production on jointly defined agendas to promote concrete actions. In particular, the design of the platform methodology leveraged the participatory approaches used in the CAAP process, which entailed working with local communities to demonstrate bottom-up approaches to improving their communities. Outputs from platform sessions have successfully helped improve the knowledge base of public officials and NGOs on critical concerns for informal settlements, relating for example to disaster risks, physical planning, and settlement upgrading. Certainly, the platform has been effective in scaling up important community concerns for discussion while also expanding the support infrastructure for community actions. For example, in Dworzark, the planning tools discussed during the CAAP process have allowed residents to negotiate the location and focus of investments made by external organisations – such as guiding the planning decisions regarding a drainage system financed by Catholic Relief Services in 2018 – ensuring that activities respond to locally-identified priorities.

The set of local networks and relationships facilitated over time by SLURC and partners, including through the CoLPs, have supported the planning capacities and knowledge of residents. In Cockle Bay, for example, community mapping has created a collective consciousness around disaster risk associated with improper land banking and the likely effects of fire outbreaks associated with unplanned development. Likewise, in Dworzark, there is evidence of the role of small-scale precedent-setting projects, such as the construction of pavements, a bridge, and rainwater collection points, in solidifying a sense of community capacity. These different engagements have allowed residents to pull together knowledge to hold transparent conversations with public officials about the existing challenges, and to highlight priorities for action. Similarly, the CiLP has created a collaborative space for public and civil society actors to interact with and foster the empowerment of community representatives, increasing the capacity of people to organise themselves, mobilise resources and work together to solve community problems.

Despite showcasing clear methodologies and approaches building on participatory practices, this engagement has generated some challenges related to community expectations. This is the case especially for vulnerable participants with insecure incomes, who sometimes expect or require compensation, especially when engagement impedes their livelihood activities. Moreover, unlike in settlements like Dworzark which have been able to collectively organise and are now better served with significant improvements, the demand for participatory processes can sometimes feel like a burden. For example, a few settlements like Colbot and CKG (Crab Town, Kolleh Town and Gray Bush) occasionally come under eviction threats by the central government, particularly after major disaster events. In these cases, participatory processes are often not seen as able to re-orient the wider inequitable relations in the city, reflective of the problem of connecting local level actions and interventions with city-wide processes and challenges. For some residents within these settlements, while capacity has been built, the inability to generate action on some pressing problems has been expressed through the frustration that: 'we have the knowledge, but not the power'.[3] In addition, several settlements still suffer from grave technological and infrastructural resource constraints, hindering the effective engagement of residents with decision makers. These challenges are linked with questions regarding how these platforms relate to other modes of representation already taking place at the community level, requiring a constant process of defining and reinforcing the added value of these 'learning' spaces.

Creating a feedback chain to scale-up in response to local/ national frameworks

Crucially, the platforms build on the momentum of previous partnerships and alliances such as PSPP, and continue to support their consolidation and institutionalisation, as well as respond to emerging challenges. As a multi-stakeholder platform, the CiLP brings together professional, indigenous and community-based actors to engage directly and contribute technical or other resources that can feed into local frameworks, such as the Freetown Transformation Agenda. Especially following the establishment of the CoLPs in 2019, there has been a huge shift through the rapid uptake of CoLPs across new communities to the co-chairing of the platform by SLURC, the FCC, and CODOHSAPA.

Likewise, the production of outputs such as practitioner and policy briefs has helped support consolidation through the translation of platform discussions into formats that can be used by policymakers. The diverse outputs seek to draw the attention of government and other service providers to the pressing development deficits in informal settlements, and to ensure that these priorities are taken seriously. As such, the learning platforms have fashioned a dynamic feedback loop between the informal settlements and the city, with the former now capable of and recognised by city and national institutions, to engage in decisions about policy, planning and practice. By bringing together diverse stakeholders in a shared conversation about the city, the platform has succeeded in building a trusted relationship, which is an important principle and foundational legacy.

Despite the clear energy and efforts to scale-up and sustain these structures, challenges remain in relation to how best to maintain their institutional legacy. In practical terms, SLURC remains the critical

Figure 16.2 CoLP members in shared t-shirts. Source: © Yirah O. Conteh

institution to convey the platform, call for meetings, and document and systematise the CiLP discussions in the form of practitioner briefs. This role can be challenging, especially at times when the appropriate resources to fund these activities are not available. Likewise, while co-leadership of the CiLP by stakeholders within the FCC is a crucial step to embedding the long-term structures of the city, such institutionalisation also requires constant vigilance to ensure that the realities and priorities of residents of informal settlements remain the key driving priority in city agenda setting. Other concerns relate to how well stakeholders can or will commit to the continued resourcing of shared activities, including building capacities to institutionalise or continue with platform activities that sit outside of the day-to-day activities of member organisations. In particular, most government ministries, departments and agencies are yet to understand how to effectively integrate locally produced knowledge into their programmes, or to work with local communities to generate knowledge that may be different to that held by universities and other research institutions.

Conclusions

This chapter sought to reflect on the role of city and community learning platforms in generating and mobilising diverse knowledge(s) to address deep urban challenges facing the city. These platforms draw on long legacies of collaborative action within Freetown and have benefitted from the momentum of consortium-building at different scales. The establishment of these two interlinked structures in 2019 have modelled an important structure through which to address deep distributional inequalities, as well as engage in an important politics of representation and recognition. That is, in addition to undertaking concrete actions across different settlements across Freetown, these platforms have fostered collaborative partnerships, building trusted relationships and respect across diverse stakeholders. It is in this reorientation of relationships, fostering of common agendas, and efforts to work across diverse forms of evidence and knowledge that these platforms offer clear lessons for how inclusive, democratic, and participatory initiatives can better respond to developmental challenges in Freetown.

While celebrating the successes of setting up these platforms, it is also clear that efforts must be made to sustain the momentum and potential of these structures as they scale up and institutionalise. These challenges are even greater given the changing priorities and demands in the context of COVID-19 and its aftermath. This includes questions of resourcing and the ability to operationalise actions emergent from platform discussions. In particular, while a number of smaller-scale precedent-setting projects have powerfully built capacities and trust, further efforts are required to ensure that these localised actions are embedded within wider urban planning within the city, and that responsible organisations are empowered to receive and act on knowledge produced by local communities. Without doing so, there remains a risk of fatigue, especially for those informal settlements that have been unable to transform their community plans into action, or for those organisations and government ministries, departments and agencies to continue investing time and commitment into platform activities.

Nonetheless, these challenges are largely to be expected at this stage of consolidation of the platforms and are reflective of the shift of the CiLPs and CoLPs from a loose network through which to exchange ideas, to a more established and durable learning space with increasing ownership from the FCC. Moreover, what is clear is the role these platforms have already played in challenging and offering alternatives to those knowledge paradigms which have underpinned inequitable processes of urban planning in the city over time. In this way, they have acted as 'impact infrastructures' for research activities in Freetown, which can be informed (in their conception, implementation, and evaluation) by the priorities and perspectives of people involved in diverse processes of change in the city, facilitating a reciprocal relationship between knowledge and practice. As such, there are clear potentials to realise by continuing to build on the strengths of these structures, negotiating the co-production and translation of knowledge across space and scales, and by harnessing this multiplicity of knowledges to inform more equitable processes of planning.

Notes

1   From an interview with Francis Reffell from the Centre of Dialogue on Human Settlement and Poverty Alleviation (CODOHSAPA), June 2019.
2   This chronogram was altered during 2020/21 given the restrictions imposed by COVID-19.
3   From a focus group interview with a Cockle Bay CoLP member in June 2019.

References

Beeckmans, L. (2013). Editing the African city: Reading colonial planning in Africa from a comparative perspective. *Planning Perspectives*, *28*(4), 615–627. https://doi.org/10.1080/02665433.2013.828447

Bockarie, M. J., Gbakima, A. A., & Barnish, G. (1999). It all began with Ronald Ross: 100 years of malaria research and control in Sierra Leone (1899–1999). *Annals of Tropical Medicine and Parasitology*, *93*(3), 213–224. https://doi.org/10.1080/00034983.1999.11813416

Butcher, S., Cociña, C., Frediani, A. A., Acuto, M., Pérez-Castro, B., Peña-Díaz, J., Cazanave-Macías, J., Koroma, B., & Macarthy, J. (2022). 'Emancipatory circuits of knowledge' for urban equality: Experiences from Havana, Freetown, and Asia, *Urban Planning*, *7*(3). https://doi.org/10.17645/up.v7i3.5319

CiLP (City Learning Platform). (2019). Practitioner brief #1: Principles of engagement for the City Learning Platform. Freetown: Sierra Leone Urban Research Centre (SLURC).

CiLP. (2020a). Practitioner brief #2: Community livelihoods opportunities. Freetown: SLURC.

CiLP. (2020b). Practitioner brief #3: Urban health: From local community action to a healthy Freetown. Freetown: SLURC.

Doherty, J. (1985). Housing and development in Freetown, Sierra Leone. *Cities*, *2*(2), 149–164.

Frediani, A. A. (2021a). *Cities for Human Development: A capability approach to city-making*. Rugby: Practical Action Publishing.

Frediani, A. A. (2021b). Freetown City scoping study. African Cities Research Consortium, University of Manchester.

Gberie, L. (2009). *Rescuing a Fragile State: Sierra Leone 2002–2008*. London: Wilfrid Laurier University Press.

Koroma, B., & Macarthy, J. (2022). Participatory planning: the role of community and city learning platforms in Freetown. In GOLD VI report: Pathways to Urban and Territorial Equality: Addressing inequalities through local transformation strategies, Cases Repository: Democratizing (2022). Barcelona: United Cities and Local Governments.

Lynch, K., Nel, E., & Binns, T. (2020). Transforming Freetown: Dilemmas of planning and development in a west African city. *Cities*, 101, 102694.

Macarthy, J. M., & Koroma, B. (2016). Framing the research agenda and capacity building needs for equitable urban development in Freetown. Freetown: SLURC.

Macarthy, J., Koroma, B., Cociña, C., Butcher, S., & Frediani, A. A. (2022). The 'slow anatomy of change': urban knowledge trajectories towards an inclusive settlement upgrading agenda in Freetown, Sierra Leone. *Environment and Urbanization*, *34*(2), 294–312. https://doi.org/10.1177/09562478221106611

Njoh, A. J. (2008). Urban space and racial French colonial Africa. *Journal of Black Studies*, *38*(4), 579–599.

SLURC. (2016). Sierra Leone Urban Research Centre Newsletter, volume 1. Accessed 25 June 2024. https://www.slurc.org/uploads/1/0/9/7/109761391/slurc_newsletter_draft_v.1_1.pdf

SLURC. (2019). Urban Transformations in Sierra Leone: Lessons from SLURC's research in Freetown. Conference report, 19 June 2019. Accessed 25 June 2024. https://www.slurc.org/uploads/1/0/9/7/109761391/urban_transformations_in_sierra_leone_conference_report_web.pdf

Part IV
Learning through SLURC

17
SLURC's work in the global context
Michael Walls

I well remember the first time I visited Freetown. It was for a meeting of the SLURC International Advisory Board and given I had visited Ghana a number of times in previous years, I had at least a sense of the region. Indeed, many things were very much as I had imagined and others very different. In contrast to my work on the other side of the same continent, mainly in the context of highland Ethiopia and the neighbouring semi-arid Somali lowlands, Sierra Leone is of course wetter and more humid, but the welcome for a foreigner such as me was equally warm. Compared to Sierra Leone's West African sibling, though, I was also struck by the poverty of infrastructure in Freetown and even more so outside the capital. Over many years, I cannot say I was surprised that there was not already an urban research centre or, indeed, a wealth of data on urban development, however patchy. But the urgency of the gap in that area was shocking and instantly apparent.

In many ways, Sierra Leone is emblematic not just of a difficult political history, recent and colonial, but also of the neglect that is a reflection of a deeply unequal world system rooted in history but played out in myriad ways in the current era.

The tides of development planning conceptually and in practice are all too changeable, as one model or another gains dominance amongst donors, states and multilateral institutions before being displaced by some new fashion. Arguably worse still is the current incoherence in that area. Countries of all resource levels have scrambled to deal with the pandemic while also addressing urgent issues of climate change and the tensions within the notion of sustainable development. However, the willingness of countries with the greatest wealth to use that position to stockpile vaccines, even as health professionals warn of the global risk if vaccinations are not distributed reasonably equitably, merely made conspicuous what we already know: wealth breeds self-interest and, however well-meaning and thoughtful the rhetoric, actions do indeed speak louder. In that respect we live in a deeply partisan world. Sadly, the pandemic has thrown into stark relief levels of inequality within and between nations that may have been exacerbated by that crisis but precede it and will outlast it.

Russia's invasion of Ukraine in 2022, during the latter stages of the COVID-19 pandemic, in addition to brutal conflicts in Syria, Yemen and Ethiopia amongst others, remind us of the volatility of the global system and, worryingly seem to herald a renewed willingness on the parts of some state actors to employ military force to further that self-interest – either within their countries, with regard to neighbours, or further afield.

One of the enormous challenges we face is that in this dynamic and polarised environment, it can be hard to sustain meaningful long-term initiatives that build on what we have in a spirit not of short-term competition, but of genuine collaboration and a willingness to tackle challenges in a methodical manner with an eye to the long-term. While the COVID-19 pandemic changed all of our lives suddenly and for over two years, the bigger crises are those of climate change and inequality, which will worsen inexorably as the pandemic recedes. Both are existential and will last far longer than pandemic or even conflict.

It is not remotely alarmist to say that we need urgently to find ways to work together much better than we have in the past if we are to mitigate, let alone meet, those challenges. Yet much of the contemporary landscape suggests we are headed in the wrong direction. That makes it infinitely more important that we seek to promote access to continuity in practice and a solid grounding in verifiable data of all kinds wherever we can, but we also need to find a spirit of cooperation – dare I say it, co-production – that is manifestly absent from large portions of our global community. And it's exactly in that regard that I am so proud to have been associated in some small way with SLURC.

SLURC is important, not because it is a UK-funded attempt to establish a much-needed urban research centre in Freetown. Not because DPU was lucky enough to be handed a significant role in that. But because it really does represent an all too rare example of what I believe to be genuine long-term collaboration between diverse actors in different countries. Also, critically, it is led by those in Sierra Leone.

It can be difficult to bring all the necessary elements together – not least because no one person typically has access to all of them. In this case, Comic Relief's initial funding was pivotal, as was the perseverance of my colleagues, Andrea Rigon and Alexandre Apsan Frediani. Even more central was the commitment and patience of our Sierra Leone partners and none more so than Joseph Macarthy and Braima Koroma. However, in the end it was absolutely a team effort: more than the sum of its parts.

That was only the beginning and in a way this is really the point I want to make here. While the journey so far has been fantastic with real progress in helping to shape the attitudes of national and local governments in Sierra Leone, and of donors, towards planning for greater equality and sustainability and in understanding the quotidian issues of those living in slums who are dependent on the most precarious of livelihoods, the work has barely begun. That is where the real challenge lies. Establishing a new organisation is exciting and fulfilling and in that, SLURC have achieved remarkable success. If we are all – SLURC, DPU, all of us – to do all we can to mitigate the huge challenges of aggressive self-interest, climate change and rising inequality, then we need to keep up that momentum. As the short attention spans of donors and governments pivot to other issues or embrace new ideologies, we need to find new ways to regain their attention in order to keep doing what we are already doing.

In that sense, I see the great challenge facing SLURC and the many other groups with a genuine commitment to co-production and meaningful collaboration in the pursuit of social and environmental justice being not just to survive, but to find a way to continue to thrive and in so doing to change the societies we live in.

In essence, development planning is about helping to expand the scope for communities to exercise the ability to survive with dignity in an often indifferent and sometimes outright hostile world. That means finding ways to keep on delivering messages that are, in essence, unpopular. For others to live with dignity, the rest of us need to accept a little less. That is not an easy thing to sell. It means we need to work out how to change the way we work together and live. To change the way we plan our cities so they are more inclusive and more liveable for all of their residents, not just those who can afford to pay. In other words, to genuinely plan for inclusivity. There are few win–win solutions: inclusivity really does mean that some will need to accept less in order for others to satisfy their most basic needs.

I'm enormously proud of the way that SLURC has embodied those principles over the years, and I look forward to the difficult but rewarding years ahead which will make the most telling difference. It is my hope that SLURC will continue to find ways to engage funders, planners and the wider development community to ensure their future, but also to incrementally advance towards the vital task of drawing together the communities that make up our diverse society.

We cannot begin to claim to be planning for inclusivity and sustainability unless we work hard to genuinely co-produce knowledge with those who do not possess the wealth to buy the resilience many of us take for granted. That is a challenge that requires fundamental social change. Hardest of all, it requires a widespread change of attitude. It requires us all to continue to persuade those who hold the power and resources to make a difference; that it is in their collective interest to seek what doesn't come naturally: a fairer and more sustainable world. We run the risk that 'sustainability' will become the preserve of the wealthy. Those individuals and societies who can afford the luxury of green energy and low-impact lifestyles while hectoring others on why they should be eschewing precisely the privileges they themselves take for granted. The reality is that the two goals must go hand-in-hand: a world in which the privileged can afford 'sustainability' while declining to extend those privileges to others is a world in which 'green planning' is just another luxury available to the few, while the planet continues on its calamitous path to increased warming. The critical challenges we face must be tackled as a whole. To put it bluntly, unless we tackle inequality with real commitment, we cannot address global warming. Just as wealthy communities have hobbled their very own pandemic responses by ignoring those unable to effectively fund their own.

Development planning is all about these concerns. SLURC remains a fantastic example of an initiative that genuinely seeks to achieve the kind of collaborative and inclusive planning that is so critical at this moment. It is only one tiny part of the equation and many, not just in Sierra Leone, require vastly more. However, the urgent need, if we are to manage it at all, will be made up by innumerable contributions of just that kind. For now, I am happy to celebrate the impressive teamwork that has got SLURC this far and to look forward to the future in which we continue to fulfil that small but vital role in partnership with a growing number of others.

18

Urban transformations and SLURC: learning, understanding and impact

Blessing Uchenna Mberu

Introduction

Africa is the least urbanised continent, but has the highest urban growth rate in the world. By 1950 Africa's urban population was 27 million people and had grown to an estimated 567 million people by 2020. It is predicted that Africa's population will double between 2020 and 2050, with two-thirds of this increase to be absorbed by urban areas (OECD & SWAC, 2020). Cities are attractive because they generally offer more choices (such as good quality housing), opportunities (e.g. employment) and services (e.g. education and health care) to residents. However, cities also concentrate risks and hazards for health and the impacts of adverse developments such as water contamination, air or noise pollution, and natural disasters are amplified in densely populated urban settings (WHO & UN-Habitat, 2010). Further, a mismatch between the rapid population growth of cities and the ability of governments to provide infrastructure and essential livelihood opportunities in urban centres enhances these challenges, with consequent losses to health and wellbeing (APHRC, 2014). The lag in planning and infrastructural development has consequently resulted in nearly one billion people – one third of all urban dwellers worldwide – living in informal settlements or slums, which are characterised by overcrowding, social and economic marginalisation, poor environmental conditions, insecurity and the near absence of the public sector and basic social services (UN-Habitat, 2001, 2003, 2006; World Bank, 2000).

African urbanisation is typified by the increasing urbanisation of poverty and the growth of slums, leading to heavy concentrations of poverty in cities, rather than being dispersed over rural areas (Chan, 2010). In Sierra Leone, the urban population rose from under one million people in 1960 to 3.4 million by 2020, representing an increase from 17% of the country's total population to 43% and an average growth rate of 3.2% between 2016 and 2020 (World Bank, 2022). According to data from UN-Habitat and the World Bank, the proportion of Sierra Leone's urban population living in slums in 2018 was estimated at 59%, which represented a substantial improvement from 97% in 2005 and 76% in 2014 (World Bank, 2022). Although there has been a consistent downward trend in the last decade and half, the proportion of the country's population living in slums remains the largest among its urban residents.

The historical city of Freetown, the capital of Sierra Leone, is estimated to have over one million inhabitants and the population is expected to double in size over the next 20 years. The port city is responsible for 30% of the nation's GDP and seen as key for the advancement of the country's economy. Beyond being a vibrant, dynamic and contested site of narratives and politics, the city's development has been marked by colonial legacies and eleven years of civil war. The civil war generated 500,000 internally displaced persons, the majority of whom remained in Freetown after the war ended in 2002, resulting in rapid population growth and a dramatic increase in population density mostly in the low-income informal settlements located by the coast and hillsides (Frediani, 2021). Sierra Leone's 2014 Ebola epidemic also marked a negative milestone for the living conditions in Freetown as it constrained urban mobility, compromised local livelihoods, disrupted education and put extra burden on an already fragile health system, with further distressing inward migration to Freetown. Other calamitous milestones in Freetown include the 2017 mudslide, annual flooding, and the COVID-19 pandemic (Frediani, 2021). The city lacks sufficient public housing, resulting in self-build solutions, the proliferation of urban sprawl, and inner-city slums. This breeds deep social and environmental disparities and provides lessons for rapid and haphazard urbanisation (Cui et al., 2019). In such a city, various information gaps and priorities have been identified, including but not limited to the importance of urban planning and implementation; the need for massive development of resilient housing and population relocation out of disaster-prone areas; addressing low-income and livelihood opportunities and the implementation of risk management, early warning systems and disaster emergency plans (Cui et al., 2019). However, most of the suggested interventions have been built on little or speculative data, and little engagement with stakeholders and vulnerable communities. Moreover, the lack of data at specific local levels across African cities has been identified as a major hindrance to answering questions critical to the health needs of the urban poor (APHRC, 2014) and further hinders urban health programming at local levels implemented by agencies and local governments in the region (Satterthwaite, 2014).

In the context of such challenges, the Sierra Leone Urban Research Centre (SLURC) has the mission of working with communities, their organisations, and other stakeholders to create capacity and produce useful knowledge leading to improved wellbeing in informal settlements. The stated aims and objectives of SLURC include the delivery of world leading research to influence Sierra Leone's urban policy and inform urban development efforts; to build the research and analysis capacities of all urban stakeholders in Sierra Leone; to provide opportunities for professional development; to engage and/or collaborate with urban stakeholders to promote equitable urban development and to make urban knowledge available and accessible to urban stakeholders, prioritising the residents of informal settlements.

Reflecting on SLURC's activities in terms of learning and its impact on understanding, practice and institution building, I draw attention to three main areas: evidence generation, community and stakeholder engagement, and building research capacity and networks.

Context relevant evidence generation

Scholars in the region have highlighted the importance and need for context-specific data and knowledge for specific cities, as part of the renewed search for pathways to address city challenges, inform policies, evaluate interventions and proffer solutions. In the 2018–2023 strategic plan, SLURC articulated the same challenge for Sierra Leone, stating that the problem of urban development in Sierra Leone is not solely the inadequate services and resources needed to make such provision, but also the severe shortage in knowledge about the conditions in which people live and the lack of capacity of the different stakeholder organisations to deal with the challenge (Macarthy et al., 2018). In generating context-specific evidence to enhance our understanding of local challenges and inform strategies that address them across urban Sierra Leone, particularly Freetown,

SLURC has played a major role. Available evidence attests to how SLURC's scientific productions have provided robust knowledge that has assisted implementing agencies and local governments to pinpoint priorities and identify appropriate interventions fit for different segments of the urban population. At the 2019 conference, SLURC presented a spectrum of research evidence, covering the integration of the health needs of informal settlements into planning; disaster risk management and urban resilience; synergies between formal and informal livelihood sectors in the Freetown economy and the policy and action nexus in the public urban space. Consequently, the work of SLURC has been characterised as providing the empirical bedrock on which we can predicate the development of our urban centres. It has provided greater understanding of the dynamics of our urban centres, and filled the data gaps in prior approaches to urban transformation by producing empirical evidence on which informed decisions and policies will be made, with consequent official acknowledgements of progress in understanding and transacting the dynamics of urban transformation (Mansaray, 2019).

Community and stakeholder engagement

In its vision, SLURC recognises that the central problem of unlocking community capabilities and improving the wellbeing of informal settlement residents is linked to addressing the lack of comprehensive information on their existing situation (UN-Habitat, 2006) and the inadequate capacity of the different actors to either deal with the problem or to draw attention to it (Macarthy & Koroma, 2016). Research programmes in urban Africa have demonstrated the value of using multiple approaches to gather empirical data that is of practical relevance to local, national, and global decision-makers and SLURC has made tremendous strides in filling these gaps. For example, Freetown is identified with flooding and for years there have been repeated cries about this intractable, naturally induced disaster. However, the Mayor of Freetown highlighted how 2018 marked a significant shift for good on that challenge, especially among slum dwellers, with credit given to research evidence provided by SLURC, which informed consequential engagement with stakeholders incorporating rich local intelligence, which had hitherto often been ignored and generally not quantified, documented, harnessed, nor incorporated into policy and action.

In its stakeholder engagements SLURC has given voice to communities and marginalised urban populations. At its 2019 conference, SLURC showcased community and stakeholder engagement in three ways. First, it brought the voice of slum dwellers and their plights to a national audience. This was typified by a young actress and dancer who grew up in the Akram Bomeh informal settlement in the East of Freetown, for whom SLURC provided a national platform to perform a spoken word piece to an audience with notable national, city and academic leaders. The presentation vividly set the picture for the conference delegates of what it was like growing up in a Freetown slum and residents' best hopes for the future. It called on delegates not to 'let our future break up; let our voices be heard. We care about our future; we want to move on to fulfil our dreams' (Shour, 2019).

Secondly, SLURC places a high value on research partnerships and has set out principles for partnerships with other researchers, research institutions and organisations, spanning ethical engagement, capacity building and co-learning (SLURC, 2020).

Thirdly, SLURC's success regarding government engagement for urban transformations in Sierra Leone was demonstrated by longstanding collaborations with relevant national and city government agencies. This is typified by the Mayor of Freetown officially expressing ownership of SLURC's research and pointing to specific uses of such data for programme implementation in the city. With at least 35% of the population of Freetown living in slums according to more stricter and realistic definitions, SLURC's work provided the platform for the city's constructive engagement with significant numbers of city residents and the development of its Transform Freetown agenda, which was designed to address the most fundamental challenges of the city across four clusters: resilience, human development, healthy city and urban mobility. Specific research inputs to environmental management, urban planning and housing were acknowledged as helpful regarding both thinking and revenue mobilisation. The community action area plans (CAAPs), which are core parts of SLURC's work, were singled out as enabling the city government to hear and see community level thoughts and planned elevation to local area action plans. Similarly, the urban risk research work of SLURC pinpointed specific areas of risk within communities that informed flood mitigation in 2018 and 2019. Further, policy briefs from SLURC on four informal communities – Dworzark, Cockle Bay, Moyiba and Portee-Rokupa – were fit for slum neighbourhood upgrading work of the City Government in partnership with the World Bank (Aki-Sawyerr, 2019).

Building research capacity, collaborations and networks

SLURC's contribution in building research capacity, collaboration and networks is captured when Brewer (2019), UCL Vice-Provost International, reported her '...joint meetings with colleagues from SLURC, Vice Chancellor of Njala University, and the Deputy Minister, to assess how much progress has been made in supporting policy development and co-creating solutions to issues of significant challenges here in Freetown.' Beyond such endorsement, SLURC is a member of various research partnerships, which continues to strengthen its place among regional and global players. For instance, SLURC is a member of the Accountability and Responsiveness in Informal Settlements for Equity (ARISE) Hub, which was launched in January 2019 and funded by UK Research and Innovation's Global Challenges Research Fund. The Hub is set up to enhance accountability and improve the health and wellbeing of marginalised populations living in informal urban settlements in LMICs – Bangladesh, India, Kenya and Sierra Leone. The Hub, composed of eleven top level research institutions across Kenya, Sierra Leone, India, Bangladesh and UK, is also engaged in building capacity for research at doctoral levels, which is consistent with SLURC's capacity building mission, as well as supporting doctoral level training for SLURC and partners.

Discussions and conclusions

The above three areas of focus, though not exhaustive of SLURC's numerous engagements, have stood out and were showcased at the 2019 SLURC conference. The meeting raised awareness of slums and challenged negative viewpoints and simplistic approaches to addressing them. It sought to shift opinions to influence policy makers and stakeholders; and provide a platform for discussion, networking, promoting collaboration and strengthening the relationship between partner institutions. Further, the theme of the conference, 'Urban Transformations in Sierra Leone: Lessons from SLURC's research in Freetown' captured profound themes of urban health, urban vulnerability, risk and resilience, urban livelihoods and the city's economy, as well as urban land use and planning (SLURC, 2019). With participants spanning a spectrum of government and non-governmental stakeholders, the conference successfully brought experts, scientific evidence, communities and policymakers together and placed urban transformation in Sierra Leone at the forefront of national discourse.

Moving forward, SLURC can only consolidate its achievements and build its future guided by equitable and inclusive urban development priorities articulated in the SDGs 2030, the New Urban Agenda and African Union Agenda 2063. Closely related to these is the new WHO Urban Health Research Agenda, especially the priorities identified for urban Africa. To this end, specific research gaps for Africa worth considering include focus on the social determinants of health, place-based solutions, health equity for marginalised population groups, urban governance (especially bottom-up approaches such as accountability, citizens science, youth engagement for evidence generation, advocacy, and community interventions), urban informal food markets, food safety, food labelling and health, mental health, waste management, climate change related vulnerabilities, health systems and human capital for health, and the role of the private sector. There are opportunities for SLURC to leverage regional bodies and regional agendas as the Africa Union Agenda 2063 and Africa Free Trade Agreement to prioritise health in cities across Africa. The experience of the COVID-19 pandemic offers an opportunity for cities to build back with more resilience around probabilistic emergency preparedness, universal health access and leaving no one behind (women, children, people with disabilities and urban refugees).

In walking these pathways into the future, collaborations and participatory approaches will be paramount for SLURC. Brewer (2019) captured this aptly when she stated that '…we believe that there is always more we can learn from each other by sharing ideas and being creative in solving problems together through collaboration.' These are approaches that SLURC has already embraced and can only perfect in securing its mission in urban transformation in Sierra Leone and beyond. Relatedly is the need to maintain momentum with stakeholder engagement and existing collaborations. The Mayor of Freetown affirmed that SLURC's '…inputs will be very seriously regarded by us at Freetown City Council. It will form part of our continued layering of the evidence we need as we work together to transform Freetown.' (Aki-Sawyerr, 2019).

References

APHRC (African Population and Health Research Center). (2014). *Population and Health Dynamics in Nairobi's Informal Settlements: Report of the Nairobi cross-sectional slums survey (NCSS) 2012*. Nairobi: APHRC.

Aki-Sawyerr, Y. (2019). Statements from keynote speakers. In Urban Transformations in Sierra Leone: Lessons from SLURC's research in Freetown (pp. 9–12). Conference report, Sierra Leone Urban Research Centre (SLURC), 19 June 2019. Accessed 25 June 2024. https://slurc.org/uploads/1/0/9/7/109761391/urban_transformations_in_sierra_leone_conference_report_web.pdf

Brewer, N. (2019). Statements from keynote speakers. In Urban Transformations in Sierra Leone: Lessons from SLURC's research in Freetown (p. 14). Conference report, SLURC, 19 June 2019. Accessed 25 June 2024. https://slurc.org/uploads/1/0/9/7/109761391/urban _transformations_in_sierra_leone_conference_report_web.pdf

Chan, M. (2010). Urban health threatened by inequities. Speech, 7 April. Accessed 25 June 2024. https://www.who.int/director-general/speeches/detail/urban-health-threatened-by -inequities

Cui, Y., Cheng, D., Choi, C. E., Jin, W., Lei, Y., & Kargel, L. S. (2019). The cost of rapid and haphazard urbanization: lessons learned from the Freetown landslide disaster. *Landslides*, 16:1167–1176. https://doi.org/10.1007/s10346-019-01167-x

Frediani, A. P. (2021). Freetown: City scoping study. African Cities Research Consortium, University of Manchester.

Macarthy, J. M., & Koroma, B. (2016). Framing the research agenda and capacity building needs for equitable urban development in Freetown. Freetown: SLURC.

Macarthy, J. M., Koroma, B., & Klingel, A. (2018). Sierra Leone Urban Research Centre Strategy Plan 2018–2023. Freetown: SLURC.

Mansaray, A. (2019). Statements from keynote speakers. In Urban Transformations in Sierra Leone: Lessons from SLURC's research in Freetown (p. 13). Conference report, SLURC, 19 June 2019. Accessed 25 June 2024. https://slurc.org/uploads/1/0/9/7/109761391/urban _transformations_in_sierra_leone_conference_report_web.pdf

OECD (Organisation for Economic Co-operation and Development) & SWAC (Sahel West Africa Club). (2020). *Africa's Urbanisation Dynamics 2020: Africapolis, mapping a new urban geography*. West African Studies series. Paris: OECD Publishing. https://doi.org/10.1787 /b6bccb81-en

Satterthwaite, D. (2014). Health in urban slums depends on better local data. Manchester, 11th International Conference on Urban Health.

Shour, F. (2019). Spoken word: Life in the slums... still I rise. In Urban Transformations in Sierra Leone: Lessons from SLURC's research in Freetown (p. 9). Conference report, SLURC, 19 June 2019. Accessed 25 June 2024. https://slurc.org/uploads/1/0/9/7/109761391/urban _transformations_in_sierra_leone_conference_report_web.pdf

SLURC. (2019). Urban Transformations in Sierra Leone: Lessons from SLURC's research in Freetown. Conference report, SLURC, 19 June 2019. Accessed 25 June 2024. https://slurc.org /uploads/1/0/9/7/109761391/urban_transformations_in_sierra_leone_conference_report _web.pdf

SLURC. (2020). SLURC Protocol for Research Partnership Version 1, April 2020.

UN-Habitat (United Nations Human Settlements Programme). (2001). Cities in a Globalizing World: Global report on human settlements 2001. London: World Bank.

UN- Habitat. (2003). The Challenge of Slums: Global report on human settlements 2003. London: World Bank.

UN- Habitat. (2006). The State of the World's Cities Report 2006/2007: 30 years of shaping the habitat agenda. Nairobi: UN-Habitat.

WHO (World Health Organization) & UN-Habitat. (2010). Hidden Cities: Unmasking and overcoming health inequities in urban settings. WHO Centre for Health Development and UN-Habitat.

World Bank. (2000). World Development Report 2000/2001: Attacking poverty. London: World Bank.

World Bank Group. (2022). Urban population (% of total population) – Sierra Leone. Accessed 25 June 2024. https://data.worldbank.org/indicator/SP.URB.TOTL.IN.ZS?locations=SL

19
Knowledge exchange as activism
Nancy Odendaal

As an academic, I am continuously humbled by the innate and tacit skills displayed by those living in very marginalised circumstances in African cities. Given that people living in informal settlements and those working in the informal economy are continuously subject to state harassment and violence, the extent to which such city dwellers can organise and engage is remarkable. In many different contexts I have encountered sophisticated organisational skills deployed towards collectively organising resources: leadership acumen that transcends much of what I have seen in middle class communities and innate technical skills that display understandings of space and place. In each context, the latter differs of course; the geographic context often dictates community priorities and associated responses. How then can researchers build on these abilities, whilst engaging with the systemic issues that require intervention and focus? Much of the answer to this question I have found in my experience working with the Sierra Leone Urban Research Centre (SLURC).

There are several themes I would like to pick up on in discussing the contribution of SLURC, as they relate to knowledge exchange as activism. The first concerns the importance of accentuating and engaging context, or geographic context, or more specifically, place. There are material qualities to the ways through which informality manifests, for example the problem solving and associated community strategies that inform endemic infrastructure solutions. I saw bridges constructed from old tyres, land reclaimed through the compaction of waste and a range of para-transit options. The second, learning from and with local logics requires relationships with a range of stakeholders that include local community and interest groups, and allies such as civil society organisations. The third understands that this work is inherently political.

It requires lobbying, a combination of the technical knowledge required to make sense of problems, and the political savvy to see opportunities to shift policy and enable the alliances to do so. In my interactions with my colleagues at SLURC, I understood that these three themes were central to their work, perhaps implicitly in some cases.

When SLURC was established in 2016, supported by the Bartlett Development Planning Unit at UCL and the Institute of Geography and Development Studies at Njala University (and funded by Comic Relief), the aim was to build the research capacity of local professionals and communities, and determine a contextually appropriate research agenda (Rigon et al., 2017). A further aim was to enable partnerships with local urban actors and local SDI affiliates. Thus, the framing of a research agenda, together with local actors, was crucial in SLURC's establishment. Enabling a knowledge exchange ecosystem requires the building of trust, and agreement of common values. I found this to be one of the most interesting talking points at SLURC advisory board meetings. Although not necessarily explicit in discussions, the common understanding of expanding the notion of what entails material practices in the city and how the informal often plays an important role in such, is key to enabling collaboration.

To this end, SLURC has established itself as a mediating platform that works with slum communities, local government and local CSOs. For example, research on livelihoods in informal settlements involved SLURC, DPU and the Federation of the Urban Poor (FEDURP), local SDI affiliates and the Pul Slum Pan People (PSPP) network that is active in Freetown's informal settlements (Rigon et al., 2017). I thought it appropriate to use SLURC as an entry point to my own research on how digital platforms contribute to and enable a knowledge generation project that essentially sees data collection as a form of collective action. In a general meeting with stakeholders in Freetown, representatives stressed the need to go beyond the use of books, journals and other publications to generate knowledge and to use podcasts, blogs, radio and online resources to disseminate data (Daramy 2021). What frames this approach is an organisational commitment to participatory action research[1] which was well displayed in the response in 2020 to COVID-19 lockdown measures.

I believe that the recent pandemic provides a fitting backstory to how important this work is. The flow of data from community to SLURC was effectively digitised when COVID-19 led to shutdowns. The use of mobile phones and video was an essential part of staying in touch with slum communities. Together with FEDURP, media specialists within the community were trained to make short videos for incidence reporting. SLURC would then edit and disseminate these. These recording experiences inform the community area action plans being prepared by SLURC and local communities. They are also available on CODOHSAPA and FEDURP's website, as the 'Know your City' TV channel. Using such perspectives captures the experiential dimensions of life in informal settlements. This capture of everyday experiences and the respect shown for tacit knowledge, was a feature of the SLURC way of working that struck me as very different to what I had been exposed to in other parts of the continent. Various methods and applications are used as needed, but clearly provide the means whereby stakeholder groups and state actors can be enrolled into networks of communication and information dissemination. The legitimacy of such networks is to some extent enhanced through the location of SLURC as a research body, as well as a policy influencer. The capture of data and putting slum communities on the map, together with the recording of stories that convey the experiential aspects of infrastructure failure and the impact of the coronavirus, are enabled through a range of technologies. The use of video in particular makes the invisible visible, as well as the SDI language for the 'Know your City' campaign.

The use of digital media to gather data is of course meaningful, but how that data is represented to the state (in cases where SLURC and partners aim at influencing debates) and harnessed to shape public opinion or to enhance neighbourhood networks, often results in visual representations that are immediately legible and digestible. Data is represented in thoughtful and intentional ways to deliver a particular message. Returning to the aforementioned themes, I found that the ways through which the material qualities of the environments within which SLURC works are engaged and portrayed, and the use of digital infrastructures to measure, capture and communicate aspects of it, are socio-technically rich and resourceful. The collaborative ventures go beyond the usual inter-academic networks and include a web of groups and organisations that form a dense informational and political infrastructure, potentially linking policy with the unique realities of Sierra Leone and thereby enabling contextually appropriate interventions. The third theme around politics is of course the most difficult to navigate. Here I believe that not only is knowledge power, but the means through information is documented, communicated and displayed, is key to shifting attitudes. Capturing the everyday and surfacing the invention required to survive on the margins, is compassionate and strategic. I believe that the SLURC experience illustrates how the research environment can be influential beyond the usual metrics of publications and funding. These are of course important factors, but here we see how impact can be achieved beyond the academy.

Note

1   Personal Communication, Joseph Macarthy, Director: Sierra Leone Urban Research Centre (SLURC). 19 September 2021.

References

Daramy, A. (2021). SLURC engages stakeholders. Global Times News, 20 June 2021. Accessed 28 September 2023. https://www.globaltimes-sl.com/archive/slurc-engages-stakeholders/

Rigon, A., Macarthy, J., Koroma, B., Walker, J., & Frediani, A. A. (2017). Partnering with higher education institutions for social and environmental justice in the global South: lessons from the Sierra Leone Urban Research Centre. *DPU News*, *62*, 2–5.

20
My journey working with SLURC: experiences and impact
Francis Anthony Reffell

I started working in urban slum development in 2007, as the Project Manager of Sierra Leone YMCA's maiden Slum Livelihood Project. Prior to that, I already had seven years working experience in community development, but this was primarily in rural localities addressing post-war poverty and challenges. As such, working in the Sierra Leone YMCA slum livelihood project was my first attempt at working in an urban space. I quickly realised that working in the urban context is totally different from the rural environment.

The key realisations, that I never encountered while working in rural settings, include the following issues.

- Forced eviction warranted by the illegality and/or informality of the occupancy of residents in target communities
- The erection of physical structures requiring approval from the ministry of land and respective line ministries before commencement of work. It is often not possible to gain these approvals, as they are usually compromised by interested parties to maintain political capital. More often than not, processes can be protracted beyond project timeframes.
- Power relations and dynamics often being quite complicated as they are fraught with conflicting roles and diverse interests.
- The prevalence of hard-to-manage community expectations, as most residents are desperate for quick-fix solutions to their challenges.

This situation prompted me to rethink how I should engage and tackle these complicated dynamics and expectations. Invariably, I reckoned that an effective methodology of development intervention in these spaces should be framed around right-based approaches. Right-based approaches embody the potential to stimulate sustainable transformation, as they focus on provoking and engendering state responses and actions, both local and national, to address community poverty and challenges. Despite this reckoning, the capacity (both personal and institutional) around right-based approaches at this time was still very limited.

As a result, in the four to five years of managing the foregoing project, I was essentially focused on social service delivery that I have known to work best, including, construction of community centres, erection of water points and kiosks, construction of community latrines, supporting community cleaning exercises, etc. This limited capacity to engage in right-based approaches – which would have laid the foundation for effective advocacy for policy and practice reforms from the very onset – gravely affected its efficacy, thereby delaying the possibility of accelerating the desired transformations of the localities I served.

Alongside these interventions though, I initiated the mobilisation of savings groups in various communities through international exchanges with SDI affiliates. They evolved into the Federation of Urban and Rural Poor (FEDURP). The emergence of FEDURP therefore, warranted the adoption SDI rituals and models. Key among them are community-led data collection practices, from which we conducted our first settlement profiling and enumeration of Kroo Bay and Dworzark communities. We talked about this first set of community data in different forums and about our work, but neither our development counterparts nor state actors gave much credence to this work, so we were left with the question of what we could do with the datasets. With hindsight, this would have been a golden opportunity to adopt right-based approaches, had it not been for the paucity of knowledge and skills.

At the same time, the Centre of Dialogue on Human Settlement and Poverty Alleviation (CODOHSAPA) was established by SDI in consultation with Sierra Leone YMCA, as the professional supporting office to provide technical support to and formal representation of FEDURP. This alliance of both CODOHSAPA and FEDURP is now the Sierra Leone alliance of Slum Dwellers International (SDI). To that end, the ensuing narrative is a reflection on the nexus between my personal professional experience and the institutional growth of CODOHSAPA/FEDURP.

It was around this same time that I had interviews with Joseph Macarthy and Graham Tipple, who were doing a scoping study for the establishment of an urban research centre. This engagement provided useful insights and learning that contributed to justifying the establishment of a research centre. Fast forward several years and the Sierra Leone Urban Research Centre (SLURC) was conceived and delivered and is now positioned as an important urban research institution.

With the advent of SLURC, the credence and value of our datasets began to grow progressively, as SLURC started referencing the work of CODOHSAPA/FEDURP in their discourses and publications. As SLURC scaled up, its works gradually contributed to the technical capacity of CODOHSAPA/FEDURP through different modes, including but not limited to direct, in-house training workshops, field practices and knowledge sharing. In the same vein, SLURC has deliberately sought collaboration with CODOHSAPA/FEDURP on a number of projects, thereby providing various platforms, both locally and internationally, where the achievements and stories of change delivered by CODOHSAPA/FEDURP are showcased.

SLURC introduced and scaled up the concept of a city learning platform (CiLP) from the Comic Relief's Four Cities Initiative known as the Freetown Urban Slum Initiative (FUSI). This concept has not only found relevance and value in the urban space discourses, but now serves as a platform of knowledge and technical exchange.

Through this space, the concept of community learning platforms was conceived. It serves as a community-based democratic space to deliberate and capture community development aspirations, and to inform the powers that be at local and state levels. These two platforms have contributed to enhancing the visibility and relevance of CODOHSAPA/FEDURP in communities, and more importantly, among state and non-state institutions as a progressive technical CSO counterpart in the urban space.

The conferences organised by SLURC have often provided opportunities for invaluable exposure. In 2017, the first conference on 'Formal and Informal Livelihood and Economy' created the platform to interact with a range of state and non-state actors and academics, with opportunities to speak on the thematic issues and to talk about the work of CODOHSAPA/ FEDURP. This engagement highlighted the importance of the informal economy to the functioning of the city, and by extension, emphasised the importance of our work in this sector. In 2019, the second conference showcased SLURC's research work and raised awareness of the challenges and negative perceptions of informal settlements. It was a rich encounter that involved a wide range of professionals, academics, community actors, government officials, and civil society activists, drawn locally and internationally. Here, CODOHSAPA/FEDURP was accorded the space to exhibit visual examples of their work, while at the same time, participating in a number of panel discussions to share their experiences and views about urban slum transformation. These spaces and opportunities profoundly enriched our visibility, and positioned us as a maverick, community-centred, non-state institution, mobilising and driving the voices and aspirations of slums and informal settlements.

I was a panellist at the international launch of SLURC: Knowledge Partnership to achieve a sustainable urban future at Habitat III in Quito, Ecuador in October 2016. This was my first experience speaking at an international conference. This increased my confidence and reinforced my profile as an urban professional. Sitting as a SLURC board member alongside high-profile academics and intellectuals provides the leverage for progressive experiential learning in human and financial resource management, which I now use in my management responsibilities.

The CAAP initiative brought insights into the potential of communities to dream and plan their neighbourhoods and communities in the context that best relates to them. This process is an effective means to meet the challenges of urban planning. It is an important step towards neighbourhood planning and special area planning models, as it has been tested, proven and is ready for implementation (see chapters 9 and 15). This can be a useful tool to the Freetown municipality for a deliberate and inclusive planning process that can lead to a progressive transformation of the city.

Contrary to the earlier assertions regarding the incapacity of CODOHSAPA/FEDURP to operate within right-based approaches, working with SLURC has changed the narrative. Foregoing narratives have expressly articulated SLURC's capacity-building efforts towards my personal and professional life and that of the institutional growth of CODOHSAPA/FEDURP. This has happened in diverse ways, including in-house workshops, practical field research work, participation in conferences, sharing of documented academic and intellectual materials, and providing toolkits for practical work. These have all contributed to shaping our understanding, knowledge, skills and practice on right-based approaches and methodologies. To that end, CODOHSAPA/FEDURP has made significant progress in positively influencing and changing the negative perspective and posture of state actors, as well as the negative public perception in relation to addressing urban poverty. As a result, there is now a significant shift from forced evictions to upgrading where possible and relocating where necessary, upholding the best internationally acceptable standards and practices.

The research outputs of SLURC position SLURC as a leader and technical expert in the urban domain and related sectors. In that respect, I wish to proffer the following recommendations:

- Expand SLURC's work to other urban centres. It is understandable that Western Urban is chosen as it is the most extensive urban centre and characterises extreme informality, poverty and climate change vulnerability. However, with an urbanisation rate of 2.75% per year, the country is expected to cross the 50% urbanisation mark by 2040. Each year, more than a hundred thousand people move to urban areas in search of employment (World Bank, 2021). This, therefore, provides an opportunity for SLURC to extend its initiatives to other growing urban areas, to ameliorate the potential 'urban catastrophe' that is currently plaguing the systemic urban planning process of the Western Urban.
- Establish progressive relationships and partnerships with universities across the country and work towards the creation and establishment of urban planning departments in the entities that are receptive to such proposals.
- Strengthen its global partnerships and networks to enrich and gain global and local recognition as a leading academic and development consulting firm in urban development and transformation, thereby positioning itself as the major port-of-call in urban space discourses and planning processes.

References

World Bank. (2021). Project information document (PID), Resilient Urban Sierra Leone Project.

21
Learning experiences from SLURC
Yirah O. Conteh

Introduction

The Federation of the Urban and Rural Poor in Sierra Leone (FEDURP) is an affiliate of Shack/Slum Dweller International (SDI) with technical support from the NGO Centre of Dialogue on Human Settlement and Poverty Alleviation (CODOHSAPA). Established on 15 February 2008, the role of FEDURP is to advocate, dialogue and coordinate with other institutions to improve conditions in informal settlements in Sierra Leone. Its processes include forming savings groups for collective savings, mapping, profiling, enumeration in all informal settlements in Freetown, and advocacy. Since its foundation, it has been very important for FEDURP to work closely with the Sierra Leone Urban Research Centre (SLURC) regarding some of these activities, as it has provided FEDURP with invaluable lessons to help strengthen the organisation. In this brief chapter we want to highlight some of the core areas where SLURC has impacted the work of FEDURP and its learning.

Data collection and ethics in research

As an institution, FEDURP had limited experience in research, mapping and data collection. Through the partnership with SLURC, FEDURP learnt about research methodologies and new techniques such as using GPS on phones for the creation of shapefiles that can then be transferred into GIS for the development of maps, or the use of different applications for effective data collection. Training and capacity building is also a very important part of increasing the effectivity and efficiency of our work and it usually involves a comprehensive training manual and access to the tools and equipment to ensure success. We joined SLURC on many projects conducting data collection and research together within most of our informal communities. The duration of contracts for fieldwork last from a couple of weeks to months, or even a year, resulting in lasting learning outcomes.

Furthermore, FEDURP learned about the importance of conducting research ethically and responsibly. SLURC helped FEDURP to understand the fundamental principles of research ethics, safeguarding and code of conduct across different types of research. The variety of research projects that we collaborated with SLURC on has helped identify new issues that FEDURP had not previously been aware of in our communities. Initially, we were just considering problems such as flooding, evictions and lack of proper planning, but when we started to work together with SLURC, more problems that people face in informal settlements became evident. FEDURP's interface with people in our communities has also changed. We now interact with residents in informal settlements in a much more professional way and we are striving every day to improve our work, which leads to communities perceiving us as their true advocates.

Intervention implementation

We are not only working with SLURC on data collection and research, for some research projects the scope extends to intervention implementation. In such cases, FEDURP has been given the responsibility to take ownership of such interventions or pilots in our communities to ensure the sustainability of these projects. One example was the 'URBAN ARK – Urban African Risk Knowledge' research project that FEDURP developed together with communities, implementing small-scale interventions within 15 settlements. The aim of the interventions was to undertake small work jointly with communities to create visible improvements and tangible impact. After identifying most of the hazards around their communities through the research project, 15 communities were selected with the help of SLURC proposals for small scale interventions that aimed to reduce the impact of these hazards. Such interventions helped, for example, to improve footpaths, drainage, water wells, and bridges. The project was designed so that the communities had to develop a proposal, with the help of SLURC, for the work they wanted to undertake in their community, including a budget. SLURC, through the research project, would then fund 60% of the intervention while the communities contributed the remaining 40%. The idea of the community contributing to the intervention cost was new, interesting, and successful. One of the main reasons for the success of this approach was that it gave communities the space to take ownership and leadership in solving their own problems and to do the work themselves. This change in attitude has now become the norm; with or without money, problems can be tackled. Other projects such as Assistive Technology for All (AT2030), community action area plans (CAAPs) and Knowledge in Action for Urban Equality (KNOW) also followed this principle and included aspects of community ownership.

Knowledge and learning exchanges

The lessons learned with SLURC were not restricted to Freetown but extend to invaluable learning and knowledge exchanges locally and internationally. SLURC gave me the opportunity to travel to South Africa, Malawi and UK on different projects and initiatives and these trips provided critical opportunities to learn from other institutions and stakeholders. Some were institutions using similar research methods to FEDURP, others were NGOs and government institutions which gave FEDURP new insights into their ways of working and ideas. However, the learning was not just one-sided. In fact, the learning opportunities were enriching for both sides and FEDURP shared our experiences from Sierra Leone with them.

We further exchanged knowledge and learning with academic institutions and their representatives, such as lecturers, professors and other important dignitaries in the academic world. While our understanding of theoretical backgrounds sharpened, they learned from us how these translate into realities on the ground.

We also gained insights into ways of leading an institution from a professional point of view. In Malawi, we focused on the collaborative aspect of FEDURP and SLURC working together on the URBAN ARK project and compared this to what they had been doing in Malawi. SLURC encouraged FEDURP to take the lead in presenting and explaining to partners the approaches in Freetown and what processes we followed to ensure successful completion of such projects. The presentation even led our partners to believe that FEDURP was an NGO rather than a CBO from informal settlements, again a credit to SLURC's training and capacity building. The trip to London for the AT2030 project offered a great opportunity to meet with other collaborators, again sharing our experiences, this time, with Global North partners and explaining how our partnership works. Credit was given to SLURC for handing FEDURP ownership of implementing the project directly in the communities together with residents. This inspired other institutions to implement similar processes on their other projects, which shows the direct impact of such knowledge and learning exchanges.

In conclusion, FEDURP are grateful to be part of this partnership with SLURC because of the exposure this has led to as well as other benefits such as the ongoing capacity building that helps progress FEDURP further each day. We are always ready to learn more and continue the partnership with SLURC.

22

The Four Cities Initiative: 'the whole is greater than the sum of its parts' – a funder's perspective

Irene Vance

Introduction

In 2012, the UK Department of International Development (DFID), matched the £10 million generated by Comic Relief's Sport Relief public appeal, thus creating a £20 million investment to support work in informal settlements in four cities in Sub-Saharan Africa: Freetown, Cape Town, Kampala, and Lusaka. This was The Four Cities Initiative (FCI), a programme that ran from 2013–2019.

Such an urban programme was new for Comic Relief. FCI was designed to test an innovative approach both to Comic Relief's grant-making and management, as well as to the way in which grantee partners addressed urban development challenges in rapidly growing urban contexts. The theory of change of FCI recognised the limitations of 'separate and individual project-funding' which all too often results in siloed and sectoral responses: consequently, FCI was based on the premise that 'the whole is greater than the sum of its parts'. With a city-wide approach, the combined impact of grants focusing on a range of issues would have greater overall impact on improving the living conditions of residents of informal settlements than single grants would.

At the heart of the FCI was collaboration, partnerships, and locally-led and coordinated interventions. Overall, it addressed six interrelated city-wide issues: i) increase access to basic goods and services, including, ii) decent jobs and stable livelihoods, iii) water and sanitation, iv) health and education, v) safety, and security, vi) policy, and giving a voice to slum dwellers. Collectively this was intended to strengthen the rights, and improve the lives, of over 1.1. million people living in informal settlements across the four cities. Each city developed its specific set of priorities and plan, reflecting the contextual and specific challenges faced by residents in its informal settlements.

In Freetown, for instance, the consortium of partners comprised five non-government organisations: Restless Development, Youth Development Movement, BRAC Sierra Leone, CODOHSAPA and YMCA (who had worked together previously), as well as UK based partners, YCARE International and Transform Africa. In 2014 Freetown launched its specific programme, the 'Freetown Urban Slum Initiative' known as 'Pull Slum Pan Pipul', against a backdrop of multiple challenges. The country had embarked upon post-conflict reconstruction, Freetown had experienced a surge of growth of informal settlements and public health services were over-stretched because of the Ebola crisis.

The Pull Slum Pan Pipul programme partners sought to maximise resources and achieve more impactful results by working collaboratively across twenty-six slum communities. Complementarities between partner specialisms, as well as their combined expertise, tackled the multiple vulnerabilities and challenges experienced by residents. Their joint programme supported community savings and loans schemes, apprenticeships, jobs and youth employment. It also supported reproductive health rights, gender-based violence reduction activities, community managed water and sanitation, tenure rights and neighbourhood improvements. Pull Slum Pan Pipul also had a strong advocacy agenda aimed at influencing national and local government to formulate policies that recognised the rights of residents of informal settlements.

This was particularly important. While an earlier enumeration and mapping model 'Know Your City', implemented by Slums Dwellers International (SDI), had contributed significantly to the community-led response during the Ebola crisis, this information had not been included in city planning. Consequently, the needs of informal settlements remained invisible, ignored by local authorities, and official policy towards such settlements remained the traditional eradication and eviction.

The knowledge gap and data needed to influence and advocate for more equitable and inclusive urban development was reported by partners to Comic Relief in their quarterly reports. This feedback from the field coincided with Comic Relief's internal grant-making strategy review that recognised the importance of more flexible, agile and responsive funding to local needs. Recognition that it was strategically important for the Freetown consortium to address this knowledge gap led Comic Relief to provide additional funding to start a new urban research centre, the Sierra Leone Urban Research Centre (SLURC). The grant also supported the collaboration between UCL's Bartlett Development Planning Unit (DPU) and Njala University in Freetown. Collaboration between academic centres in the Global North and South tested the assumption that research can contribute to a more effective urban development system. In addition, the creation of such a new urban research centre recognised that local researchers have a better understanding of the socioeconomic, legal and cultural context. Consequently, locally generated knowledge production can be strategically well placed to influence policy and enhance advocacy to achieve systemic change in urban development.

Bridging the knowledge gap

In early 2016, SLURC was launched with a very ambitious vision. The goal was to achieve a fully functioning and sustainable research centre in three years, with its own governance and management structure. From Comic Relief's perspective, this highly ambitious endeavour reflected two rapidly emerging, interrelated shifts in international development aid discourse. First, donor and philanthropy grant makers wanted to redesign their investment strategies so that funds went directly to Global South grassroots organisations and communities. Second, a movement, known as ShiftThePower, that started at the 2016 Johannesburg Global Summit on Community Philanthropy, challenged traditional top-down working and decision-making paradigms. The movement called for new behaviours, mindsets and working approaches that would shift power and resources and promote more equitable and people-led development. Comic Relief was an early advocate of ShiftThePower, adopting it in the FCI collaborative city-wide approach, in which local agencies led the process. This was identified as a pilot in this new approach to bring about more equitable urban development.

I took up the grant management of the FCI programme portfolio in 2016. At that time SLURC was in its infancy, recently launched and in its start-up phase. What follows are my personal reflections as a grant manager of SLURC's early years and its contribution to Freetown's urban development policy and practice.

Building longer term institutional capacity

From the outset, one of the keys for the centre's success was its emphasis on long term sustainability. Two priorities were resolutely addressed in the first year: setting up a financially autonomous legal and governance structure, comprised board members from Njala University, the DPU, and local civil society. The centre was co-managed by a committee of two SLURC co-directors and two UCL lecturers, who would gradually withdraw from management and transition SLURC towards full, locally led governance.

The second priority focused on putting in place a strategy for the long-term financial sustainability of SLURC. Typically, discussions around sustainability between funders and grantees are left to the final year of a project and are framed as exit strategies. In SLURC's case, the rapid increase in demand for its research and training services highlighted the need to build administrative, financial and accounting systems and to develop a robust financial strategy to secure additional resources beyond the life of the Comic Relief grant. Hence, modifying the budget allocation ensured that in the first year of operations, SLURC acquired the services of a consultancy firm to guide and craft the transition of the centre from project-based finance to institutional finance, putting in place a back office, internal financial systems capable of managing multiple research projects and diverse funding flows from different sources. Over time, the enhanced operational and governance structures and sound financial planning, enabled SLURC to secure additional funding for several research projects and to establish partnerships with a range of organisations, thereby expanding its reach with global networks.

Early progress was made in fulfilling its research mandate to strengthen the evidence base on urban issues, by completing several flagship action-research studies, working in close collaboration with the SDI affiliate, the Federation of Urban and Rural Poor, FEDURP. The dissemination of research findings and the training workshops carried out with a range of city stakeholders, positioned SLURC as a broker and coordinator of dialogue between citizens and city officials. The evidence-based dialogue played a pivotal role in fostering a step change in the mindset of government thinking towards informal settlements. This was the critical shift from negative attitudes and practice of evictions towards a supportive response, that recognised the need for public investment in upgrading rather than eradication. Harnessing the new knowledge and data published by SLURC, the Freetown partners engaged in an advocacy campaign to stop evictions, lobbying for an 'upgrade where possible and relocate only where necessary' policy agenda. Continual engagement with Freetown City Council and the Lands Ministry contributed to a positive shift in their thinking and treatment of people living in informal settlements.

Knowledge is power[1] – action is more powerful

A key milestone for the collaborative efforts of the partners complemented by SLURC's evidence-based research culminated in the recognition of informal settlements in the National Development Plan. Yet, the best made plans and policies require commitment from national and local authorities, if the evidence and research findings, policy briefings and development plans are to be translated into action. The election of a new mayor of Freetown in 2019 marked such an opportunity for SLURC and partners to accelerate their change agenda. A new era of cooperation of trust-based relationships was marked by the invitation from the city authorities to SLURC and civil society partners to take an active role in the formulation of the new mayor's Transform Freetown Framework.

A cornerstone of SLURC's work was the design of a comprehensive monitoring, learning and evaluation framework. This enhanced the two-way flow of information, creating a feedback loop between key decision-makers at city level, as well as facilitating the participation and engagement within and between communities. This was critical in giving greater voice and diversity to community groups to not only express their views, but also to contribute to the design and implementation of a new vision and programme of action, with immediate effect and for the future of Freetown.

Final reflections

Assessing the programme wearing my funder's hat, it was commendable to know that in three years SLURC made significant progress towards reaching its expected outcomes. It increased its capacity to carry out locally led urban research and achieved significant improvements to the quality and quantity of knowledge of informal settlements. In addition, it provided tangible examples as to how research and data influences urban policies. Equally important, SLURC made significant strides towards establishing itself as an independent and sustainable urban research centre, capable of punching above its weight in informing urban development debates at the national and international level.

Viewed from an 'anti-logframe' perspective and recognising the complexities of shifting policy and influencing mainstream practice in urban development agendas, SLURC's progress was by no means linear. Challenges and risks – some predictable, some less so – had to be addressed throughout project implementation. One key takeaway from the experience of supporting the creation of SLURC is the critical importance of providing core and unrestricted funding to local partners, which provides them the flexibility to pivot and adapt their work and their strategy in an ever-changing local context and political landscape. This is increasingly gaining traction in international funding circles.

In addition, the creation from scratch of a research centre, not only as a stand-alone entity, but as a key player in a collaborative consortium with a diverse range of key city stakeholders, residents and communities, requires additional funding that goes beyond supporting initial institutional capability. Dedicated resources are crucial if a collaborative partnership is to continue on a sustained and permanent basis. Sustainability also required investment in capital assets; for example, acquiring and owning their own premises, which can be used as collateral and for borrowing purposes.

Finally, from a funding perspective, the SLURC and the Freetown consortium experience illustrates the benefits of supporting the complementarity of skills and expertise, through simultaneously resourcing a set of partners. The mix of northern and southern academic institutions that collaborated in the co-creation of SLURC, together with the consortium of local actors, played to the strengths of each organisation. Northern based research partners provided their extensive experience working at a global level. The Freetown based researchers, together with national entities and community-led organisations, have a much deeper local knowledge and an interpretative reading of the nuances of local decision-making, which is critical in gauging key tipping point moments, where a set of conditions converge that propel forward and accelerate an urban reform agenda. These conducive moments are unpredictable and progress is far from linear. In those lull periods, when the political environment is less than conducive, SLURC's research endeavours – gathering evidence and updating information in an urban context that is constantly changing – is well placed to make valuable contributions to present and future urban planning and policy reform. So, all in all, I can conclude that it was a very good decision by Comic Relief to test the water with this innovative city-wide programme, moving away from smaller individual projects.

Note

1   'Knowledge is Power' is SDI's mantra, referring to data collection and management by slum dwellers, which is used as a negotiating tool to inform their advocacy for change with local authorities.

23
SLURC: a reflection from the national government perspective
Alphajoh Cham

Land use planning and urban development has never been a national priority in Sierra Leone until recently with the development of the new Medium-Term National Development Plan (2019–2023) (MTNDP). The strategic objective of the MTNDP in promoting spatial development is to ensure an 'effective land management and administration system that is environmentally sound and sustainable for equitable access to and control over land, including the provision affordable housing for low- and middle-income groups to alleviate poverty and promote economic growth.' The MTNDP also incorporates policy actions that address the issues of rapid urbanisation, including the development of a national spatial development plan and strategy. The implementation of the MTNDP thus far has not been effective due to many challenges, including very limited technical and financial resources.

The historical lack of national recognition of the functional relevance of land use/urban planning in the design and implementation of national development projects and programmes has resulted in reduced internal rates of return on urban investments and the creation of agglomeration diseconomies and negative externalities, which ultimately impede economic growth and prosperity. The planning system in the country is faced with several challenges, which include weak legislative frameworks or instruments which do not address the emerging multi-dimensional and multi-sectoral urban issues, institutional fragmentation, overlapping and conflicting mandates coupled with weak coordination and collaboration amongst institutions responsible for planning and land management, and weak technical capacity within these institutions.

To strengthen its research capability, the Ministry of Lands, Housing and Country Planning (MLHCP) established in 2015 a directorate of planning, policy and project development. The ministry has been collaborating through this directorate with the Sierra Leone Urban Research Centre (SLURC), which has provided much needed support to the Ministry in its research and development efforts. SLURC took an active role in the development of the MTNDP. The ministry has also participated in SLURC's development programmes, including training workshops, conferences, seminars and study tours. SLURC's interactive and user-friendly website serves as credible source of research materials.

Ultimately, the collaborative partnership between MLHCP and SLURC helped to re-shape or re-direct the ministry's policy directive, putting urban planning and housing development at the centre of its development agenda. The new strategic focus of the ministry is sustainable and climate-resilient urban development under the leadership of Turad Senesie, to address the rapid urbanisation growth rate through integrated spatial and land use planning, and the provision of affordable housing with the five key policy objectives.

1. Promote integrated spatial planning and strengthening development control through effective monitoring and surveillance.
2. Strengthen the legislative and institutional frameworks for effective land governance and urban planning.
3. Enhance tenure security to protect land and property rights by transitioning from the registration of instruments to biometric title registration.
4. Improve efficiency and cost-effectiveness of delivery systems in cadastre, registration, valuation and real estate services to boost productivity and domestic tax revenue generation.
5. Promote the investment climate to provide affordable housing and promote slum upgrading.
6. Mainstream environmental sustainability in the implementation of programmes and projects.

The results of the new policy directions of the Ministry in supporting the development agenda of the Government of Sierra Leone are already visible. The Government of Sierra Leone has secured a US$41.1 million grant from the World Bank to develop an efficient and accessible land administration system in support of the New Land Reform in Sierra Leone. The project will support the development of an integrated digital land information system (LIS) with automatic land administration processes, the establishment of a new national geodetic network for accurate surveying and the development of new base maps that will support integrated urban planning.

The World Bank is also supporting the Government of Sierra Leone through the Resilient Urban Sierra Leone Project (RUSLP) under the arm of the Ministry of Finance, to improve integrated urban management and resilient urban infrastructure, enhance service delivery and promote disaster emergency management in the country. The project will specifically support the development of spatial master plans for the Western Area and six cities in the provinces. The government's strategy for urban development focuses on a spatial approach to transform urban centres through planning and investment in basic services, informal settlement upgrading, low-income housing, and local government fiscal enhancement. The project's balanced approach includes: (i) strengthening institutions and integrated urban planning systems, enhancing local revenue generation to safeguard fiscal sustainability and disaster preparedness; and (ii) investing in urgent local infrastructure in poor urban and large-scale metropolitan areas crucial for sustainable development of the country, will provide a foundation for subsequent urban sector investments. Over the longer-term, the project aims to strengthen cities' institutional and financial capacity and develop the appropriate integrated urban planning tools and instruments to enable the country to fully capture urbanisation dividends.

One of the key objectives of the World Bank-funded Sierra Leone Economic Diversification Project under the Ministry of Finance is to improve the business environment and capacity building in the housing sector. The project will streamline and modernise the construction permit system that will reduce time, cost and red tape for the private sector, while reducing administrative operational cost for the public sector. This initiative will help improve the enabling environment for private and public investment and is consistent with the strategic objective of the government to prioritise private sector-led growth as a key means of job creation, poverty reduction and economic diversification.

The government is also receiving financial support from the World Bank to implement the Sierra Leone Integrated and Resilient Urban Mobility Project under the Ministry of Transport and Aviation. The project will improve the quality of public transport, address climate resilience, improve road safety in selected areas and enhance institutional capacity in the transport sector. It will contribute to the implementation of one of Sierra Leone's principal measures required to mitigate and adapt to climate change, supporting Sierra Leone's transition to a low-carbon and climate-resilient economy, with mobilisation of resources to enhance climate resilience. One of the main climate change mitigation measures stated in the country's nationally determined contributions (NDC) includes the absolute reduction of emissions by promoting use of public transport.

The MLHCP is in the process of developing a national urban policy for Sierra Leone. With its rapid rate of urbanisation and no integrated policy in place, Sierra Leone runs the risk of un-controlled urban sprawl, poor urban basic service delivery, and fragmented urban management. A new national urban policy will provide a blueprint for sustainable urban development and economic development. It will further promote social and income equity, provide employment opportunities, and ensure efficient service delivery infrastructure. SLURC's research work will be critical to informing the formulation process. The ASK-UK Change by Design methodology adopted in the development of community action area plans (CAAPs) with a participatory, inclusive and integrated approach in local communities, for example, could serve as good basis to address the issues surrounding informal settlements and slum development, while empowering communities in urban design and planning, particularly women and the youth. This approach will ensure community ownership and promote the lasting sustainability of programme implementation.

Successful implementation of all these projects will fundamentally transform the urban planning landscape in Sierra Leone and SLURC will have a critical role to play in that regard. I see the long-term impacts of SLURC's collaborative research work in Sierra Leone in strengthening the research base, in providing credible and reliable data and information that will inform the policy decision process in the areas of effective urban planning and urban development, in technical capacity building, and institutional reform. My hope is that SLURC will continue to consolidate its impressive achievements and sustain them.

Appendix: Protocols for research partnerships

Sierra Leone Urban Research Centre, August 2019

This appendix sets out some principles for research partnerships between the Sierra Leone Urban Research Centre (SLURC) and other researchers and research institutions. It also helps our partners to better understand SLURC's objectives and ways of working, and we hope it will help create mutually beneficial and solid partnerships. The document also suggests some practical ways in which some of these principles could be implemented within the research partnership. These can be discussed further and adapted to the specific need of each partnership within the framework of the overall principles. This is a living document, so we appreciate feedback and are available to further discuss the rationale of any part of this document.

We would like to ask our prospective partners to familiarise themselves with our Strategy Plan 2018–2023 to get to know us a bit more. However, to set the context of this document, below are our overall vision, mission and objectives that underpin all our work.

Our vision

Sustainable, socially and environmentally just urban settlements where no one lives in deprivation and slum-like conditions; where all have access to a decent living condition with opportunities to influence policy decisions; a world where no one is left behind.

Our mission

Work with communities, their organisations and other stakeholders to create capacity and produce useful knowledge leading to improved wellbeing in informal settlements.

Aims and objectives

The objectives of SLURC are as follows.

i.   To deliver world leading research in order to influence Sierra Leone's urban policy and inform urban development efforts.
ii. To build the research and analysis capacities of all urban stakeholders in Sierra Leone.
iii. To provide opportunities for professional development and further the experience of academic staff and students in Sierra Leone.
iv. To contribute to public debate on equitable urban development and the needs of the urban poor.
v.   To nurture a collaborative research environment in Sierra Leone.
vi. To engage and/or collaborate with urban stakeholders to promote equitable urban development.
vii. To make urban knowledge available and accessible to urban stakeholders, prioritising the residents of informal settlements and their organisations.

Strategy actions

In order to achieve its vision and mission, the strategy of SLURC is to undertake activities in the following key areas of operations.

i.   The production of quality relevant research that will inform urban development policy and practice.
ii. Collect, collate and disseminate relevant knowledge products to its stakeholders with ease of accessibility.
iii. Conduct relevant training activities to address the identified capacity gaps of urban development stakeholders, including informal settlement communities and their organisations.
iv. Provide a platform for development and policy dialogues on urban development challenges.

SLURC has a number of overall principles that apply differently to specific aspects of the research process. By signing this document, you commit to work with SLURC in ways that:

1. Engage ethically with different groups

- SLURC is grounded in working with residents of informal settlements to improve their wellbeing as per our vision and mission. Therefore, our research work is informed by a strong normative mission and is directly accountable to the informal settlement residents.
- Our ethics commitment is not only about 'no harm'; we explicitly seek to bring benefits to the residents and communities involved in the research.
- We check that all our research complies with our values and policies.

1.1. Partnering with communities

- Our relationship with communities is the most important SLURC asset and an ethical engagement is of the utmost importance to preserve this relationship.
- Our research is co-produced with communities. This means doing research in ways that respect community knowledge and their ways of knowing.

1.2. No harm and sensitive data

- Data collected can be very sensitive and can even be used to justify an eviction. Researchers should discuss with communities, their representatives and other organisations working with them about the potential risks and prioritise a cautionary approach to prevent harm from the misuse of data or the publishing of research results.

1.3. Communities' involvement in setting the research agenda

- This is a fundamental principle for SLURC. Because of our ongoing work, we are often able to understand if a proposed project responds to some needs of communities. However, whenever possible, our research proposals are presented and discussed early in the process (ideally well before submission) with community learning platforms. SLURC strives to reverse top-down research processes where the research agenda is developed outside Sierra Leone with little participation of local communities.

Communities will be involved in:

- providing feedback on the research proposal
- monitoring and evaluation of the research process
- dissemination of the results
- identifying the legacy
- thinking of future/follow up research.

- Because of this work with communities, research projects should budget sufficient resources (both money and time) for researchers to sustain the engagement process and to cover community members' expenses in the process.
- We have witnessed that sometimes a lack of time and resources compromise the ethical engagement with communities.
- Doing research in this way takes more time and therefore more resources, but it also has a higher demonstrable impact (therefore, still delivering good value for money).

1.4. Benefit to communities

- For SLURC, the ethical principle of causing no harm is not enough. We want our research to bring benefits to communities. While there may be no direct immediate benefit to research participants, the research should work towards benefiting urban communities consistently within our mission and objectives.
- SLURC acknowledges the fundamental role that community members play in their research and the trade-off between participating in the research and getting a livelihood for their family, where there is not a direct benefit from participating or advising the research process. Therefore, we require projects to budget for community members according to SLURC community engagement practice across different research projects. It is also important that payments and arrangements with community members are managed by SLURC staff directly and are consistent across projects.
- SLURC see communities as co-producers of knowledge and therefore train community members to work as researchers in the

collection and analysis of data (see also under capacity building). Through SLURC's work, we developed a code of conduct for data collection that we ask all our partners to follow.

- It is important to explain to community bodies and research participants the objectives of each research project and how they will be involved in it and provide an opportunity to provide comments and feedback.
- Towards the end of each research project when findings are presented to communities, it is important to discuss with communities about existing knowledge gaps and the type of follow up research that the community may want and make this information available to other researchers working with SLURC.
- Moreover, SLURC seeks to renew the relationship with communities and find new ways to benefit members. Research partners are asked to contribute to these efforts.

1.5. Avoid duplication and fatigue

- An important part of the ethics is to avoid duplication and research fatigue, which may also lead to standard answers based on what communities think researchers expect to hear. Therefore, before planning any field activities, every researcher must familiarise themselves with existing research, the data available and methods used.
- We also encourage getting in touch with other researchers who have worked either on the same settlements or in similar research areas to discuss the synergies of respective projects.
- Every project should budget sufficient resources and commit to fill out a research log where research activities, and the type of data collected, are clearly listed. As well as working towards making datasets available to other researchers once the research is completed.

1.6. Legacy

- In line with the mission and principles of benefitting local communities, the legacy of projects is a very important aspect for which every project should budget and plan accordingly, in consultation with community and other stakeholders.

1.7. Knowledge dissemination

- As part of the legacy and SLURC mission, researchers should think and plan research outputs for different audiences (e.g. podcasts in local languages, leaflets, policy briefs, documents to be used by local organisations). We ask research partners to discuss with the research team and SLURC communication officer about how to translate research into outputs for a broader audience (including the media) and allocate time to produce such outputs.

1.8. Diversity and safeguarding vulnerable research participants

- We often conduct research involving marginalised individuals within poor communities. While we may not be able to change local power relations, we need to have a research approach sensitive to these and able to manage the complex intersection of different social identities including gender, age, ethnicity, ability, religion, class, and sexuality. This may also require having diverse teams, with female and male researchers, as well as with diverse abilities, ethnic identities and religious beliefs.
- Researchers will follow SLURC's safeguarding policy to deal with complex ethical situations they may witness during their research.

1.9. Ethical clearance

- SLURC has its own ethical approval process, which all projects involving SLURC researchers should follow.

2. Build capacities

- Through our research activities we aim to benefit local universities and other stakeholders.
- We ask that researchers working with SLURC plan enough time for disseminating research outputs and some teaching during their trips to Sierra Leone. We suggest that within the duration of a research project, the researchers plan visits to local universities. Moreover, it would be important to budget projects in such a way to create opportunities for graduates to work as paid interns.
- We consider communities to be co-producers of knowledge and acknowledge their unique expertise on their social reality. Through

research projects we also aim to build community capacity through training and their participation with the research project, including data analysis.

- SLURC is still a fairly young research organisation and we value partnership as an opportunity to build the research capacity of our staff. Therefore, we value your support in the research management, particularly in complex multi-country projects.

3. Enable co-learning

- SLURC is a learning organisation and aims to reflect and produce learning for all the stakeholders involved in its activities. We ask partners to plan time to participate in exchanges and discussions with other actors about learning on different aspects of the research process, including ethical issues.

4. Promote synergies, coordination and good use of resources

- SLURC researchers and their stakeholders in Freetown are often invited to travel to other countries, particularly the UK. The travel and visa arrangements are in themselves a huge investment, particularly in terms of time on already very constrained resources, in a tight multi-project environment. Coordination amongst international research partners is fundamental in order to organise trips in such a way as to maximise the use of researchers' time in the UK for more than one project. Sometimes, just adding one or two days to a stay would allow a researcher to work on a different project with very low budget impact and potentially reducing the need for another trip. This has also a positive impact in terms of emissions, which is important given that Freetown is highly impacted by climate change.
- This means that as soon as you have the intention to invite any SLURC researcher or other stakeholders abroad, you need to communicate your potential dates with SLURC and the other involved research partners (contact details will be provided by SLURC).
- Similarly, as soon as you intend to travel to Sierra Leone for field work, it is important that you communicate this to the SLURC team and other research partners. This will ensure that a realistic schedule can be organised and we ask you to be as flexible as possible to ensure your visit fits with other commitments.

- Moreover, there may be a need for equipment or documents to be brought to Sierra Leone and we would ask these to be available to help out SLURC and other research teams if possible.
- SLURC has entered into agreement with institutions that offer special rates to SLURC associates and very good value for money. We encourage all research partners to use their services. We have also prepared a document on life and work in Sierra Leone which can be useful, particularly to those new to the country.

5. Guarantee co-ownership of data

- SLURC works with its research partners, both research institutions and communities, in a spirit of co-production. Data produced through research co-production belongs to all these actors and this has implications in terms of ownership and its use that need to be taken into account.

5.1. Complementarity and integration

- As per the above, SLURC strive towards creating synergies, complementarity and integration of data from different research projects to ensure the knowledge co-produced across different projects is more valuable than the sum of single projects and is better able to address the knowledge needs of urban Sierra Leone. This requires studying existing research and the inventory of existing data, checking and filing the SLURC log of research activities and an integrated and ethical data management process.

5.2. Data management

- We ask our partners to help manage data safely and in such a way to be easily retrievable by other researchers. Substantial time should be spent planning how the data relates to existing SLURC data and SLURC data management systems to facilitate integration. This also implies that adequate budget is allocated for data management throughout the project, particularly at the end. The data management plan is a particularly important document that will need to be produced in partnership with SLURC staff responsible for knowledge management.
- SLURC also plays a fundamental role as knowledge broker in Sierra Leone. We have a resource unit with over 1,000 items, the largest

collection on urban Sierra Leone. We ask all research partners to make use of this open access platform, but also to contribute to it by emailing any document, paper, book, map, or database to SLURC staff responsible for knowledge management. This will be promptly uploaded or, if restricted by copyright, will be added as a physical resource available in the office or on external platforms. We also ask partners to send SLURC any outputs from the research so that they can be added to the resource unit.

6. Encourage co-authorship

- While there are disciplinary differences in terms of what constitutes authorship, SLURC encourages authorship to be discussed at the beginning of the research project.
- Co-authorship is an important tool for decolonising research and addressing the epistemic inequality in knowledge production between Global North and Global South.
- For SLURC, authorship recognises different contributions beyond writing and involves taking part in the analysis and production of data, as well as taking responsibility for the final output. Co-authors may have played different roles in the production of a research output, but these were all fundamental to the output.
- SLURC and its partners adopt an open/inclusive approach where those involved in the research process are invited to contribute to an output. There is therefore an obligation to communicate the intention of producing a particular output and giving other people an opportunity to participate.
- SLURC understands that space for individual writing is also important but if it is linked to a collective project then communication and discussion with other researchers is important.
- SLURC research projects are strongly intertwined both thematically and geographically. SLURC encourages all researchers to be aware of other research conducted by SLURC, and researchers who worked in partnership with SLURC and to cross-reference this work in a spirit of acknowledging and building on each other's knowledge. This contributes to outputs that are strongly grounded in comprehensive local research. All SLURC research outputs and projects are available on our website, and our researchers are available to point you to relevant work.

- SLURC encourages all researchers to share with the SLURC network and researchers via email any outputs as soon as they are in a sharable format. SLURC can let you know the most suitable way for sharing (most likely a small mailing list of active researchers associated with SLURC).

Annex 1 – Code of conduct for data collection
Annex 2 – SLURC safeguarding policy
Annex 3 – SLURC strategy plan 2018–2023
Annex 4 – Life and work in Sierra Leone

I have read the protocols for research partnership with SLURC and the related annexes and discussed any concerns that I had. I commit to follow the protocols and their principles in my research activities with SLURC.

Full name   ———————————————

Role   ———————————————

Institution   ———————————————

Signature   ———————————————

Index